CANADIAN ISSUES

Essays in Honour of Henry F. Angus

Edited by
ROBERT M. CLARK

Topics of widespread concern to Canadians interested in the social sciences and to the general reading public are dealt with in this volume of essays by a group of Canada's leading scholars in political science and history. The book is presented in honour of Henry Forbes Angus, Head of the Department of Economics, Political Science, and Sociology at the University of British Columbia from 1930 to 1956, and the authors are all his former students, colleagues or associates. Included also are a bibliography of publications by Dean Angus, and, with his consent, a thoughtful and humorous article of his entitled "Administration and Democracy."

HENRY FORBES ANGUS was born in Victoria, in 1891. He received his school education in Victoria and subsequently attended the Lycée Descartes at Tours (France) and McGill University from which he received his B.A. in 1911. He proceeded to Balliol College, Oxford where he obtained a B.A., first class, in 1913 and a B.C.L., also first class, in 1914. He won the highly prized Vinerian Law Scholarship at Oxford in 1914, and was called to the Inner Temple Bar in the same year.

Henry Angus served throughout the First World War: in India from 1914 to 1916 and in Mesopotamia from 1916 to 1919. He was promoted to the rank of Captain and mentioned in despatches. He returned to British Columbia after the war, and in 1919 was appointed Assistant Professor of Economics at the University of British Columbia. In the same year he obtained his M.A. from Oxford. He was promoted to Professor in 1929 and made Head of the Department of Economics, Political Science and Sociology in 1930. From 1949 to 1956 he was also Dean of Graduate Studies.

Professor Angus was made a Fellow of the Royal Society of Canada in 1939 and was its President in 1951–1952. He has honorary degrees from McGill University and from the University of British Columbia. He was a member of the Royal Commission on Dominion-Provincial Relations, 1937–40, and a member of the Royal Commission on Transportation, 1949–51. From 1941 to 1945 he was Special Assistant to the Under Secretary of State for External Affairs.

Since 1955, Dean Angus has been Chairman of the Public Utilities Commission of British Columbia.

HENRY F. ANGUS

CANADIAN ISSUES

Essays in Honour of Henry F. Angus

Edited by

ROBERT M. CLARK

Published for the University of British Columbia
by University of Toronto Press

Reprinted in paperback 2015
ISBN 978-1-4426-3917-1 (paper)

Foreword

I am delighted to join with other friends and colleagues of Henry Angus in doing honour and paying tribute to him.

I came to know him first in 1927 soon after my return from Geneva to Canada and to the University of Toronto. We had a common interest in international affairs, in Canadian-American relations, and in Canada's domestic and foreign policies. We soon became fast friends, and I learned to respect him as a scholar and as a man. We were associated as members of the research committee of the Canadian Institute of International Affairs. Together we attended the conferences organized by Dr. James T. Shotwell under the auspices of Carnegie institutions for the study of Canadian-American relations, and we were both delegates to other international conferences across the world and to many national meetings on a variety of topics. In all of these undertakings he impressed me with the clearness, the accuracy, and the sharpness of his mind in debate, on committees, in public addresses, and in the books and articles he wrote.

When in 1944, during the Second World War, I came to the University of British Columbia, Henry Angus, like so many other University colleagues, was in the service of the Canadian Government. Happily for me and for the University, he returned to us, despite attractive and persuasive offers to take on other work. As Head of the Departments of Economics, Political Science, Sociology, Anthropology and Criminology, and later as Dean of the Faculty of Graduate Studies, he proved a warm and loyal friend and an able and distinguished colleague, to whom I often turned and to whom I will always be grateful because of his wise counsel and advice.

In due course he retired from active university life. Retirement for him has meant a new and important career as Chairman of the Public Utilities Commission of British Columbia. It is greatly to the credit of the Government of this Province that it has used and continues to use men like Henry Angus, whose wisdom, experience, and vision contribute so much to the progress and welfare of British Columbia.

With all his new responsibilities, Henry Angus maintains an active interest in University affairs and until only recently he served as a special lecturer. We shall continue to turn to him for counsel and guidance.

NORMAN MACKENZIE

Preface

The purpose behind the preparation of this volume has been to publish a number of essays worthy of the man the contributors wish to honour, Henry Forbes Angus. It may be that he or other readers will ask: "Must I praise the leaves where no fruit I find?" But I trust that their verdict will be more favourable.

The bibliography of publications by Dean Angus at the end of this volume indicates the diversified range of his writings. His interests in the social sciences extended even more broadly. The contributors are all former students, colleagues, or associates of his. They were invited to write upon any topic in political science or economics of significance in Canada, and each chose a topic in which Dean Angus is interested. Despite the variety of topics selected, there still are several other fields in which he had a keen interest. These include constitutional law, Canada's relations with the Far East, civil liberties and the position of Oriental minorities in Canada, transportation, and the role of graduate education in Canadian universities.

In 1957 I began looking for contributors to this volume, with the expectation that it would be published early in 1959. My unexpected diversion to the preparation of a report for the Canadian Government on old age security delayed publication. By the fall of 1960 the few authors who had sent in their essays two years previously had revised them, and all the remaining articles had been written.

The reader probably will discover that he cannot agree fully with all of the opinions expressed by the contributors. As editor I have considered it no part of my duty to beckon in from the ends of sundry limbs a few of the more controversial authors, including myself, who are clinging to them.

Having served as a junior colleague of Dean Angus from 1946 until his retirement in 1956, I wish to refer to some of his qualities for which academic colleagues of those days think of him with keen appreciation. As a department head, and later as a dean, he was a man of unsurpassed fairness in dealing with his colleagues. He expected us to be candid in criticizing his policies and he never resented such criticism. We knew him as a man of courage. This was evidenced, for example, by his vigorous defence during the Second World War of the legitimate interests of Canadians of Japanese origin. Now as in the past we have found pleasure in the obvious zest with which his logical and penetrating intellect attacked and mastered problems which had been baffling to us. This quality was illustrated in the outstanding work he did as a member of the Royal Commission on Dominion-Provincial Relations. The report of this commission, which was published in 1940, is probably the most significant document in the history of government finance in Canada since Confederation. For the high reputation of this report Dean Angus, in my judgment, deserves much of the credit. We continue to value his independence of judgment, typified by the thoughtful statement of reservations which he appended to the report of the federal Royal Commission on Transportation of which he was a member.

Students and colleagues alike have admired his precision of thought and language, and his habitual economy in the use of words. His dry wit has made memorable many a conversation and some of his writings. This rare capacity to use "the stainless steel of perfect English prose" is well illustrated in a speech he gave in 1957 to the Vancouver regional branch of the Institute of Public Administration of Canada, entitled "Administration and Democracy." He has been prevailed upon to allow it to be included in this volume.

Dean F. H. Soward and Dean George Curtis at the University of British Columbia and Miss Jean Houston at the University of Toronto Press have been generous in giving me helpful advice on the numerous occasions when I sought it. Friends of Dean Angus will be grateful to President Norman A. M. MacKenzie and other members of the Board of Governors of the University of British Columbia, who have made possible the publication of this collection of essays.

ROBERT M. CLARK

Vancouver
January, 1961

Contents

Contributors

JAMES A. CORRY, Hardy Professor of Political Science, Head of the Department, and Vice-Principal (Academic), Queen's University

JAMES H. AITCHISON, Eric Dennis Memorial Professor of Government and Political Science, and Head of the Department, Dalhousie University

JOHN N. TURNER, associated with Stikeman & Elliott, Barristers & Solicitors, Montreal

FREDERIC H. SOWARD, Associate Dean of Graduate Studies, Head of the Department of History, and Director of International Studies, University of British Columbia

EDGAR W. MCINNIS, Professor of History, York University

J. DOUGLAS GIBSON, General Manager, The Bank of Nova Scotia, Toronto

JOHN J. DEUTSCH, Professor of Economics and Vice-Principal (Administration), Queen's University

RONALD M. BURNS, Deputy Provincial Treasurer, Manitoba

ANTHONY D. SCOTT, Associate Professor of Economics, Department of Economics and Political Science, University of British Columbia

ALBERT S. WHITELEY, Member, Restrictive Trade Practices Commission, Ottawa

ARCHIBALD W. CURRIE, Professor of Economics, Department of Political Economy, University of Toronto

A. E. DAL GRAUER, Chairman, British Columbia Electric Company Limited; Chancellor of the University of British Columbia

JOSEPH A. CRUMB, Professor of Economics, Department of Economics and Political Science, University of British Columbia

STUART M. JAMIESON, Professor of Economics, Department of Economics and Political Science, University of British Columbia

ROBERT M. CLARK, Associate Professor of Economics, Department of Economics and Political Science, University of British Columbia

Administration and Democracy

HENRY F. ANGUS

The ambitious objective of "Government of the People, by the People and for the People" has been approached by a series of steps which have brought most of those who exercise political power under the control of the adult population. First taxation, then legislation, and then the tenure of office of the chief executives have become subject at the national level to the will of an elected parliament and, at other levels, to the will of elected legislatures or councils. In many cases executive offices themselves have been filled by election. The sphere of action of appointed persons has been restricted to the exercise of judicial functions and to administrative, as distinct from executive duties—administrative duties that is to say which involve no important element of policy formation.

The elected personnel—as is obvious at election times—is inclined to address the electorate in obsequious tones and to placate it with the most extravagant promises. It seems to conform to Bernard Shaw's definition of a coquette by "exciting expectations which it has no intention of gratifying." In short, the victory of democracy has been, in appearance at least, complete—so complete, one is tempted to say, as to be embarrassing, for the new rulers sometimes find it difficult to ape the "majesty" that should "hedge a king" and may even find some difficulty in the all-important task of exercising power effectively.

The first of these two difficulties is met—in a parliamentary democracy—by separating dignity from power. The second is a difficulty which all rulers experience, however small their realms. It increases with the size of the realm and also with the scale and complexity of government and it can make power itself seem futile and its exercise frustrating. Rulers may perform executive functions but they must rely on administrators and, in a democracy as much as in any other form of government, efficiency depends on the maintenance of suitable relations between top executives and their administrators. As government becomes more complicated and its activities more varied the chief of these administrators become more and more skilled, more and more professionalized, more and more specialists or experts.

Inevitably a great deal of real power must pass into the hands of the administrators. This obvious fact can be illustrated by going, in time and space, well beyond the bounds of democracy and taking a Hindustani proverb that boldly likens the rulers to monkeys and the officials to the calendars (or, as we should say, the organ-grinders) who make them dance to amuse the public. A ruler would put the same idea into different words and so, no doubt, would an administrator. The ruler would not compare himself to a monkey nor would the administrator compare himself to an organ-grinder. But there can be little doubt about the facts and, this evening, we are concerned with realities and not with semantics. Detached observers from such vantage posts as the judge's bench or the professor's chair have chosen to describe these facts such sensational titles as "The New Despotism" and "Bureaucracy Triumphant." The terms may be new, they may express a certain nostalgia for the Rule of Law, but, let me repeat, we are concerned with realities and they are very old. As I am attempting, in an after-dinner address, to discuss a serious topic in not too serious a tone, I shall use the terminology of the Indian proverb.

Let us leave out of sight for the moment the intermediaries who have retired or are on the point of retiring vanquished from the field: kings and presidents, judges, parliaments, and even local government bodies. There remain the two protagonists in the modern struggle for power: the People and the Administrators. The former have the weight of numbers and, in the last resort, irresistible power. The latter find themselves confronted not with monkeys but with a lion. But a sleepy lion may be more tractable than a sensitive monkey and the administrators have no inconsiderable advantages: they are, intellectually speaking, a selected group and belong to the most effective age groups in the country; with the slightest skill in camouflage they can make themselves inconspicuous and practically invisible by allowing the attention of the public (if, indeed, a sleepy lion is capable of sustained attention) to concentrate on the intermediaries (the monkeys, who are by nature exhibitionists and only too anxious to display themselves); the administrators can bide their time and choose their time.

To these obvious advantages modern administrators have added others: within a limited range they can make laws (discreetly called regulations) and interpret them. They have not stolen these powers which have been thrust upon them in order to enable them to act with speed and vigour. They are not in the faintest danger of losing these powers, provided that they do not abuse them. They must not, of course, arouse the sleepy lion. If he shows signs of being restive they must see to it that the monkeys are the first object of his wrath. They must not irritate the sensitive monkeys but, if the latter become meddlesome, they should interest them in pulling the lion's whiskers. It is possible, of course, to make a false step, but an experienced administrator can have an amusing life and, under modern conditions, a reasonably long one.

Although today I must count myself among the administrators, I am not an experienced administrator and claim no competence in the game of skill that I am describing. I should be compared to the critic who confidently offers advice to artists although his own creative achievements are beneath contempt. Administrators as a class will continue to be alert and agile—the principle of survival of the fittest will see to that. But what of the public—the lion, whose attention is fixed on the monkeys and who is oblivious of the organ-grinders?

It is impossible to deny the lion one's sympathy, poor baffled brute with a ballot in his paw when he would prefer a steak. "Why should we starve with ballots in our hands?" The lion can—and, on occasion does—brush the monkeys aside and replace them by others. But his philosophy at election times is more often that of Aesop's dog who declined to change his fleas because the newcomers might be hungry. The lion cannot divide and conquer by sowing discord between the monkeys and the organ-grinders. The organ-grinders have succeeded in establishing the bewildering principle that, at least in all matters of policy, responsibility must devolve on the monkeys. The organ-grinders have security of tenure, the monkeys may disappear at the whim of the lion. Among monkeys the principle of the survival of the fittest can operate with startling speed. Alternative monkeys are constantly pressing forward; only the inert disillusionment of the lion stands between them and the succession. It is the duty of the administrator not to have favourites except, of course, when he marks his own ballot. As organ-grinder he must treat one monkey just like another, even if one is an affectionate creature and the other a fair devil. The lion need have no such scruples.

The administrator's duty not to have favourites may not be easy in spite of the strong traditions by which it is supported. It means, in practice, that he must act as if he were totally indifferent to the purposes of the executive whom he obeys and to the spirit of the legislation which he is called on to apply. He may, of course, have principles and convictions of his own but they are not for display. He may believe in private enterprise or in state socialism; may consider progressive taxation essential for social justice or utterly dishonest; may have old-fashioned or new-fangled ideas about education, criminology, or planning. We have no crime consisting in an "offence of opinion," but opinion must not influence official behaviour or official speech. Private conversation is another matter. It is notorious that organ-grinders discuss with one another the merits and demerits of their respective monkeys. In a civilized country such conversation in which administrators speak irreverently about their political superiors is an innocent form of amusement. We have no difficulty in understanding that a soldier may die bravely in battle even if he dislikes the régime, laughs at his general, and is professionally contemptuous of the plan of attack. Every politician knows that the behaviour and language which commends him to the electorate is not calculated to impress a civil servant who may be quite as well-educated, quite as cultured, and quite as sophisticated as he is himself. He has his own type of expert skill but it is not the same as theirs.

It is these political chiefs—the monkeys—whom we must consider next. They are by definition successful politicians; they have been chosen by the People; they are monkeys who can, for a season, speak in the name of the lion. They are confronted with organ-grinders whom they suspect of believing that they can always make them dance. The wiser monkeys know better. They know that, provided that they do not attempt to do too much, they can have their own way in the things that matter most to them particularly in policy formation and, indeed, that their organ-grinders will welcome a good deal of originality. It takes greater skill for a monkey to train an organ-grinder than for an organ-grinder to train a monkey. But it can be done. The political chief must never come into conflict with his professional advisers on matters of which he knows nothing and of which they know a great deal. Misunderstandings may easily occur if the political chief thinks he knows a great deal and his administrators think he knows nothing. Misunderstandings occur even more readily if the administrators forget that there is one important matter about which their political chief undoubtedly knows more than they do. He and he alone can make policies acceptable to the electorate, within limits of which he is the best judge. The monkey, that is to say, has a lighter touch than the organ-grinder when it comes to soothing the lion. The principle of the survival of the fittest takes care of this point.

And all the examples confirm this opinion. For example: the British minister who told Queen Victoria that the civil servants could govern the country admirably but would provoke a revolution within a few weeks; the Labour minister who said that experts should be on tap but not on top; a New Zealand minister who told me that in pressing an easy money policy on the governor of his central bank he came to learn by heart every hostile argument which he would have to encounter in the legislature and that eventually his policy was loyally executed by the man who had opposed it.

All this is old history. So too is the reverse case of the minister who resigns because of the uncorrected error of the civil servant. There is nothing here to suggest Bureaucracy Triumphant or the New Despotism. The novelty arises when the monkey induces the organ-grinder to try to make the lion dance. The temptation must at times be very great, certainly it has occasionally proved irresistible. In complicated matters legislation cannot foresee every contingency. It has to be supplemented at short notice by authoritative rules dealing with points of detail and these rules themselves may have to be interpreted. Who is in a better position to make the supplementary rules than the man who will have to administer them? Who is in a better position to interpret them than the man who must apply them? There must, of course, be controls. The making of rules may require ministerial approval; their interpretation may be subject to review by the courts. But if controls were too rigid they would destroy the very convenience which is desired. Some risks of injustice may be deliberately accepted. In this matter monkeys and organ-grinders are in cordial agreement, but what about the lion?

The lion, remember, personifies the People. What do the People expect from government, of which the day-to-day aspect is administration? The answer is simple. They expect too much. To steal a phrase from André Siegfried, the People want a high price for wheat and a low price for bread. In the same inconsistent way they want generous social services and low taxes, or high wages with low prices. A successful politician (as André Siegfried suggests) must promise these incompatibilities. An administrator cannot deliver on such a promise.

The People, again, want to be able to complain to someone in authority if things go wrong—and to be able to defend themselves vigorously if they are complained against. The administrator must do what the politician tries not to do. He must act decisively and must, therefore, make enemies—one at least in every dispute and quite likely two. He must reconcile himself to being disliked because of the very impartiality which he considers his highest duty. The exception which does not constitute a precedent, the discretion which takes the edge off a rule when a powerful interest is concerned, the cutting through of red tape to reach a speedy decision, and the excessive use of red tape to protect established interests—annoying as these things may be to persons with tidy minds—seem to those who profit by them the very essence of good administration. Unfortunately most administrators have tidy minds. For the exasperated public the remedy seems obvious. They appeal from the administrator to his political superior, appeal, that is, from the organ-grinder to the monkey. Or, better still, they approach the monkey first and leave it to him to cajole the organ-grinder.

I do not wish to give the impression that the public is altogether opposed to integrity. Quite the contrary. But the public is sceptical of integrity being universal and, if there must be bias, no one wants to lose by it. If there is a possibility of pressure resulting in concessions it may well seem to be the height of folly to let others be first in seeking them. The administrator's duty is clear. It has not altered with the coming of democracy. In ancient China the government had official historians. On one occasion the historians annoyed the government by describing its acts as murders. There was no rule of law and the government had the historians executed. Their successors were duly appointed and proceeded in a matter of fact way to chronicle the murder of their predecessors. The government had learnt its lesson.

It is not merely to spare your blushes that I have gone to a distant time and place for my example of administrative probity. I wanted to take an extreme case and I wanted to prepare the way for a discussion of the administrator as an educator. He is constantly meeting newly elected persons, who are making their first acquaintance with what he might call administrative ethics and what the elected person might call administrative behaviour. It may require almost infinite tact and patience to acquaint an elected person with what he may expect from his administrative staff. The organ-grinder must exercise these qualities when dealing with new monkeys, who fresh from managing the lion think that they can easily manage the organ-grinder. The newly elected person is fresh from a successful election. He knows what the public wants, what it will and what it will not approve. He is all set to educate his administrators and there is much that he may usefully do. He can, if he is careful, restrain administrative zeal or dispel administrative apathy, while not himself trespassing on the sphere of the administrator.

Perhaps it is the fault of our system of popular education, which is not as cynical as it might be, that the public thinks that it has a right to expect to be well governed. We no longer applaud the poet who wrote:

How small of all that human hearts endure
That part which laws or kings may cause or cure.

A right which may not unreasonably have been claimed against an autocratic sovereign when the "things that are Caesar's" were relatively few and unimportant continues to be claimed against a government concerned with matters of detail affecting everybody—a government that is itself the choice of the People, who should learn to say dolefully *"Tu l'as voulu, Georges Dandin!"* or, crudely translated "You asked for it."

But the public does not think that it is in fact well-governed. It has a compendious four-letter word for government—so compendious that it includes legislature, executive administration, and local authorities as well. It is not as obscene as some four-letter words, but it is as contemptuous as any and has done more harm than most. It is the word "THEY." The public has never learned to say "WE" when it refers to government. It avoids the first person as scrupulously as Proust advised French novelists to avoid writing in the first person if the theme of the novel were homosexual.

Now Proust's advice applied only to novelists and may have been successfully disregarded by the more ingenious of them. It should be the aim of political education in a democracy to make people speak of their government in the first person, to say "These are *our* traffic regulations; *we* do not allow litter in the parks; *we* punish drivers who are under the influence; *we* insist on proper municipal planning; *we* discountenance favouritism of every sort; *we* detect and punish tax evasion whether at the border or on income tax forms." The third person should be reserved for transgressors: "*They* go to gaol!"

This may be a counsel of perfection. The lion is a stupid brute at best and it may well be that he is incapable of being educated. The experience of organ-grinders has been with monkeys and they are eminently teachable. The organ-grinders cannot expect to do much with the lion. The lion is a suspicious animal and is allergic to organ-grinders. It is much better that they should approach him through the good offices of the monkeys who—partly by the process of natural selection—have acquired some skill in dealing with lions. It is, as we have seen, their specialty.

The reasons for the lion's distrust are obvious. He thinks—or perhaps more accurately he verbalizes his emotions—in moralistic terms. He is quick to insist on his rights, meaning the rights according to the moral system or ideology which the lion professes at the moment. This ideology is profoundly influenced by his immediate interests and, as these interests change rapidly, the most inconsistent "rights" may be claimed in complete good faith and with the utmost conviction. The apparent inconsistency does not puzzle the monkeys in the least. They understand it perfectly and are adept in exploiting it. It is quite otherwise with the organ-grinders, men with tidy minds who are apt to think in legal rather than in moral terms. There is only one system of law and, therefore, only one set of legal rights in any one country at any one time. But to measure all claims to rights by the existing system of law is more than the lion can endure. He insists that administrative boards should be freed from the control of the courts and be guided by justice and equity, and relies on the courts to control the administrative boards.

The lion's extremely subjective and extremely flexible view of right and wrong enables him to indulge in the most intense form of self-pity whenever his immediate wishes are frustrated. Self-pity is the lion's favourite emotion and up to a point he enjoys it. But he can easily become dangerous. The organ-grinders then take shelter behind a screen of monkeys and the monkeys do their best—at the peril of their career as monkeys—to appease the lion.

The moral of all this is that administrators would be mad to hope to dispense with elected personnel (the monkeys) who are experts in the difficult matter of making decisions which will be acceptable to the electorate (the lion). The administrators should give advice when asked for it and give it frankly, however unpalatable they may expect it to be. They should never attempt to destroy elected personnel, except of course by the process of giving them enough rope to destroy themselves, which means offering good advice, however distasteful it may be to the electorate, and never pressing for its acceptance. Above all administrators should never, never, advise elected personnel how to appease the electorate. In the first place they are less competent in this matter than the elected personnel; in the second, natural selection should be allowed to take its course. There is of course nothing to stop administrators offering themselves as candidates for election (organ-grinder into monkey!) but, if elected, they should be scrupulous in obeying the canons of the new position and should not attempt to remain organ-grinders. They should remember that they have become monkeys and that, as such, they are fair game for the lion.

CANADIAN ISSUES

ESSAYS IN HONOUR OF HENRY F. ANGUS

Constitutional Trends and Federalism

JAMES A. CORRY

As a minimum courtesy, those who are offered a discussion of constitutional trends and federalism should be told what is to be discussed under the heading. I shall interpret the first limb of my topic broadly and refuse to be limited to constitutional matters in the strict sense. In addition to trends in formal amendment, in judicial interpretation, and in the development of constitutional usages and conventions, I shall speak about social, political, and economic trends that make a significant impact on the working of federal constitutions, trends that affect the balance of the constitution.

To allay somewhat the fears aroused by a proposal to plunge readers into this morass, I shall interpret the second limb of the topic narrowly and restrict discussion to the three Anglo-American federations, the United States, Australia, and Canada. They are the only ones with enough in common for ordinary folk to generalize about, or to find readily comparable. What I can say of all three will be very general indeed. What I can say in particular with any assurance will be limited to Canada.

One very good reason for limiting discussion to these three federations is that they were all constructed, and have been operated, by the same kind of people with the same kind of basic ideas about the role of government, in a broadly similar social and physical environment. The men who framed these federations and set the main lines of their working were the heirs of the English liberalism of the seventeenth and eighteenth centuries. Without saying how far the Americans of 1789 and the Canadians of 1867 were democrats in the sense in which we now use the word, they were liberals with a profound belief in individual freedom. In particular, they had an abiding faith in economic freedom, and saw this faith amply justified by the way in which free men had been able to carve out goodly heritages in the new continental domains that lay before their eyes.

Believing that individual men could shape their own destinies by their thought and effort, they did not want much of governments except that they should be both responsive and responsible.

They wanted governments to be responsive at every level in maintaining a regime of public order congenial to individual freedom and enterprise, and in judiciously helping energetic people to help themselves. They wanted governments to be responsible in the sense of being accountable under law for encroachments on individual freedom of action. To this end, governments as well as individuals should be subject to law enforced by independent courts.

When the circumstances of the several times and places counselled political unity of the separate colonies, it did not seem inappropriate to liberal minds that the price of union should be continuance of the states, or provinces, in self-governing dignity. (In Canada, because of Quebec, it was not only appropriate but imperative.) Indeed, they should be autonomous, responding to the enfranchised within their boundaries, rather than mere field agencies of a distant national government. As Woodrow Wilson, a latter-day heir of the liberal tradition, made clear to us, self-determination of individuals is easily translated into self-determination of small nations.

If the self-determination of individuals and small states is to be preserved, there must be order based on law. Accordingly, an attempt was made to state with some precision the limits of legislative authority at both levels of government. While the framers of these constitutions did not, in any instance, provide expressly that the courts should police the distribution of legislative power, what other result could they have contemplated? Both the Canadian and the Australian constitutions were acts of the British Parliament which, of course, the courts would interpret when litigants contested their meaning. And even if *Marbury* v. *Madison*[1] was not directly within the vision of the framers of the Constitution of the United States, one could have predicted it as a consequence of the circle of ideas in which they and their generation moved.

What I have been taking too long to say is that the general design of these three federations was shaped under the influence of liberal

[1](1803) 1 Cranch's Reports 137. In this case, the Supreme Court of the United States asserted, and established, the right of the Court to determine the constitutionality of legislative and executive action, including of course the questions whether federal legislative acts encroached on state power, and *vice versa*.

ideas. They began, and continued for some time, under the impulse of individualism, legalism, and *laissez faire*. From an examination of these three constitutions comes the definition of federalism we have found meaningful: general and regional governments of co-ordinate authority each independent of the other in its appropriate sphere, ruling over the same persons and the same territory under the benign surveillance of a court. This is classical federalism in the Anglo-American mode.

Classical federalism saw the national and state governments in the system as independent entities, each going its own way in the enjoyment of its own powers under the check of a watchful electorate with a minimum of either association or collision. Because the electorates would limit narrowly the actual use made by governments of their extensive legislative powers under the constitution, the governments would not run foul of one another as long as each minded its own business. If some forgot themselves and encroached on the domains of the others, the courts would remind governments of their place. Indeed, the genius of place would have its way, in Virginia and Massachusetts, in Quebec and Nova Scotia. Both unity and genuine diversity would flourish.

Making allowances for the imperfect realization of ideals in action, for the general untidiness of political processes, and for one major breakdown in the Civil War in the United States, the classical federalism worked with considerable success until the First World War. Thereafter it was subjected to increasing trials and was finally transformed into something quite different in the depression of the thirties, something which is called co-operative federalism, or the new federalism. Although the change has been effected without striking amendments in the formal constitutions of any of the three countries, the alteration in the working governmental structures of the United States, Canada, and Australia has been profound. Whether the essential reality of these structures can now be called federal at all depends, of course, on one's definition of federalism. At any rate, the reality has moved far away from what I have called classical federalism.

There has been a persistent and rapid acceleration in the centralizing at the national level of the prime initiative in government, if not so much in the formal exercise of governmental power. The umpiring of each of these federal systems seems to be slipping out of the hands of the judges into the hands of the politicians, where decisions are taken on a view of policy rather than as a matter of law. The co-ordinate governments no longer work in isolation from one another, but are increasingly engaged in co-operative ventures in which each relies heavily on the other. Before considering the outlines of these developments, we should remind ourselves of some of the forces thrusting in this direction.

Great improvements in transportation and communication within the free trade area that each federation provides have knit the economic life of each federation into an interdependent whole. The separate chambers of the states are insulated no longer. Instead, conduit pipes and high-voltage wires link them together transmitting economic pressures and economic shocks throughout the country. The exercise by one government of its undoubted powers often has serious repercussions on some or all of the others by the transmission of political pressures and political shocks.

Economic individualism has been displaced by a mixed economy of a strongly collectivist cast. In part, it is a private collectivism of giant corporations, national trade associations, and national trade unions which we are always being driven to try to match by extending the authority of national governments. In part, it is a public collectivism in which *laissez faire* has given way to a dispensation where governments are many things to all men.

Governments intervene in the social and economic spheres in at least three different and important ways. First, they respond to complaints of social and economic maladjustment with regulatory action in one sector of affairs in ways which impinge on other sectors and other governments. Second, to meet their housekeeping needs and to finance the services they provide, the several governments in the federation taken together impose a weight of taxation which seriously affects economic decisions, the level and distribution of economic activity. The dominant economic theories of the time gravely warn governments to give serious thought to finding the least burdensome and disruptive, or perhaps I should say the most beneficial, way to raise a given total of public revenues. Because it is so hard for seven governments in Australia, eleven in Canada, let alone fifty in the United States, to take thought effectively together, the tendency is for the national governments to take strong leadership in taxation policy. Third, because economic concentration and the tinkering of governments have diminished greatly the self-adjusting capacity of the economy, the national governments have gone a considerable way towards assuming responsibility for over-all guidance of the economy.

The experience of national action gained in two world wars,

improvements in communications, additional bundles of social and economic data improved in reliability by statistical techniques, to say nothing of electronics, have made it easier for the national governments to take the initiative on a wide front. The fact that, in the last ten years of uneasy peace, these federations have had to remain girded for war has strengthened the case for the dominance of the national governments in the field of taxation. But the material factors, to which for the most part consideration has been restricted so far, will not alone account for the decisive leadership the national governments are taking. In countries where governments are as responsive to popular moods as they are in Australia, Canada, and the United States, there must be widespread acquiescence in, if not active support for, the enlarged role of the national government. If the people of the several states and provinces remained stubbornly determined to find their principal collective expression as tarheels or bluenoses, we should not have arrived where we are. So it seems necessary to put as a major factor in the superseding of the classical federalism some nationalizing of sentiment.

The cautious phrasing of this statement may seem to some quite unnecessary. Of course, we have become Americans, Canadians, and Australians. What began as sheer expediency has come to have an independent and inspiring value of its own. We have become nations in Renan's sense that our people are conscious of having done great things together in the past and want to stick together to do great things in the future. We now see many things we did not always see in the past that we want to accomplish in unity together, and are willing to use our national governments as means to these ends even if pursuit of them entails sacrifices of interests, both individual and parochial. Certainly this is true as far as it goes, but it does not go the length of saying how many things, of what kinds, and at what sacrifices.

Some say the nationalizing of sentiment has gone so far that the vitality of federalism which depends on some balance of provincial and national feeling has been destroyed. There are some awkward facts in the way of such a conclusion. There has not been any strong swelling of sentiment in favour of drastic centralizing amendment or of reducing the states and provinces to administrative instruments of national governments. If we leave aside the income tax amendment of 1913 as perhaps equivocal, Americans have not put forward, let alone approved, any formal amendment to enlarge national power at the expense of state power. Perhaps an obliging Supreme Court has made any such action unnecessary, a point to be considered later. Since 1867 Canadians have put forward and pushed through two amendments, and two only, which enlarge the powers of Parliament at the expense of the provinces, the unemployment insurance and old age pensions amendments. Two other important facts about Canada are to be noted. First, repeated efforts to get agreement on a method of amending the portions of the British North America Act which define provincial powers and privileges have failed completely. Secondly, all attempts to get general agreement on a comprehensive and enduring settlement of federal-provincial public finance have also failed. We have, it is true, negotiated, since the Second World War, three successive sets of federal-provincial tax agreements but only because the federal government, in the end, relied on its constitutional advantages in the field of taxation and negotiated separate agreements with each province that was prepared to deal.

It is clear that national unity is not strong enough to bring Canadians to agreement on these matters. Of course, Quebec has been in the forefront of the resistance, but she has not been there alone by any means. On the other hand, it must be said that all the discussions just referred to have been directed at getting the agreement of provincial premiers and cabinets who have a vested interest in provincial status and power which the several provincial electorates perhaps do not share fully. Having no provision for plebiscites on such issues, we do not know what the electorates would say. Yet there is no evidence that the provincial electorates have been dismayed, or even disturbed, by the reluctance of their governments to make concessions for the sake of agreement.[2]

In Australia, formal amendment requires approval by majorities of the electorates of four of the six states, as well as by a nation-wide majority. The Australian Parliament has proposed some twenty centralizing amendments and only two of these have secured the needed popular majorities. Most of the Australian writers I have read still insist, in the face of these verdicts, that "the States are no longer vital political entities in any basic sense,"[3] and that these impressive refusals of enlarged authority to the Commonwealth Parliament do

[2]Equally, of course, one has to say that on June 9, 1957, there was little evidence of the restiveness of the Canadian electorate over twenty-two years of Liberal rule.

[3]S. J. Butlin, "The Problem of Federal Finance," *Economic Record* LVIII (1954), p. 11.

not spring from any loyalty to federalism as such. The electoral vetoes are explained rather as votes against paternalism in general or against the particular proposals in question on the ground that they should not be enacted by any legislature, state or national. This explanation does not carry full conviction to me, partly because until I know more, I would be disposed to regard a vote for *laissez faire*, hopeless and misguided though it may be, as an unequivocal vote for the classical federalism.

In Canada, we have no plebiscites of this kind to explain one way or the other, unless the rejection of the Liberal party in the 1957 and 1958 national elections can be interpreted as a rejection of the centralizing policies of the Liberal Government. Of course, we do not need plebiscites at all to know that the Quebec electorate is generally opposed to centralization, whether it be by formal amendment or through the informal drift of prime initiative to Ottawa. In a negative way, as noted above, the other provincial electorates have shown that they see no urgency for nation-wide agreement on at least some broad and vital issues. But we do not know what positive views, if any, these other electorates have on the question of the piecemeal centralizing of initiative in the national government.

We do know something of the attitudes of the provincial premiers and cabinets to this question. The positions they adopt and the courses they pursue over a period of time probably reflect the balance of opinion in their respective provinces. Therefore it seems highly significant that in the recurring tax negotiations and agreements of recent years, all provincial governments except Ontario and Quebec have given up, for three successive five-year periods, the right to levy personal and corporate income tax and succession duties in return for guaranteed annual grants from the federal treasury. In fact, Ontario did give up personal and corporate income tax for one five-year period, and for a second period has given up the right to levy personal income tax. So it too has been a participant, if not so fully committed as the other eight English-speaking provinces, in transactions with a strongly centralizing effect, increasing the leverage of the national government on the policies of provincial governments as well as on the economy of the country.

In these negotiations and deals, Quebec alone has had a completely consistent position. From 1945 on, Premier Duplessis always refused to enter into a tax agreement with the national government. So far, his successors have given no ground for expecting a reversal of this position. Since 1951, this has entailed a considerable sacrifice in the revenues they otherwise could have had for provincial purposes. They do not want grants from Ottawa. They do not want Ottawa to assume burdens for purposes that lie within the scope of provincial legislative power, such as grants to the universities. All they want of the national government is that it should get out of their way, allow them effective freedom to tax heavily personal and corporate incomes and successions, and allow their government to carry the full cost of whatever services it decides Quebec is to have. The Quebec premiers want to go it alone, and so far have been prepared to take the risks and pay a price for provincial autonomy.

Generally speaking, the other provincial premiers do not appear to be willing to pay the price of being genuinely masters in their own houses. They either press for, or acquiesce readily in, federal assumption of burdens relating to costly services which traditionally, to say the least, have been regarded as provincial responsibilities: education, highways, welfare, electric power development, and so on. We are now to have provincial health insurance schemes, in aid of which the federal government somewhat reluctantly promised large federal grants. As far as one can judge, the strongest pressure for the Dominion to take up this costly venture came from Premier Frost, of Ontario.

All federal commitments for objects that are either constitutionally or traditionally the responsibilities of the provinces increase the dependence of the Dominion on personal and corporate income tax and reduce the room for effective provincial exploitation of these tax sources. The provincial premiers do not stop at the point of encouraging new direct federal expenditures. Each goes on to urge, in addition, that the Dominion's proposals for compensating the provinces for giving up these tax sources are quite inadequate, and that its grants to the provinces should be greatly increased. At each round of negotiations, these grants are sharply increased. In effect, the provincial governments, Quebec excepted, are doing all they can to ensure that the Dominion will continue its dominant role in public finance and fiscal manipulation, and that genuine provincial initiative will be correspondingly curtailed. The provincial electorates, Quebec again excepted, do not seem to mind.

Of course, a just appreciation of the lines pursued by provincial premiers in tax negotiations must take account of their dilemmas. The requirements of national defence have always to be taken into account. Given the level of provincial services and expenditures established in response to electoral demand, if not social need, most provincial governments could not make ends meet at all by scorning tax agreements and the large federal grants they produce, and levying their own personal and corporate income taxes. Partly because of the concentration of control of the economy, a very large proportion of the high personal and corporate incomes are pooled in two or three provinces. The other seven or eight provinces must either acquiesce in a much lower level of government services or conspire with the Dominion in a scheme for taxing and redistributing this pooled wealth. I think it is correct to say that the reflective members of the Canadian community in all provinces, except perhaps Quebec, have decided that the first alternative is unfair and unjust, and therefore approve the second.

Ontario is the province which would best be able to go it alone. Indeed, Ontario would profit immensely from complete dismantling of the tax agreements. She did, in fact, oppose the first post-war tax agreements, adhering to the bucolic vision of former Premier Mitchell Hepburn who had said many years earlier that Ontario wouldn't be made a milch-cow for the rest of the Dominion. By 1951, Ontario changed her mind, acquiesced in the policy of centralized taxation, and entered into a tax agreement. The change of mind was, in part at least, due to a recognition of some justice in the claims of the poorer provinces that much of the wealth pooled in the richer provinces is produced by the skill and effort of people in other provinces, and that some of it should be redistributed for their benefit. That is to say, Ontario has loyalties that go beyond her boundaries and distract her from any crusade for a self-centred provincial autonomy.

Indeed, a self-centred states' rights or provincial autonomy is no longer practicable. It is not practical at all for states and provinces in these three federations to think of themselves as did the American states before, and even after, the Civil War, or as the older Canadian provinces tended to think of themselves until after the First World War. They cannot think of themselves as independent principalities, bowing only to federal dictates on foreign policy and foreign trade and a few other matters. They threw all this away when they allowed themselves to be drawn into an interdependent economy which undermined whatever secure economic base they may previously have had within their own boundaries. Even the rich and powerful states in the federation compromised their positions when they brought within their walls the Trojan horse of big enterprise with nation-wide interests and outlook, which, by its very nature, cannot be loyal to any self-centred provincialism. In so committing themselves, states and provinces gave up the power to develop or maintain widely differing economic relationships and sharply divergent social and cultural patterns. In fact, before interdependence had gone very far, the

American states found they could not live together half slave and half free, if I may use a term which points to the fateful differences but does not express them fully. In this discovery, they pointed up a lesson for all federal systems to learn in their maturity, if not before.

Alberta soon found it was not free to follow the genius of Social Credit in building the New Jerusalem in the foothills. If Saskatchewan under the C.C.F. had attempted full-scale socialism it would have run into much more trouble than the mere timidity of free enterprise about exploring for oil. Actually, the C.C.F. in Saskatchewan has chosen to work within the postulates of the mixed economy, which is the dominant economic pattern for the country as a whole. It has found there room for considerable experiment and variety in adapting the mixed economy to the distinctive genius of Saskatchewan for public and co-operative enterprise.

If it is said that Quebec has managed so far to maintain a culture markedly different from that of the other provinces, it must be recalled that for most of its people and over most of its area, Quebec culture has rested, until very recently, on a base of relatively self-sufficient agriculture. The very rapid industrialization in Quebec in the last fifteen or so years has caused sharp internal stress and strain. Much of the stress is due to the unremitting pressure exerted, for example, through trade unions and corporate enterprise to establish there the urban industrial pattern accepted by the rest of Canada. Quebec is being caught up in the logic of the interdependent economy and of large-scale industrial enterprise.

A province cannot now hope to run successfully against the tide of national development unless, of course, it associates with enough other provinces to turn the tide, in which event we have national not provincial action. The most it can hope to hold is freedom for minor adventure, for embroidering its own particular patterns in harmony with the national design, for playing variant melodies within the general theme.

It can hope to be free to decide to have rather more public ownership and rather less private enterprise, more or less social security and provincial regulation of economic life. It can hope to adjust policy on education and conservation of natural resources to distinctive provincial needs and aims, and so on. But it is everywhere limited in the distance it can go by having become part of a larger, although not necessarily a better, scheme of things. Its main role now is to lighten the curse of bigness.

In support of this conclusion I have so far produced only big nationwide enterprise, the interdependent economy, and some admittedly equivocal evidence on the nationalizing of sentiment. This testimony alone is not enough. Economic interdependence does not always draw communities together; big cartels do not always foster integration effectively, as witness the world wars of the twentieth century. There must be, in addition, a will to work together in solving the problems posed by interdependence. If that will emerges, it will find its main instrument in the initiatives of the national government and the national legislature. But it is not clear to me that there are firm popular majorities in the several states with this united will. It is little more than twenty years since an almost spontaneous mass revolt took place in Alberta and more such may well be possible, even if somewhat unlikely. The truth is the bulk of the people are not really aware of what is at stake in federal-state issues. They probably want the best of both worlds, state governments that respond fully to regional aspirations, and a national government with power to spawn an increasing range of services, deploring only the outrageously high taxation.

Whatever may be the truth about popular loyalties, it seems clear that sentiment is rapidly being nationalized among the *élites*, meaning by this term no more than the leaders of minority groups, the persons whose occupations or interests lead them either into close relationships with governments or into sustained reflection about it.

The active persons in many occupations and interests have been drawn into national associations. Whether or not these organizations become pressure groups in the strict sense, association in them has marked effects on those who take part. Their horizons are widened and they breathe the large air of broader understanding and sympathies. The relations of French-speaking and English-speaking Canadians have improved immensely in recent years. Much of both the decline in recriminations and the rise in generosity comes from the meeting each year in national associations of one kind and another of relatively small numbers of persons of the two language groups who reach not only understanding but friendship. They recognize themselves and one another as Canadians.

Associations of this kind break down barriers and clear ground for common action. When the members of such associations find they have common problems, they are led easily to think of attacking them on the broadest possible front, which is the national front. The welfare *élite* increasingly pins its hopes on the national government, for initiative and the setting of standards at the least. The agricultural *élite* still wants governmental action at both state and national levels but wants the essential frame of policy determined at the latter level.

The trade union *élite* wants national standards in labour matters. In Canada, the education *élite*, if that is a permissible description of the National Conference of Canadian Universities and Colleges, has been pressing strongly for federal subventions to university education.

Most striking of all are the changing attitudes of the business *élites*. In the long retreat of *laissez faire* in the first third of the century, substantial business interests fought many determined rearguard actions from the bastions of state power and judicial review, in an effort to stem the advance of federal legislative action. Over the last twenty years, they have almost given up the struggle, not so much because *laissez faire* is a lost cause but rather because events have made them change their minds. Industrial concentration has proceeded at a rapid pace. One industry after another has come to be dominated by a few great corporations. These mammoths and a number of more nebulous but nevertheless very real industrial combinations have deployed themselves in a nation-wide arena.

The men who control them are compelled to think in nation-wide, if not national, terms. They do not want *laissez faire*, nor the free fluctuating market, nor the unco-ordinated tinkering of many state or provincial governments. Instead, they want stability in prices, in labour relations, in monetary, fiscal, and other governmental policies, so that they can engage in long-range planning for their industry. They want the economy to be manageable, and, within limits, to be managed with a foresight which takes their nation-wide concerns into account. Because foresight on the scale that they want implicates the national government and its powers at many points, they want to be able to bring a persuasive influence to bear upon the national government. Instead of being closeted with their attorneys to find ways of frustrating national governments, they are now in conference on friendly terms with presidents, cabinet ministers, and senior officials at the national capitals. A wise precept says, "If you can't lick 'em, join 'em," and one may guess that the great managers would now consider a partnership with the national government if suitable terms could be arranged.

This is not quite the managerial revolution but it is a profound change. Adolf Berle calls it "administered capitalism" in a brilliant paper[4] in which he sketches the anatomy of the change and discusses

[4]"Evolving Capitalism and Political Federalism" in A. W. Macmahon (ed.), *Federalism, Mature and Emergent* (New York: Doubleday and Company, 1953).

its significance for federalism. He speaks only about the United States, but it is possible to discern the outlines of a similar change taking place in Canada on a smaller scale and at a somewhat slower pace. In the last twenty years, Canadian business interests have not challenged seriously the constitutional validity of federal legislation in the courts. Significantly, the one case in this period which reproduced some of the atmosphere of battles long ago was brought by grain traders (who still believe in the free market) seeking to have declared unconstitutional a wartime regulation of the federal government which, in effect, denied them windfall profits arising from decontrol of the price of barley.

From 1912 to 1932, interests engaged in the insurance business urged the courts again and again to hold that the Parliament of Canada had no constitutional power to regulate the business of insurance. By 1941, Canadian financial interests, including the insurance companies, had become the strongest supporters of the main recommendations of the Royal Commission on Dominion-Provincial Relations, recommendations which proposed to stabilize public finance and restore confidence and credit mainly through greatly enlarged action by the federal government. Shaken by widespread defaults in the depression and terrified by the revolt against financial orthodoxy in Alberta, they were driven to take a nation-wide view of their affairs, and to pin their hopes on the national government.

The tax agreements, which were first undertaken as a wartime measure and which have continued to the present, give the sole power of levying personal and corporate income tax, and, in most instances, succession duties, to the national Parliament. These far-reaching fiscal powers joined to federal monetary powers have been used courageously and with considerable effectiveness to stabilize the economy during the war and post-war periods. The fiscal initiative of the national government has not only kept the attention of business leaders focused on Ottawa but has also earned a grudging appreciation from the clear-headed ones. Despite incantations about free enterprise and imprecations about the scandalous tax burden, few of them want to return to a situation in which each of eleven governments dips into personal and corporate incomes as it sees fit. National government planning in fiscal matters is the least of the horrible evils that must be endured in a polity where high taxation seems inevitable.

To say that business leaders in Canada are coming to look more favourably on the federal government does not mean that they have all succumbed to this temptation or that those who have really favour all that the federal government does. Those whose interests are concentrated on the development and exploitation of the natural resources of a single province are naturally more concerned with the positive policies of the provincial government than with those of the national government. Big business with nation-wide interests sees more readily how helpful the national government could be. At the same time, it finds the federal government's scrutiny of combines and monopolies somewhat hampering and can be expected to urge on the courts a narrow interpretation of the power of the federal government in this field. All that is asserted is that nation-wide interests establish some kind of bond with the national government.

There is considerable ground for thinking that the business and other *élites* are coming to accept the pre-eminence of the national governments and to concentrate their efforts on ways and means of getting effective influence in the national political arenas. In the main, they are the active leaders of opinion, and they are likely, in the long run, to carry electoral opinion in most states and provinces. If this is so, the federal balance is being tipped decisively in favour of the national power, and it is hard to see how state governments and national governments can continue to be genuinely co-ordinate authorities. In constitutional law, the states may long continue to be co-ordinate, but politically they are likely to sink to a subordinate position.

Much the greater part of this paper so far has been taken up with speculation about the focus of opinion and sentiment in electorates and influential groups. It has had to be speculation because, as far as I know, this aspect of federal trends has not been studied with detailed care. Nevertheless, in these democratic aggregates with which we are concerned, sentiment and opinion, molded and canalized no doubt by material factors, will decide where power lies. Because power alone can balance power, the provinces and states have to keep strong and vigorous bodies of opinion on their side if they are to stop the aggrandizement of national governments.

For a long time, it was thought, admittedly with something less than accuracy, that the boundaries of power were pretty clearly marked out by the constitution. In practice, uncertainties about these boundaries were dealt with, if not always completely clarified, by the courts. In the classical federalism, the courts were the arbiters of the system. Even if it would not be quite correct to say that they held the balance between state governments and national governments (since, allowing for some exceptions in the case of the Judicial Committee of the Privy Council, the courts did follow the election returns) they nevertheless tipped the balance one way or the other from time to time. Here we come on a constitutional trend of the greatest importance. The courts are retiring, or being retired, from their posts as the supervisors of the balance.

If the consistent course of decision in the last twenty years is a reliable index, the Supreme Court of the United States has retired. By very wide interpretations of the interstate commerce clause, and of the general welfare clause as it relates to the federal spending power, the Court has come very close to holding that Congress can direct the economic life of the country—and influence its social and political structure through the spending power—as it sees fit. It has not excluded the states from intervention in the areas of economic life formerly thought to be their exclusive preserves, but rather has enabled Congress to oust them by over-riding legislation. At the same time, by restrictive reinterpretation of the due process clauses, it has freed both state legislatures and Congress from the restraints formerly imposed by these clauses on legislative regulation of economic affairs. Judicial review by the Court continues to be important in two main matters, in restraining the states from encroachment on fields that are either clearly exclusive federal domain under the Constitution or have been occupied by federal law, and in the safeguarding of fundamental civil liberties against encroachments by governments. Insofar as the federal balance is concerned, "recent judicial doctrine encourages the determination of both power and action by legislation, so that for most purposes, the national policy-makers are the arbiters of the federal system."[5]

Of course, this does not necessarily mean that Congress is rapidly denuding the states of all effective power. The states do not lack defenders in Congress, and so far state interests have been treated with circumspection, if not generosity. It does mean that contests about state power have to take place largely in the national political arena, and that a flexible method of experimental shifting of powers back and forth between the nation and the states has been achieved. It also means that, in federal relations as in many other aspects of our affairs, leadership in social adjustment to rapid and complex change has shifted from courts to legislatures, and law has been replaced in part by policy.

[5]Harvey C. Mansfield, "The States in the American System," in *The Forty-Eight States* (New York: The American Assembly, 1955), p. 30.

It would be quite wrong, however, to say that the Supreme Court of Canada is retiring from its post as supervisor of the federal balance in Canada. Indeed, the Supreme Court has recently proclaimed its strict adherence to the classical federalism by holding that neither the federal Parliament nor a provincial legislature can constitutionally delegate any portion of the exercise of its legislative powers to the other.[6] Ironically enough, it seems clear that Parliament can delegate its legislative powers to a provincial cabinet or other provincial executive agency or even to a tramp in the street, and that provincial legislatures can equally delegate their powers to the Governor-General in Council or to some agency of the federal executive.[7] The reason that the Parliament and the legislatures cannot delegate to one another is that their capacity for lawmaking is limited by the British North America Act to the classes of subject exclusively conferred on them therein. The Supreme Court sticks to the notion of exclusive and rigidly separated spheres of power. There is here no encouragement for experimental trading back and forth of legislative power between the nation and the provinces.

There is, however, some ground for thinking that the Supreme Court is being retired from this post, or perhaps rather being relieved of many of its duties at this post, by forces outside itself. It is well known that, on the whole, the Judicial Committee of the Privy Council gave a narrow restrictive interpretation of the powers of Parliament under the B.N.A. Act and a correspondingly wide interpretation to the powers of the provincial legislatures. Faced with this condition and seeing no hope of drastic constitutional amendment, those who have been concerned over the past twenty years with finding means of national action which would meet what they thought were, or would be, national needs have tried to turn the flank of the constitutional obstacles.

One of the reasons for persuading the provinces to give up personal and corporate income tax and succession duties by agreement to the Dominion was to give the Dominion massive fiscal powers. On the assumption that the power of the Dominion over its "public property" conferred by section 91.1 gave by implication a wide federal spending

[6]*Attorney General of Nova Scotia* v. *Attorney General of Canada* (1951) Supreme Court of Canada Reports 31.

[7]*Prince Edward Island Marketing Board* v. *H. B. Willis, Inc. and Attorney General of Canada* (1952) 2 Supreme Court of Canada Reports 392.

power, big spending programmes were undertaken. Vigorous use of its constitutional powers over monetary and foreign trade policy, of its constitutional–and contractual–fiscal powers, and of its assumed spending power for objects within the exclusive legislative authority of the provinces, has given the federal government enormous leverage on the provinces as well as on the national economy. This has been achieved without undertaking much legislative action of dubious constitutionality on which the Judicial Committee of the Privy Council or the Supreme Court would have had a chance to rule.

At first glance, it seems extraordinary that no one has challenged the constitutionality of the assumed spending power before the Supreme Court. It accounts for a very large portion of the heavy taxation about which everybody groans. Yet a little reflection will show that proof of the unconstitutionality of federal spending for objects outside federal legislative power would prove far too much for almost anybody's comfort. A great many of the substantial interests of the country now derive advantages from such spending, and the rest of them have not given up hope of doing so. The provincial governments which, as pointed out earlier, are always urging new projects on the federal government do not want to challenge it. Federal spending now supports so much of the established political, social, and economic structure of the country that prudent men hesitate to take steps that might wipe it out.

More generally, it can be said that neither the provincial governments nor big business interests are testing federal legislative action in the courts as vigorously as they used to. No spectacular cases challenging federal legislative power have recently come to the Supreme Court. An arbiter who is rarely appealed to is still an arbiter, but his importance diminishes *pro tanto*. Perhaps this is happening to the Supreme Court of Canada. I say perhaps, because conclusions based on trends of twenty years or less may turn out to have been merely temporary aberrations.

The negative side of the development is that the Court is not being asked to rule against Parliament so often. On the positive side, Dominion-provincial conferences, notably those held to negotiate about tax agreements every five years, have become clearing-houses for many disputed issues between the Dominion and the provinces. One can almost say that the various stresses and strains of the system are negotiated into tolerable compromises in the course of hammering out the next tax agreements. In Australia, where fiscal power and policy have also been centralized and the states are dependent for a large part of their revenues on the central government as in Canada, annual premiers' conferences perform, somewhat more systematically, functions similar to those of the Dominion-provincial conferences. The Australian premiers' conference mediates between the states and the nation in much the same way as does the United States Senate. Because of the discipline imposed by cabinet government in Australia —and Canada—regional interests cannot express themselves as freely in the national parliaments as they do in the United States Senate. They do express themselves through the state and provincial premiers in negotiations with the national governments. The Australian and Canadian mechanisms differ from that used in the United States, but they also give the appearance of a political process replacing, or at any rate supplementing more extensively than in earlier years, the judicial process.

The political processes have a flexibility and an easy adaptability to the dominant moods of the country that constitutional amendment and judicial interpretation both lack. There will continue to be regional aspirations which, even if they cannot have free play in a mature federalism, still have to be recognized and reckoned with. There will still be regional resistance by the people in the poorer areas against the tribute levied on them by the metropolitan areas. All these stresses and conflicts need to be negotiated and compromised in *ad hoc* arrangements, particularly where the electorates do not seem disposed to say clearly whether they are federal or unitary in spirit.

At any rate, we are likely to have to live for a long time with the equivocal structure called co-operative federalism. It has arisen because several separate governments share a divided responsibility for regulating a single economic and social structure. It is most unlikely that any constitution could be devised which would enable each to perform its specific functions adequately without impinging seriously on the others. So their activities are inevitably mingled, and co-operative arrangements must be worked out. In the result, formal powers are not co-terminous with operating responsibilities; the two levels of government as well as the several state and provincial governments interpenetrate one another in many places and ways. Under the heat and pressure generated by social and economic change in the twentieth century, the distinct strata of the older federalism have begun to melt and flow into one another.

Little can be said about co-operative federalism in the compass of a paper and it is a subject on which saying a little is not very useful.

The ramifications of co-operative federalism in the United States are bewildering, precisely because so many more promising applications of it have been made there than in either Canada or Australia. The most effective instrument of its vertical, or federal-state, manifestations in the United States has been the federal grant-in-aid, which has been used with great flexibility, ingenuity, and imagination, if not always with fully satisfying results.

Its achievements are very largely due to two features of the American governmental structure, the strict separation of powers at both state and national levels and the loose structure of command within the state executives. The separation of powers shields the formulation and operation of co-operative schemes from the more niggling reservations of politicians. Because state administration is not fully integrated under the command of the governors, many governors cannot control effectively the arrangements that state officials make with officials of the federal government. In some measure, perhaps, the exigencies of government in Washington deny the President and his staff effective control of officials at their end.

The result is that federal and state officials, many of whom have a professional devotion to their tasks, are relatively free to develop administratively satisfactory arrangements for the federal aid programmes. Nothing like these conditions prevails in Australia or Canada, because of responsible, cabinet government. Federal and state cabinets will not—indeed cannot—keep political considerations out of co-operative federalism. More than that, there is an integrated command of administration under premiers, prime ministers, and cabinets. Officials know they have to be sure of the support of their ministers before taking significant positions in matters as political as Dominion-provincial relations.

These differences explain in large measure why the federal grant-in-aid is less used and less flexible in Canada and Australia. To help with the imbalance of state and provincial revenues and responsibilities as well as to meet effectively the special cases of the poorer states, efforts have gone instead into securing a federal monopoly of levying the progressive taxes in return for which large unconditional grants are made to the states and provinces. Having possessed themselves of these revenues without federal conditions or controls on their use, the states and provinces develop their own services and programmes as they see fit. Federal-state co-operative arrangements are not undertaken except where there are special and compelling reasons, as for example in the administration of proposed health insurance schemes in Canada. The tendency is for the states to become dignified and haughty pensioners rather than partners of the national government.

Given the political conditions in which it would have to be worked, it is not clear whether Canada and Australia could really secure the important advantages that the technique of the federal grant-in-aid offers. On the other hand, it must be said that the broad fiscal powers that the Australian and Canadian national governments have secured are important, if not indispensable, instruments for maintaining stability and coherence in the public finance system and in the economy at large. The maxim that the power to tax is the power to destroy has a special poignancy for present-day polities with the prevailing high levels of taxation. Perhaps we exaggerate the practical usefulness of cyclical budgeting which broad fiscal powers make so attractive in theory. But it would be difficult to exaggerate the menace to economic stability and rationality of a number of unco-ordinated taxing authorities each trying to dip deeply into the flow of income. Perhaps the American economy is sufficiently productive to stand it without serious distortion and disruption. The Australian and Canadian economies almost certainly are not.

Whatever the different configurations of co-operative federalism are and however well they may be working, the ingenuity and resource that have gone into the adaptation of the classical federalism to the complexities of the twentieth century in the last two decades are remarkable. In the mid-thirties, the prospects that polities with significant federal elements in their constitutions could survive the tribulations from which they then suffered seemed dim. The prospects now appear to have improved greatly. We can at least hope to operate big government with a moderate amount of centralization, and at the same time preserve many of the values of wide participation and decentralized decision. Those who want to get back the substance of the classical federalism will have to reduce greatly big business, big government, and economic interdependence.

The Speakership of the Canadian House of Commons

JAMES H. AITCHISON

"Impartiality on the part of the Speaker is the supreme law of his office. It is essential that every member should have the conviction that when our colleague ascends the throne of the Speaker he ceases to be the man of the party and becomes the man of the whole house."[1] When Lapointe moved the election (for the second time) of Lemieux to the Speaker's Chair he formulated in these words the prime requirement of the Speakership of the popular branch of the legislature of a parliamentary democracy patterned on the classical British model. It is important that it be realized that it is not democracy as such nor any of the values democracy is designed to establish and maintain that makes impartiality imperative. The Speakership of the House of Representatives of the United States is a position of political power expected to be used by its incumbent to promote the political objectives of his party, of his wing of his party, or of himself. It cannot be seriously argued that this fact indicates that democratic values are less cherished in the United States than in Canada, or that the means of maintaining them are there less well understood, or that as a result the United States is less democratic than Canada. Yet any permanent impairment of the impartiality of the Canadian Speaker would be a certain sign of the permanent deterioration of Canadian democracy and of the permanent erosion of democratic liberties.

The reason for the difference is obvious enough: in the United States there is a plethora of checks and balances designed to hinder

[1]Canada, House of Commons, *Debates*, 1926, p. 1. Hereafter when the reference is to the Debates of the Canadian House of Commons, the word *Debates* only will be given. When the remarks quoted or referred to were made at the beginning of a new Parliament on the occasion of electing a new Speaker no citation will be given.

the exercise of arbitrary power; in Canada, as in all countries that have successfully adopted the British form of parliamentary government, the checks are few. Gordon Churchill, the present Minister of Veterans Affairs, listed them in 1956 as freedom of speech, freedom of assembly, and freedom of organization. There are others, none of which, however, would long survive the loss of these three. But in themselves they are insufficient. The rules of procedure of the House of Commons must indeed afford some protection to the Cabinet for it is too much to expect that without such protection there will always be enough day-to-day restraint on the part of Opposition parties to enable the Cabinet fully to present its case and to carry on the government of the country. But for Churchill's three checks to be effective the rules must also enable the Opposition parties to expose any tendency to arbitrariness on the part of the Cabinet. Given a set of rules which, if impartially interpreted and applied, would enable both Government and Opposition to perform their essential functions, it is obviously essential that the will of the Speaker who interprets and applies them be indifferent as to the effects of his decisions on the fortunes of parties and individuals. The impartiality of the Speaker, in a British institutional framework, is thus of key importance. Baldwin was not exaggeratng when he said that the Speaker of the British House was "the linch-pin of the whole chariot"; nor was O'Connor, who capped him by saying that the Speaker was "the centre stone upon which the pillars of our mighty Empire rest."[2] No doubt the impartial Speaker better symbolizes the spirit of democracy than does the partisan Speaker of the American House of Representatives, and no doubt its value as symbol is part of what both Baldwin and O'Connor had in mind. But they had in mind much more than that, for the real importance of the impartiality of the Speaker lies not in its symbolic value but in the necessary function it has to perform in an institutional framework of a special type. With that impartiality the few checks to arbitrariness within the system are effective; without it, the system, of which the checks are integral parts, collapses.

The requirement is therefore a logical, not a moral, requirement. In his recent *Science and Human Values* the physicist, Bronowski, informs us that as new facts have come to light scientific concepts have had to be changed to conform to them. So it is with the Speakership. The modern British Speakership differs greatly from what it was in

[2]United Kingdom, House of Commons, *Debates*, 5th series, vol. 179, pp. 10, 14.

the days when the chief function of the Speaker was to be the mouthpiece of the Commons. It had to change to conform to new facts, and ultimately to the new institutional and value facts of the nineteenth century. British statesmen of a century and more ago discerned clearly what the new political habits and political ideals of Britishers implied for the Speakership. The institution of the Speakership is thus not just a fact that happens to be this or that and need only be described. Nor does its most essential feature—impartiality—require a new moral judgment. Given the characteristic institutional facts of the British form of parliamentary democracy, impartiality is essential if the moral judgments, made when the state becomes democratic, are to be implemented.

Changes in the political institutions and value judgments of a society are less rapid than are modern physicists' discoveries of new facts. For over a hundred years we have not had to alter our idea of what the Speaker's office needs to be. There have been some institutional changes, however, both in Britain and Canada, that have made even more imperative a strict regard for the rules. The influence of the monarchical element in the constitution has almost entirely disappeared; the power of the second chamber, legal and political in Britain and political in Canada, has been sharply curtailed; there are disturbing signs that the outraging point of the parliamentary membership of the Government party, within and without the Cabinet, has become very high. As these checks have weakened, the checking function has more and more been left to the Opposition parties in the Commons and adequate performance by those parties has been made more difficult by the dislike (very strong and very evident in Canada) for minority governments and by the inexorable necessity in the positive state to grant large legislative and judicial power to administrative bodies and officials.

In the perspective of these institutional changes, which is the only perspective in which the appalling events that took place in the Canadian Parliament in 1956 can properly be viewed, the most appalling event of all is one to which little attention has been drawn. I refer to the occasion when the Prime Minister of Canada got on his feet to argue that the Speaker had not lost the confidence of the House because he still retained the confidence of a majority of the House. He thus equated the requirement of confidence in the Speaker with the requirement of confidence in the Government. That the Prime Minister of Canada should make so desperate and spurious an argument is itself a distressing event. But the most depressing feature of it is the deadly accuracy with which it registered the depth of degradation that had occurred. In this perspective, too, should be judged the power of another Prime Minister to wave the Speaker to his seat.[3] Nor, as in certain other areas, is it to the point for Britishers or Canadians to quote British precedents dating before the Reform Act of 1832.[4] It is now a very grave matter for a government to tamper with, or even be cavalier about, the position of the Speaker whose impartiality provides opposition parties with the protection that is so vitally required.

II

A definitive account of the Speakership of the Canadian House of Commons would require more research than I have been able to undertake and more space than is here available. A cursory examination of the all-too-frequent occasions on which the House has elected a new Speaker suffices to establish beyond a doubt that after Confederation Canadian parliamentarians were well aware that impartiality was the primary qualification for the Speakership. Reference to the paramount need for a Speaker to be impartial, "to hold the scales even," to be possessed of a "judicial spirit," occur with monotonous regularity in the remarks of Prime Ministers disclosing, and Opposition leaders supporting, the choice of the Government. This is not one of the many habits which were carried over from the Parliament of the Province of Canada to the Parliament of the Dominion of Canada. In 1852 Hincks even expressed the opinion that "the person filling the situation should be one whose political sentiments were in unison with the majority of the people, and who was known to favour those measures of progressive reform which the country sought,"[5] and was not criticized for it. No doubt a certain degree of fairness was expected and obtained from pre-Confederation Speakers: otherwise the allegation that Hincks made Sandfield Macdonald Speaker in order to neutralize him does not make much sense. But in the complicated and fluid parliamentary situations of the fifties and early sixties the

[3]On May 25, 1959. See the *Ottawa Citizen*, Feb. 12, 1960.

[4]As did Mr. Percy Somerset in *Punch*, Nov. 25, 1959: "It is hard to see very much sense in the contention that an ex-Speaker ought never to take any other job for the rest of his life. Addington, after he had been Speaker, became Prime Minister, though no Member of the present House seemed erudite enough to remember as much."

[5]*Toronto Globe*, Aug. 24, 1852.

Speakership was contested more frequently than not and this contest, not the Address, was often the first test of party strength in a new Parliament. The incongruity of making much ado about impartiality in purely partisan contests may have been the reason why nothing was said about it. One of the results of the solid majorities obtained after Confederation was to make it futile to contest the Speakership. The Canadian House of Commons has been divided only twice on the election of the Speaker: by Macdonald in 1878 on the occasion of Anglin's second election, as a means, in the last session before dissolution, of reviving the case that had been made against the Government the previous year for giving printing contracts to Anglin; and by Bennett in 1936 because Casgrain had dismissed House of Commons employees before even being elected by the House. Both were simply registering a protest against bad practice and neither bothered to put up an alternative candidate. The result of the election having become a foregone conclusion, it was now possible to pay full respects to what had long been the main feature of the British Speakership. It became the interest of Opposition leaders to stress that feature and, on the principle that a person is more likely to achieve a high level of performance if it is confidently expected of him, to proclaim complete confidence that the Government's choice possessed the required virtue.

It is less certain that the rationale of impartiality in the Speakership was always fully grasped. It may well have been sensed by many in a dim sort of way, but I suspect that for a long time most could have explicitly justified it only as an application of the British principle of fair play. The absence of an adequate and understood rationale is, I think, indicated by Laurier's attempt to provide one. "Our system of government rests," he said, "on the basis of free and untrammelled discussion, and the duty of presiding over the deliberations of the House of Commons, where this free and untrammelled discussion must take place, is, we must admit, one of the most difficult and delicate, when we remember that the object is, as it ought to be, to maintain absolute impartiality."[6] This argument ignores the plain fact that parliamentary decisions are not the result of truth emerging victorious after a fair encounter with error on the floor of Parliament. The point that the primary function of the rules is to protect the minority in the House was often made. "The rules of the House are made for the protection, not so much of the majority as of the

[6] *Debates*, 1899, p. 9062.

minority," said Speaker Lemieux in 1925, "The majority can always protect itself."[7] In insisting on the strict interpretation of the rules Knowles in the pipeline debate said: "The government has two protections. It has its majority and it has the rules. The opposition has only the rules. . . . That is the reason for the tremendous weight of responsibility that rests upon the occupant of the chair in seeing to it that the one and only weapon available to the opposition is not lost to it."[8]

This is excellent as far as it goes, but it does not go beyond the walls of Parliament. Pugsley, who led the Liberal obstruction against the Naval Bill in 1913, offered an extra-parliamentary ground: "When you protect the minority in Parliament, you are protecting the interests of at all events a large number of people, whose interests have as much right to be protected as those of the majority."[9] The fact that the protection of minorities inside the House is required for the protection not only of minorities but of the whole people outside the House was rarely expressed. The language used by Laurier in 1913 did express a deeper insight than his language of 1899. "The rules of the House," he said, "are certainly the bulwark of freedom."[10] And in 1953 St. Laurent in proposing Beaudoin used language reminiscent of that used by Baldwin and O'Connor in 1924: "Another very essential quality is a sense of responsibility toward the Canadian people, for the office is one of the cornerstones of democracy in this country." But neither attempted a demonstration. The failure to spell out clearly the whole argument suggests that few were fully seised of it. That the full rationale of the impartial Speakership was not widely understood contributed greatly, I suspect, to making possible the evident and serious lapse from impartiality in 1956.

III

The need for impartiality in the Speaker has, with rare exceptions, been unquestioned by Canadian parliamentarians and repeatedly asserted by them. The rationale of impartiality has been partly, if not fully, understood. But what of the record? Have Speakers of the Canadian House of Commons been, in fact, impartial? On the

[7]*Debates*, 1952, p. 2736.
[8]*Debates*, 1956, p. 4330.
[9]*Debates*, 1913, p. 6375.
[10]*Debates*, 1913, p. 6383.

answer to this question there is no agreement. One view is that until the unfortunate lapse in 1956 the impartiality of Canadian Speakers never fell far short of, and, much more frequently than not, equalled, the impartiality of British Speakers. It was the opinion of Beauchesne that none of the Speakers under whom he served during the long period he sat at the Clerk's table was partial.[11] Another view, put forward by those who would condone the obvious partiality of 1956, is that Canada never had an impartial Speakership. A third, maintained stoutly by Forsey,[12] is that the record was good until 1930 but that about that time a marked deterioration set in. If there is a break in the record, it did occur about 1930. But is there such a break?

For the answer to this question the critical Speakerships before 1930 are those of Cockburn (1867–74), Anglin (1874–9), and Marcil (1909–11). In proposing Cockburn's re-election in 1873 Macdonald made the dubious point that none of his decisions had ever been reversed. When he said that, like all other Speakers, Cockburn may have given decisions that were not acceptable to individual members, Rymal of North Wentworth came in with a "Hear, hear!" Cockburn's second election, though unopposed, was greeted with "loud applause from the ministerial benches and a solemn silence on the part of the opposition."[13] On May 15, 1873, he was loudly cheered by the Conservatives for ruling Huntington out of order on Macdonald's initiative, when Huntington was trying to ensure that certain evidence would be placed before the Select Committee to inquire into the Pacific Railway negotiations. After the session was over the *Hamilton Times* referred to "Mr. Speaker Cockburn of the Commons, whose unfortunate failing it is to sneeze whenever Sir John takes snuff and whose movements are popularly supposed to be controlled by a wire extending from his spinal column to the Premier's desk."[14] It was also said scornfully of him that he had had his decisions reversed in a friendly House. But the main charge of the Opposition against him was that he had failed to take the Chair on August 13 until the Black Rod was at the door of the House, and that he had

[11]Stated in personal interview, June, 1958.

[12]E. A. Forsey, "Correspondence," *Canadian Forum*, Sept., 1956, pp. 143–4; "Speaker and Pipeline," *Canadian Bar Review*, XXXIV, pp. 880–2; and especially "Constitutional Aspects of the Canadian Pipe Line Debate," *Public Law*, Spring, 1957, pp. 9–27.

[13]*Debates*, Scrapbook Record in Parliamentary Library, March 5, 1873.

[14]Reprinted in *Sarnia Observer*, Oct. 24, 1873.

deliberately done so in order to prevent Mackenzie from protesting against the prorogation. For this Mackenzie took the first occasion that offered in the second session of 1873 to rebuke him. "Speakers of the English House of Commons," summed up the *Stratford Beacon*, "shew conspicuously in history for the jealous care and courage with which they have watched over and protected the interest of the minority and guarded the privileges of Parliament against usurpations: but Mr. Cockburn will appear in history in a different guise."[15]

There is little evidence that Cockburn had done anything in the first Parliament to justify the solemn silence with which the Opposition greeted his second election. Holton on May 14, 1868, complained about the rules being rigidly enforced against the Opposition, but it is clear that his complaint was directed against the Government, not the Speaker; for he announced the intention of the Opposition to make the refusal of indulgence reciprocal, and succeeded in preventing Howland from getting a suspension of a standing order. Six days later Mackenzie complained that language had been applied to the Opposition which had been ruled out of order when used against a minister, but on that occasion he and Holton got what they wanted. And some, at least, of his decisions were unfavourable to the Government: on May 16, 1868, for example, he ruled against the objections of Government supporters to an Opposition amendment. A striking feature of the first Parliament, like some of the other early Parliaments, is the extent to which the Speaker remained in the background. Not only were none of his decisions reversed; none seemed to have been appealed. It was only in the short second Parliament of 1873 that any real exception was taken to his conduct. The solemn silence was probably an earnest of what was to come and Rymal, after all, was the licensed humourist of the House.

Nor are the Opposition's strictures on his conduct during 1873 to be accepted without examination. The year of the Pacific Scandal was no ordinary year. The Liberals were prepared to believe the worst of the Prime Minister and of anyone connected with him. Their diatribes against Cockburn were exceeded by their diatribes against the Governor-General and had, perhaps, as little justification. The only "reversed decision" I have been able to find is not a hitherto undiscovered appeal: the House merely defeated a motion to receive an election petition after Cockburn had given it as his opinion that the petition should be received.[16] The Opposition press (for example,

[15]Reprinted in *Sarnia Observer*, Nov. 21, 1873.
[16]*Debates*, Scrapbook Record, March 24, 1873.

the *Halifax Citizen* of March 25) called the vote the first Government check, but Cockburn's argument would seem to be better than that of the majority, and he was probably technically right also in ruling Huntington out of order on May 15. It is true that he was twenty-five minutes late in taking the Chair on August 13, but his tardiness is greatly weakened as evidence of collusion with the Government when it is realized that punctuality was never a great virtue of his: he had been late no fewer than nineteen times earlier in the session, on one occasion by as much as thirty minutes, and no one seems to have taken any objection. After the acerbity of 1873 had receded into the past he was not remembered as a partisan Speaker. "His tact and courtesy," says Wallace, "did much to establish a high tradition in the Speaker's Office."[17] We need not, perhaps, accept this at its face value, but it is significant that when the Liberals criticized Macdonald for not continuing Anglin in 1879 they simply pointed out that the question of continuing Cockburn in 1874 had not arisen because he had not been re-elected to the House; they made no reference to his alleged partisanship.

Despite his printing contracts, Anglin's impartiality was never even impugned. In criticizing the contracts in 1877, Conservative debaters emphasized repeatedly that they were not suggesting that his decisions had been influenced by them in the slightest degree. The law had been broken, they argued; Anglin was not in law even a member of the House, and hence he could not be its Speaker. On April 7, Macdonald gave his highest testimony to the ability and impartiality with which Anglin had filled the chair. Two days later he came very close to suggesting that Anglin had been influenced. "Who knew," he said, "that in 1874, the Government held the Speaker, the First Commoner of the land, in the hollow of their hand? Who knew that the Speaker was, week after week, and month after month, and quarter after quarter, receiving his commission at the hands of the Government for which he signed receipts." But he checked himself in time. He had no hesitation in saying, he continued, "that the hon. gentlemen were again and again disappointed at the result of their actions, because Mr. Speaker rose superior to their inducements." The Government saved Anglin for the balance of the session by having the matter referred to the Committee on Privileges and Elections which conveniently did not report until the dying moments of the session. In the interval before Parliament assembled for its last session before dissolution Anglin had resigned his seat and had been re-elected to

[17]*Dictionary of Canadian Biography.*

the House. In protesting against his re-election to the Chair, Macdonald reiterated that he did not wish to say anything against him in his character. He protested because the Speaker should be, like Caesar's wife, not only pure but free from suspicion, and because Anglin had sat in the Chair for two years after he must have been told that his contracts were stopped and that his dealings with the Post Office were within the description of parliamentary corruption. Anglin gives every evidence of being a very conscientious Speaker who considered difficult questions with great care before giving a decision. In *A Canadian Portrait Gallery* Dent says that his rulings "were always rendered with strict impartiality and justice."

The campaign against Charles Marcil in the Conservative press was led by the *Toronto News*: it began shortly after the general election of 1908 and was carried on for some time after he was elected Speaker on January 20, 1909. The burden of the charge was Marcil's method of electioneering which was to promise to get, and to boast of having got, public works on a large scale for his constituency (of Bonaventure in the Gaspé Peninsula). "IT IS INCONCEIVABLE," thundered the *News*, "THAT SUCH A PERSON SHOULD BE CHOSEN TO PRESIDE OVER THE MOTHER OF PARLIAMENTS." The British practice of re-electing a Speaker "WOULD HARDLY WORK OUT SATISFACTORILY IN A COUNTRY WHERE A MAN WHO HAS DISTINGUISHED HIMSELF AS A WHOLESALE BRIBER OF A CONSTITUENCY IS CONSIDERED FIT TO BE A SPEAKER. But even in the Dominion Parliament there has heretofore been some effort to appoint to the speakership men who would hardly descend to the Marcil methods."[18] Marcil remained a member of the House until his death in 1937 and apparently retained to the very end his lively interest in constituency favours. According to Bennett, "he was ever mindful of the claims of those who lived in the Gaspé peninsula," and King said of him that it "was not surprising to discover that his last word was one of grateful acknowledgment to a minister of the Crown for something the minister had been able to do which was of assistance to the constituency represented by Mr. Marcil and to adjoining constituencies."

But Marcil was also very likable and very popular. Although Borden was urged by some of his followers to do more, he contented himself, when Laurier moved Marcil's election, with saying that it might be permitted him to say, "without in the slightest degree desiring to be disrespectful, or to be understood in any offensive sense, that the very judicial quality with which the Speaker of the House

[18]Reprinted in *Halifax Evening Mail*, Jan. 3, 1909.

is invested would negative any idea in the mind of any one of us, and I am sure in the mind of the hon. gentleman himself, that the person filling such a position could be a suppliant for favours from the administration from day to day in respect of his constituency." Marcil had been Deputy Speaker in the previous Parliament and in proposing him Laurier appealed to the judgment of the members of that Parliament that he had discharged his duties as such "with grace, with dignity, with impartiality and with marked ability." Borden agreed that he had conducted himself with dignity and impartiality and tact. For aught that appears to the contrary his performance as Speaker was as acceptable as his performance as Deputy Speaker. "He was a gentleman of the old school," was Woodsworth's obituary comment.

In campaigning against the selection of Marcil the *News* spoke of "all the traditions of dignity and honor and fair play that have grown about this high and responsible office,"[19] and it was the Canadian, not the British, office it had in mind. Many expressions of confidence in the Speakers of the first sixty-four years of the Canadian House are to be found in *Hansard*. In opposing a salary for the Deputy Speaker in 1885 Casey said that "the Speaker . . . is so utterly apart from the political contests of the House that it is very seldom that any suspicion of political leanings can rest upon his position in the Chair; and it goes without saying that any such suspicion is out of the question in the present instance."[20] Despite the heat generated by the protracted debate on the Naval Bill in 1913, Pugsley became bitter, not about the conduct of the Speaker, but about that of the temporary chairmen of the Committee of the Whole House. He had such confidence in both the Speaker and the Deputy Speaker that he thought that points of order should be referred for decision from temporary chairmen to either. Laurier did not agree that this should be done, but he too bore "testimony to the impartial motive of Mr. Speaker."[21] The following year Laurier moved that the Deputy Speaker, like the Speaker, be debarred from taking part in electoral contests while in office. Borden agreed that the position of Deputy Speaker should be assimilated to the Speaker's but did not think that Laurier's was the way to do it. "If we are to make formal rules and to embody them in a resolution of this House, why is there more necessity for doing it in respect to the Deputy Speaker than in respect to the Speaker?" he

[19]Reprinted in *Halifax Evening Mail*, Jan. 14, 1909.
[20]*Debates*, 1885, p. 3351.
[21]*Debates*, 1913, pp. 6363–8, 6391–2.

asked. "We have not attempted to do it in the case of the Speaker and nevertheless the status of the Speaker is acknowledged in this House, and my right hon. friend himself has borne testimony to the fact that the duties of Speaker under all Administrations have been satisfactorily and worthily discharged by the men who have been selected for that important position."[22]

No answer was made to this argument. When Foster proposed Sévigny in 1916 he remarked that in his long parliamentary career he had been under eight Speakers, four of them Conservative and four Liberal; all had worthily upheld the traditions that clustered around the Speaker's Chair; the balances had been fairly held; equal justice had been dealt out to both parties. "If disadvantages and difficulties had existed in connection with the Speaker's tenure of office it may be said to their credit that they have overcome them, and that they have maintained the dignity of the office according to its traditions." Laurier, though he reflected on the administration's custom of making its selection from among the most prominent and most devoted of its followers, and upon the fact of Sévigny's being a Nationalist, agreed nevertheless with what Foster had said "as to the character and ability of those of our colleagues who have in years past had the honour of being Speakers of the Canadian House of Commons." Laurier expressed perfect confidence in Rhodes in 1917 (his only blemish was in being a Tory) and when Rhodes was re-elected in 1918 he said: "Both as Speaker and Deputy Speaker he certainly was entitled to the encomium which has been passed upon him by the Prime Minister. For he performed his duties with impartiality, which is the first qualification for the Speakership of this House, with dignity and with full knowledge of Parliamentary law." It is generally conceded that there is no question about the impartiality of either Rhodes (1917–21) or Lemieux (1922–30).

There is more to be said about the period prior to 1930; the evidence so far presented all suggests that a high standard of impartiality was consistently achieved. But very fine things have been said also about most of those who have been Speaker since 1930 and there have been few open charges of partiality. The weighty opinion of Beauchesne has already been given. The applause that greeted the nomination of Bowman in 1935 indicated, according to King, then Leader of the Opposition, that all members on his side of the House very cordially approved of the choice. It seems to be the general opinion that Bowman, in being Speaker for only one session, was given

[22]*Debates*, 1914, p. 1368.

no real chance to prove his worth in the Chair. The non-committal quality of this judgment is itself evidence that, at the very least, he could not have been flagrantly partial. Casgrain (1936–40) came in under a cloud. Bennett was justified in dividing the House in his election. He made it clear that Casgrain did not possess the confidence of the House as a whole and in this he was supported by Woodsworth who was "not at all sure" that Casgrain possessed the necessary qualifications of fairness, impartiality, and ability to leave partisanship behind, and who recognized that it might be "extremely difficult for a man to resign the post of chief whip of a party and at one jump accept the more or less judicial position of Speaker of this house." In nominating Casgrain, the Prime Minister had referred to the noble tradition in the British Empire "that where members of the bar receive appointment to the bench they leave behind their partisanship and adopt a judicial character which is beyond question." That tradition, he thought, was equally true of those who had been strong party men and had come later to occupy the position of Speaker in the House of Commons and he believed that it would be equally true of Casgrain. In winding up the debate he asked the House to withhold judgment until Casgrain was actually in the Chair. "If I had not the utmost confidence in what I believe will be the impartiality and fair play of the gentleman I have nominated," he said, "I would not for one moment think of urging the house to take action immediately." Bennett was quite content that Casgrain's election be carried on division. As it turned out, King's confidence appears to have been justified: Beauchesne's verdict is that Casgrain was "the most partisan of politicians; the most impartial of Speakers."[23] When his successor was elected Blackmore said that "if the reputation which was so well established by the Speaker who occupied the chair in the last parliament is maintained . . . we shall be fully satisfied."

Elected in May, 1940, Glen was, by June, 1941, already being congratulated (by Ross and Coldwell) upon the "magnificent way" in which he was conducting the affairs of the House. "I am afraid," he said, "when all men speak well of me." In 1943 the selection of Bradette to be Deputy Speaker was received with great satisfaction by the House. "I am sure," said Coldwell on that occasion to the Speaker, "we shall have in our Chairman of Committees, one who will follow your own example, if I may say so, and be fair at all times to all members of the house." A year later Church said of Glen that "in the discharge of his duties here since the war started [he] has been most

[23]Stated in personal interview, June, 1958.

fair to all parties in the house."[24] When Glen's successor was elected Coldwell hoped that when the time came for him to lay down his care of office the House would regard him with the same esteem and respect that it had for Glen.

Church also paid a tribute to Fauteux (1945–9).[25] But it was the most casual of tributes; it included Fauteux's predecessors, and occurred early in Fauteux's Speakership; and Church's main interest seems to have been to compliment Beauchesne, the Clerk of the House. I have been unable to discover any other Opposition tribute to Fauteux and there is no disguising the fact that his performance in the Chair caused great dissatisfaction. This is evident from the pages of *Hansard* itself. In the absence of compliments to Speaker Fauteux the compliments to Deputy Speaker Macdonald were pointed; and on one occasion the House's preference for the latter was made startlingly explicit. One of Fauteux's failings was to delight in the neatness of the logic with which he impaled members when he gave a ruling on his own initiative: they could not discuss his ruling before he gave it because, he pointed out, they did not know what it was going to be; and they could not discuss it after he had given it for that was prohibited by the rules. Yet the trouble with Fatueux was incompetence rather than partiality, and if there was partiality it was not the result of failure to maintain a standard well understood by himself.

When Macdonald succeeded to the Speakership in 1949 there was a return to (expressed) satisfaction with the Speaker. His election was greeted with enthusiasm on all sides. Pouliot (whose word in this connection is as good as that of any member of the Opposition) praised him in 1951 and so did Drew. "We now have a Speaker who, according to my experience, has been without parallel," was Pouliot's tribute in 1952.[26] When Macdonald's term drew to its close he received the most fulsome praise from all corners of the House. No pre–1930 Speaker had fairer words spoken of him than he.

IV

There remains, nevertheless, a persistent belief that the fair words used by Canadian parliamentarians about their Speakers since 1930 are to be taken at less than their face value. The explanations for the

[24]*Debates*, 1941, p. 4042; 1943, p. 702; 1944, p. 1261.
[25]*Debates*, 1945, 2nd sess., p. 1916.
[26]*Debates*, 1951, pp. 4746, 4037–8; 1952, p. 2121.

fair words are various. For some they are the result of the view that it seldom does harm and may do good to praise the Speaker. Others suggest that they mean no more than a recognition that the Speaker has done about as well as could be expected in a very difficult position, the difficulty consisting of the Speaker's being dependent on the Government for future preferment. There is the interesting theory that politicians, required by their trade constantly to say nasty things about one another, tend to compensate by overdoing it whenever an opportunity arises to use, safely, the language of praise. (So readily does insincerity come to politicians!) And there is the opposing view, probably true of some of the more idealistic politicians, that the fair words are due to a natural and generous disposition to see human beings and their behaviour in the most favourable light. Whatever be the explanation, the twin facts are that fair words have been used and that there has been something less than perfect confidence in nearly all Speakers since 1930.

Evidence for the latter fact can be found in *Hansard* itself. Bennett's lack of confidence in Casgrain was so evident that Lapointe charged him with persecution. The occasion was Bennett's angry accusation that Lapointe had instructed Casgrain and that Casgrain, regardless of his previous indication of his views, had followed Lapointe's instruction. Lapointe retorted that all who had sat in the previous Parliament knew how Bennett had directed the debate and the way he had instructed the Speaker.[27] In 1952 (after Macdonald had been Speaker for three years) Fulton contrasted the position of the Speaker in the United Kingdom with that of the Speaker in Canada in a manner which made his lack of perfect confidence perfectly plain:

> . . . I speak in no sense of criticism in referring to the position of the Speaker here as not being the same as the position enjoyed by the Speaker of the House of Commons in England. If that is so it is so for no other reason than that it has been our custom to change our Speakers with every parliament. . . . the custom there has resulted . . . in the Speaker's having a more independent position than he has here.
>
> When the Speaker there rigidly applies some rule, enforces limitation of debate or disciplines a member, there is never any feeling that it is done for reasons of partiality. The Speaker there is absolutely impartial and that is recognized.

[27]*Debates*, 1936, pp. 488–90.

> It seems to me that until that same fundamental principle is accepted here and we can have the same curtailment of debate as is possible over there, which would be accepted without any suggestion inside or outside the house that there was unfairness or partiality, it will be extremely difficult for us to adopt these restrictions which the hon. member for Halton has set forth in the resolution.[28]

Green, as if to emphasize the greatness of the tribute he was paying to Macdonald, began his praise by saying: "I suppose the members of the opposition parties are the ones who *usually wonder* about the actions of the Speaker." And in complimenting Beaudoin on his election he said: "Those of us who sit in the opposition side *always* watch carefully the way in which the presiding officer carries out his duties."[29]

But if parliamentarians after 1930 were uneasy despite the fair words used by some of them about their Speakers, is it not possible that the same could be true of parliamentarians before 1930? Is there any evidence that despite the multitude of fair words spoken about pre–1930 Speakers there was also lack of perfect confidence in some of them? The answers are that it is possible and that there is evidence.[30]

There seems to be some reservation in Foster's remark, made on the occasion of Edgar's death, that Edgar's decisions had been "as fair and as equitable as he in his position could make them."[31] The cheers that greeted the naming of Brodeur in 1901 indicated to Laurier only that his election was acceptable "at all events" to the Government side of the House and although Brodeur had been Deputy Speaker in the previous Parliament, Hibbert Tupper would only go so far as to say that "we fervently hope . . . that the hon. gentleman . . . will be so

[28]*Debates*, 1952, p. 1213. For another expression of Fulton's uneasiness and a powerful plea by him for a permanent Speakership, see *Debates*, 1955, pp. 5565–6.

[29]*Debates*, 1952–3, p. 5439; 1953–4, p. 371. Italics mine.

[30]My evidence all comes from the period after 1891 and therefore does not run counter to Ward's conclusion that Speakers down to 1891 "checked members on both sides of the House impartially" (Norman Ward, "The Formative Years of the House of Commons, 1867–91," *Canadian Journal of Economics and Political Science*, 1952, p. 437). Ward's generalization is of the kind that is ordinarily difficult to make with confidence.

[31]*Debates*, 1891, p. 9061.

able to observe the great traditions of that high office . . . that he may confidently rely upon the support of the gentlemen who sit either to the right or left of the Chair." Borden failed to echo Laurier's praise of Brodeur when the latter was superseded by Belcourt, and although Borden made the polite assumption that Marcil would be uninfluenced as Speaker by his fondness for the pork barrel, there appeared "to be some skepticism among opposition members."[32] Sproule (who was soon to become Speaker himself) was not wholly reassured by the fact that the new rule concerning irrelevance, introduced in 1910, was the British rule word for word and for much the same reason that Fulton gave for having doubts about the proposals of 1952. "I do not wish to insinuate," he said, "that any Speaker would be partial in his ruling, but the Speaker of the English House of Commons continues to occupy that position no matter what party is in power, whereas the Speaker of this House is elected for every new parliament and is taken from the side of the House which for the time being is controlled by the ministers, so that if he gave a ruling that might be considered a partial one, there would be no redress."[33]

In the debate of March 24, 1913, already referred to, Emmerson blurted out: "So far as lies within his power, he may seek to be immune from association with either of the political parties; but there is no use disguising the fact that the party which appoints a Speaker looks to him as one of its own, as a part of the Administration as it were."[34] It is true that in the same debate Pugsley and Laurier indicated their confidence in the then Speaker. But were they and the many witnesses, before and after them, to the impartiality of Speakers, disguising what Emmerson alleged to be a fact? Did Emmerson blurt out what were the real feelings of Opposition members? That he gave expression to an uneasiness among Opposition members that was far more general than they cared to admit is borne out by the discussion of the Speakership by the journalist S. D. Scott at the time of the controversy over Marcil:

> The speaker comes from the party ranks and knows that in four or five years he must return to them. He looks to his party and the government for rewards. He applies to ministers for favors for his county to assist in his re-election. In the nature of the case his sympathies are with the party in power.

[32]*Halifax Herald*, Jan. 25, 1909.
[33]*Debates*, 1909–10, pp. 8377–8.
[34]*Debates*, 1913, p. 6313.

> . . . While [previous Speakers] were generally selected for the speakership with regard for their natural ability and knowledge of parliamentary law and usage as well as their judicial character and the respect in which they were held, they did not cease to be party men, though they were expected to hold their partisanship in abeyance during the hours when the house was in session, and they were in the chair. *Some* of them, notably the late Hon. Peter White, thoroughly fulfilled these expectations and all of them did so *most* of the time.[35]

Confidence in the impartiality of Speakers before 1930 was probably not substantially greater than confidence in Speakers since then. It was recognized that given the cluster of practices surrounding the Canadian Speakership they had done well, even remarkably well, but because of those very practices it was not to be expected that the high level of impartiality displayed by British Speakers would always be attained. It had not always been attained and could not be taken for granted. The very frequency of tributes to the impartiality of individual Speakers itself indicates that impartiality was not taken for granted.

Forsey, however, puts forward two additional grounds for his belief in a marked deterioration since 1930. One is that the practices themselves have, in his opinion, become worse. He relies mainly on the fact that since 1930 proportionally more Speakers have become Cabinet ministers after serving in the Chair. But it is not the number of Speakers who subsequently became ministers that is significant for the possible motivation of their conduct in the Chair; it is whether or not any Speaker might hope to become a Cabinet minister. In 1952 Ward reported that three of the first six Speakers aspired to the Cabinet. To this Forsey replies that "the point is not what they aspired to but what they got."[36] This point would be valid only if election to the Chair put a term to Speakers' hopes. What we are interested in is their conduct in the Chair and while that conduct may not have been affected by their aspirations while in the Chair, it is the nature of those aspirations that is relevant. Whether or not they were subsequently realized is irrelevant. Most Canadian Speakers continued as active politicians after the interval of their Speakerships,

[35]*Halifax Herald*, Jan. 25, 1909. Italics mine.

[36]Ward, "The Formative Years," p. 436; Forsey, "Constitutional Aspects," p. 22.

many of them were re-elected to the House, and nearly all of them, on their election to the Chair, had belonged to the group that had at least some claims to be considered for Cabinet office. Macdonald gave it as a reason (or was it an excuse?) for not putting Kirkpatrick into the Cabinet that no Speaker had been so "transferred," but so far as I have been able to discover the principle that no former Speaker should be appointed to the Cabinet was never enunciated in Canada in the nineteenth century,[37] and no objection was taken on grounds of principle when the first Speaker (Ouimet in 1892) was so appointed. Even before that first case there was, therefore, no reason why a Speaker (while in the Chair) should have been without hope. All of the three Speakers referred to by Ward aspired to Cabinet office while in the Chair, and the third of them, White, aspired in spite of the fact that the other two had been disappointed. After 1892 the thought "If Ouimet, why not me?" in the absence of any countervailing opinion of any strength would not require the frequent occurrence of new cases to have the effect, or nearly the effect (on the assumption that Speakers are prone to yield to temptation), that Forsey suggests the greater frequency of cases since 1930 has had.

For Forsey writes as if the greater frequency of appointment to the Cabinet were itself evidence of deterioration, an assumption which requires for its validity an inexorable connection between the existence of a temptation and the yielding to it. Whether Speakers before or since 1930 resisted temptation or yielded to it is not, however, relevant to the point I am now trying to make, which is simply that if there were temptations after 1930 there were also temptations (and strong ones) before 1930. That they were stronger after 1930 than before is by no means established by the fact of greater frequency of appointment to the Cabinet. There were other methods by which compliant Speakers could be rewarded, among them other kinds of appointment as well as printing contracts and pork barrel appropriations. In his discussion of the Speakership already referred to, Scott treated the appointment of Kirkpatrick to the Lieutenant-Governorship of Ontario and the prospective appointment of Sutherland to the Bench as if they were on a par with the appointments of Ouimet and Brodeur to the Cabinet. The increasing size of the Cabinet has made Cabinet office more readily available and it may have simply become relatively more

[37]On the contrary. Macdonald wrote to White that his "claims to cabinet office are not to be in any way affected by [his] having accepted the Speakership." Quoted by Ward, "The Formative Years," p. 436.

desirable in the eyes of ex-Speakers. Kirkpatrick, it is true, would have preferred Cabinet office, but the other reason Macdonald gave for refusing it—the existence of a general impression among supporters of the Government that Kirkpatrick had generally decided against them and had been afraid of the Leader of the Opposition—was not likely to stiffen the backbones of those of his successors who had similar ambitions. The inference that Kirkpatrick got his Lieutenant-Governorship despite his failure to satisfy Government supporters, and that in future even a Lieutenant-Governorship could not be taken for granted, was not implausible.

The absence of comment in 1892 is itself significant: the close connection maintained between the Speaker and party was manifested in a novel way, but the connection itself was not news and the addition of a novel way to the old ways was unimportant. How close the connection was, or was thought to be, is indicated by the fact that White, after a single session as Speaker and before Ouimet had entered the Cabinet, was reported to have had a conference with Abbott over Cabinet reconstruction. The Prime Minister wanted him to take Haggart's place, it was reported, but the difficulty was to get rid of Haggart.[38] And two of the three appointments to the Cabinet before 1930 were worse than those of the last two decades, for both Brodeur in 1904 and Sévigny in 1916 *resigned* the Speakership to enter the Cabinet, whereas Casgrain, Glen, and Macdonald were not appointed until their terms of office in the Chair had expired with the dissolution of Parliament.

In brief, if bad practices since 1930 resulted in poor performance, the practices before 1930 (and before 1904) were in all conscience bad enough to produce the same result. And where the question is that of yielding to temptation, just where is the breaking point anyway? Even if the temptations have latterly become somewhat stronger, it does not follow that recent Speakers have succumbed. Glen had before him the example of his immediate predecessor's appointment to ministerial office and he subsequently became a minister himself; yet he was one of those of whom, conspicuously, fair words were spoken. Beaudoin eventually succumbed, but the fact that his immediate predecessor entered the Cabinet did not prevent, on his election to the Chair, the universal expression, in terms of unprecedented enthusiasm, of confidence in him.

Forsey's second ground for believing in a deterioration since 1930

[38] *Halifax Morning Chronicle*, Nov. 14, 1891.

is the marked increase since then in appeals from the Speaker's rulings.[39] He concedes that the number of appeals from a Speaker's rulings "is not, of course, by itself, conclusive evidence of his competence or impartiality or the reverse." But he insists that "the glaring contrast between the very few appeals down to 1930 and the enormous number since certainly suggests that something has happened to the Canadian Speakership in the last quarter century, and that conclusions drawn from that period are, to say the least, not necessarily valid for the whole of Canadian history since Confederation."[40]

A final assessment of the significance of the number of appeals for the impartiality of Speakers must await a fuller analysis than has yet proved possible. There are, however, a number of considerations that suggest that Mallory's instinct, in scouting the importance of the increase in appeals, is right.[41] They are:

(1) The number of appeals since 1930 should be adjusted to take into account the increased length of sessions.[42]

(2) In not a few cases, the appealers disavowed any intention of reflecting on the Speaker's impartiality. "Mr. Speaker," said Green to Glen on one occasion, "I have the utmost respect for Your Honour's

[39]His figures are: no appeals in the first thirty-nine years of the Dominion, only seventeen in the first sixty-three years, and seventy-five in the twenty-three years from 1931 to 53 inclusive ("Constitutional Aspects," p. 20). I have found five more in the last period, two in the Speakership of Bowman, and three in that of Casgrain.

[40]Forsey, "Constitutional Aspects," p. 21.

[41]J. R. Mallory, "Correspondence," *Canadian Bar Review*, XXXIV, p. 883.

[42]Ward reports that the right to challenge the Speaker's ruling was often referred to before 1891 ("The Formative Years," p. 437). References to the right were no doubt prompted by dissatisfaction with particular rulings. But Ward does not say how frequent the references were, and my own impressions are that they were not very frequent, that references to the right of appeal from the rulings of chairmen of Committees of the Whole House were more frequent, and that the latter occurred at such long intervals that even leading parliamentarians were unsure of the procedure to be followed. For such uncertainty see the discussions of May 1, 1885 (pp. 1510–13), June 6, 1899 (pp. 4448–57), and July 24, 1903 (pp. 7342–52). Even as late as 1926 Meighen was unsure (p. 3985). But if the issue is to turn merely on the score with respect to appeals, and if the frequency of references to the right were to count as well as the frequency of the exercise of the right, the number of times the right was referred to but not exercised since 1930 would have to be discovered.

judgement. However, I believe that like the rest of us Your Honour is subject to human error. In this case I think the decision is wrong, and with great respect I would appeal your ruling to the house."[43] Some of the disavowers may not have been wholly sincere but there is no reason to assume that all or most of them were wholly insincere.

(3) In 1927 the Speaker became unmistakably responsible for deciding not only as to the form of a motion to adjourn the House to discuss a matter of urgent public importance, but also as to whether debate on the matter was urgent. Thereafter members who voted on appeal against the Speaker's decision that debate was not urgent or, after the Speaker's coup of 1932, against his ruling that his decision was not appealable, had good reason for doing so, quite apart from any feeling that the Speaker had been partial. They wanted, for obvious political reasons, to put it on record that whatever was the Speaker's opinion as to the urgency of debate, *they* thought that debate was urgent. No doubt, also, they wanted to force the Government and its supporters to go on record in the opposite sense. After 1932 there is no ground whatever for imputing partiality to a Speaker for ruling that his decision on the question of urgency was unappealable; he was merely following the precedent set, and confirmed by the House, in 1932.

(4) There are a number of other cases where the fact of appeal warrants neither the inference that the Speaker's ruling was partial, nor the inference that the appealer thought it partial. Fauteux may have favoured Prime Minister King, and Knowles may have thought he did, in ruling that King was not out of order in referring to previous debates when lecturing the House about the frequency of the appeals, but Knowles's chief reason for appealing on that occasion must surely have been to provide a moment of high comedy and to deflate the Prime Minister by cutting short his preaching.[44] The facility of the appeal procedure encourages members, once it has become an established practice of the House, to use it frivolously or as a vent for chagrin or anger. Any member acting alone can appeal a ruling. Normally rendered helpless by the Government's disciplined majority, it is only natural for a member to have recourse to the one form of demonstration always available to him when he or his motion is ruled out of order. If, with the help of four others, he can disrupt the normal course of business for half an hour by forcing a division, so much the

[43]*Debates*, 1943, p. 2817.
[44]*Debates*, 1948, pp. 1047–8.

better! Few even among the more responsible of the chronic appealers could honestly maintain that they have appealed only when they thought the Speaker's decision was wrong; fewer still could honestly maintain that they have appealed only when they thought that the ruling was influenced by partisan considerations. And there have been some cases where Opposition parties have voted on different sides in an appeal division.

(5) No fewer than five of the eighteen appeals against Black's rulings (1930–4) and three of the four against Bowman's (1935) were made by Labour or U.F.A. members. These members did have a tendency to think that the cards were, and were being, stacked against them; Heaps and Woodsworth in particular found it difficult to believe that the rules, fairly interpreted, precluded them from discussing subjects they thought important at the times they thought they should be discussed or from moving amendments they thought ought to be moved. It by no means follows that their doubts about the reality of fair play were justified, and on at least one occasion in the following Parliament Lapointe seems to have satisfied Woodsworth that his suspicions were unfounded.

(6) The case of Fauteux, against whose rulings there were twenty-eight appeals, is a special case. Angered by the logic-chopping that prevented them from presenting their views on a point of order, members gave vent to their anger by appealing; profoundly dissatisfied with the quality of some of his rulings, they registered their dissatisfaction in the same way. The situation became so bad that Knowles felt constrained to quote Macaulay on the need "never to suffer irregularities, even when harmless in themselves, to pass unchallenged, lest they acquire the force of precedents."[45] But although the number of appeals during this Speakership was swelled by reason of loss of confidence in the Speaker, it does not follow that the more modest number of appeals during other post–1930 Speakerships is evidence of a like loss of confidence. There is only one case (the pipeline debate) where appeals were used as part of the deliberate tactic of obstruction.

My conclusion is that Mallory is substantially right in holding that the increased number of appeals is evidence of little more than a change in the recognized tactics of opposition. He takes from Ward the suggestion that the absence of appeals in early decades is due to the certainty that the Speaker would be sustained. Forsey retorts, with

[45]*Debates*, 1949, 2nd sess., p. 2003.

justice, that the same certainty has obtained in recent decades. But the retort does not dispose of the matter. For it is a fact that the certainty *was* a reason for not appealing in the earlier period. "My experience in the past has shown me there is not much use in appealing to the House," said Pugsley in 1913.[46] And it is significant that the first sharp rise in the number of appeals occurred in the one-session Parliament of 1926 when the political battle was fiercely joined, when neither the Liberal Government nor the Conservative Government that superseded it had a majority, and when the Government side lost two of the five divisions on appeals. The number of appeals fell off immediately after the election of 1926 and did not pick up again until after the election of 1930. Forsey may legitimately ask why the tactics again changed despite the continuing certainty that the Speaker would be sustained.

One possible answer is that the pressure exerted on the parliamentary timetable by depression and the emergence of the positive state so crowded Opposition members that they were forced to use any available form of protest. "If we do not have the opportunity to express ourselves otherwise then we have to take the only course left open to us," said Fair of Battle River in defending appeals in 1951.[47] Another is that modern parliamentarians found a use, or thought they had found a use, that Pugsley and his contemporaries and predecessors had failed to discover: to give a chance to the electorate to confuse an opinion about the merits of a ruling with an opinion about the merits of the issue that was the occasion of the ruling. In 1944 Lacombe objected to a proposal to increase from five to twenty the number of members required to force a division on an appeal, on the grounds that "when a minority group numbers less than 20 members, it will be impossible for them to force a vote without the support of members from other groups with political tenets inconsistent with their own." What would be the use, he asked, of such members moving amendments if they were deprived of the privilege of forcing a vote on the decision of the Speaker?[48] The force of habit once developed is another factor.[49] In making eight of the twenty-two appeals in the Parliament of 1930–5 Labour and U.F.A. members were partly re-

[46]*Debates*, 1913, p. 9703.

[47]*Debates*, 1951, p. 2665.

[48]*Debates*, 1944, p. 1247.

[49]A striking example of the force of habit is to be found in the fact that six of the twelve appeals against the rulings of Macdonald, who succeeded Fauteux, occurred in his first short session. The members had not adjusted

sponsible for developing the new habit. But the responsibility was not theirs alone. The other fourteen appeals were made by Liberals, six of them by King's immediate lieutenants, and three of them by King himself. Forsey's theory of the deterioration of the Speakership is at bottom a demon theory and the demon is King. King's special deviltry with respect to the Speakership consists of having "promoted" Casgrain and Glen to the Cabinet. With more justice King could be charged with helping substantially to develop a new habit of parliamentary warfare, a habit which he himself was later to deplore, and which constitutes Forsey's evidence for his baneful effect on the Speakership.

V

If the demon theory were sound the sensible reform would be to establish a set of practices that would make it very difficult for a new demon to produce the same deleterious effect. Most of the cluster of practices surrounding the Canadian Speakership are of very long standing and nearly all of them are wholly bad. The degree of impartiality attained by Canadian Speakers has been attained in spite of them, not because of them. The practices in the United Kingdom symbolize impartiality. "I care little about the form except as an expression of a principle," said Blake on the occasion of Ouimet's election in 1887. But he agreed that "as a symbol of a principle, the form is of importance, and that principle is vital." But the British forms do more than symbolize: they exemplify the rule of abundant caution. They serve to guarantee substance; they seek as far as possible to ensure the indifference of the will by fostering the indifference of the feelings. The Canadian practices neither symbolize nor exemplify.[50] That Canadian parliamentarians were right to feel uneasy

themselves to the fact that a new man was in the Chair. It was in this session that Knowles quoted Macaulay but the experience that produced the frame of mind to which Macaulay's thought was congenial was the experience of the preceding Parliament.

[50]I find no evidence to support Mallory's contention that in 1956 the Canadian Speakership was "just approaching the point reached in the United Kingdom during the tenure of Mr. Speaker Shaw Lefevre" ("Parliament and Pipeline," *Canadian Bar Review*, XXXIV, 723). The Canadian practices from the beginning have been different from the British; there has been no need in Canada to work out the symbolizing and exemplifying practices, for it has been recognized from the beginning that the British model provided these; if there has been any change in Canada it has been one of retrogression.

in the absence of the proper forms is shown by what happened in 1956. All that was necessary to produce that result was a combination of an arrogant and unscrupulous Government and a Speaker unable to withstand its pressures.

The worst of the Canadian practices, and the progenitor of most of the others, is that of electing a new Speaker for every Parliament.[51] There have been only four exceptions: Cockburn, the first Speaker, was re-elected for the short second Parliament of 1873; Rhodes, first elected for the last session of the Parliament of 1911–17, was re-elected for the Parliament of 1917–21; Lemieux was elected for three successive Parliaments and served from 1922 to 1930; and now Michener, Speaker of the short twenty-third Parliament of 1957–8, has been re-elected for the twenty-fourth Parliament.

The most obvious and serious disadvantage of the short term is that the Speaker, whose function is essentially a judicial one, is not unequivocally put in the position where he has nothing to lose by doing right and nothing to gain by doing wrong. But it has other disadvantages. It aggravates the difficulty, already somewhat greater in Canada than in Britain by reason of Canada's smaller House, of getting competence in the Chair; and there is no doubt that the Canadian House has suffered severely on occasion from incompetence. Moreover, the fact that the Prime Minister is faced with finding a new Speaker immediately after a general election, when he is usually engaged in forming a new Cabinet or reconstructing an old one, means that the Speakership becomes involved in the process of cabinet-making. It is normally an alternative to Cabinet office. In the United Kingdom a new Speaker is required only when the office becomes vacant by death or resignation. This usually occurs during the life of a Parliament and the selection of a new Speaker is divorced from the political process of cabinet-making. The choice usually falls on a back-bencher who can more readily cut his party ties than can one who has, or has had, strong claims to ministerial office. In the United Kingdom, too,

[51]There is a common impression that this practice and that of alternating a French-speaking Canadian with an English-speaking Canadian originated after Confederation. Neither did. Both originated at the beginning of the Union of the Canadas and were in full force throughout the whole of the Union. The elections of Blanchet in 1879 and of Kirkpatrick in 1883 constituted a reversion to a former practice, as Blake pointed out on the latter occasion. Macdonald had merely briefly hoped, and briefly attempted, to establish better practices on the broader foundation provided by Confederation.

Opposition leaders are consulted and they are usually given time to sound out the rank and file of their party. The man whose name is presented to the House has already in a very real sense been agreed upon by the two front benches and found to be acceptable to the rank and file of both parties. The involvement in Canada of the choice of Speaker with the highly personal and political work of cabinet-making effectively precludes such consultation and sounding out.[52]

Two further Canadian practices are associated with the fact that with us the Speaker is more effectively the choice of the Prime Minister than is the case in the United Kingdom. In Canada the election of the Speaker is moved by the Prime Minister and until 1953 was seconded by another minister, whereas in the United Kingdom both movers and seconders are always back-benchers. In both countries the procedure reflects the underlying reality. For Canada to adopt the British practice without changing the Canadian reality would be a mockery. The other practice, of revealing who was to be Speaker in advance of the meeting of Parliament, has recently been discontinued. King was sharply criticized for following it, the last time by Bracken who asserted that it was an affront to the best parliamentary tradition and, to that extent, an invasion of the rights of the House. But King had a very good defence. The practice, he asserted, had been in effect since Confederation; it gave members an opportunity to decide whether they wished to approve or oppose the choice; honourable members would have resented it very strongly if he had changed the practice and had given to them and to others no intimation in advance as to whom the Government had in mind to nominate; he should have been commended for what he had done.[53] To represent

[52]In 1951 Sir Winston Churchill was unexpectedly confronted with the task of finding a new Speaker in the few days between the general election and the opening of Parliament. It is interesting that his choice fell on a former minister, that Attlee, though consulted, did not have time to sound out his party thoroughly, and that his party insisted on putting up a rival candidate. By timing his resignation to coincide wth the end of the Parliament of 1955–9, Mr. Speaker Morrison gave the British Government another opportunity to behave badly. The opportunity was warmly embraced. It should, therefore, be understood that in advocating the adoption by Canada of the British cluster of practices, it is the pre-1951 British practices I have in mind, not the bad British precedent of 1951 and the even worse precedents of 1959.

[53]*Debates*, 1945, 2nd sess., pp. 4–6. Ward and Forsey have convinced me between them that the name of the Speaker-to-be was not always

that the recent change constitutes a marked improvement in procedure is to indulge in pretentious nonsense. The interest of the general public does not, however, extend to knowing in advance the name of the person to be elected. It stops short at knowing that there has been effective consultation with all groups in the House and that the person to be nominated is generally acceptable to them. But until such consultation becomes a fact in Canada, the old practice followed by King is to be preferred to the new. The practice in operation since 1953 of having the Leader of the Opposition second the Prime Minister's nomination is no substitute for effective consultation.

Consultation is desirable even in those cases where it need only be *pro forma*. Such cases are not infrequent in Canada for the Speaker and Deputy Speaker are required by standing orders to be of different linguistic origin and sometimes after a general election when there has been no change in Government the Deputy Speaker of the previous Parliament has been promoted to the Speakership.[54] A Deputy Speaker of proved competence who has satisfied the House generally as to his impartiality has no possible rival and in his case consultation is not strictly necessary. No amount of consultation would have enhanced the general acceptability of Beaudoin in 1953.

But Beaudoin's case is evidence enough that general acceptability, whether established by consultation or otherwise, is insufficient. The only effective way to guarantee impartiality is to establish the practice that a Speaker will be re-elected as often as he wishes to remain in office *provided he remains impartial and continues to respect the symbols of impartiality*. That is all that the much misunderstood term "a permanent Speaker" means. It is now recognized that the security of tenure of the British Speaker, like that of a judge, is the best guarantee of his impartiality. But "permanency" of tenure developed for a

---

revealed in advance. It was, however, usually revealed in advance—often through a Government "organ." King's innovation lies rather in the formality of the announcement by which he made his decision known. His defence remains a good defence even if his assertion about the invariability of the practice is not strictly accurate.

[54]A Deputy has never been promoted when the Government has changed and Meighen was simply being silly in charging King with not following a custom in not promoting (*Debates*, 1922, p. 3). Nor has the Deputy always been promoted when the Government has not changed. I am indebted to Professor Mallory for the information that standing orders and not merely custom require the Speaker and Deputy Speaker to be of different linguistic origin.

quite different reason. It was recognized when a new Parliament assembled that many of its members were probably capable of becoming good Speakers, as good, perhaps, as the Speaker of the previous Parliament. But the House did not know who they were. The one man the House was sure of was the Speaker of the previous Parliament. It would have been a gratuitous reflection upon him, and contrary to the interests of the House, to take a chance on someone of unproved quality and to lose into the bargain the advantage of his experience.

That is the kind of thinking that was responsible for the establishment of the permanent Speakership in Britain, and all that is required for the establishment of a permanent Speakership in Canada is the development of the same kind of thinking here. No new machinery is required. Nor is there any danger. A Speaker who failed to satisfy in every way need not be re-elected. Manners Sutton was dropped in 1835, not because there was any dissatisfaction with his rulings but because he engaged in political discussions with Wellington. No doubt the same treatment would be meted out even today to a British Speaker who failed to live up to the high traditions of his office. Even judges hold office only *quamdiu se bene gesserint.*

It is no wonder that no Speaker has been refused re-election in the United Kingdom since Manners Sutton. Consider the incentive there to behave well. In Canada a Speaker knows that, however conscientious, competent, and impartial he may be, he will probably be superseded after the next general election. In the United Kingdom the Speaker knows that he will be superseded only if he is partial or otherwise behaves badly. The fact that Canadian Prime Ministers have seldom promoted a Deputy Speaker to the Speakership who has not as Deputy Speaker won the confidence of Opposition members, and that not a few Deputy Speakers have both earned and received promotion, suggests that the mere possibility of reward for good behaviour has had a beneficent effect. In the United Kingdom the stigma attached to the loss of office would be a greater punishment for bad behaviour than the mere loss of office itself.

But, says Forsey, a permanent Speakership is now impossible in Canada:

> It is possible that if Mr. Beaudoin had fulfilled his early promise, he might have become our first "permanent" Speaker; and when he retired, full of years and honours, the French-Canadians might have accepted a "permanent" English-Cana-

dian Speaker until he chose to retire; and so on, back and forth. But that chance is now gone. Mr. Beaudoin has forfeited it. . . . In the next Parliament, English-Canadians will certainly insist that it is their turn in the Chair; in the following Parliament the French-Canadians will equally insist that it is theirs.[55]

To suggest that we can establish a permanent Speakership in Canada only if the first permanent Speaker is a French Canadian is a wholly unwarranted reflection on the French-Canadian people. Far from making a permanent Speakership impossible, the failure of Beaudoin to fulfil his early promise, by making unmistakably clear the dangers inherent in our present practices, provides an unparalleled opportunity to change those practices. No calculation of petty political advantage, no assertion of and concession to petty racial pride, can excuse the failure to seize that opportunity. To assign the question of a permanent Speakership to future Parliaments to determine in the light of circumstances that develop in the crucible of history[56] is to abdicate responsibility. The crucible of history has now produced highly favourable circumstances; their like will seldom recur. If those with power to act now in the political arena do not act, it is idle to expect that future Parliaments will. Love requires deeds for the demonstration of its warmth and the sincerity of the words professing it, and love of Parliament is no exception.

It is true that no Prime Minister acting alone can establish a permanent Speakership. What is needed is a series of acts by a succession of Prime Ministers. We can begin to feel confident that we have a permanent Speakership only when a Speaker has been re-elected after a change in Government. But a great deal more could have been done during the election of 1958 toward the establishment of a permanent Speakership than was in fact done. The Prime Minister could have suggested to the leaders of the other parties that the time had come to make a beginning; that all should agree that Michener should be continued as Speaker whatever the party in power as long as he proved worthy of office and was willing to remain in it; that a public announcement of the agreement be made; and that Michener be

[55]Forsey, "Constitutional Aspects," pp. 24–5.

[56]"I have nothing to say on this occasion with regard to the question of a permanent Speaker; that is a matter for future parliaments to determine in the light of circumstances that develop in the crucible of history." The Prime Minister in moving the re-election of Michener on May 12, 1958.

unopposed in his constituency. If the leaders of the other parties had agreed the foundation for a permanent Speakership would have been firmly laid. It would have been very difficult for them to have refused, but if they had, or if they had agreed and had been unable to prevail upon their party organizations in the Speaker's constituency not to run opposing candidates, the Prime Minister could still have announced (provided that Michener concurred) that Michener would be his recurring candidate for the Chair and if opposed in his constituency would stand not as a candidate of the Conservative party but as "Mr. Speaker."

That the Prime Minister had earlier thought that the time was ripe for a beginning is indicated by his offer of the Speakership to Knowles in the summer of 1957. If the offer was only for the twenty-third Parliament which was expected to last, and did last, only for a few months, it was the emptiest of gestures. If it was not an empty gesture it implied that the Conservative party would not oppose Knowles at the next general election and if returned to power would move his re-election to the Speaker's Chair. The failure, after this, of the Prime Minister to make a beginning during the election of 1958 suggests that he had come to realize the possible use of the Speakership to win marginal support in Quebec. Is his failure to make a beginning since the election due to the possibility that it might be of service in the same way in 1962 or 1963? If such a thought justifies inaction the prospect of reform is slight, for party leaders can never be sure that the Speakership will not be a convenient counter of conciliation at the next election or at the election after the next election.

It is sometimes an advantage for a politician to have his hands tied and he can be little blamed for not giving what, on sound principles, he has precluded himself from giving. The re-election of Michener to the Chair certainly does not prejudice the establishment of a permanent Speakership, but in itself it does little to advance it. As a precedent it is of less weight than the re-election of Cockburn and Lemieux whose first terms were of normal length. The Prime Minister was careful not to claim any credit for moving the re-election of Michener and no credit is due him. But politicians have often less plausibly claimed credit, and for the Prime Minister to have claimed credit in this instance would have had the desirable effect of committing him in some degree.

More could have been done but the opportunity afforded by the events of 1956 is by no means irretrievably lost. Party leaders need only agree that in the future no worthy Speaker will be jettisoned.

All the rest is detail. That the present incumbent is English-speaking, that he has shown himself a worthy Speaker, and that he may therefore become the first Speaker to be re-elected after a reversal of party fortunes if the change is made now, are not adequate reasons for not making that change now. French Canada can have no legitimate objection. As it turned out, English-speaking Canadians did not insist on the selection of an English-speaking Speaker for the Parliament of 1957–8. They did not have to: the linguistic composition of the Conservative party in the House made it a practical necessity. Had Beaudoin fulfilled his early promise he, a French Canadian, might have become a "permanent" Speaker. His failure created the present opportunity. Lemieux, after all, served for three successive Parliaments. When he was elected for the third time, Guthrie, the Leader of the Opposition, objected that it was the turn of an English-speaking member but he was immediately repudiated by White of Mount Royal and supported by no one. Gardiner of Acadia supported the re-election of Lemieux because the U.F.A. group for whom he spoke knew of none in the House better qualified. "We can quite understand," he said, "and I trust our French-Canadian friends will recognize this as well, that in the years to come we may have a well-qualified English speaker in the chair for many sessions of parliament." "None of us felt very badly over the breaking of that old established custom;" said Carmichael, Progressive member for Kindersley, a little over a year later, "indeed, we were all quite satisfied to have Your Honour occupy the position for the third consecutive parliament."[57] There is no reason why the next "permanent" Speaker after Michener should not be a French Canadian and every reason why he should be. In view of the paramount importance to the proper functioning of our political system of establishing complete confidence in the impartiality of the Chair, French Canada is not entitled to demand more. Such is the nature of Canadian politics, however, that continuity in the Chair is much more likely to be established if party leaders are committed in advance. Let them tie their hands now.

The impartiality of the Speaker is not an end in itself. Its proximate end is to secure the impartial interpretation and application of the rules. It is therefore absurd to insist on impartiality in the Chair and to place the interpretation of the rules at the mercy of the majority of the day. In appealing, on December 13, 1957, a ruling of Chairman Rea that was in strict accordance with a ruling made by the Speaker

[57]*Debates*, 1926–7, p. 277.

a few days before, the Conservative Government showed how little it really cared for the institution of Parliament. The defence it offered for its conduct was wholly spurious, and in view of the fuss the party had recently made about its concern for the proper functioning of Parliament, shameless. It was a minority Government, it urged, and was therefore entirely in the hands of the House. This is like the criminal's absolving himself from responsibility for the crime he is about to commit by pointing out that others have the power to stop him. The Liberals, in fleeing behind the curtains in sufficient numbers to enable the ruling to be reversed, are in no better case. They succeeded merely in demonstrating how demoralized and neurotically fearful they had become. How is it possible they could have thought that the Government might dissolve if a ruling, made by a chairman selected by it from its own supporters, were sustained by the House? Parliament is sick, says Forsey. The unprincipled behaviour of both major parties on December 13, 1957, would seem to confirm his judgment.

The case for the abolition of appeals is overwhelming even in the absence of a permanent Speakership. Appeals are almost always made by Opposition members and are almost always lost. When the ruling is a good one, an appeal adds nothing to the prestige of the Speaker; when the ruling is bad, a bad ruling is confirmed by a vote of the House. The use that I have suggested Opposition members have latterly discovered for appeals is an illegitimate one and should be denied them. Appeals are ineffective as a means of obstruction, for the Canadian closure, once invoked, is inexorable. There has, however, been a persistent belief among Opposition members that the appeal procedure affords them some protection. Since there is always a possibility that the Government will avail itself of it, the procedure, on the contrary, is a positive danger to Opposition members. It has also been frequently asserted in the Canadian House that the abolition of appeals would be inconsistent with the position of the Speaker as a servant of the House and the fact that the House is master of its own procedure. But there are no appeals in the British House where the Speaker is equally the servant of the House and the House the master of its procedure. The Speaker best serves the House if his rulings cannot be reversed, and the House best serves its own interest by controlling its procedure through the deliberate amendment of the rules when necessary, and not through the determination by majority vote of the application of the rules to particular cases. If the latter is what is meant by "control of procedure" the rule book becomes largely superfluous and Opposition groups are shorn of protection. The abolition of appeals would not deprive Opposition members of the power of registering dissent from the Speaker's rulings: greater recourse could be had to the substantive motion, if necessary. The substantive motion should be sparingly used, but it need not imply that the Speaker's conduct is censurable,[58] and it has the advantage that it leaves standing the particular ruling that occasioned the dissatisfaction.

[58]An interesting use of the substantive motion to review the Speaker's ruling but not to censure the Speaker was made in the British House in July, 1957. It received the blessing of neither Butler nor Gaitskell but it would well repay study by those interested in the reform of Canadian procedure. Somewhat similar discussions have been occasionally permitted in Canada—sometimes on the orders of the day and at least once on a supply motion. The use of such occasions would probably now be ruled out of order.

The Senate of Canada—Political Conundrum

JOHN N. TURNER

No political subject provokes more dissatisfied public comment in Canada than its Senate. Rare is the year that passes when someone of note in this country has not been on his feet voicing criticism and seeking the reform or outright abolition of the Upper House. It is probably fair to say that most Canadians who are aware of the subject feel that the Senate has outlived its usefulness and has become a superfluous appendix to the political system. Indeed, the prestige and authority of the Senate has probably fallen to its lowest level in Canadian history.

This was not always so. During the 1930's, when Mr. Dandurand and Mr. Meighen led their respective parties in the Upper House and when it harboured an illustrious group of other distinguished politicians, it was the forum of lively debates and commanded the interest and respectful attention of the public. Today the debates in the Upper House are so dull, dreary, and futile that the press rarely thinks it worthwhile to give them any coverage. Even more symptomatic of its decay is the political fact that recent governments of the day seem to have abandoned and ignored it. Saddest fact of all, the Senate has become an object of ridicule. Cynics call it the most exclusive club in the country, a haven of old men, retired politicians, and contributors to party funds.

Talk of reform of the Senate is cyclical; it is a political vogue—sometimes more in fashion, sometimes less. And the arguments have not changed since Confederation. The reputation of the Upper House has always been challenged because of the senility of many of its members. It has always been criticized because of its lack of activity. The label of a political haven is not new, nor are the abuses in the system of appointments.

These accusations have dogged the Senate throughout its history. Yet nothing is done. The abuses do not abate. With the resignation of a people not easily disturbed from the status quo, the Canadian public seems to have grown accustomed to its survival. Perhaps the prevailing attitude is more one of bridled frustration: the average Canadian may dislike the persistence of the Senate as an institution but he has begun to grow weary of being able to do anything about it. Such a widespread feeling must harbour some truth. And after a little study it becomes apparent that the solution of the problem is far from easy. What type of reform is there to be? Is an elective Senate to be substituted for the present system of appointments? What would this do to the balance of power between the Senate and the House of Commons? Would it mean that each Chamber would compete as the expression of public mandate? If the system of appointments were to be changed, how would it be changed? And if the Senate is to be reformed or abolished, would this not require an amendment to the British North America Act? Would such an amendment require the unanimous consent of the provinces? Would the provinces be likely to consent to an amendment which curbed or eliminated the Upper House? It is characteristic of the subject that each suggestion seems to provoke more problems than it cures.

Any mental exploration in this direction does not go far before one realizes that the Senate is one of those typical Canadian situations: a constitutional impasse. The solution depends upon constitutional mechanics that either do not exist or do not work. In order better to understand the nature of this conundrum, a review of the origins of the Senate must be made. The question must be studied in historical terms and placed in relief by tracing the original pattern of the Senate in the fabric of Confederation as it was woven by the statesmen of the day and comparing it with the current design.

Historically, the Senate was the political embodiment of two competing systems: federalism and the British parliamentary tradition. Federalism, especially as it developed under the American experience, contemplated that the Senate should be a bastion of sectional or provincial rights. The British parliamentary tradition that only the House of Commons, controlling the purse-strings by its unique power to initiate money bills, should exercise the mandate of the people as its sole elective expression, dictated that the Senate should be a nominative rather than an elected body.

Federalism implies a compromise between the principles of popular representation, which recognizes the weight of population, and of territorial equality, which recognizes the essential partnership of the units that comprise the union. The Canadian Senate was the creature of federalism. Had there been no provision made for an Upper House in 1867, it is certain that Lower Canada and the Maritime Provinces would not have entered the Confederation. Lower Canada was suspicious of a union in which the growing population of Upper Canada threatened to place its own peculiar institutions at the mercy of an English-speaking Protestant majority. The Atlantic Provinces feared that they would be dominated by the populous areas to the west. It was to meet and allay the suspicions of the weaker partners that the principle of popular representation was diluted so as to grant each geographical division the same numerical representation in an Upper House.[1] Consequently, the Maritimes, Ontario, and Quebec were each given the same number of seats.[2] Undoubtedly the American experience was a factor and a precedent. The problem was, however, a Canadian one and the solution was a typically Canadian version of the compromise in that territorial equality was achieved on a geographical rather than a strictly provincial basis. There was a certain concession, in other words, to the force of population.[3]

Against this historical background, reinforced as it is by the "com-

[1]Support for this proposition that the Senate was conceived as the Canadian incarnation of "provincial" rights is clearly derived from the debates and proceedings in the various legislative houses in the two Canadas and the Maritimes and from the proceedings at the Quebec and London Conferences of 1864 and 1866. See an excellent summary in "Memorandum for Senator Robertson, Re: The Senate—Reasons given by proponents of Confederation for constituting a second chamber," by J. F. MacNeill, Law Clerk and Parliamentary Counsel to the Senate, February 16, 1950.

Mr. Arthur Meighen expressed this particular responsibility of the Senate in words that summarize exactly the original aim: "The Senate has the particular duty of standing guard over the Constitution as it applies to all sections of Canada, of making certain that provincial rights are maintained inviolate, that the relationship which the British North America Act established between the provinces on the one hand and the Dominion on the other hand is respected, whatever may be for the time being the arbitrary action of a bare majority." "The Canadian Senate," *Queen's Quarterly*, XLIV (1937), pp. 153–4, a revision of a speech made at an earlier date before the Canadian Club in Montreal.

[2]It is noteworthy that when the western provinces entered Confederation they formed a fourth geographical division and that the traditional balance was upset by the entry of Newfoundland. For the basis of numerical representation in the Senate, see British North America Act, 1867, ss. 21–22, 147; B.N.A. Act, 1915; B.N.A. Act, 1949.

[3]R. A. Mackay, *The Unreformed Senate of Canada* (London: Oxford University Press, 1926), pp. 37–9.

pact theory" of Confederation,[4] one might suggest that any tampering with the machinery of the Senate would be bound to arouse the constitutional sensitivity of the provinces. Moreover, if the "compact theory" were to be admitted, and since an amendment to the B.N.A. Act would be required to alter the constitution of the Senate, it is arguable that the unanimous consent of all the provinces would be necessary to effect any such change.

All this would make some practical sense if provincial rights were really at stake in reform of the Senate. The plain truth of the matter seems to be that the Senate today has very little to do with the provinces. Political theory and principles are often not reflected in practice. Although the Senate was historically the embodiment of the compromise of Confederation and was meant to ensure the protection of provincial rights, it is doubtful whether, since 1867, the Upper House has ever found occasion to act in the defence of a province against the federal authority or against another province. Again, in practical terms, it is doubtful whether today any provincial government would look towards the Senate as its spokesman or champion.

The role intended for the Upper House by the statesmen of Confederation was never achieved. Certain factors came into play which these men could not have foreseen. Other institutions usurped the role of the Senate as the protagonist of provincial rights. Over the early years of the development of the country, it was the courts that formed the line of first defence against the encroachment of the central power on the area of provincial jurisdiction. A federal system with its fabric of checks and balances and its division of powers between the central and local jurisdictions cannot function without the intervention of a final interpreter. In the United States, the Constitution gives this role to the Supreme Court. In Canada, the final arbitrator during the formative years of the Confederation was the Judicial Committee

[4]The "compact" or "treaty" theory of Confederation states that the Canadian constitution is really the crystallization into law by an Imperial statute of an agreement made by the provinces after full consultation or discussion. A logical consequence of this theory is that the B.N.A. Act cannot be amended without the unanimous consent of the provinces. The theory is attractive but of doubtful historical validity. See The Senate of Canada, *Report Pursuant to Resolution of the Senate, 1939, to the Honourable the Speaker by Parliamentary Counsel Relating to the Enactment of the British North America Act, 1867, Any Lack of Consonance between Its Terms and Judicial Construction of Them and Cognate Matters* (Ottawa: Queen's Printer, 1939), Annex 4, pp. 134–52.

of the Privy Council in London. Any Canadian student of political science is familiar with the trend of the famous decisions of this Board during the Watson-Haldane era. The residual powers in the B.N.A. Act were virtually rewritten in favour of the provinces. The intentions of the framers of the Canadian Confederation towards a strong central power (fashioned in the psychological aftermath of the American Civil War) were frustrated by a series of judicial decisions which, by the turn of the century, had left the residual power with the provinces.[5] In this climate of judicial protection, the Senate's historical purpose became otiose.[6]

The framers of the B.N.A. Act might conceivably have anticipated that the courts would impinge upon the Senate. They could hardly have predicted, however, the phenomenon which has made provincial representation in the federal Cabinet far more important than that in the Senate. The development of the power of the Cabinet in the British parliamentary system over the last hundred years is notorious.

[5]The Senate of Canada, *Report Pursuant to Resolution of the Senate, 1939, passim.*

[6]Today, however, there is some argument that since the abolition in 1949 of civil appeals to the Privy Council (leaving the Supreme Court of Canada as court of final resort) the tendency of the judicial decisions in favour of the provinces may have been checked and the provinces may have to seek protection elsewhere. Time has not run sufficiently to permit an opinion on this delicate point. What can be said with some confidence is that the judicial climate has surely changed. The nine members of the Supreme Court are federal appointees. It is hardly conceivable that any of these men are avowed advocates of provincial rights. Their sympathies tend to lie with the federal authority. This suspicion is especially widespread in legal circles in the province of Quebec. In that province, the political question is compounded with the legal one. Many lawyers in Quebec resent the fact that many of the decisions of the Supreme Court on matters originating within that jurisdiction are decided by a majority made up of judges schooled in the common rather than the civil law.

Of course, if there is something to this argument, the Senate will fare no better in provincial eyes than the courts. The personnel of the Upper House comes almost exclusively from the ranks of federal politicians who, although they may have certain allegiance to the respective provinces of their origins, owe their appointments to Ottawa and not to any of the provincial capitals. Furthermore, it is rather unlikely that the attitude of a man whose political thinking has been given national scope throughout his active political life will adopt the cause of a more provincial view in his later years.

Partly discipline, enforced by the whips in the House of Commons, and concentration of authority in the Prime Minister and his Cabinet have meant that the real power in Parliament has shifted from the Commons to the Cabinet. Translated into Canadian vocabulary, this means that having representation at this focus of authority is the strongest protection a province can have. And it has become a tradition that each province must be represented in the Cabinet at Ottawa.

An important reservation must be made at this point. The type of protection which is achieved does not go to the maintenance of provincial rights in constitutional terms; the protection is primarily economic. Representation in the Cabinet guarantees each province some share of the federal spoils. A federal Cabinet minister is less interested in the preservation of the constitutional rights of his province than he is in ensuring that it receives its due share from the national coffers. For instance, Quebec is traditionally entitled to about five or six ministers in the federal Cabinet. In practice, however, these men have not contributed the staunchest voice to the upholding of that province's constitutional approach to the Confederation.[7]

The very fact of the practical politics of a federal system tends to protect the component units to the federation. In a parliamentary democracy, operating in a federal state, no political party can hope to retain a majority in the legislative forum unless it succeeds in winning support (to a greater or lesser measure) from each of the geographical

[7]The current political issue of federal grants to universities has been a case in point. This legislation was conceived under the administration of Mr. Louis St. Laurent, a son of Quebec. Yet the provincial Government refused to allow its universities to accept the monies made available to them by the federal Government because it refused to concede the principle that, since education was a provincial matter under section 93 of the B.N.A. Act, the funds necessary to support education should be taxed by the province and not by the federal authority. To have accepted the federal monies would have been to concede that the central Government had the right to tax for this purpose in the first place. Expressed in other terms, this meant that the province insisted on the principle that it be allowed to tax for the support of matters guaranteed to it under the constitution; a federal handout was no substitute for a constitutional right. For several years there was an alarming lack of mutual appreciation of the psychology of each side to the dispute. In the end the solution was disarmingly simple: the federal Government would yield one per cent of its tax rate to the province. It is certainly not the public impression that the federal Cabinet ministers from the province of Quebec had much to do with effecting this compromise.

sections of the country. In Canada, this truth is self-evident. Unless a political party obtains a sizable number of the 65 seats allocated by statute to the province of Quebec it stands little chance of forming a stable government at Ottawa. Conversely, the ultimate protection of French-speaking Canada lies in its ability to dispose of these seats as its interests are fulfilled, tolerated, or rewarded.

Indeed, if the provinces were to look to a federal institution for protection they would have to seek it elsewhere than on the floor of the Senate.[8] As a practical matter, the Senate lacks the necessary power to act effectively on their behalf. Legally, it is true, the Senate enjoys legislative equality with the House of Commons, except in one very important respect: section 53 of the B.N.A. Act limits the initiation of money bills to the Lower House.[9] Otherwise the chamber can initiate, amend, or reject all legislation as it sees fit. There are, however, several reasons why the Senate cannot exercise its power to the legal limit. The most self-evident is that the Senate is an *appointed* chamber and, accordingly, cannot compete in a democratic system with the *elected* House of Commons. If the Senate had really been

[8]As a matter of legislative record, the Upper House has never been called upon to decide more than a few rather unimportant questions involving the rights of any province or against the Dominion: Honourable Senator Norman Lambert, *Reform of the Senate,* reprinted from the editorial pages of the *Winnipeg Free Press,* pamphlet no. 30 (April, 1950).

[9]B.N.A. Act, 1867, s. 18: B.N.A. Act, 1875, s. 1. The restriction on the initiation of financial measures is, however, a severe curtailing of the Senate's power. Since any legislation of importance tends to involve the imposition of a tax or the raising of money, a sizable domain of legislation is thereby deprived the Senate. There has, moreover, been a continuing dispute between the members of the two Houses about whether the Senate has even the power to amend financial legislation. The House of Commons maintains that it has exclusive jurisdiction over money (Rule 78 of the Standing Rules). Despite this opinion, the better view is that the Senate has and always had since it was created the power to amend bills originating in the Commons appropriating any part of the revenue or imposing a tax by reducing the amounts: The Senate of Canada, *Report of the Special Committee Appointed to Determine the Rights of Senate in matters of Financial Legislation under the Chairmanship of the Honourable W. B. Ross, K.C., Dated May 9, 1918* (Ottawa: Queen's Printer, 1945); E. Russell Hopkins (Law Clerk and Parliamentary Counsel to the Senate of Canada), "Financial Legislation in the Senate," *Canadian Tax Journal,* VI (1958), pp. 320–5, 1958.

considered by the "Fathers" of Confederation as a court of last resort for the provinces, surely they would have given it the kind of power that can only come in a democratic society from the authority of popular election. Why they did not do this can only be understood in terms of a logical conflict which faced them between the ideas of British parliamentarianism and federalism. Federalism would have dictated that the Canadian Senate be given the power to enforce the principle of territorial equality by conferring upon it a joint mandate from the people by reason of its being a freely elected legislative body. This was the formula of the United States and it has been the choice of all subsequent republican governments fashioned on the bicameral system. Why was the American precedent not followed? The answer is that a second elective chamber was considered by the Canadian statesmen of the time to be inconsistent with the British parliamentary tradition in which the mandate of the people resided only in the House of Commons and more recently in the Cabinet. An elected Senate would have been a dangerous departure in their eyes and would have tended to compete with the Commons; and it was not their intention that this should happen. The Senate was to have a restraining influence on legislation, not an initiating or aggressive one. Macdonald spoke of the Senate "as the controlling and regulating, but not the initiating, branch" of Parliament. It was to be merely the "House which has the sober second thought in legislation," and nothing more.[10] The Upper House was conceived in negative terms, the parliamentary strain proving stronger than the federalist urge. Yet the statesmen of Upper Canada had to speak the language of federalism and the Senate was the lip-service which was paid. The Senate was a mere psychological palliative for the weaker partners to the Confederation, because the nominative principle as embodied in the Senate is irreconcilable with a true federalism. Provincial rights cannot thrive under a system whereby the appointments are made by the federal government. Of this the founders were fully aware. They were striving for a strong union, and they saw in appointment by the central government the means of weaning the various sections from their particularism. "They granted the forms demanded by sectional sentiments and fears, but they made sure that these forms should not endanger the political structure."[11] The end result was a constitutional

[10]*Parliamentary Debates on the Subject of Confederation of the British North American Provinces* (1865), p. 35.

[11]Mackay, *The Unreformed Senate*, p. 44.

hybrid: the Senate was a still-born offspring of British and American political nepotism.

Once the nominative idea was accepted, it was inevitable that the Senate should never exercise any real power; nor, as it has been suggested, was it intended that it should. After Confederation, the status of the Upper House dwindled steadily. Although it was given in the beginning the semblance of equality–indeed, constitutionally (except for the initiation of money bills) the Senate has the same power as the Lower House–its power slipped gradually to the Commons. Originally, several ministers were chosen from the ranks of the Senate. During the years of Mr. Bennett and Mr. King this representation dwindled to that of a ministry without portfolio.[12] Today the Senate contains no portfolios; all important legislation must therefore be initiated in the Commons since that is where the responsible ministers sit.[13] The Senate has been reduced, therefore, to the work of revision and the words of Macdonald have become prophetic.

Has the Senate, in fact, cast a "sober second thought" on legislation? A review of the statistics indicates that the Senate amends or revises between 15 and 20 per cent of the bills sent up to it from the House of Commons.[14] Most of the amendments relate to detail and to improvements in drafting. Charges have frequently been made that the Senate has been active in amending legislation only when a majority of its members are opposed to the Government of the day and that at other times it is docile and entirely useless. The statistics do not substantiate this criticism.[15] Amendment can often mean the same as outright rejection and some bills have met this fate as a result of amendment by the Senate.[16]

The most controversial feature of the Senate as a legislative body

[12]Since 1926, there has been only one portfolio represented, briefly, in the Senate: Honourable Senator Gideon Robertson, Minister of Labour, 1930–2.

[13]Among exceptions to the general rule were Canadian and British Insurance Companies Act, 1932; Canadian National–Canadian Pacific Act, 1932; Canada Shipping Act, 1934; Admiralty Act, 1934.

[14]J. N. Turner, "The Senate of Canada, 1924–48," thesis in two volumes submitted in partial fulfilment of the requirements of the Honours B.A. at the University of British Columbia, May, 1949, pp. 46 *et seq.*

[15]*Ibid.*

[16]Amendment to Industrial Disputes Investigation Act, 1924; Amendment to the Pensions Act, 1925; Amendment to the Lord's Day Act, 1938; Amendment to the Farmers' Creditors Arrangement Act, 1934.

is its power to reject any bill regardless of its importance or how many times it may have been passed by the Commons. In practice, however, the "veto" right has been used mostly against less important legislation. The most important bill vetoed by the Senate during the last thirty-five years was the Old Age Pensions Bill of 1926.[17] Today the veto is in virtual disuse. Between the years 1929 and 1948 only five Government bills failed to pass the Senate.[18] No bill of importance has been rejected since 1940.

There is much to be said for the theoretical function of the Senate as a chamber of revision. Professor R. A. Mackay (as he then was) stated the argument succinctly in his classic treatise on the subject:

> Much of the legislation which passes the House of Commons is in very crude shape. Even in the case of departmental bills the drafting is often incredibly bad. As for the House it is by no means a model legislature: it is too busy with politics, too large, and contains too many members who are unfamiliar with the technical work of legislative science. As a result much slipshod work is done there, and the burden of recasting a considerable part of the most important legislation falls upon the Senate.[19]

And again:

> The House of Commons is not a good legislative machine. The party turmoil, the harassing parliamentary and administrative duties of the Ministers, the attendance at caucuses and committees required of private members, the constant anxiety of all members to court the public and the press, all militate against good legislation.[20]

[17]The reasons for the rejection were varied. Some senators considered it impractical in view of the fact that it provided for a partnership plan between the federal and provincial authorities to which most of the provinces were opposed. Other speakers maintained that the matter of old age pensions was a provincial matter; others criticized the mechanics and the motives of the bill. The bill was repassed by the Commons in the next session and sent up to the Senate again, this time, however, with the added mandate of a general election behind it. The bill passed the Senate.

[18]Turner, "The Senate of Canada," appendix "G."

[19]Mackay, *The Unreformed Senate*, p. 107.

[20]*Ibid.*, p. 108.

Mr. Arthur Meighen once had this to say:

> The Senate has a more prosaic task. Its duty is to see that great principles upon which the Dominion has reposed are carefully reflected in its Statutes, to design legislation so as to meet the realities of business, to review and temper proposals of the other House so as not unnecessarily to discourage enterprise or restrict the area of employment; to oppose the ravages of partisanship from whatever source they come, and at least to give public opinion time and opportunity to be deliberate and to be understood; to be governed not so much by emotional appeal or fleeting spasms of popular fancy, but to listen to the accountant, the operator, the employer, the employee and the unemployed, and to make sure that legislation when finally passed will work with fairness and facility. The Second Chamber should be a workshop and not a theatre. For this function the Senate was created, and this function it must with thoroughness and fearlessness perform.[21]

Unfortunately, the legislative record of the Senate during the past twenty-five years has not fulfilled these hopes; it has been far from impressive. Except for a brief interlude of Conservative administration in the early 1930's and for the immediate post-war period, the chamber scarcely justified the outlay of expenditure for its upkeep. The Senate has been neither a workshop nor a theatre. Since by far the greater bulk of legislation now originates in the Commons, the Senate has become and is now utterly dependent upon the Commons for its business. It cannot function until it receives bills from the other chamber. Thus, for weeks on end, while the Commons debates the Address in Reply to the Speech from the Throne, the Senate must sit idle. It has been estimated that three out of the average five months in every session are spent by the Commons in idle debate, that is to say, debate that does not bear directly on legislation. The Senate, then, is faced with an enforced unemployment, and it is not unknown for the chamber to adjourn for long periods immediately after the Speech from the Throne and for shorter periods throughout the session. On an average the Senate is adjourned for 40 to 50 per cent of the tenure of each Parliament.[22] Even when the Senate is sitting, there is often

[21]"The Canadian Senate," pp. 152–63.
[22]Turner, "The Senate of Canada," appendix "A."

little or no business transacted. A cursory look through *Hansard* is convincing.

On the other hand, during the closing days before the prorogation of a session, the Senate is almost deluged with legislation. The debates in the Upper House are full of bitter comments on this feature of Canadian parliamentary practice. Mr. Meighen expressed the sentiment of the members of the Senate vehemently in these words:

> It is little less than a travesty that this chamber, prepared for work, ready to serve the people of this country, should be compelled to wait more or less idly for weeks, perhaps for months, while discussions, which are no doubt necessary under any democratic system, are proceeding in the other chamber, and that a plethora of legislation should be thrown at us in the latter part of each session, when we have no opportunity to do what we ought to do in the way of reviewing it, and all that the other House expects of us is that we shall pass it without thought, without amendment, and without delay.[23]

Despite the fact that this irritating procedure is a regular occurrence, the Senate has only on one or two occasions seen fit to hold a bill over for a future session until its committees could argue it carefully and give it due consideration.

This abuse of the time of members of the Senate (among whom may still be numbered several of Canada's outstanding citizens) has been aggravated under the present Conservative administration. Frequently, the present Government has asked for immediate Senate approval of a bill, without even a lapse of the two days required by the Senate rules for tabling. This is clearly contemptuous treatment of the Upper House.[24]

Modern parliamentary custom has undermined the legislative position of the Senate. Ministers no longer sit in the Upper House; important legislation is no longer introduced there (and financial measures cannot be); and the pressure of time imposed upon senators by the last-minute flow of legislation deprives them of the opportunity of exercising a sound judgment or of suggesting useful modifications. The "sober second thought" is now merely a hollow echo from an optimistic past.

[23]*Senate Debates*, March 8, 1934, p. 140.

[24]Note in respect of the Hospital and Diagnostic Service Bill, *Financial Post*, July 5, 1958, p. 4.

What useful purpose does the Senate have today?[25] Neither in its federal nor legislative aspects has the Senate accomplished its purpose. If this is so, there can be no logical impediment to its reform or abolition. The argument, however, is more severe. The waste of talent in the Senate of recent administrations has made that chamber a functionless oddity; but it has been the abuse in the method of appointments which has bankrupted its reputation in the country.

It was originally hoped that the Senate would be an impartial and reflective body. The Fathers of Confederation were not unaware of the partisan use to which the appointment procedure could be put, but they hardly foresaw the proportions it would reach. They expected that the legislature would have some control over the appointments and thereby limit the extent to which political patronage could be pushed; but two developments in the post-Confederation era completely dashed any such hopes.[26] The first was the gradual dominance of the Prime Minister over the Commons and later over his Cabinet —a development which had not been foreseen in 1864. Consequently, appointments to the Senate have become his virtual preserve as his personal patronage. It is not surprising, therefore, that they have been made on the basis of partisanship.[27] The second feature has been the

[25]In recent years, there have been suggestions to the effect that the Senate may have a new role as a sort of counterweight or balance to the civil service. Legislation is now so technical and complicated that the members of the House of Commons engrossed in debate and in a variety of political business cannot hope to study it adequately. Consequently the civil service assumes a power in direct proportion to the complication of the legislation. This is the modern problem of the empire of the expert. It has been suggested that the Senate, with its more leisurely procedure and with the wealth of experience both political and financial among its membership, should be assigned a greater proportion of the work of current legislation. If, of course, this is to be done, the present timetables would have to be revised and a method agreed upon whereby the difficult legislation be introduced at an earlier date so as to be made available to the Senate. Certain of the committee work accomplished by the Senate has been outstanding. There have also been proposals from time to time that senators be chosen to head and staff royal commissions instead of judges. This would relieve a busy judiciary from an onerous task, but one wonders whether the public could be as convinced of a senator's impartiality.

[26]Mackay, *The Unreformed Senate*, pp. 45–9.

[27]As a reward for political loyalty, party appointment has become an all but unbroken tradition. During his nineteen years of office Sir John Macdonald appointed only one Liberal and one Independent—John Mac-

peculiar phenomenon of Canadian politics whereby governments change but seldom and the cycles of power are long and slow. The long periods of office enjoyed by both parties have meant that the membership of the Senate has been coloured by one political complexion and then another—and in extreme hues. For instance, the tenure of office of the Liberal Government between the years 1935 and 1957 left the Upper Chamber a virtual monopoly of the Liberal party.[28]

Because of the partisan source of the appointments, the nominations have fallen largely into three categories: Cabinet ministers who are weary of the burdens of office (or who have become burdens themselves); old political war-horses who have lost their seats or who are tired of running elections; and what the Americans call "fat cats," meaning rich men who have been generous subscribers to the campaign funds of the party. Party affiliation does not always mean the best appointment. Despite the fact that most of the ex-ministers are very useful senators and that some of the wealthy appointees bring to the debates an informed understanding of financial problems, the general standard of contribution to the debates by most of the senators is paltry.

---

donald of Toronto (Liberal) and Donald McInnes from British Columbia (Independent): Mackay, *The Unreformed Senate*, p. 174, n. 1. Sir Wilfrid Laurier appointed none but Liberals and, except during the period of Union Government, Sir Robert Borden appointed none but Conservatives. Recent Prime Ministers have continued to pay homage to the custom, and during the past thirty years there were only five appointments across party lines. R. B. Bennett summoned his personal friend, Patrick Burns, a Liberal from Calgary, in 1931, and Prime Minister King appointed Charles L. Bishop, a former member of the Press Gallery and a Conservative, in 1945. Senator John Hackett from Montreal was a well-known Conservative when he was appointed by Prime Minister Louis St. Laurent in 1954. Senators Molson and Savoie were probably independents and no doubt their appointments in 1955 met with a good deal of back-room opposition from party ranks.

[28]The standing in the Senate on June 10, 1957 (the date of termination of Liberal power) was 78 Liberals, 5 Conservatives, 2 Independents, 1 Independent-Liberal, and 16 vacancies. Almost three years of Conservative regime has not yet succeeded in restoring the balance. As at Jan. 20, 1960, the membership in the Senate was divided politically as follows: Conservatives—22; Liberals—73; Independents—2 (Molson, Savoie); Independent Liberals—1 (Cameron); vacant—4.

Senators are appointed for life.[29] The fact of a life appointment means that the age of several senators has become a handicap to the proper functioning of the chamber. This is an abuse which is especially vulnerable to criticism. The reasons advanced, of course, in favour of life tenure are independence and security. Surely, both motives could be met by providing for a compulsory retirement age with continuation of the stipend until death.

In recent years, a senatorship has become like a carrot dangled before the noses of the party faithful. Prime Ministers have perfected the skill of withholding vacant senatorships until the very eve of an election before sprinkling them among the most faithful and deserving of the party flock. Thus, from July 20 to October 14, 1935 (the day of the general election), no less than seventeen Conservative senators were appointed (ten of them members of Parliament fleeing from the impending storm); and in the two months preceding the 1945 election, eighteen Liberals (eleven of them from the Commons) were made senators. The fact that there were sixteen vacancies on June 10, 1957, was a rather amusing example of Liberal over-confidence.[30]

Curiously, despite the falling prestige of the Senate among the public, a seat in the Upper House is still very much in demand. Campaigning for the vacancies is heavy. At the present time, the traditional Irish-Catholic seat in Montreal is unfilled and many are the visits made on behalf of the candidates to the Prime Minister's office in Ottawa, or to the Cardinal's Palace in Montreal. A few years ago, when it became known that Prime Minister St. Laurent intended to appoint the first Jewish representative to the Senate, the battle for that honour became almost a free-for-all. The Jewish communities in Montreal and Toronto were locked in what amounted to civil war until the pressure was finally relieved by the appointment of Mr. David Croll from Toronto. So the price must still be worth the game. The question is how long will the Canadian people continue to put up the trophy!

[29]B.N.A. Act, s. 29.

[30]The situation had become somewhat less than comical in the year 1955, when virtually a fifth of the complement of the Senate was vacant, provoking the introduction of a bill (Bill H-10, introduced in the Senate on March 29, 1955, by the Honourable Senator Euler) to provide that vacancies in the membership of the Senate be filled within six months of the occurrence of the vacancy. Needless to say the bill had little chance of success and was killed on second reading.

Political considerations have succeeded in depriving the Senate of any independence. Party appointments to the Senate produce, naturally enough, party senators; and their independence, their calm judgment, their impartiality tend to vanish when subjected to strain.

> The senators take their seats in the Upper House, not as critics, not as legislators whose one object is to produce good statutes; but as violent partisans, men whose minds have become warped and twisted with long party controversy, and whose chief end in life is to promote the interests of those whom they have always supported and to whom they owe their position.[31]

In view of this gradually deteriorating situation, it is not surprising that talk of reform has been on the lips of Canadians since Confederation.[32] Proposals for reform have been of two kinds: administrative and constitutional. The former have been broached usually by the senators themselves and have sought to achieve greater efficiency in the use of the time of the Upper House. It has been frequently suggested, for instance, that legislation be introduced into the second chamber at an earlier stage in the parliamentary session. From time to time, the Standing Rules have been improved so as to allow for a better conference procedure between the two houses. Proposals of this kind do not, however, go to the heart of the matter. The present system of appointment and the reluctance of the Cabinet to find a use for the Senate are symptoms that more radical measures are needed. The institution itself must be remodelled.

Constitutional reform might be of several kinds. The following are the suggestions that are most frequently advanced: (1) reform in the method of appointment; (2) a fixed and limited term of office with an age limit for appointees; (3) limitation of the "veto power"; (4) adoption of the elective principle; (5) outright abolition.

[31]R. M. Dawson, *The Principle of Official Independence* (Toronto: Grundy, 1922), p. 247. The opposite view that senators lose their partisanship upon appointment and are glad to break the shackles is held by Arthur Hannay, "Canadian Senate a National Asset," *Maclean's Magazine*, April 15, 1925, p. 49. Dawson's opinion is generally the one commonly accepted: see Senator Perley, *Senate Debates*, June 20, 1906, p. 823, and Laurier and Foster, *Commons Debates*, April 1, 1912, pp. 6821–4.

[32]This includes several debates in the Senate itself. For a history of reform proposals, see Turner, "The Senate of Canada," pp. 69–85.

"Whatever be the virtues of an ideal system of appointment," wrote Stephen Leacock, "the Senate is a mere parody of it."[33] Who could help but agree? Suggestions for changing the method of appointments adopt a variety of forms. It is frequently advocated that instead of senators being chosen from the ranks of the political parties, distinguished citizens from all walks of life be nominated in their stead in order to give the Upper House a true variety of experience. A little reflection upon the present scheme of things would lead one to conclude that the suggestion is hardly reconcilable with practical politics. It might be well to consider whether under any system of appointment (or election) party loyalties and allegiances could be eliminated. The hackneyed axiom that man is a political animal is never more applicable than in politics, and it is quite conceivable that no matter how he managed to reach the Upper House a senator would still retain to a greater or lesser extent the political beliefs and sentiments he had before his summons. Again, it has been suggested that the appointments be given over to the provincial governments on the ground that provincial interests would thereby receive fuller representation in the Senate. Against this proposal, of course, is the observation that if the system of appointments is abused under the present system when they emanate from the federal authority, there would be little likelihood of an improvement if the appointments were to come from the provincial capitals. The innovation would do little towards alleviating the partisan spirit in the Upper House, and, indeed, the appearance of diverse political allegiances from different provinces would probably intensify it. Moreover, the inevitable consequence would be to make senatorships spoils for provincial politicians, a class on the whole much less able than their federal counterparts. "Why thrust Dominion politics into the provincial legislatures?" asked Sir George Ross when discussing the proposal in the Senate. "The smaller the pit, the fiercer the rats fight. The pit is small enough now, and the rats do fight fiercely, and if there is anything more to be fought for it will only intensify the struggle. . . .[34] Finally, since the Senate is hardly equipped to be an adequate forum for the defence of provincial rights, the very purpose of the proposal would seem groundless. In any event, no matter what change was made in the method of appointment, this would not cure its present ills.

[33]"The Canadian Senate and the Naval Bill," *National Review* (London), LXI (July, 1913), p. 995.

[34]*Senate Debates*, 1908, p. 112.

A Senate chosen by the nominative process, no matter how impartially, is destined to remain essentially a secondary chamber and to labour under the shadow of the House of Commons. Remedies that would have the Senate chosen by various public bodies, such as the universities, trade unions, Chambers of Commerce, and so on, while they would undoubtedly salvage the dwindling popularity of the Upper House, would hardly succeed in restoring it on a plane with the popular chamber.

Some of the same observations could be made about the suggestion that senators be appointed for a fixed term and subject to a compulsory retirement age. While eliminating one cause of ridicule, the achievement of a less senile Upper House would fulfil no object if the members of the Senate were still given little or nothing to do.

Another brand of reform relates to the limitation of the "veto" power granted the Senate by virtue of its having co-ordinate powers with the House of Commons, except in the matter of the origination of money bills.[35] The Canadian Senate has more legal power than any other second chamber in the world, with the possible exception of that of the United States. It can amend any bill in any way it wishes; it can throw out any bill, even a money bill, if it chooses;[36] it is subject to none of the restrictions usually placed on the powers of upper houses. "If there was a deadlock between the House of Commons and the Senate, nothing short of revolution could solve the difficulty . . . no constitutional remedy within our grasp could bring the Senate to a different view."[37] So said Sir Wilfrid Laurier on one occasion, and from a purely legal standpoint he was correct; but his statement certainly did not rest on grounds of fact. For the Senate has never defeated the real will of the people or obstructed it when that will was clearly expressed. The history of Canadian government proves conclusively that the Senate has never overstepped its bounds as a secondary fixture in the parliamentary system and scarcely deserves the tirades hurled against it on this score.[38] Therefore, a limitation of the "veto" power would merely be a further emasculation of the chamber without any compensating cure of an abuse. A Senate without power to reject legislation would be handicapped yet more severely in its constitutional role as a restraining influence on legislation.

[35]B.N.A. Act, ss. 17, 18, 53.
[36]See note 9, *supra*.
[37]*Commons Debates*, 1908, 1571–2.
[38]Turner, "The Senate of Canada," p. 117.

A Senate elected directly by the people would have the obvious advantages of being at once popular and strong. Undoubtedly, were such a constitutional amendment passed, the Senate would recoup immediately its lost prestige and would regain much of the power shorn from it under the present system. There would also be the accompanying benefits of having the minority parties represented in the Upper House and of bringing the Senate more into line with the political complexion of the House of Commons. These advantages cannot overcome the historic objective taken in the Confederation Debates, already discussed, that an elective upper house cannot be reconciled with the Cabinet system under the parliamentary tradition.

Those who seek abolition argue that the Senate has failed to fulfil its purpose. It is not and has never been the bastion of provincial rights. Its function as a restraining influence on legislation has been rendered almost obsolete by the method in which bills are sent to it for review mostly during the closing days of the session. It is said that the work of the Senate could be equally well accomplished by a parliamentary drafting commission of technical experts charged with preparing legislation before it reaches the Commons. There is much to be said for the elimination of an institution when it no longer has a role to play.

Why is it that the discussion never ripens into action? There are a number of very good reasons. Undoubtedly, from a realistic point of view, the strongest is that power corrupts. A prime minister once in office is loth to foment any agitation which might result finally in his being deprived of a very convenient source of patronage with which to humour his party followers. Again, the cause of reform has suffered from the wide divergence in opinion as to how it should best be accomplished. There has been little unity of purpose among the various sections of the movement, with the usual result that the Senate weathers the storm without much difficulty. The root of most of the inaction, however, may be that constitutional reorganization of the Upper House would require an amendment to the B.N.A. Act, and, in view of the fact that the very procedure of obtaining such an amendment is a matter for dispute, or, at least, of doubt, that would be a delicate business.

The crux of the problem is whether an amendment to the B.N.A. Act affecting the Senate would require the consent of the provinces or whether the federal government could amend of its own motion. The B.N.A. Act, as originally enacted, contained no provisions for its own amendment. An Imperial statute, it could be varied only by subsequent legislation of the Parliament of the United Kingdom. In the year 1949, however, the Canadian Parliament passed a statute known as the British North America Act (No. 2), 1949, whereby an amending procedure in relation to matters within the competence of the federal legislature was added to section 91 of the Act.[39] The statute was in the form of an address to the British Parliament requesting the appropriate addition to the Act and the amendment was duly enacted by the United Kingdom Parliament.

Under that statute, jurisdiction was transferred to the Parliament of Canada to amend the constitution of Canada with the following five important exceptions: (1) matters coming within the classes of subjects assigned exclusively to the legislatures of the provinces by the B.N.A. Act of 1867; (2) rights or privileges granted or secured to the legislature or the government of a province by any constitutional act; (3) rights or privileges granted or secured by the constitution to any class of persons with respect to schools; (4) constitutional provisions regarding the use of the English or the French language; and (5) the constitutional requirement that a session of Parliament must be held once a year and that a general election must take place at least every five years, with a proviso for possible postponement of an election in cases of real or apprehended war.

Certain remarks are apposite. In the first place, power is given to the Canadian Parliament to amend the constitution only in its federal aspects. This is underlined by the incorporation of the amending power into the existing section 91 of the Act relating to federal powers. Consequently, it must be implied that for matters beyond its competence, the federal Parliament would itself have no statutory jurisdiction to amend the Act which serves as the Canadian constitution and would be bound to follow the procedure adopted by Parliament in achieving the 1949 amendment; that is to say, an act would be passed requesting the appropriate legislation from the Parliament of the United Kingdom to alter the particular provision of the B.N.A. Act.

The vital question is, therefore, on what grounds can the Imperial Parliament act? What amount of internal agreement as the basis of an address from Canada to Westminster would suffice for British action? In other words, the real issue is whether the British Parliament would be justified in enacting a change in the constitution desired by the Dominion Parliament in relation to a matter beyond its competence under the 1949 amendment and strongly objected to by one or more of the provinces. Recent interpretations, based on the

[39] 13 Geo. VI, c. 81.

conception of Dominion autonomy, maintain that Britain would not be required to look behind the request at all but would be sufficiently warranted, if not bound, to comply with the request of the Dominion Parliament *per se*. In respect of the attitude to be taken by the Imperial Parliament, therefore, there are strong grounds for believing that any amendment could be pushed on the authority of the Canadian Parliament alone.

There are cogent reasons, however, why the Dominion Parliament would not submit an address on this subject to the Imperial body on its own authority. Constitutionally, the issue is not very clear. The "compact theory" of Confederation, which maintains that the union was a result of a contract or treaty, inevitably leads to a conclusion that an amendment to the constitution requires the unanimous consent of all the provinces.[40] However, there is some disagreement as to the historical validity of the compact theory, and inasmuch as it is contested, its corollary of unanimous consent is also in jeopardy.[41]

There is some reason to suppose that a procedure along the lines of that suggested by the late Hon. Ernest Lapointe, Minister of Justice, might be adopted. According to the scheme he proposed at the Dominion-Provincial Conference, 1927, in the event of ordinary amendments being contemplated, the provincial legislatures should be consulted, and a majority consent of the provinces obtained, while in the event of vital and fundamental amendments being sought, involving such questions as provincial rights, the rights of minorities, or rights affecting race, language, and creed, the unanimous consent of the provinces should be obtained.[42] While the proposal begs the

[40]For the compact theory and its effect on amendments to the constitution, see Sir George Ross, *The Senate of Canada* (Toronto: Copp Clark, 1914), pp. 15–36, 109–19; "Amendment of the B.N.A. Act" in Annex 4 of the *Report Pursuant to Resolution of the Senate, 1939, Re: British North America Act* (Ottawa: King's Printer, 1939), pp. 122–34; for the compact theory of Confederation, see "Letter and Memorandum of Hon. Howard Ferguson, Premier of Ontario, to the Prime Minister of Canada, September 10, 1930," *ibid.*, pp. 134–39; and "The Compact Theory of Confederation," by Norman McL. Rogers in *Proceedings of Political Science Association*, 1931, pp. 205–30, as cited in excerpts in *ibid.*, pp. 139–48.

[41]For opinions hostile to the compact theory, see "The Compact Theory of Confederation," by N. M. Rogers; Wilfrid Eggleston, *The Road to Nationhood* (Toronto: Oxford, 1946), pp. 19–34.

[42]Dominion-Provincial Conference, November 3–10, 1927, *Official Precis of Discussions* (Ottawa: King's Printer, 1928), pp. 11–12.

question in not defining the difference between an "ordinary" and a "fundamental" amendment, it seems reasonable to suppose that Senate reform would fall under the latter classification. Undoubtedly, a measure seeking the reform or abolition of the Senate would be beyond the competence of the Canadian Parliament and could not be achieved solely in virtue of the B.N.A. Act (No. 2), 1949.[43]

Notwithstanding the constitutional issues involved in any amendment seeking the reform or abolition of the Senate, no matter whether unanimous consent were necessary or not, there would still remain the moral and political considerations. Even if the Dominion Parliament were successfully to petition the Imperial Parliament for an amendment of this sort—and this writer is of the opinion that no legal objection could be taken by the United Kingdom to an amendment which would abolish or reform the Senate—there would be a serious issue on moral or historical grounds unless the provinces had previously given their consent to such an amendment. It is an indisputable fact that Quebec and the Maritimes were induced to accept the federation by the promise of equal representation in the upper chamber, and any measure seeking to alter either the representation or the composition and powers of the Senate would be affecting the vital interests of those provinces.

Admittedly the moral argument depends on historical grounds and because the nature of the original compact is a disputable point, the Canadian government might conceivably argue that it was under no moral compunction to seek out the unanimous consent of the provinces. Politically, however, if any Government at Ottawa were to proceed in such a fashion towards the passage of any amendment looking to the curbing of the prerogatives of the Upper House without first having obtained the consent of the provinces it would be endangering its existence; indeed, it would be committing political suicide. Notwithstanding the argument that has been made in the foregoing pages to the effect that the Senate no longer serves any

[43]Whether the consent of the Senate itself would have to be obtained is another matter. Sir George Ross maintained that it would have to agree to its own reform: Ross, *The Senate of Canada*, p. 118. In a sense, however, that is admitting that the Senate could not be reformed in any other way short of revolution, should it prove intransigent. However, discussion of the point is really academic: if Senate reform or abolition received the mandate of the people in a general election, there is little likelihood that the Senate would oppose any measure passed to implement that decision.

useful legislative purpose and is now otiose as a means of safeguarding provincial interests, the probabilities are that the provinces would be sorely exercised if an attempt were made by the federal government to reform or eliminate it. At the conference of January, 1950, between the provinces and the Dominion, strong objections were expressed by the provinces to the amendment of the B.N.A. Act as represented under the B.N.A. Act (No. 2), 1949. It was strongly represented at that time that the provinces should have been consulted before such action was taken and this representation was made so forceably that Prime Minister St. Laurent gave definite undertakings that the application of the B.N.A. Act (No. 2), 1949, would be held in abeyance pending the production by the provinces of a better method of amending the constitution. Insofar as the clauses in the B.N.A. Act that affect the Senate are concerned, the reports of the proceedings of the conferences which took place in the years 1950 and 1951 amongst the attorneys-general of the different provinces have shown that all of the provinces except Saskatchewan insisted that no change be made in any clause affecting the Senate without the unanimous consent of the provinces in certain cases and majority consent in others. It is fair ground to assume, therefore, that the federal government would never contemplate action in this regard without the consent of the provinces.[44]

How the provinces would react to Senate reform is a moot question. If the reform sought an abridgement of the powers of the upper chamber, it is unlikely that the provinces would agree to it, as matters now stand. The same situation would apply to any scheme looking to the rearrangement of the representation in the chamber: unanimity would be extremely hard to obtain. On the other hand, any measure indirectly augmenting provincial powers, such as an amendment stipulating that senatorial appointments should be made by provincial legislatures, might meet with a different response; and it is not inconceivable that an amendment of this sort would achieve proclamation. Still, the issue must remain in the realm of speculation.

Now, finally, the conundrum can be stated. The Senate, in terms of current facts, no longer plays a useful part in the government of Canada. Its historical purposes have been lost. It no longer operates (albeit through forces beyond the control of its own members) as a restraining influence on legislation. Its initial historical function, that of representing and protecting the rights and interests of the provinces, was never discharged; and it is scarcely equipped with the necessary

[44]*Senate Debates*, 1951, pp. 147–8; 1955, pp. 502–5.

mandate for that role today. Consequently, the argument for its abolition is difficult to resist. However, the attainment of this goal or, indeed, of any appreciable reform, would require an amendment to the B.N.A. Act which is constitutionally beyond the scope of the federal government alone. The better view is that the unanimous consent of the provinces is required and, certainly, in view of the expressed attitude of nine of the ten provincial governments on the subject, practical politics would dictate that such consent must be sought and obtained. Yet the current climate of provincial sensitivity (limited by no means to Quebec alone) would indicate that, notwithstanding the experience of almost a hundred years, which should demonstrate that the provinces have never depended upon the Senate for help in their wars against successive federal ministries, provincial authorities would look askance at any attempt to abridge whatever constitutional rights are consecrated to the provinces in the institution of the Senate. Political bodies are notoriously long in dying; in a federal state they live well past the age of usefulness.

Canada and "Colonialism" in the United Nations

FREDERIC H. SOWARD

The series of volumes on "Canada and the United Nations" produced by the Department of External Affairs, of which a dozen have now appeared, are widely recognized as among the most useful sources of information upon the issues which confront the United Nations and the attitude which Canada has taken towards them. A recent volume, *Canada and the United Nations 1956–57*, draws attention to "the great interest in the problems of dependent peoples" which was noticeable at the Eleventh General Assembly. Although the report admitted that there was no meeting of minds on many issues, it believed that "there was more candor and less rancor than in the past" and that some compromise solutions were adopted which may help to secure a peaceful adjustment of the many difficulties confronting the administering powers in their handling of dependent peoples.[1] Such difficulties are seldom recognized by Canadians as being of pressing concern. As a Canadian who once served on the Fourth (Trusteeship) Committee has written, "Questions affecting the unity and autonomy of the Ewe tribe of coastal Togoland, or the land rights of the Wa-Meru in Tanganyika, or even the adequacy of French reforms in Tunisia, do not stir in the breasts of Canadians the kind of lively emotions that are naturally felt by the parties directly involved."[2] It is not unfair to say that in discussions of these colonial issues at the United Nations their delegates have pursued a minor, not to say self-effacing, role. Recently, however, there have been signs of some change of attitude which may reflect a realization of the necessity for Canada's helping to bridge the gap that undoubtedly exists between the so-called "colonial" and "anti-colonial" powers in

[1]*Canada and the United Nations 1956–57* (Ottawa, 1957), p. 4.

[2]F. H. Soward and Edgar McInnis, *Canada and the United Nations* (New York, 1956), p. 207.

the United Nations, if progress is to be made in settling disputes in this and other areas.

The foregoing summation of the Canadian attitude on colonial issues may surprise those who are aware that Canada has played on more than one occasion a really significant role in the United Nations. But a little reflection will soon make clear why such an attitude of disinterested detachment was perfectly natural. Unlike so many other members of the United Nations, including almost the whole of the Western Hemisphere and most of the Afro-Asian group, Canada did not win her freedom by revolution from the parent state or imperial power. Because of the absence of bitter memories there is not the almost instinctive support of colonial complaints against a metropolitan power which comes so readily from so many states. With a population very largely of European origin, Canada has never experienced the painful realization which has been the lot of Asian and African states that superiority may be claimed and enforced because of a difference in the colour of the skin. As Sir Ivor Jennings has pointed out, in writing of British colonial policy, "the imperialist Puritans of the Victorian era . . . obeyed the Ten Commandments, and added an element, incorporating the colour bar."[3] Unlike her four associates in the British Commonwealth of Nations, the United Kingdom, Australia, South Africa, and New Zealand, Canada did not become a mandatory power after the First World War. By this abstention she escaped both the burden of administration and the criticism of their policies which has been the lot of those countries. As a strong supporter of NATO, Canada is well aware that besides the United Kingdom five more of her allies in that grouping, Belgium, France, Italy, The Netherlands, and Portugal, are either administering powers with trusteeship agreements or are governing colonial peoples, while a fifth, the United States, is responsible for a strategic trusteeship area in the Pacific. No state readily becomes a candid critic or a discriminating supporter of its allies and associates when they are under a steady drumfire of criticism, much of which is undeserved. Such a reluctance is intensified, in Canada's case, by the knowledge that she is quite unversed in the arts of colonial government. Within her metropolitan area, Canada has had and still has her own problems in being responsible for the welfare of Indians and Eskimos, but few would claim that such an experience offers a firm base for criticizing the administration of the Cameroons. When these considerations are com-

[3]Sir Ivor Jennings, *Nationalism, Colonialism and Neutralism* (Leeds, 1957), p. 6.

bined with the normal Canadian caution, it is not surprising that Canada has been one of the most unobtrusive participants in the handling of colonial questions at the United Nations.

At the very outset, when the San Francisco conference was debating the provisions of the Charter on Trusteeship, which appear in chapters XI, XII, and XIII, the voice of Canada was seldom heard in the drafting committee. As the Canadian delegation subsequently reported, they "took no active part in the discussions but followed them with close attention." They preferred to be reticent because of "the lack of any direct responsibility of the Canadian government for the administration of colonial dependencies."[4] On the other hand, the delegation appreciated the opportunity which would undoubtedly be presented to the Soviet Union in future of exploiting the anti-colonial feeling, shared by many members of the United Nations. It was among the few which voted against the proposal that permanent members of the Security Council should likewise be permanent members of the Trusteeship Council whether they were responsible for a trust territory or not. This decision, adopted by an overwhelming majority, gave the Soviet Government a chance of embarrassing its former allies, which it has ever since skilfully exploited.

Three years later another example of tactful silence on the part of Canada was afforded when there was an extensive debate in the Fourth (Trusteeship) Committee of the General Assembly upon the refusal of South Africa to negotiate a trusteeship agreement for South West Africa as the other mandatory powers had done with respect to their mandates. A resolution was adopted, another one of a long series, which expressed regret at South Africa's failure to accept Assembly recommendations that it place South West Africa under trusteeship, and called on the Union Government to submit annual reports to the Trusteeship Council. The volume on *Canada and the United Nations, 1948* notes that the Canadian delegation "took no part in the debate on this question either in the Fourth Committee or in the General Assembly." It likewise abstained on the vote when the resolution was carried by 43–1 (South Africa)–5.[5] The fact that the four other states abstaining on the resolution were all from the Commonwealth indicated a sense of group loyalty, except in India's case where abstention was followed on the ground that the resolution was not strong enough. In 1951, when the Fourth Committee, after

[4]Department of External Affairs, *Report on the United Nations Conference on International Organization* (Ottawa, 1945), p. 49.

[5]*Canada and the United Nations 1948* (Ottawa, 1949), p. 152.

another lengthy debate, voted to hear petitioners from South West Africa, the Canadian delegation again took no part and again abstained on the vote of 37–7–7. The reason given was that the delegation was "not prepared without closer examination" to reject either South Africa's view that the action was illegal or the opposing argument that the Committee was "morally justified" in getting information from petitioners because of South Africa's failure to accept the advisory opinion of the International Court of Justice that the United Nations should exercise supervisory functions over its annual reports on the territory and the transmission of petitions.[6]

A continual source of dispute in the United Nations has been the uncertainty which obscures the relationship of the Trusteeship Council to the Fourth Committee and the General Assembly. By the terms of the Charter, the Council is a "principal organ" of the United Nations. But in article 85 the Council is described as "operating under the authority of the General Assembly," and assisting that body in carrying out the functions of the United Nations with regard to trusteeship agreements. Since the Trusteeship Council is equally composed of administering and non-administering powers, its debates and votes are more evenly balanced than in the General Assembly where the anti-colonial powers and the Soviet bloc command a majority. As a Burmese delegate remarked in the Eleventh Assembly, it was sometimes whispered that the Council "was too much of a friendly or even a family party." It is to be expected that the anti-colonial powers will bend every effort to bring the Trusteeship Council as much as possible under Assembly control. In the same manner they are constantly endeavouring to enhance the authority and prestige of the Committee on Information from Non-Self-Governing Territories, set up under the jurisdiction of the Fourth Committee, which appraises the information received from the administering powers for some sixty territories not covered by trusteeship agreements which have been voluntarily listed by the colonial powers. On the degree of supervision to be exercised, the Canadian position has been "to resist unreasonable extensions of the authority of the General Assembly by resolutions interpreting the Charter."[7] In 1950, for example, when there was a

[6]*Canada and the United Nations 1951–52* (Ottawa, 1953). But Canada, which had supported in 1946 a resolution disapproving of the union of South Africa with South West Africa, did vote with the majority 39–5–8 urging South Africa to reconsider her position. *Canada and the United Nations 1957* (Ottawa, 1958), p. 76.

[7]*Canada and the United Nations 1949* (Ottawa, 1950), p. 168.

heated debate on the relationship between the Trusteeship Council and the General Assembly, the Canadian delegation consistently resisted "all attempts to have the Assembly prescribe in detail the manner in which the Trusteeship Council should carry out the functions assigned to it by the Charter."[8] They had no desire to see it become either a territorial agency or a rubber stamp in the hands of the General Assembly. The Canadian representative on the Fourth Committee opposed an amendment which claimed that the administering authorities had "a clear obligation to implement the recommendations of the Assembly and of the Trusteeship Council."[9] He did so because of Canada's preference for "the desirable element of flexibility" in the operation of the trusteeship system, and her concern lest the administering powers, as they had indicated in the discussions, would be alienated by the persistent attempts to put pressure upon them to do what the anti-colonial powers thought advisable.[10] Let the Assembly content itself with "broad questions of policy" and leave the Trusteeship Council some freedom of action, has been and remains the Canadian position.[11] Consequently, Canadian representatives will oppose, by vote if not always by voice, attempts to give precise instructions to missions visiting trust territories; to set exact time-tables for independence of trust territories; to extract political information about non-self-governing territories by extending the scope of article 73; to increase the tendency of the Fourth Committee to hear petitioners who prefer to voice their grievances before such a body rather than in the Trusteeship Council, which is more directly concerned with their problems.

Canada is also less suspicious of administrative unions between trust territories and other colonies which have occurred in Africa than are the Soviet bloc and the anti-colonial powers. In 1949, she attempted unsuccessfully to temper resolutions criticizing them. On the other hand, she is distinctly dubious of attempts to broaden the authority of the Committee on Information from Non-Self-Governing Territories so as to blur if not eliminate the distinction between trust

[8]*Canada and the United Nations 1950* (Ottawa, 1951), p. 127.

[9]*Ibid.*, pp. 127–8.

[10]For the effect of constant harassing criticism upon an experienced colonial administrator who sat for several years on the Trusteeship Council see Sir Alan Burns, *In Defence of Colonies* (London, 1957).

[11]Cf. the volumes for *1950–52*, p. 129; *1952–53*, p. 78; *1953–54*, p. 82. The report on *Canada and the United Nations 1949* (p. 164) comments that in the Fourth Committee "A good deal of the criticism was irresponsible, although by no means all of it should be dismissed as ill-intentioned."

territories and dependencies. In short, on these and allied questions Canadian representatives on the Fourth Committee normally play a responsive rather than an originating role, seldom sponsoring a resolution or taking part in a debate and frequently abstaining on resolutions. In keeping with this prudent restraint the Canadian delegation has consistently and resolutely avoided following up any hint that Canada's candidacy would be well received for membership on the Trusteeship Council, the Committee on Information from Non-Self-Governing Territories, or the Committee on South West Africa. Such a modesty is less evident when there are opportunities for membership in the Security Council or the Economic and Social Council! But it is in keeping with the conviction that the colonial area is not one of direct interest to Canada. Let Guatemala or Burma, Haiti or the Philippines, serve on "colonial" committees. Canada would gladly stand aside. The old soldier's advice in the First World War to the green recruit "up the line" for the first time to "Never volunteer" is the kind of maxim which Canadians have thoroughly appreciated in the Fourth Committee.

It is probably too soon to point to a definite shift from this cautionary attitude, but there are some indications that it may be in progress. One reason for this change, if such it is, may be found in the changing composition of the United Nations for which Canada has been in part responsible. It is generally conceded that in the Tenth Assembly the Canadian delegation played a prominent part in breaking the deadlock over admission of new members, which had existed for several years.[12] After a series of complicated manœuvres, the Security Council and the General Assembly agreed upon an increase in membership from 60 to 76 in December, 1955. Once that had been achieved it was easier for other states to secure admission, and in 1956 and 1957 Sudan, Morocco, Tunisia, Japan, Ghana, and Malaya were also accepted for membership. Then Guinea was accepted. As a result, the United Nations now has 82 members of whom no less than 29 belong to the Afro-Asian group. If they vote as a unit on any important question, they can prevent its adoption, since a two-thirds majority is required for such an Assembly resolution. Conversely, if they combine with the Latin American group of 20 and the Soviet bloc of 9, they can carry any important resolution by the required majority.[13] Such a solidarity is not impossible but is improbable, since Afro-Asian and

[12]Cf. Soward and McInnis, *Canada and the United Nations*, pp. 229–30.

[13]Cf. F. H. Soward, "The Changing Balance of Power in the United Nations," *Political Quarterly*, Oct.-Dec., 1957, pp. 316–27.

Latin American groups are, fortunately, not monolithic in their political behaviour. But the best chance for securing a wide measure of agreement among these three groups is in the colonial sphere. It is to the Soviet's advantage to proclaim its enthusiasm for independence everywhere, except among Soviet satellites, and to claim, as a Romanian representative did in the Fourth Committee in 1957, that "the existence of dependent territories is an anachronism which should be eliminated from the contemporary world."[14] In view of the fact that almost two-thirds of the Afro-Asian group have won their independence since the Second World War it is to be expected that they will be strongly tempted to accept such arguments.

Under such conditions it is obviously advisable for the western powers to reduce the tension as much as possible in colonial debates in order to avert closer union between the Soviet bloc and the Afro-Asian group and to prevent dissatisfaction over the handling of colonial issues colouring the attitudes of Afro-Asians on other important questions such as disarmament. That this consideration was appreciated by both administering powers and states which are neither colonial nor anti-colonial, among which Canada would include herself, was apparent in the Eleventh and Twelfth Assemblies. Its importance was heightened by the Suez crisis, which kindled anew the smouldering suspicions of imperialism in Asia and Africa. The following examples may illustrate this argument.

In 1956, the Trust Territory of British Togoland, in a plebiscite held under United Nations auspices, voted to join the Gold Coast in order to constitute the new independent state of Ghana. At the Eleventh General Assembly the United Kingdom asked for approval of this union and the termination of the Trust Agreement. It took pains to have its Minister for Colonial Affairs present the case to the Fourth Committee and to include in its delegation the Finance Minister of the Gold Coast Government. The resolution for this purpose was sponsored by four Commonwealth countries—Canada, Ceylon, India, and Pakistan—three African, two Asian, and two Latin American. It was adopted by the Assembly with the impressive vote of 63–0–9.

However, the French Government had less success in its parallel attempt to have the Trust Territory of French Togoland, where the people had voted in August, 1956, in favour of a constitution for the "Autonomous Republic of Togoland" and for the end of trusteeship,

[14]Quoted in F. H. Soward, "Canada, the Eleventh General Assembly and Trusteeship," *International Journal*, Summer, 1957, p. 171.

likewise freed from control. In this case the plebiscite did not take place under United Nations auspices, and the new government, which would remain in the French Union, possessed only partial autonomy, as the Soviet delegate and others were quick to point out. Here too the Minister of Overseas Territories, M. Defferre, came to New York for the debate. Forewarned no doubt by his advisers of the slim chances of success, he consented to a modification of the original request. As a result the initiative was taken by a group of states, Canada, Denmark, the Dominican Republic, and the United States, which, with some assistance from Liberia and Yugoslavia, set to work to find a compromise solution. They sponsored a resolution which advocated the appointment of a special commission to visit French Togoland, examine the working of the new constitution, and report to the next Assembly upon its findings. The resolution described the reforms already introduced as being of real significance, and congratulated the people of French Togoland upon the progress which they had achieved. After prolonged debate and much negotiation off-stage, in which the Canadian representative took an active part, this resolution was carried by 53–16–7, the Arab states (angry because of Suez) and the Soviet bloc providing the most consistent opposition. Subsequently, Canada, Denmark, Guatemala, Liberia, the Philippines, and Yugoslavia were called upon to designate nationals to serve on the Commission. It was the first time Canada had accepted such an assignment. Under Liberian chairmanship the Commission carried on its investigations in the summer of 1957.

Such victories for moderation did not, however, preclude the adoption by the Fourth Committee of other resolutions in a more familiar vein, criticizing British administration in Tanganyika or the French in the Cameroons. They did not prevent a sharp attack upon Portugal, led by Iraq and India, for her failure, in response to an enquiry from the Secretary-General, to list any of her territories as non-self-governing. Portugal had advanced constitutional reasons for her refusal. On this issue the United States, Canada (who spoke in both the Committee and the Assembly), all the members of the "Old Commonwealth," sixteen European, and several Latin American states successfully stood by Portugal. Their chief objections were levelled at the attempt to set up an *ad hoc* committee to study the application of chapter XI of the Charter to newly admitted members and to report on the explanations they had given about the status of their territories. As the American representative told the Fourth Committee, "It was for every member state and it alone to decide upon the territories in respect of which it was to provide information."[15] The vote in the Assembly on a resolution which was obviously aimed at Portugal was 35–35–5, the closest vote of the session and an unexpected defeat for the anti-colonial powers.

If the West won that round, however, the Soviet Union scored in another when, for the first time, she secured adoption of a resolution sponsored by herself upon colonial issues. By skilfully choosing the issue of speedy independence for trust territories and adroitly accepting amendments from states like India and Syria to limit the recommendations to African territories and to replace the original reference to a three- to five-year limit by one which called for independence or self-government "at an early date," the Soviet delegation secured a substantial majority for its resolution in the Fourth Committee of 38–13–11. Canada voted with the administering powers, five European states, the United States, and Peru in opposition to the resolution. She shared the view of the United Kingdom spokesman that "it was impossible for the Administering Authority . . . conscientiously to declare an estimate of the time required for the attainment of self-government." Five Afro-Asian states were absent when the vote was taken and Turkey abstained. All the rest supported the Soviet resolution as did seven Latin American states.

In the Twelfth Assembly, the Canadian delegation continued to play the slightly more active part in colonial debates which it had assumed in the Eleventh Assembly. On the perennial question of South West Africa it "warmly supported" a resolution introduced by Thailand which, in a new approach to the deadlock, proposed that a Good Offices Committee, composed of the United States, the United Kingdom, and a third member to be named by the President of the General Assembly (Brazil was selected), should discuss the problem with the Union of South Africa with a view to securing agreement on the territory's retaining an international status.[16] Canada's representative also introduced an oral amendment to a Liberian resolution critical of South Africa in an effort to soften slightly its wording, but was defeated 20–40–9. In accordance with its previous attitude, Canada also spoke and voted with the minority of 29 states which opposed a

[15] *Ibid.*, p. 176. The report *Canada and the United Nations 1956–57* (p. 99) said the proposed resolution "seemed to harbour a threat against one of the foundations of the Charter, that of the constitutional sovereignty of member states."

[16] *Canada and the United Nations 1957* (Ottawa, 1958), p. 76.

resolution concerning the administration of non-self-governing territories submitted by seventeen others, chiefly from the Afro-Asian and Latin American groups. The latter, who had not forgiven their defeat on the Portuguese position in the Eleventh General Assembly, recommended that a committee of six be established to report on the transmission of information and study a summary prepared by the Secretary-General of the replies received from members on this question. On this occasion, the resolution carried in the General Assembly by 41–30–10, but, lacking the required two-thirds majority for an important matter, did not become effective.

In keeping with its previous acceptance of a measure of responsibility for reaching agreement on the future status of French Togoland, the Canadian delegation took the initiative in presenting a resolution on that question to the Fourth Committee. It was also sponsored by Colombia, Denmark, Ireland (a new and welcome associate), and Liberia, and proposed, in effect, to follow up some of the principal unanimous recommendations of the United Nations Special Commission on Togoland. These proposals had already been examined and favourably received by most of the Trusteeship Council.

As explained in its report, the Special Commission felt that the Statute of Togoland had been "broadly interpreted and liberally applied," and that, in consequence, French Togoland possessed a large measure of self-government. However, it drew attention to important restrictions which limited the extent of autonomy, and stressed the desirability of ensuring wider and freer exercise of political freedom by the opposition parties. It hoped that the wishes of the Togolese would prevail on the future relations of the territory with France, but expressed no view on the maintenance or termination of trusteeship.[17]

The appeal of the resolution was heightened by the fact that since the Commission had reported, France had transferred further substantial powers to the Togolese government. Moreover, new elections for the Legislative Assembly on the basis of universal adult suffrage, such as the Commission had favoured, were to be held in 1958, and the governments of both France and Togoland were quite willing to have them supervised by the United Nations. Accordingly, the resolution called for acceptance of this invitation and for a report upon the conduct and results of the election, which would be transmitted

[17]Cf. the report of J. L. Delisle, Canadian delegate on the Commission, "United Nations Commission for Togoland," *External Affairs*, Nov., 1957, pp. 340–5.

to the Trusteeship Council and next General Assembly. The Administering Authority was also invited to inform the Council of the developments in Togoland arising from the transfer of additional powers which had been announced, and "any wishes which may have been expressed by the Legislative Assembly concerning the new Statute and the termination of the Trusteeship Agreement. . . ."

In introducing this resolution, the Canadian representative, Mr. Harry O. White, M.P., expressed his country's satisfaction at the fact that, through membership in the United Nations Commission on Togoland, Canada had been given an opportunity for contributing a "modest share" to the study of the Togoland problem. He told the Committee that Canada, as a country which had benefited "from a period of internal autonomy or self-government with the experienced co-operation of the parent country," could not be adverse to the idea of Togoland's having a constitutional relationship with France "on a partnership basis." In Mr. White's view, the resolution would provide "all the essential procedures for the progress and orderly attainment of the trusteeship system," and would help the people of Togoland to complete the last stage in their constitutional evolution. If the various steps described in it were taken, it should make possible "the eventual termination of the Trusteeship agreement." He therefore felt that the United Nations should not then refuse "to accede to the wishes of the autonomous Republic of Togoland" and drew attention to a statement made by the French representative in the Trusteeship Council that, if after termination of the Trusteeship Agreement the Togolese Assembly should vote to terminate the union with France, his Government would "undoubtedly have no choice but to accept."[18]

Although several amendments were proposed by Latin American and Afro-Asian states and Yugoslavia, some of which the sponsors accepted after three weeks' debate, the resolution was carried substantially in the form desired by its sponsors. One change of minor importance provided for the election of the proposed Commissioner to supervise the elections by the Assembly instead of his being appointed by the President. An effort of eleven powers, Burma, Ceylon, Ghana, Guatemala, Haiti, India, Indonesia, the Philippines, Syria, Uruguay, and Yugoslavia, to make less precise the undertaking by the Thirteenth Assembly to reach a decision, if so requested, concerning the termination of the Trusteeship Agreement was defeated.

[18]Canadian Delegation to the United Nations General Assembly, Twelfth Session, *Press Release No. 19*, Nov. 6, 1957.

The draft resolution as amended was approved by the Assembly 50–1–29.[19] In the general debate, Ghana and Syria again tried and failed to water down the resolution.

The Canadian delegation deserves commendation for the manner in which it handled a delicate situation. By its initiative in sponsoring the resolution, it secured a reasonable solution which did not facilitate as speedy a termination of trusteeship as, to judge from their attitude in 1956, the French and Togolese governments may have desired, but clearly paved the way for it. Had Canada and the other sponsors not acted when they did, anti-colonial states, as in 1956, would have seized the initiative. They would almost certainly have presented a resolution less conciliatory in tone and more grudging in its attitude towards the termination of trusteeship, because of the suspicion with which such countries eye the policies of administering powers in general and, because of recent events such as Suez and Algeria, those of France in particular. If these countries had been the first to present a resolution, it would have had priority in the debate and would have reduced the good effect produced by the unanimous report of the Commission and the approval with which it had been greeted in United Nations circles. By accepting amendments proposed by Ecuador and Venezuela, and three of the seven amendments presented by the eleven-power anti-colonial group, the sponsoring powers blunted the opposition to their resolution.[20] As a consequence, France and the Autonomous Republic of Togoland were in a position to implement the programme which they agreed to undertake and the anti-colonial powers were not left with the impression that Canada was simply an uncritical supporter of policies favoured by her colonial allies. The fact that a Haitian, Ambassador Max d'Orsinville, thoroughly experienced in trusteeship matters, was elected to supervise the elections also facilitated action.[21]

[19]Cf. "A Formula for Togoland," *United Nations Review*, Jan., 1958, pp. 16–17, 43–9; *Canada and the United Nations 1957*, pp. 77–9.

[20]The sponsoring powers were also helped by the United States, which successfully presented a useful oral sub-amendment to the eleven-power amendments.

[21]When the elections were held, the opposition were unexpectedly successful, and their leader, M. Sylvanus Olympio, well known as a petitioner by the Fourth Committee, appeared as Prime Minister and a member of the French delegation to the Thirteenth General Assembly. The General Assembly unanimously adopted a resolution endorsing an agreement reached between the governments of France and of Togoland

It may not be too much, therefore, to expect that Canada, having twice successfully played a conciliatory rôle in the Eleventh and Twelfth Assemblies, will become accustomed to the fact that such a part is one which she may be required to repeat. There are few other states in the General Assembly which are in such a position, the Scandinavian states, Japan to an increasing extent, and, on occasion, Ireland being among them.[22] Such countries can accept the task of attempting to reconcile the opinions of colonial and anti-colonial powers, since they are not regarded as doggedly partisan for either one point of view or the other. On other issues they have shown in the past that they are prepared to strive patiently and persistently for middle-of-the-road solutions without sacrificing any major principles. To present a constructive resolution in the Fourth Committee which an administering power may not always relish, or to criticize a propagandist one sponsored by a Soviet or anti-colonial power with a frankness and freedom from self-interest which an administering power cannot possess, is a task which Canadian representatives may not enjoy, but will find increasingly hard to evade. Nor should it be forgotten that much can also be done in United Nations circles by unobtrusive negotiation. The draftsman of a formula or the chairman of an *ad hoc* group concocting a draft resolution is seldom a dramatic or a conspicuous figure. He is usually most successful when his efforts are least in the public eye. But he can be a most useful public servant in the international as well as the national sphere. Is it too much to expect that Canadians should occasionally play such a part in discussions of colonial questions?

Since this article was forwarded to the editor events have sharpened its thesis. The United Nations has expanded with unexpected rapidity

---

that Togoland would obtain independence in 1960. Accordingly, the Republic of Togoland became fully independent on April 27, 1960.

[22]In an editorial on the United Nations during 1957, the *Economist* quoted the Assembly resolution on Togoland as an illustration of the "preference for compromising rather than what the Secretary General has called illusory voting victories." It praised the work of what it termed "greater Scandinavian group" in which, it said, "Canada may perhaps be counted as foremost among the 'honorary Scandinavian' powers." But for their efforts, the *Economist* said, "The United Nations might now be entering 1958 in much worse shape." "New Year Irresolutions," *Economist*, Dec. 28, 1957, p. 1106. Ireland provided the Chairman for the Fourth Committee at the Thirteenth Assembly.

to a total of 99 members at the end of 1960. No less than sixteen African states and Cyprus were admitted during the Fifteenth General Assembly. As a result, the African states, with a total of 23, constitute the largest single group in the Assembly. Together with the Asian states they total almost one-half of the membership of the United Nations. Moreover, their number is bound to increase as other regions, such as Tanganyika, attain their independence. Emerging as they have done from the status of a colony of the United Kingdom, France, or Belgium, or as a trust territory of the United States, France, or Italy, the new countries are particularly susceptible to the emotional appeal to end colonialism immediately which was voiced so harshly by Mr. Khrushchev at the opening of the Fifteenth General Assembly. It was significant that the Assembly gave unanimous assent to a debate upon this issue during the session. The new members are also certain to turn a critical glance in the Fourth Committee upon the position of the Portuguese colonies in Africa and to voice a vigorous protest against the policies of South Africa.

The breakdown of authority in the former Belgian Congo, so soon after the new state gained its independence, and its crying need for technical assistance have thrust upon the United Nations a very heavy responsibility. Its task has been complicated by the Soviet charges that the Secretary-General has acted as a tool of western imperialism. In an effort to offset the Soviet bid for African support, the leading western powers are stressing their interest in working through the United Nations to meet the need for "newly developing African countries to shape their long term modernization programs," as President Eisenhower did in his address to the General Assembly on September 22. Canada could not, of course, be unaffected by such developments. The request for the despatch of Canadian airmen and soldiers with special skill, as in communications, to serve with the United Nations forces in the Congo, the appeals for Canadian technicians especially those who are bilingual, and the announcement that Canada would contribute to a special fund for African states, such as Nigeria, entering the Commonwealth of Nations are signs of the times. Obviously, the relations of Canada with the newly emergent states are bound to play an increasingly important part in the shaping of Canadian foreign policy.

Neighbour to a Giant

EDGAR W. McINNIS

The relations of Canada with the United States have been conducted from the beginning on two interconnected levels. The most immediate interest has of course been centred on the direct contacts which are so vital from the Canadian point of view. Trade has been of prime importance ever since the commercial hinterland of the St. Lawrence region was partitioned as a result of the American Revolution. Boundaries and boundary waters have given rise to repeated controversies right up to the present day. And at various intervals there have been situations arising out of American policies which Canadians have viewed with alarm as actual or potential threats to their independence, and apprehension about matters ranging all the way from armed menace to economic infiltration has periodically agitated Canadian opinion.

At the same time it has never been wholly possible to divorce these direct relations from the respective attitudes of the two countries in the wider sphere of world politics. Even when the United States followed a policy of isolation, and even when Canada had no independent voice in foreign affairs, the world situation had inevitable repercussions on their mutual interests. Neither could be wholly indifferent to the European balance of power or to its implications for their own national aspirations. The attitude of Canada, with its British connection, was occasionally a matter of concern to the United States; the attitude of the United States toward Europe, and especially toward Britain, was inevitably of still greater concern to Canada. When these attitudes were in harmony, one possible source of difficulties was eliminated; when they diverged, the difference was only too apt to be reflected in Washington's attitude toward Ottawa.

Since the Second World War there has been a decided shift of emphasis toward the second of these two levels. The assumption of the leadership of the free world by the United States—an acceptance, by that time inescapable, of the responsibilities that go with power and the inevitable bearing of the world situation on American national interests—has been of decisive significance for all free nations, and not least for Canada. The power and resources of the United States are the indispensable bulwarks without which the strength of the free world would be utterly inadequate to resist the pressures against it; and the acceptance by the United States of this new role, with all its formidable burdens, has made it possible for Canada on her part to make a contribution to the common cause that might otherwise be beyond her attainable capacity.

For Canada too has stepped into a new and more positive role in world politics, and one that is only possible for her because she can act with more powerful associates. It is true that while Canada is relatively new to the field of formal diplomacy, she has had a long experience in the realities of international affairs. Her dependence on Britain throughout the nineteenth century meant a continuing consciousness of how Britain might be affected by changes in the balance of power, and consequently of how her own national interests might be favoured or jeopardized by shifts in European alignments. But it was only after the First World War that Canada embarked on her first uncertain ventures into the complexities of an independent foreign policy, and not until the Second World War that she undertook to play a positive and constructive role as a full member of the international community.

In consequence, Canada and the United States are now operating on a major scale, in proportion to their respective size and resources, in a field in which they previously occupied a position of semi-spectators. Not only has this resulted in the assumption by each of them of vastly enlarged responsibilities—it has also placed a new and major emphasis on their respective foreign policies as vital factors in their own mutual relations. It is not only the matters directly at issue between them that affect the attitudes of Ottawa and Washington toward each other. For Canada at least, the course of the United States in world politics is an even more constant and pervasive preoccupation—something that, for many Canadians, has in recent years become a matter of almost daily concern.

The reasons are easily appreciated. Canada is a country whose geographical situation is offset—or, if you prefer, complemented—by its economic and political interests. Physically there is little to fear from external enemies. There is more than formerly, in the dawning age of intercontinental missiles, but even this is relative. Canadians may be potential long-range targets for hydrogen warheads. They do not live under the constant prospect of a mass invasion by hostile forces that are poised just across the border. Yet none of this gives them immunity from the vicissitudes of international politics. Their economic welfare is inseparable from the fortunes of a world in which they must trade to live; their strategic interests cannot be divorced from the political connections that bind them inescapably to the other democratic nations that make up the free world. The concept of Fortress America, so attractive to the isolationist remnant in the United States, is one to which few Canadians have ever been tempted to subscribe.

The basic fact is that Canada, as much as almost any other nation, has to base her foreign policy on a reasoned and realistic concept of the kind of world she must try to promote if she is to build the kind of nation to which she aspires. Yet no nation, not even the most powerful, can determine this solely by its own strength and resources. Still less can a smaller power such as Canada achieve its aims by its own unaided efforts. It must act in concert with other like-minded states, and especially with larger states, if there is to be a combination of power that is adequate to implement the positive policies which will advance the national welfare or hold in check those factors that would be adverse to the national interest.

The active participation of the United States in the concert of free nations is thus a development whose significance cannot possibly be overestimated. For Canada in particular, it not only offers a broad basis for co-operation with the larger neighbour with whom it is virtually imperative for her to work in the maximum harmony; it also releases her to a major degree from that long-standing dilemma between Britain and the United States, the two basic poles of her external policy, with a consequent increase in her own freedom to pursue a positive course in foreign affairs. Yet while the abandonment of American isolation has relieved Canada of certain very real problems, there are times when American world leadership has raised other problems in their stead. The two nations are inescapably bound up with each other; and as the smaller of the two, Canada is constantly and inevitably affected by the actions of her most powerful, her most generous, and at times her most exasperating friend.

One thing is fundamental at the outset. The two countries share an identity of basic aims—an identity so complete that it is normally taken for granted in any discussion of their relations. They share the desire for a stable and a peaceful world in which are preserved to the utmost those essential human values which are traditional in their own social and political structures. To protect these values, the western democracies have united to create the necessary deterrent to the forces that threaten to destroy them. Canada was one of the early advocates of such a deterrent, which found its embodiment in NATO; and Canada recognized from the very first that an essential condition for its effectiveness was participation by the United States as the indispensable bulwark of the whole Atlantic community.

This concentration on the North Atlantic region as the essential key to the whole problem of security comes more naturally to Canadians than it does to various segments of the American public. By tradition as well as by interest, Canada has consistently been European-minded. There has been none of that deliberate turning away from Europe, none of that jejune apprehension that innocent virtue was in constant peril of being compromised by the sinister wiles of the corrupt Old World, that marked the era of American isolationism. There has been none of that tendency, which still lingers in some quarters in the United States, to emphasize the Pacific as an area of paramount interest that should take precedence over the Atlantic. Yet if the appreciation of the concept of an Atlantic community is less automatic in the United States than it is in Canada, acceptance of the basic idea has been firm and sustained. Differences in the backgrounds of the two nations may have resulted in some differences in the understanding of what the idea implies, but there is no significant divergence about the vital bearing of the balance of power in Europe on the security of the whole free world.

This means that Canada, in one of the vital areas of foreign affairs, is committed not only to acting in concert with the United States, but to the carrying on of this co-operation within the wider framework of the Atlantic coalition. Yet while this fact often determines methods, it does not change the essential problem. The maintenance of an effective deterrent is fundamental to Canada's national interest. So is the search for a way to ease international tensions without placing the national interest in jeopardy. Neither of these aims can be pursued realistically without the full collaboration of the United States, and it is consequently of prime importance that the policies of the United States should be in harmony with Canadian needs and objectives.

How to assure this desirable result is perhaps the major problem in Canadian foreign policy. It is here that a nation in Canada's position runs slap up against the limitations that attach to the status of a Middle Power. Canada's contribution to the security and stability of the free world is by no means negligible. She is a country of large resources, not only in natural products, but also in processing facilities. She enjoys to a notable degree the high living standards and the advanced level of technology that are common to other western industrial democracies. An important consequence is that, when the western democracies embark on some enterprise or confront some crisis that calls for substantial contributions, Canada is expected—and to do her justice, Canada expects—to provide such contributions on a scale second only to that of the Great Powers with whom she is allied. But that does not mean that she carries a comparable weight in framing the decisions on which the demands are based. It is the Great Powers, and first among them the United States, that determine the lines of action, often with limited consideration for or even consultation with their smaller associates. More often than not it appears that Canada's responsibilities are quite out of proportion to her influence when matters of great moment are at issue.

This is of course merely the outcome of the inexorable facts of life. However great Canada's responsibilities may be, they still fall well short of those of a Great Power. No grouping of other states hangs on Canada's decisions for guidance; no alliance depends for its effectiveness on the willingness of Canada to take the initiative. The United States, in contrast, must recognize and accept these burdens that go with leadership. Every decision in Washington on major issues must be designed to confound its foes and satisfy its friends—and how disastrous it is if the effect is the other way round! In certain circumstances—though these are becoming rarer—the United States can even take the risk of acting alone. But few of America's associates can go it alone in major matters of world politics—indeed, in many such matters, they often find it hard to act at all until they know what the United States has decided, and whether the decision is one that they can accept and join in implementing.

In dealing with this situation, the United States on its part has certain priorities. It must first of all consult its own national interests, and try to frame policies which will both express that interest and command the support of its friends. And in seeking this support there are some friends who inevitably take precedence over others. Sometimes this is because they can contribute more to the achievement of a given objective. In other cases it may be because they can make intolerable nuisances of themselves if they dissent from a particular policy. Britain, for example, is clearly more important than Holland or Belgium because of its world position and its larger potential. France may have to be wooed more subtly than Italy or West Germany because of the complexity of its external problems and the touchiness of French national sentiment.

In these circumstances a smaller state, even one that can claim to be of middle rank, has relatively little leverage. It is clearly of the first importance to Canada that American policies shall contribute to the use of the deterrent in the way that is of maximum effectiveness. If those policies are marked by either weakness or rashness, the consequences will fall on Canada as well as on her associates. Yet it is only on rare occasions that Canada can exercise a substantial or significant influence over the process by which decisions are reached in Washington. If the larger powers are in agreement, dissent by Canada carries little weight. If the United States is at odds with its chief allies, it will seldom change its attitude out of regard for Canadian opinion. The frequently repeated claim that Canada serves as a bridge or an interpreter, while it may be justified on some special occasions, is more often a myth that is cherished for the sake of self-esteem. Canadians enjoy a good reputation in the United States as people who can usually be relied on to behave themselves; but when it is a case of trying to modify American policies, they are apt to find that they are liked, and trusted, and ignored.

When it comes to problems outside the Atlantic area, this lack of effective leverage is even more apparent. Canada usually has a very real stake in the solution of these problems. Her interest in peace and stability is global in its scope, and any significant change—either favourable or adverse—in almost any part of the world is bound to have ultimate implications for her own national well-being. Yet Canada lacks the resources that would enable her to operate actively on a global scale. It is a tribute both to her international reputation and to her sense of responsibility that in recent years she has been drawn into a series of commitments in areas with which she had previously had little direct concern—in Korea, in Indo-China, in Sinai. In principle, however, she must refrain from dispersing her limited strength if that strength is to make any effective contribution anywhere. Her first concern is the Atlantic region, and it is here that her main efforts are naturally concentrated. Elsewhere the initiatives and the burdens that go with them must be entrusted to others, and again they fall chiefly on the United States.

What this means in effect is that Canada relies very largely on the United States to protect her interests, and particularly her broad general interests, in those areas outside the North Atlantic where she cannot herself operate on any significant scale. For this to be effective,

Canadian interests must be virtually identical with American interests as the United States conceives them. The preservation of the free world in general is a recognized American interest; but it is only as Canada is incidental to this, or to objectives that are still more specifically American, that she can count on sharing the benefits of American policies. Where views or interests diverge, the United States inevitably follows the course that is dictated by its own viewpoint.

Yet Canada too has a national viewpoint; and while it rests on the same fundamental postulates as that of the United States, there is no guarantee that the two will always coincide when it comes to application to specific issues or to the means of implementing agreed objectives. It is always possible that on this level the interests and outlook of the two countries will be at odds. It is even possible that the United States may be mistaken in its assessment, not only of what measures will best serve the common cause, but even of what actions will be in the best interests of the United States itself. In such a case, Canada is faced with the need to balance the importance of harmony within the Atlantic alliance, and particularly harmony between Canada and the United States, against the dangers inherent in the ill-judged course on which the United States seems resolved to embark.

These factors are illustrated by the case of China. It is more than probable that if American opinion had not been so vehement toward Chinese communism, Canada would have recognized the Peking Government at a fairly early stage. As matters stood, the incentive for taking such action was never quite strong enough during the decade that began with 1949 to make it worth risking a profitless controversy with the United States. It seemed preferable to temporize until some new development created a more favourable atmosphere. But this did not mean that Canada went along with American policy or was prepared to accept a share in its consequences. On the contrary, it was repeatedly made clear that Canada had no intention of getting involved in a conflict over Formosa; and when at one stage it seemed highly probable that the United States might engage in a shooting war over the offshore islands of Quemoy and Matsu, Canada firmly dissociated herself from any participation in this kind of adventure.

Against this area in which the primary interest of the United States takes precedence, one may cite the interest of Canada in the Commonwealth which the United States does not share in anything like the same degree. The divergence is unlikely to provoke any crisis that is nearly so acute as the kind that could arise over China, but it does result in differences in outlook and emphasis that hamper full co-ordination of policies. American opinion is imperfectly aware of the revolutionary transformation that has taken place in that ancient bugaboo of American radicalism, the British Empire, and has little emotional appreciation of how important the new association, with its lack of constitutional ties or organic expression in formal institutions, can be for the whole free world. In particular, there is only a limited realization that the newer members of the Commonwealth have a link with the democratic West whose maintenance and strengthening might be a decisive factor in the ultimate alignment, not only of free Asia, but of emergent Africa as well. Canada, actively aware of these considerations, finds herself constrained to refrain from endorsing the occasional American actions that seem to be born of either impetuosity or irritation in dealing with a country such as India, and to counsel a longer view with its implied need for the exercise of such traditional Canadian qualities as moderation and restraint. Failure to get such views accepted is unlikely to lead to a major quarrel; but what could happen is a course of action by the United States which, by alienating Asian or African leaders in the newer nations, could break the ties of those nations with the west in general and thus wreck the prospects of a favourable balance of power in which Asia and Africa are potentially so important, and with which Canada's long-range interests are so intimately linked.

Thus while Canada and the United States unquestionably share an identity of aims, that is no guarantee against sharp differences on questions of method. And in the present world situation the tolerable margin for error, even in method, has drastically narrowed. The consequences of a major mistake in calculations by the United States will fall not only on that country, but on all its associates. It is conceivable that if the United States became involved in a purely local crisis or a brush-fire type of war, Canada could remain detached, although the possibility that any brush-fire might spread into a major conflagration must always remain a cause for acute apprehension. What is certain is that a wrong decision by the United States in a crisis of major importance holds the risk of precipitating a war in which the whole free world would be involved. And as Mr. Khrushchev, with his usual endearing candour, pointed out to Mr. Pearson during their talks in 1955, in any war between the Soviet Union and the United States, Canada would be right in the firing line. That unassailable fact gives Canada a pretty big stake in American foreign policy. It gives her a right to make her views heard, and to advise or to encourage or to warn when policies are in question that affect not only the United States, but Canada not least among the other members of the western alliance.

In summary, this is a situation in which mutual relations involve mutual responsibilities. Canada, which is as anxious as other free nations to see the United States exercise world leadership, must accept the consequences of that desire. There must be an appreciation of American initiatives, a readiness to give the utmost support that is compatible with reason and common sense, an avoidance of petty criticism and carping on minor aspects. But leadership, if it is to be effective, must also recognize the conditions that are needed for success. It must be leadership on a basis and in a direction that others are prepared to accept. It must be based on consideration for the views and interests of all the parties involved, on adequate consultation when those interests are in question, on adequate forewarning before any irrevocable action. The United States has every right to expect reasonable support from countries such as Canada that look to it for leadership; it cannot expect them to surrender the right of reasonable dissent if mistakes in leadership threaten disaster to all parties involved.

It is against this background of common world interests that the direct relations of the two countries must constantly be viewed. If co-operation is to be effective in the wider sphere, harmony must be sought in their normal dealings with each other. The two levels of relationship are now inseparable, and if there are serious strains in one, that fact cannot help but be reflected in the other.

It is too much to expect of any two nations that harmony between them should never be disturbed; but to most of the rest of the world, the easy relationship between these two North American states is a matter for admiration and envy in spite of the minor irritations that accompany it. The virtually unguarded frontier is so well established, and so widely taken for granted, that other peoples have come to regard it as almost a natural phenomenon. In fact, of course, it is the result of a long and sometimes arduous process of mutual concession and mutual forbearance. Disraeli once remarked that a nation is a work of art and a work of time, and this same description applies very aptly to the relations that Canada and the United States have succeeded in evolving. It has taken time to create the mutual confidence that is the solid foundation, and it has taken the kind of imagination that is the artistry of statesmanship to overcome the obstacles that threatened at times to bring about a different and less happy result.

Now no good thing of this magnitude is without its price, and both parties have had to pay a price, and not least the smaller country that had the larger stake in the outcome. The United States, with a giant's strength, has had to refrain from using it like a giant. The few occasions when it has yielded to the temptations of power are the exceptions that emphasize the rule. Power and rapacity were both held in check sufficiently to leave Canada the means of national existence. Canada on her part has had to avoid imposing on this restraint by irresponsible provocations, to refrain from actions that the United States might feel—whether rightly or wrongly—were a threat to the national interests, and even to consent to sacrifices which the United States in the last resort showed itself determined to exact.

Some of these exactions aroused a good deal of bitterness at the time, based on a feeling of injustice, but they have not been frequent enough or damaging enough to leave behind a lasting sense of enmity. There is no Canada Irredenta. Canadians have become reconciled to letting Maine have the Aroostook country. They still wish that they might have been conceded the Alaska panhandle, but Canada is unlikely to revive a claim to it as of right. At best she would explore whether a reasonable bargain could be arranged, knowing that even this would risk provoking across the line a burst of patriotic oratory that would dwarf any Fourth of July within living memory.

In fact, whatever irritations Canadians may on occasions express, there is an underlying recognition of the inevitable consequences of the disparity in size between the two countries. In theory they are sovereign equals, and every now and then Ottawa has occasion to remind Washington of this fact. In practice the exercise of sovereignty must be adjusted to the realities of a power world. It is not that there is any real fear of retaliation from the United States if Canada should happen to offend; it is simply that Canada has the good sense not to risk hampering the maximum closeness of co-operation by actions that would create unnecessary friction without serving any indispensable national interest.

After all, Canada is, for the United States, only one of many associates, though one hopes a valuable and trusted one. Perhaps just because she *is* trusted, and because she refrains from making needless trouble, the United States at times gives less thought to Canada than to some of its more erratic and more temperamental friends. Certainly Canada is not normally a major American preoccupation. But the United States *is* major for Canada, and the desire for good relations conditions all actions and decisions, not only in matters of foreign policy, but even in domestic affairs.

Now there are two sides to this situation. One is the basic realization that the destinies of the two countries are inescapably linked, and that whatever controversies may arise between them, it is unthinkable that these should be pushed to the point of a major breach. The second is a necessary corollary. If harmony is to be maintained, it must be a continuing process, and one of reciprocal give and take. Part of the process is the readiness of both sides to consider the interests of each other and avoid infringing on them; and it is particularly important for the larger of the two parties to recognize that what may seem to be a relatively minor decision dictated by its own interest may in fact be an adverse blow of major proportions to its smaller neighbour.

That is why the relatively small controversies arising from direct relations sometimes bulk so large in Canadian eyes. Just because the big fundamentals can be taken for granted, it is possible to pay a lot of attention to the secondary irritations. At times these result in a rather carping undercurrent of anti-Americanism. It does not mean that Canada is likely to turn against the United States and take up an attitude of national hostility. But it does indicate a feeling that the United States in its self-absorption is disregarding the feelings or ignoring the interests of Canadians in things that are important to them, and is thus impairing the harmony that both parties really desire.

To no small extent, this is the consequence of the steadily increasing integration of the North American continent. Waterways and energy resources, primary products and processing facilities, capital investments for economic progress and defence arrangements for mutual security, have all taken on an importance that transcends national boundaries. Yet the boundary remains important as a symbol of the determination of both nations to retain their identity and to pursue their separate and sovereign political development. It is the problem of reconciling this political separatism with the pressures toward functional integration that lies at the root of many of the controversies in which the two countries have lately been engaged.

Take the St. Lawrence Seaway. Here is an immense navigation artery, with a vital power potential incidental to it, reaching into the heart of the continent. If the whole thing had been under the direction of a centralized government, it would have been fully developed long ago. Because the border cuts across it, local interests were able to sustain a long campaign of obstruction and sabotage. Canadians have a certain feeling that when agreement was reached, it was on the wrong basis and for the wrong reasons. But at least agreement was ultimately reached, and although there will still be periodic wrangling over particular details, they will no longer be serious enough to block the great undertaking in which the two countries are now engaged.

A second example is the controversy over the Columbia, and the right of Canada to divert its waters within her own borders. When the Boundary Waters Treaty of 1909 was negotiated, it was the United States which insisted that each country must have unrestricted control of the full flow within its own territory, and Canada yielded only reluctantly to this claim. When, however, it came to applying this to the Columbia, there were strenuous objections that the United States would suffer grave damage if the provision were actually implemented. To a detached observer it was interesting to see the American advocates exerting every device of Yankee ingenuity to prove that a principle on which the United States originally insisted should not be applied to the disadvantage of the United States in circumstances which it did not have the imagination to foresee.

Of course, this question too will ultimately be settled on the basis of a workable compromise. It might have been settled all the sooner if the United States had been readier to cease invoking dubious legal technicalities and concentrate on practical arrangements. Canadians have seldom been inclined to base their dealings with Washington on rigid legalism. In their search for a really lasting agreement, they have felt that the soundest basis would be one that was mutually advantageous and mutually acceptable. In the case of the Columbia, this approach offers the United States a chance to wriggle out of its legalistic blind alley, and to press for a settlement in which Canada would make the usual substantial concessions beyond its legal obligations, and it now seems certain that this is what will actually happen in the end.

Canadians, in fact, have found by experience that in Uncle Sam they are dealing with a hard-boiled sentimentalist. He has a genuine and spontaneous interest in others. He wants everyone to like him, and he is puzzled and hurt if they don't. When he sees someone who needs help, his response is generous and ungrudging—always so long as it is prompted by spontaneous impulse and by his own free will. When he is asked to show his friendship by giving way in a bargain, that is a different matter. That is when the spirit of the Yankee trader takes over, when interest replaces sentiment, and when the idea of making any material sacrifices in the name of friendship becomes an outrage to all his business instincts.

This has been particularly evident in matters of trade, in spite of the protests of intelligent and influential citizens in the United States who realize fully that Canada and the United States are each other's best customers, and that Canada must sell if she is to be able to buy. The goodwill of the Administration has acted as a brake on domestic pressures for tariffs and quotas against Canadian products, and voluntary limitations by Canada on certain categories of exports have further helped to head off formal restrictions. Because this has resulted in a relatively small number of tariff increases, some Americans feel that Canadians have done a lot of unnecessary worrying about things that never happened. That, however, is an over-simplification of the situation. The things that were feared may not have happened immediately, but there remains real reason to fear that they may yet happen, and if they are prevented this year, there is still no assurance that next year they may not come to pass. It is this uncertainty that continually haunts Canadian exporters, and that makes it hard to plan with any confidence for costly long-run developments.

With all these impediments, the flow of goods between the two countries still exceeds that across any other international border in the world; and behind this is a flow of capital whose balance has been heavily in favour of Canada. Now of course, American investors are not pouring in these billions simply because of their love and admiration for their northern neighbour. They are doing it because they are finding sound investments with a sound return; and one reason why the investments are sound is that Canada can be relied on to deal fairly with foreign enterprise. This is not something that the average foreign investor can take for granted in this turbulent and uncertain world.

There is naturally some concern on the part of Canadians about the extent to which certain sectors of the economy are under outside control. American control extends to approximately three-quarters of Canada's petroleum industry, 55 per cent of her mining, and slightly under one-half of her manufacturing. There is an understandable feeling that this might lead to a diversion of Canada's economic development along lines that are in the interests of the American investor rather than of the Canadian nation. There have even been some concrete examples of this danger, such as the purported rejection of an order for motor-cars for Communist China on the ground that American laws would prevent acceptance of such an order by a Canadian subsidiary. Such examples are relatively rare, and on the whole the interest of the American investor in the soundness and prosperity of the Canadian economy is a reasonable guarantee against actions that would be damaging to both. Yet the guarantee is not absolute, since American political pressures as well as American private interests are involved; and one may speculate whether the United States itself, in a comparable situation, might not develop an anti-foreign agitation that would be a good deal more vociferous than the relatively subdued anti-Americanism that has occasionally cropped up in Canada.

There are some parallels in the sphere of continental defence. Probably few Americans realize that the defence of North America was integrated as long ago as 1940, and that present arrangements are far closer and more binding than any between the United States and the Latin American countries with which public opinion, and at times the Administration as well, often seem so obsessed. There have been joint manœuvres, joint planning, and arrangements for a joint air command, and these have involved a willingness on the part of Canada to admit not only American troops, but even American military establishments, to Canadian soil. One of the major undertakings, the Distant Early Warning or DEW line, aroused particular concern because of the fear that by conceding American authority over the project, Canada might be in danger of surrendering her sovereignty over her northern areas. This concern was certainly exaggerated. What is really significant is the ability of Americans to operate on foreign soil, and of Canadians to accept a foreign operation within their borders, with an absolute minimum of friction—a striking tribute to the tact and good sense of both parties. Yet one may be permitted to wonder whether, if there were an American area in southern California or even Alaska which Americans could not enter without previous clearance from Ottawa, it would be accepted with the same equanimity.

And here it is pertinent to venture beyond foreign affairs and to emphasize that American domestic as well as external policies are of legitimate and even critical interest to Canada. It is quite impossible to insulate what goes on inside so great a country from the effects outside. Agricultural price supports may seem to Americans to be their own affair, but if they lead to a piling up of surpluses that eventually have to be dumped on the world market, other agricultural producers are bound to feel concern. The gyrations of a political figure like the late Senator McCarthy may have been something that sensible Americans felt sure they could deal with eventually, but if their delay in dealing with this phenomenon resulted in a loss of reputation and influence by the United States, that loss was felt by the whole free world. The American Constitution, with its separation of powers, is a remarkable and original document; but to the extent that it affects the ability of the Administration to take firm decisions on long-range policies, it is part of the structure of the free world, and its defects as well as its advantages are of direct importance to millions of people outside the borders of the Republic. Outsiders who make free with comments on American politics are not indulging in wanton interference, but are giving expression to an unavoidable interest in developments which directly affect them, yet over which they can exercise no direct control.

Yet when all these things are said, there remains the solid fact of a basic identity of aims and of mutual agreement on fundamental principles. Canada and the United States are friends in spite of the fact that they are also neighbours, and that is something pretty unique in international relationships. It took both parties to create this desirable relationship, and Canadians would like to feel that their appreciation of the American contribution is reciprocated by an American recognition of how fully Canada has also played her part. If Canada fully realizes that the United States is the indispensable pillar of the free world, the United States on its part may have more than a little reason to value the spirit of good neighbourhood on the part of Canada—the most patient and the most understanding and the most reliable friend that the United States has in this turbulent and critical world.

Some Problems of Canadian Trading Policy

J. DOUGLAS GIBSON

During 1957 and thus far in 1958,[1] there have been much discussion and a good deal of controversy about Canadian trading policy. It is not too much to say that a reassessment has been going on and, though it has not yet produced any clear result, there has been some change in the emphasis of policy and more important changes may be in the making. At no time since the end of the war have there been so much concern and questioning about the direction which Canadian trading policy should take.

[1]This article was completed in May, 1958. It has not been practicable to revise it in the light of the developments of the two following years since this would involve the preparation of a basically new study related to a considerably changed environment. However, as a matter of interest the figures in the tables have been brought up to date and a few comments are made in this note concerning the changes of emphasis brought about by the developments of the past twenty-seven months.

On the one hand, some tendencies have turned out to be more favourable or less unfavourable than this article suggests. Of first importance, the concern expressed about restrictionist tendencies in American policies has not been fully justified. Though the story is still unfolding, the American political system has thus far shown heartening resistance to economic pressures which in the past would have produced a much more protectionist response. Moreover, in the rest of the world, progress toward freer trade has been more rapid than the tone of this article would suggest is likely. We have in fact gone a long way toward restoring a multilateral trading world in the West, and interestingly enough Canada and the United States who have both worked long and persistently in this direction are finding the competition severe. Another way in which the picture has turned out better than expected is that the recession in business which was under way when this article was written was checked and followed by a sizable recovery both in Canada and in the United States. This, no

There are several reasons for this developing interest and concern. In the first place, a business recession began in the fall of 1957 and it has now gone far enough and continued long enough to suggest that it will probably be the most significant reaction since the war. As business has eased here, in the United States, and abroad, competition has become increasingly severe and lay-offs more common with the result that demands by domestic producers for protection against imported goods have broadened and strengthened. Protective actions and threatened actions by the United States have stirred up recollections of the thirties when Canada was treated as an unneeded marginal supplier, and of course have added strength to the proposals that Canada should follow a more protective approach herself.

The business recession, however, while heightening and focusing demands for more protection, is not the underlying reason for the widespread questioning of trading policy. The fundamental reason is a growing concern among Canadians about their economic relations with the United States. Signs of a less liberal trend in American commercial policy beginning several years before the present recession, the almost continuous threats against one Canadian export commodity or another, the great difficulty of gaining access to the American

---

doubt, explains in part why American trading policies have not become seriously restrictive and why the world-wide trend toward freer trade has not been reversed.

On the other hand, some developments have been less favourable than indicated by this article. The deficit in Canada's balance of payments has proven more persistent and much larger than implied by the article. In part, this reflects a remarkably high propensity to import, supported by business recovery, and in part it reflects the growing effectiveness of competition from overseas countries. The expectation that Canada could readily run a surplus with the overseas world if only these countries would remove their special import restrictions has not been well founded and, in fact, Canada is barely balancing her current transactions with countries other than the United States. Moreover, from a competitive point of view, developments in Europe have been discouraging. Britain has not found a way to bridge the gap between the outer European trading countries on the one hand and the Common Market countries on the other. Indeed, the division is much more sharply defined than when this article was prepared. Nor do Canada or other Commonwealth countries appear unduly concerned about this problem, at least judging by their actions or lack of action. Canadian ability to compete in the overseas world is probably less evident than it was two years ago and the prospects are by no means reassuring.

market for more highly processed and manufactured goods, and a United States surplus disposal programme which is far from consistent with the code of fair commercial behaviour envisaged in GATT—the General Agreement on Tariffs and Trade—all these developments have fostered the view that the United States is unlikely in the reasonable future to provide leadership toward a freer world trading system. They have resulted both in a sense of frustration and in a feeling of concern over Canada's great dependence on the United States. The extremely large current deficits which Canada ran with the United States in 1956 and 1957 added to the state of concern and brought into active political discussion the question of whether more of Canada's imports could be obtained from countries with whom she has less trouble in balancing her accounts. Furthermore, the notable growth in American ownership of Canadian resources and of some manufacturing industries, though contributing very substantially to the development of the country, has been arousing deep-seated Canadian fears of losing the substance of economic and, indeed, of political independence.

Related to this concern over American policies has been a growing and widely held feeling of frustration arising from the slowness of progress toward freer trading practices on the part of other countries—an attitude which frequently expresses itself in criticism of GATT. Canadians rightly believe that they have played the game toward GATT both in letter and spirit. Indeed, GATT has occupied a central place in Canada's post-war trading policy and there was one occasion at least when this country went to quite extraordinary lengths to play the game—when in 1947 action on the critical balance of payments position was postponed simply in order not to upset the then current tariff negotiations going forward under that Agreement. In the last few years, a reaction has been building up. Why should Canada abide by GATT when so many others, including the United States, take it less seriously? Why should her customs administration, brought into line with GATT principles away back in 1948, provide reasonable access to the Canadian market when the customs procedures of many other countries still have a strong protective bias? These and other questions in like vein keep cropping up, frequently with protective intent.

However, all the reasons for the current reappraisal of Canadian trading policy are not negative. In addition to concern about American policies, to a desire to avoid undue dependence on the United States, there is a positive wish to broaden the basis of Canada's trading relations and particularly to increase trade with Britain and the Commonwealth. Moreover, whatever we may think about it, it so happens that an experiment which may be of great economic and political significance has begun in Europe—the Common Market designed to bring together gradually the economies of France, West Germany, Italy, Holland, Belgium, and Luxembourg. The further plan for a Free Trade Area which would bring Britain and certain other European countries into association with the Common Market, though far from settled, is obviously of great importance to Canada.

This is, therefore, an appropriate time to review the direction of our trade and to consider possible changes with a view to arriving at a broad policy appropriate to Canadian interests. This paper offers a few observations on this subject.

I

First, to review the main facts concerning the direction of Canadian trade. There is no doubt about Canada's close relations with and dependence upon the United States. As is well known, the greatest flow of trade in commodities and services on earth goes on between these two countries. About two-thirds of Canada's external transactions are with the United States—60 per cent of her commodity exports go there, over 70 per cent of her imports come from there, and an even higher proportion of the exchange of services, including tourist trade, freight, and interest and dividends is with the United States. As will be seen from Table I, which shows changes in the

TABLE I

CHANGES IN THE DIRECTION OF CANADA'S TRADE

Exports	Percentage going to					
	U.S.	Britain	Other Commonwealth	Continental Europe	Latin America	Other countries
1927–9	39	21	8	23	3	5
1937–9	35	38	11	9	2	4
1955–7	59	17	5	10	4	4
1958–9	60	16	6	11	3	4
Imports	Percentage coming from					
	U.S.	Britain	Other Commonwealth	Continental Europe	Latin America	Other countries
1927–9	67	16	5	8	3	2
1937–9	63	17	10	6	2	2
1955–7	72	9	4	5	7	3
1958–9	68	10	4	7	6	4

direction of Canadian trade, the big change since before the war has occurred in exports, though there has also been some further increase in the already dominant share of Canadian imports provided by the United States.

Before the war the proportion of Canadian exports going to the United States was generally in the range of 35 to 40 per cent. It used to be regarded as an established feature of the Canadian economy that from 60 to 65 per cent of Canada's exports would be sold in overseas markets. Today, the position is reversed; overseas markets are taking barely 40 per cent and the United States 60 per cent at a much higher level of trade. The truth is that Canadian exports to the United States have expanded greatly, and indeed the growing American market for industrial materials has been the leading factor in the post-war growth of the Canadian economy. Recently, the physical quantity of Canadian exports going to the United States has been almost three and one-half times as great as in the years just prior to the war (see Table II). In contrast, the quantity of shipments to Britain and the Commonwealth was actually slightly less than in the years immediately before the war, though somewhat larger than in the late twenties.

The major discouraging feature of the change in Canada's trading position is thus the relative decline in the importance of trade with Britain and the Commonwealth. In the late thirties, Britain alone was taking close to 40 per cent of Canada's exports—slightly more than the United States—and Britain and the Commonwealth and Empire were taking about half of the total. In the last few years, Britain has been

TABLE II

CHANGES IN THE PHYSICAL VOLUME OF CANADA'S TRADE
(indexes base 1937–9 = 100)

Exports	Amount going to				
	U.S.	Britain	Other Commonwealth	Other countries	Total exports
1927–9	109	55	69	208	99
1937–9	100	100	100	100	100
1955–7	340	89	96	250	203
1958–9	363	89	109	258	214
Imports	Amount coming from				
	U.S.	Britain	Other Commonwealth	Other countries	Total imports
1927–9	129	113	59	152	121
1937–9	100	100	100	100	100
1955–7	351	159	124	471	307
1958–9	330	186	124	550	306

taking only 17 per cent of Canada's exports and the rest of the Commonwealth only about 5 per cent—in all less than one-quarter of the total (see Table I). In other words, from a statistical point of view, the great change in Canadian export trade since the late thirties has been away from the Commonwealth and toward the United States, though if we go back to the late twenties as the basis for comparison it will be seen that a large part of the shift toward the United States was from Continental Europe as well as from Britain (see Table I).

While Canadian exports to Continental Europe were drastically cut in the thirties, they have increased substantially in recent years and the proportion is now slightly higher than in the years just before the war. The relative importance of Latin America as a market for Canadian goods, though still rather small, has increased considerably. Actually, close to 20 per cent of Canada's exports today go to countries other than the United States and the Commonwealth compared to 15 per cent in the late thirties and about 30 per cent in the late twenties. Canada has substantially increased her trade with Germany and Japan as these countries have recovered from the war and as their needs for basic materials and food have risen. Her trade with Switzerland and Norway has expanded notably and there has been a striking advance in trade with some Latin American countries, including Venezuela, Mexico, and Colombia.

When it comes to imports, the share of Britain and the Commonwealth has declined quite sharply, from close to one-quarter prior to the war to only 13 per cent recently (see Table I). The proportion coming from the United States has increased to over 70 per cent as compared with 63 per cent before the war and that coming from third countries has also increased to some extent particularly in the form of petroleum from South America.

In other words, trade with the Commonwealth has come to play a considerably less important part in the Canadian economy while trade with the United States has become of pre-eminent significance. It is worth noting, too, that Canadian trade with certain other countries, including some in Europe, some in Latin America, and Japan, has been of increasing importance.

With regard to the balance of Canadian trade, the picture has changed quite radically both in nature and degree. Prior to the war and for some time thereafter, it was customary for Canadians to think of using a surplus earned in their transactions with overseas countries to settle all or a large part of a deficit resulting from their business with the United States. Canada is still running a surplus with overseas countries, both in the Commonwealth and outside, but this surplus is much smaller relative to the scale of transactions than it used to be. Meanwhile, the deficit which Canada is still running with the United States has grown enormously and is out of all proportion to the surplus arising from her overseas business (see Table III). There is no prospect whatever of balancing the kind of deficits Canada has been running with the United States in the last few years by earnings from overseas trade. In fact, of course, most of the deficit has been met, not by current receipts, but by a heavy capital inflow mainly from the United States.

TABLE III
BALANCE OF CANADA'S CURRENT TRANSACTIONS

	Annual averages in $ millions of the balance of all current transactions, including merchandise and tourist trade, freight, interest, and dividends, with			
	United States	Other countries	All countries	Balance as percentage of total current receipts
1927–9	− 345	+227	− 118	7.0%
1937–9	− 114	+249	+ 135	9.2
1955–7	−1414	+251	−1163	18.5
1958–9	−1185	− 95	−1280	19.4

The big deficit of the last few years with the United States results from the fact that Canadian imports have increased sharply rather than from any unfavourable change in the direction of exports and imports. Indeed, as has already been emphasized, the share of Canadian exports going to the United States has increased markedly as compared with before the war and considerably more than the proportion of imports. However, in the last few years the increase in total imports has been much greater than the rise in total exports, and the balance of "invisible" or service transactions has also become increasingly passive. Had it not been for the huge capital investment programme in Canada and the great additional demand for imports to which it gave rise, this country's trading position would have been much better balanced. The fact is that Canada has been enjoying an extraordinarily high rate of economic development by virtue of importing additional capital goods financed by increased American investment in Canada and by increased Canadian borrowing in the United States.

II

Even such a brief statement of the facts of Canada's trading position makes it clear that the Canadian economy has been enjoying a good deal of stimulus from the United States in the post-war period. The increase in Canadian exports to the United States has not only been great by any standard of comparison but it has turned out to be substantially greater and better sustained than almost anyone anticipated in the early post-war period.

At the end of the war, Canada was particularly concerned with rebuilding her overseas trade and was still not too sure about the breadth and reliability of the American market. For a short time, indeed, this country did succeed in almost restoring the pre-war proportion of overseas trade, in part by virtue of making available reconstruction credits. Unfortunately, by the end of 1947 Canada was in serious balance of payments difficulties and was in no position to continue financing a large volume of exports on credit. In these circumstances she found it necessary to turn increasingly toward the American market.[2] And, in fact, that market was receptive and took up a good deal of the slack left by reduced overseas demands. For base metals, lumber, pulp, and certain other industrial materials the United States turned out to be a big and rapidly expanding market. It is true that the Americans did not buy Canadian wheat, or more than a few manufactured items, but they were ready to purchase many industrial materials from Canada in greatly increased quantities.

This mounting United States demand, particularly for mineral and forest products, has been the leading impetus in Canada's economic growth during the past decade. It has been more than a broad demand ready at hand as goods were produced. It has also shown itself in the active and vigorous interest of American concerns in Canadian resources, in the large-scale investment of capital, and in the provision of American know-how and skills. In the pulp and paper industry, in the mining and smelting of base metals, in the development of iron ore, in asbestos, in uranium, and perhaps most of all in petroleum, the American influence is clearly evident. Whether represented by direct investment by a United States parent concern, by the purchase of a controlling interest in a Canadian business, or by a United States government contract to buy metals, the basic motivation has been the same—to develop nearby sources of supply of industrial materials for an economy which has been rapidly outgrowing its own natural resources. In other words, the American economy has been ready to

[2]For a discussion of attitudes and expectations at the time, see article by Kenneth R. Wilson in J. D. Gibson (ed.), *Canada's Economy in a Changing World* (Toronto, 1948).

provide large amounts of capital to hasten the development of Canadian resources and the result has been to speed up the growth of the whole Canadian economy.

Moreover, for some years after the war this beneficial tide of American economic influence was associated with American policies in the sphere of international economics that were far-sighted and expansive and which were in line with basic Canadian interests. The development of the European Recovery Program with its provisions for off-shore purchasing was of great help to Canada directly, in overcoming her balance of payments problem in the two years following 1947. It meant that, though Canada was no longer able to provide substantial credits to European countries, her exports to Europe did not decline nearly as sharply as they otherwise would have. In a broader sense, the European Recovery Program was a great imaginative step toward re-establishing a workable economic order, and suggested that the United States was prepared to accept the full implications of leadership in the sphere of economics as well as in that of defence. Actually, as events showed, the European Recovery Program did a great deal to aid European recovery and to lay a better basis for a freer multilateral system of world trade. Though the United States would not agree to establishing a world trade organization, tariffs were reduced to a significant degree under GATT and as time went on import and exchange controls were gradually lessened in many countries. With the Korean war and the development of NATO, American military aid provided more dollars which helped to lubricate the channels of trade; and through the years assistance to underdeveloped countries also became of growing importance.

Canada had no difficulty in adjusting herself to such United States policies and indeed in actively co-operating and in accepting a reasonable share of the costs and responsibilities. As long as the broad direction of American policy was toward freer trade and exchange, toward rebuilding an international economic order, Canada's economic relations with the United States were generally good and the liberal trend of Canadian trading policy was not seriously challenged. However, in the last few years as American commercial policies have changed direction and become more protective, Canadians have become more and more concerned about their trading relations with the United States and more divided as to the kind of trading policies they should pursue.

Whatever happens, of course, it is as clear as anything can be in this uncertain world that Canada will continue to enjoy a very close relationship with the American economy. Canada has done very well in the post-war period, largely by adapting herself to the growth of the American economy and by pursuing policies which have facilitated the appropriate economic development. Different policies might have been pursued, of a more protective character, or directed more toward supporting trade with the Commonwealth and Europe, or designed to achieve a higher degree of ownership of Canadian resources. But there is much to suggest that the policy which was pursued was in fact that most conducive to economic growth and improving living standards.

There are great advantages in living in close proximity and in close association with the United States. This fact may perhaps be more apparent to a country like Australia, which suffers from remoteness from the United States and Britain, than to Canada which is naturally quite conscious of the irritations and difficulties of living in very close proximity to a giant, friendly and well-disposed though the giant is. The advantages in terms of markets for basic materials are obvious. Less obvious, but also of great importance, is the accessibility of capital, know-how, and supplies of every kind and description from across the border. This certainly promotes efficiency and at times contributes significantly to economic stability. It was a great help in the war effort and in the rapidity of the post-war reconversion. On several occasions, the availability of American goods has been an important factor checking inflation; the last instance was in the recent boom. Indeed, the fact that American equipment and materials were readily available in the recent boom is cushioning the present recession, since much of the extra demand which has now receded was met by imports rather than domestic production. Canadians usually think of themselves as occupying a marginal position in relation to the American economy, and in many ways so they do. It is therefore of more than passing interest to find an important instance in which things have worked the other way—in which the American economy has been marginal to the Canadian.

Though it may seem a contradiction after two years of record-breaking deficits with the United States, it would also appear that Canada is making some progress in overcoming her traditional balance of payments problem. The recent big deficits reflect the fact that Canada has been buying much more than she has been selling, that in effect she has been borrowing capital goods to hasten her economic development. Since a goodly part of this economic development is geared to supplying the American economy it may be expected as time goes on to add substantially to United States dollar earnings. This has been the trend in the post-war period, as is indicated by the notable increase in the proportion of Canadian exports going to the United States, and this trend will probably continue. In the last few years the Canadian investment programme has been extraordinarily high even for a growing country, and looking ahead the average rate of investment is likely to be somewhat lower with correspondingly reduced needs for imports. Thus, the trend is likely to be toward a closer balance of transactions between the two countries. This is not to suggest that the current account deficit with the United States is likely to disappear, or that the United States is likely to provide Canada with satisfactory access to its enormous market. The deficit will probably be with us for a long time to come but it may well be of decreasing relative importance and a matter of less urgent concern to Canada, particularly if she sticks to a flexible exchange rate policy.

Having said this, however, it is also perfectly clear that there are going to be continuing problems for Canada in her trading relations with the United States—problems which because of their importance to Canada will get almost constant attention in this country. In the first place, post-war experience suggests that goods from other countries are only likely to obtain improved terms of entry into the American market when that country finds she really needs the production concerned. Exhaustive studies showing the advantages of freer trade to the United States in terms of living standards, costs, efficiency, and the maintenance of export outlets appear to make little political impression in that country. The only argument for freer trade that seems to have much effect in the United States is the necessity of working along with the allied countries of the free world and of countering communist penetration, and this argument more frequently results in financial aid than in lowered trade barriers. Certainly, there is as yet no official indication that the United States sees any merit in reducing its protective barriers except as a means of gaining concessions from other countries. Though it may be difficult for Canadians to accept, the record thus far suggests that the United States will only give better access to more highly processed forms of Canadian basic products very gradually, and as a result of continuing pressures from Canada and from American companies who have interests in Canada. The evidence also suggests that Canada will be fortunate to get much improvement in the limited access which she now enjoys in the American market for manufactured goods and that she will continue to find American agricultural policies administered in a manner injurious to her interests. It is to be hoped that this is too pessimistic a view, but it is the sort of conclusion that the experience of recent years suggests.

It is often stated by well-intentioned Americans that the growing United States interest in Canada safeguards this country against unreasonable American commercial policies. This is only partly true and only over rather long spans of time. For example, the fact that important American oil companies have a stake in western Canada does not assure Canada of an adequate developing market for oil in the United States, as recent events indicate. These companies have much larger interests in the United States than in Canada, and often large interests in other oil-producing regions including the Caribbean area and the Middle East. Their policies for Canadian development, though frequently in line with what Canadians conceive to be in their national interest, will not necessarily be so. Moreover, the views of the big international oil companies, which are generally those with interests in Canada, do not always carry the day in the United States, and they are not always prepared to fight major battles on issues which may not appear to them to be of major importance. American concerns which own pulp, newsprint, mining, and smelting facilities in Canada are strong and important allies in the struggle to maintain the best possible entry into the United States for the basic products which they are making in Canada. But it does not follow that such concerns will work to improve access to the United States market for more highly processed forms of these basic products, and indeed it may not be in their interests to do so if they already have adequate facilities for such processing across the border.

There can be no doubt that the long-term trend is toward the export of Canadian basic commodities in more highly processed forms. We have come a long way since the early part of the century when logs and mineral concentrates were frequently exported to the United States instead of newsprint and refined metals. By the end of the century we shall undoubtedly have made substantial further progress. But if past experience is any guide, progress will be gradual and there may be considerable periods when no progress is made at all.[3] Speeches on the subject will continue to be frequent and politicians will continue, rather inaccurately, to deplore Canada's status as a hewer of wood and a drawer of water. But unless these statements, and the

[3]For an analysis of the relationship between the American tariff and Canadian development, see The Bank of Nova Scotia, *Monthly Review*, Oct.-Nov., 1955.

Canadian policies which may be associated with them, have a significant impact on American commercial policies, the results are not likely to amount to much. And, thus far, American policies have been unresponsive to Canadian protests and pressures.

From a Canadian viewpoint perhaps the most depressing aspect of American trading policy in recent years has been in the sphere of agriculture. Though Canadians were not naïve enough to expect any real liberalization of trade in farm products, few of them foresaw the full implications for Canada and other countries of the American policy of maintaining support prices well in excess of world prices. It was clear quite early in the post-war period that the United States was going to limit imports of farm products when price supports were in effect. What was not so apparent, but was also a logical consequence of setting excessive floor prices, was that the United States would become involved in subsidizing exports to an extent which would seriously curtail the export opportunities of Canada and other countries in competing products. Thus, in the case of milling wheat, of which Canada is generally a lower-cost producer than the United States, she is not only kept out of the American market but finds herself up against highly subsidized competition in third markets.[4] Canadian reactions to such policies are not improved by the mantle of virtue with which some American spokesmen cloak such unfair trading practices, implying that the programme is essentially one of relief to the needy. While there has undoubtedly been an important humanitarian element in the distribution of surplus commodities, the essential purpose is to dispose of surpluses and, indeed, the programme has been used as a means of assuring future commercial markets. What is most discouraging, however, is the continuance at somewhat reduced levels of the root cause of the surpluses—high support prices.

In addition to the difficulties of gaining access to the United States market and the problems resulting from the American surplus disposal programme, Canadian trading relations with her neighbour are now confused by the development of a business recession. The two earlier readjustments in business in 1949–50 and 1953–4 did not greatly affect trade or trading relations between the two countries. But they were minor reactions, and it now seems clear that the present recession is of somewhat greater dimensions. There can be no doubt of course that if the recession continues for long it will result in increased

[4]See article by Lucy I. Morgan, "Exporting the U.S. Farm Surplus" in *Canadian Banker*, Summer, 1957.

pressures for protection in the United States; there has already been evidence of this tendency in base metals and oil. How great the protective pressure becomes depends on the extent and duration of the recession. Certainly nothing like the Smoot-Hawley Tariff of 1930 appears in the making and the kind of severe depression which might bring it about does not seem likely. Moreover, Canadian supplies in the United States are less marginal today than they were in the thirties.[5] The United States is more dependent upon them, and many Canadian suppliers are an integral part of a corporate and marketing structure and cannot be readily cut off from it. If new protective measures against Canadian industrial materials are being considered, this country has more friends at court than was the case in the thirties, in the shape of the many additional American companies which have developed sources of supply in Canada. But, though nothing like the thirties appears to be threatening, the effect of the recession is obviously restrictive to trade and, at least until very recently, American reactions have appeared to be disappointingly normal and protective in nature.

This leads to my final point. What has perhaps been most disturbing to Canadians is that the American reaction to the change in the world economic climate has been largely defensive in nature. There has been little sign of the imaginative leadership which is needed to prevent the free world from slipping into a new web of protective controls, or even possibly from breaking up into regional economic blocs. Protective reactions by the United States to the downward movement of business increase the probability of similar reactions on the part of other free countries, particularly in view of the inadequacy of liquid exchange reserves. It has taken the better part of a decade to restore a reasonable volume of international trade, to reduce the restrictions, to lay the foundations of a new international economic order. These important gains are now threatened. More than that, the free world is now faced with an economic challenge from Russia. The Russians have not been quick to see the possibilities of economic penetration open to a country which controls and directs its trade in the interests of its political objectives. But there is widespread evidence that they are now making up for lost time, both in the realm of foreign aid and trade. For those who remember the success of German policies pursued

[5]See article by J. Douglas Gibson, "The Changing Influence of the United States on the Canadian Economy," *Canadian Journal of Economics and Political Science*, Nov., 1956, pp. 423–4.

on a much smaller scale in the late thirties, the danger of the new Russian economic offensive is obvious. The present is no time for restrictive and defensive policies on the part of the West. It is rather a time for imaginative action of the kind that produced the Marshall Plan and set up the various economic agencies of the United Nations.

III

Concern about trading relations with the United States, about the big deficits in Canada–United States trade, and about growing American ownership of Canadian resources and industry have led to heightened interest in the possibilities of increasing Canadian trade with Britain and the Commonwealth. The Canadian Prime Minister's initiative in reopening the subject in London in the summer of 1957, his suggestion of a substantial diversion of Canadian purchasing from the United States to Britain, the visits of Canadian business men to Britain and British business men to Canada, the Commonwealth trade conference in Montreal in September, 1958, are all indications of the Canadian desire to be less dependent on the United States, as well as to have better economic relations with Britain. And it is perfectly natural that Canada should turn toward the Commonwealth connection. In addition to the links of tradition and history, there are the facts that Canadian trade with the Commonwealth used to be considerably more important than it now is, and that Canada has no payments problem with Britain and the Sterling Area.

There may indeed be real possibilities of increasing trade in both directions with Commonwealth countries. The recent trade missions have expressed a good deal of optimism. Britain is now more interested than she was a few years ago in developing her sales to Canada and she has been making sizable investments in this country which work to support the growth of her trade. The Imperial Preference rates in the Canadian tariff are in many cases low, there are no import or exchange controls, and there is both interest in, and goodwill toward, British products. In the other direction, it is probable that Canada could sell more to Britain if import controls were further reduced and eliminated. With regard to the other members of the Commonwealth, Canada is a growing customer for such products as bauxite, sugar, vegetable fibres, and oils. Canadian exports to these countries, though restricted by their import controls and national economic policies, may be facilitated to some extent by the provision of aid and long-term credits and by direct investment. Assistance to underdeveloped countries in the Commonwealth, through the Colombo Plan, has resulted in some significant sales of capital goods and recently certain additional assistance has been provided for the purchase of Canadian wheat. Direct investment in Commonwealth countries may help to support our trade by producing a demand for Canadian parts and equipment in lieu of finished products.

One particular part of the Commonwealth in which there are specially interesting possibilities of increasing trade is the British Caribbean area. Trade between these countries (many of which have now joined the Federation of the British West Indies) and Canada is largely complementary. What more natural than the sale of Canadian flour, fish, lumber, and a variety of manufactured goods for sugar, bauxite, tropical products, and tourist services? This trade is likely to expand substantially over the years and it may be supported by additional Canadian investment. However, it must not be forgotten that the British West Indies are part of the Sterling Area. So long as they are dependent on substantial aid from Great Britain and so long as the Sterling Area has a dollar shortage, it is questionable whether Canadian goods will be permitted the same freedom of access as British goods.

But though there are opportunities for developing trade with Britain and the Commonwealth, their scope is rather limited in relation to the total volume of Canadian trade. It seems, for example, to be out of the question to restore the relative position which the Commonwealth occupied in our exports during the thirties. The truth is that the proportion of total Canadian trade done with Britain and the Commonwealth has been declining for decades. The rather high proportion of the thirties was probably no more than a temporary interruption in the long-term downward trend, and was the result of the depression and the highly restrictive policies of the United States. The slower growth of the British economy when compared with that of the United States and certain other countries, and the serious balance of payments problems of the Sterling Area, have combined to limit the expansion of Canadian trade with the Commonwealth. Britain has kept tight control of her imports and, while Canada has maintained her relative share, British imports have been more or less stable at a time when those of the United States and many other countries were increasing rapidly. In the overseas Dominions, markets for Canadian goods have been restricted by import controls motivated by national economic policies as well as by the dollar shortage. Australia, South Africa, and India are determined to develop their own industries and are not content to go on importing things like automobiles, farm implements, and appliances from Canada or even from Britain. The result has been that a good deal of Canadian trade in manufactured goods with Commonwealth countries has been lost or limited to the supply of parts.

At times it has been suggested that Canada might try to join the Sterling Area and get inside the ring of import controls. However, this would not get around national protective policies, as the Brtish themselves can testify. Moreover, the proposition of joining the Sterling Area simply does not make sense in view of the preponderance of Canada's trade and her very close economic ties with the United States. With only 22 per cent of her exports going to countries of the Sterling Area and a mere 13 per cent of imports coming from these countries, Canada would not fit into the Sterling Area. Canada's propensity to run surpluses with Sterling countries and big deficits with the United States would be a most unwelcome attribute from the standpoint of the other members, most of whom have a weakness for dollar deficits themselves.

Though it would run counter to GATT, it would be possible to increase the Imperial Preferences as was done in the thirties with a view to stimulating Commonwealth trade. However, such action has not been advocated by any of the larger members of the Commonwealth and it would be in direct conflict with the trend of the post-war period which has been toward reducing the preferences in order to develop trading opportunities elsewhere. This has been true of Australia and South Africa as well as of Canada, and from Britain's standpoint an increase in the preferences would seem distinctly inappropriate at a time when she is trying to work out new trading arrangements with the Common Market countries of Europe. The position today is very different from what it was in the thirties. The Canadian economy is much larger and more closely connected with the United States. Even if they imposed no import or exchange restrictions, the Commonwealth countries could not begin to take half of Canada's exports as they did for a while in the thirties. Canada cannot retire into the Commonwealth. It is neither big enough nor sufficiently oriented in her direction.

However, one specific suggestion has been made which would increase Canadian trade with Britain and is also consistent with GATT, that is the British proposal that Canada and Britain form a free trade area. This would mean that both Canada and Britain would remove all tariffs and import restrictions against each other, but maintain their existing tariffs and other restrictions against all other countries, including other members of the Commonwealth. This would be done gradually over a period of years. It would certainly give Canada better access to the British market, particularly through removing the import restrictions which for years have limited Canadian sales in Britain to a rather short list of industrial materials and grains. However, it would probably not help the Canadian farmer very much, since the British farmer's basic protection lies in a subsidy system rather than in tariffs or import controls. Since there is no British tariff on wheat and since many other farm products enter free or at fairly low rates under the Imperial Preference, it is questionable whether joining in a free trade area with Britain would extend the market for Canadian farm products more than moderately. Canada might gain with respect to some specialized farm products such as apples, canned goods, and tobacco where the trade is now under quota or cut off, and she might recover the market for some of the manufactured products which have been virtually eliminated from Canadian-British trade.

From the point of view of Britain's export opportunities, the Canadian market would become more accessible. Canada would gradually remove the Imperial Preference rates against British goods and permit them completely free entry. While many of the preference rates are low, some very low or non-existent, others, including those on textile products, represent significant protection to the industry concerned. In Canada, competition from imported goods is evident in almost every conceivable line of manufactures. To remove tariffs against Britain, even though many of the existing rates are low, would create serious problems in some industries and further sharpen competition in a number of others.

From the standpoint of both countries an agreement to form a free trade area would have developing and important effects on the pattern and rate of economic growth. Though the initial changes would be small, its gradual implementation would increasingly indicate broadened market opportunities in both directions. Canadian manufacturers would be faced with much stronger British competition in some lines, but there would also be opening to Canada a much bigger market on which to base plans for industrial expansion. A free trade area would probably give a good deal of impetus to British investment in Canada. While there would obviously be many problems, the proposal has important advantages and, if Canadians are really serious in their desire to develop a counterpoise to growing American influence, this is one of the possibilities which should be carefully considered.

However, before reaching any conclusions about trading relations with Britain, it is essential to consider the other economic developments which are going forward in Europe. The outstanding event has, of course, been the formal beginning of the Common Market early in 1958. This decision may turn out to be of tremendous significance: it may be the beginning of an economic entity second only in importance to the United States. It certainly has major implications for Canada, both directly and indirectly through its consequences for Britain.

As to its direct economic implications, they are not on balance encouraging. The countries of the Common Market are in fact averaging their tariffs to outside countries over a period of twelve to fifteen years. At first sight, this may not seem disturbing, but the net result is almost certain to add to protection. The point is that the countries with lower tariff structures, Holland, Belgium, and, to a lesser degree, West Germany, are reasonably accessible markets for Canada. They will be increasing the degree of protection. France and Italy, which are less accessible markets for Canada, are committed to some gradual tariff reductions, but it is difficult to know if these will make much difference to outside countries. Moreover, the effect of providing a Common Market will certainly be to give an increasing impetus to trade within the area, and generally to reduce the proportion of business done with outside countries like Canada. From a Canadian point of view, this tendency has added significance in that the dependencies of the Common Market countries are to be included and some of these are producers of basic commodities of a kind competitive with Canadian sales to the area. And because of the special agricultural plans envisaged in the Common Market treaty, it would appear that wheat and certain other farm products are to be permitted entry only to the extent of the net deficiency of the entire area.

Whatever we in Canada may think of these plans, it is extremely doubtful whether we can do much to change them. They have been agreed upon by the countries directly concerned and they are being reviewed by GATT. Moreover, while we may object to them on economic grounds, they are part of a broader concept of political unity which is of profound significance to the western world and which is also in Canada's underlying political interests. From Canada's point of view, the remaining area in which effective negotiation seems useful is the basis on which Britain and possibly other members of the Commonwealth associate themselves with the Common Market.

From her own standpoint, Britain cannot afford to be completely dissociated from the Common Market, either politically or economically. She would not only lose out in her exports to Europe which are still of major importance in her trade, but she would probably fall behind the expanding industries of the Continent in efficiency and thus lose out in overseas markets as well. She has, therefore, been planning with a number of other European countries to participate in a Free Trade Area with the countries of the Common Market. The principle here is the same as in the British proposal of a free trade area with Canada—the countries of the Free Trade Area agree to gradually establish free trade with the Common Market countries while retaining their tariffs and other protective arrangements against other countries. The picture is highly complex and its complexity has been accentuated by the problem of fitting in overseas dependencies and by the fact that Britain does not find it practicable to join in the Common Market's agricultural planning arrangements.

The way in which Britain works out her relationship to the Common Market is clearly of prime importance to the rest of the Commonwealth and Empire. Newly independent members like Ghana and Malaya do not wish to be placed at a disadvantage in the European market as against French, Belgian, and Dutch dependencies, or even as against British colonies which might automatically become part of the Free Trade Area. It is true that Britain's refusal to join the Common Market's agricultural arrangements leaves access to the British market by Commonwealth countries unaffected for such products. But some Commonwealth countries may want better access to the Common Market than is envisaged under the new arrangements, and this would involve negotiation and perhaps reciprocal bargaining with the Common Market countries. In any case, Britain is having considerable difficulty in working out the arrangements for the Free Trade Area with the countries of the Common Market, and some of these countries have expressed interest in obtaining better access to Commonwealth markets as part of a deal with Britain. All this suggests that Commonwealth discussion and examination of the problem posed by the Common Market is urgently required.

What might come out of such discussions is difficult to say—there are various possibilities. However, from a Canadian standpoint, some of the questions are clear enough. Do Canadians want to see their access to the markets of Continental Europe, and possibly of Britain, restricted further at a time when they are concerned at the extent of their dependence on the United States and concerned about the direction of American commercial policy? Obviously, they do not. But the real question is the cost. Probably a means of associating Canada and other overseas members of the Commonwealth with the Common Market could be found, perhaps in the form of an extra level in the preference system—the lowest rates for Imperial Preference, the middle rates for Europe, and the next level for most-favoured-nation countries, including the United States. This would be contrary to GATT. It would not be well received in the United States despite that country's support of the Common Market, and it might encounter a very unfavourable reception if, as seems likely, the new middle rate schedule for Europe were to be worked out largely by raising the general tariff rates. But if the trend is toward restriction of world trade, if the United States does not give leadership toward establishing an effective system of world economic order, then such possibilities cannot be dismissed. In any case, they should be examined thoroughly so that Canada's trading policy can be based on an intelligent assessment of the practicable possibilities rather than on emotional or defensive reactions.

IV

If these comments lead to any conclusion, it is that there are no easy solutions to Canada's trading problems. Canadians are concerned about being too dependent on the United States and about the extent of American control of Canadian resources and industry. Yet they also recognize that the growth of the United States market and American investment in Canada have been the leading factors in Canada's post-war development. Canadians are concerned about and irritated at the recent protective tendencies in American commercial policy. Yet they are also aware that there are no real alternatives to the United States as an outlet for the greater part of their export surplus and as a source of supply for the majority of their import needs.

But while they must face the realities of their dependence on the United States, Canadians cannot afford to see their country become a mere economic division of the United States. That would undermine Canada's national identity and leave a substantial part of her economic system in a state of chronic depression. After all, the Canadian transportation system is an east-west system and this is also true of the latest additions to it—the oil and gas pipelines and the St. Lawrence Seaway. The truth is that Canada still needs a large overseas trade for the efficient operation of her economy. She also needs a large overseas trade in order to provide her with some bargaining power in her economic relations with the United States.

Thus, it is sensible for Canada to look for ways and means of improving her economic relations with the Commonwealth and with other overseas countries, as she has been and will probably continue doing. Unfortunately, as was noted earlier, many of the steps that might be taken in this direction are in conflict with the principles of GATT and would in fact involve serious discrimination against the United States in particular. This applies, for example, to the possibility of increasing the Imperial Preferences or to the idea of adding a new tier to the Imperial Preference system designed to give a middle preference to western Europe. Indeed, it is probably true that no really substantial and early expansion of Canada's trade with the Commonwealth and Europe could be achieved without discriminating in a major way against goods from the United States.

There may, of course, be circumstances in which such discrimination would be justifiable or even necessary; the increase in the Imperial Preferences put into effect under the Ottawa Agreements of the early thirties is probably a case in point. It may also be that the best arrangements that can be worked out in the existing circumstances will involve some discrimination. It may not, for example, be possible for Canada to protect her trading interests in the Common Market countries without getting into some discriminatory arrangements. But it is well for Canadians to remember that the principle of non-discrimination is a sound one and one which is very much in the interests of a country heavily dependent on international trade.[6]

When all is said and done, Canada is still an international trader with a profound interest in an expanding multilateral system of world trade and exchange. At the end of the last war, she was very conscious of this basic interest as her actions in the realm of trade, aid, and international co-operation and planning made clear. As time went on, as the United States market expanded, as world requirements for industrial materials grew in every direction, and as defence demands also increased, it began to look as though the world almost had to buy from Canada regardless of what kind of trading arrangements might be operative. But whatever substance there may have been in this view, and the demand for Canadian basic commodities was for years

[6]See article by H. F. Angus, "Canada's Interest in Multilateral Trade" in Gibson (ed.), *Canada's Economy in a Changing World.*

broad and insistent, it no longer describes the facts as they now exist. With rapid expansion of the resource industries of other continents, with technological advances opening up new vistas of production and threatening old methods and old materials, and with the present temporary slackening in world demand, Canada's interest in an orderly multilateral system of international trade is again quite apparent, if there ever was any serious doubt about it.

For some commodities, of which grain is the most important, Canada's interest in the freest possible access to world markets is entirely obvious. The same thing is true of such commodities as nickel, copper, aluminum, lumber, and asbestos. It is also true, though in lesser degree, of products like newsprint, pulp, and iron ore where the great majority of Canada's exports go to the United States. And even in the few cases where American demand is sufficient to absorb the entire exportable surplus, it is still desirable to have access to and connections with markets in other countries.

Thus, despite its descent into the role of whipping-boy, GATT and the principles of multilateral trade associated with it remain a prime Canadian interest. If progress toward a freer system of world trade has been checked for the present, it is of vital importance to Canada, as well as many other countries, that the free world should not become involved in beggar-my-neighbour restrictive policies and in bilateral deals at the expense of natural trade. The sorry record of the thirties stands as a clear warning of what could happen in world trade, and the appearance of Russia as a vigorous political trader has the same ominous characteristics as that of Germany in the middle thirties.

While American trading policy leaves much to be desired, it is at least a real improvement over that followed in the early thirties, and American economic policy in general has become much more outward-looking. Moreover, it should never be forgotten that the United States is literally carrying the burden of responsibility for leadership of the free world on her shoulders. For a country which was isolationist and inward-looking as recently as two decades ago, the change constitutes a revolution. It is scarcely surprising that there are some inconsistencies and lags in American policy, of which that concerning trade is a major one.

In the circumstances, therefore, it would seem the part of wisdom for Canada to use whatever influence she may have in support of a multilateral system of world trade. To break with GATT, to get involved in major discriminatory policies, could well turn out to be costly to Canada, as well as against her underlying interests. Canada's ability to influence American trading policy is clearly limited. But she should keep trying, keep putting her case before the American Administration, before Congress, and before the American people, as best she can. Perhaps Canada has a little more influence with Britain, though that too can be overstated. It is to be hoped that Canada and the other Commonwealth nations in their negotiations will provide a salutary lead against restrictive policies and that this lead will have a significant effect on American policies.

Changing Trends in World Trade

JOHN J. DEUTSCH

In the past twelve years there has been a revolution in the conditions of world trade. The changes which have occurred have been more rapid and more far-reaching than most of us would have thought possible. Consequently the problems of today are almost unrecognizably different from those of a decade ago. At the end of the war the international trading community was a highly fragmented, disjointed, and unbalanced structure. It was the heritage not only of wartime destruction but also of the anarchy of the 1930's. In this situation two urgent tasks had to be undertaken. First there was the need to restore production in the war-wrecked economies; and second there was the need to formulate an agreed framework of policy to govern the longer-run development of international economic relations.

One of the most striking features of the immediate post-war years was the profound imbalance which existed between North America and the rest of the world. The United States and Canada emerged from the war with greatly strengthened economies and with greatly increased industrial capacities. On the other hand the important industrial systems of Continental Europe and of Japan had come to a virtual standstill. Great Britain was gravely weakened by shortages and debts. In the underdeveloped areas of the world many countries were set on the road to political independence under conditions of uncertainty and grinding poverty.

These enormous disparities between North America and the rest of the world dominated international trading arrangements throughout most of the post-war period. The imbalance manifested itself in the universal dollar shortage, in the widespread discrimination against dollar trade, in inconvertibility of currencies, in the widely differing rates of growth and prosperity, and in the varying impact of the pressures of inflation. During the early post-war years the United States and

Canada supplied close to 30 per cent of total world exports, compared to about half this proportion before the war. The United States held more than 50 per cent of the world's monetary reserves and continued to achieve large surpluses in its balance of payments. The availability in the United States of private capital for international investment had fallen about to zero. Consequently most of the overseas world had to finance its international transactions on a hand-to-mouth basis. This condition resulted in the development of an intricate pattern of bilateral arrangements which threatened to reduce international trade to a system of barter.

The rates of economic growth in the United States and Canada during the period 1947–53 were significantly larger than the historic averages for these two countries. North America presented itself as an island of outstanding strength and dynamism. In most of the rest of the free world the rates of growth were disappointingly slow and it appeared that these areas were condemned to falling even further behind.

This picture of the international scene during the period prior to the Korean War produced certain attitudes and theories regarding world trade which had an important effect on subsequent events. It was argued that the dollar shortage was a chronic and persistent phenomenon that, very probably, could never be overcome. On this basis it was contended that discrimination against dollar trade was a permanent necessity, that convertibility of currencies into the dollar would not be possible for the foreseeable future, and that the stubborn surplus in the United States balance of payments could be financed only by some system of gifts and grants. These conclusions were founded on the assertion that the rate of increase in productivity and of economic growth in North America would inevitably outstrip the rates of growth in the rest of the world. It was explained that these other countries, faced by the North American leviathan, had no choice but to try to shelter themselves behind a screen of protective devices. Such were the new theories of international trade which the post-war difficulties had inspired in certain quarters.

The developments in world trade since the end of the Korean War have brought about an extraordinarily rapid obsolescence in these theories and attitudes. Virtually none of the predictions have come true. The facts of world trade as they exist at present are entirely different from what had been so confidently foretold. The outstanding fact of today is that the great imbalance has disappeared. The dollar shortage is gone. Indeed, the concern over the mighty dollar has been replaced by a fear that it might become too weak. The supposed chronic surplus in the United States balance of payments has given way to a large deficit. Actually the United States has had an over-all deficit almost steadily since 1950.

This amazing reversal is the outcome of many factors. The cold war and the policy of foreign aid have resulted in an enormous increase in United States government expenditures abroad. These expenditures in other countries together with United States government loans are now running at about $9 billion a year, an amount equivalent to nearly two-thirds of total United States imports. Meanwhile, United States commodity imports also have risen substantially, by about 50 per cent since 1950. These increases in United States outlays abroad have entirely transformed the international payments situation. The magnitude of the change can be portrayed by recounting that the world's receipts of United States dollars for all purposes was only $3 billion in 1938, was $18 billion in 1948, and is about $30 billion a year at the present time. This huge sum flowing out into the channels of world commerce has enabled the great trading nations of Europe and elsewhere to rebuild their monetary reserves and has removed any necessity for continued discrimination by these large trading nations against dollar exports from North America. The gold and foreign exchange holdings of western Europe have tripled since 1950. The world distribution of monetary reserves among the large industrial countries is now better balanced than at any time since the 1920's.

Aside from the effects of United States policy there have been significant developments elsewhere. These developments are even more fundamental and are less transitory in their longer-run implications. The astonishing recovery of western Europe, Great Britain, and Japan has restored the basic competitive balance between the great industrial nations of the free world. North America is no longer the one great industrial giant which needs to fear no one. Indeed the United States and Canada are now being confronted with the keen competitive pressure of large industrial complexes overseas which recently have demonstrated even greater vitality. The importance of North America has receded and the circumstances of world trade are being determined to a much greater extent elsewhere. The average annual rates of growth in economic output in western Europe between 1953 and 1959 were twice as great as in the United States and Canada. In particular, the rates of growth in West Germany and Japan in this period were three times that in North America. This striking disparity in rates of expansion was made possible, in part, by the ability of these countries to capture a larger share of the world market. The United States share of total free world exports fell from 21 per cent in 1953 to 18 per cent in 1958, while the combined share of the three other leading industrial nations, namely Great Britain, West Germany, and Japan, rose from about 17 per cent to 22 per cent. These three countries together now constitute a larger and more dynamic source of world trade than does the United States.

In recent years another massive and dynamic factor has intruded on the international trading scene, namely the Soviet Union. In this country also, the rate of economic expansion has been substantially faster than in North America. The Soviet Union is now the sixth largest trading nation in the world and its share of world trade has been rising more rapidly than that of the United States. The Soviet industrial system is the second largest in the world. The significance to international trade lies in the fact that the Soviet economy is very large, is highly self-sufficient, and is highly controlled. Its ability to intervene in world markets is extremely powerful, and this ability is an important factor in determining the kind of world trading community in which we now live. In the sphere of economic relations there is no iron curtain in front of which the rest of the world can, unhindered, order its own affairs by the traditional methods of free societies. The long arm of the Soviet Union reaches out to the Middle East, to South East Asia, to Africa, and to the Carribbean whenever it is expedient to do so, and it can change the course of events, both economic and political.

In the field of monetary affairs and finance the world situation has changed very significantly. At the end of the war capital for international lending and investment was almost non-existent, and could be obtained only from the government of the United States, and to a certain extent from the government of Canada. Now, capital for international loans is again available to some extent from nearly all of the large industrial countries, either directly or through international institutions. During the last three years there has been a remarkable growth of private foreign lending from the United States—now running in the amount of about $3 billion a year. While this private capital is concentrated in particular fields and areas, nevertheless it has reached a volume in real terms which is today greater than the outflow of private capital from the United States in the heyday of the 1920's. The amounts of capital available for international lending are still inadequate over a large part of the world, but there has been very great improvement.

Perhaps, basically, of even more importance is the fact that the overblown monetary systems of the principal industrial nations have now been restored to more normal proportions. The very large increases in the supplies of money brought on by the war and post-war reconstruction caused strong inflationary pressures, which periodically produced severe shocks to world trade in the form of payments crises. The sterling crises of 1947, 1949, and 1951 and the successive devaluations of the French franc were menacing weaknesses. The economies of the industrial nations have now grown up to, or have absorbed, the excessive liquidity of their monetary systems. In the last two to three years more effective steps were taken to prevent further excesses from reappearing. In these circumstances the danger of payments crises is greatly reduced. In the United States and Canada we are no longer shielded by the greater inflationary pressures elsewhere. We now have to consider the possibility of having payments crises ourselves. We can no longer indulge in inflationary fiscal and monetary experiments on the assumption that we will be saved by the excesses of other countries. If we do this we would be likely to price ourselves out of the world market. It is this changed situation in the world scene which is at the back of our present anxiety about our ability to hold our markets.

The developments I have described make it clear that there has been a remarkable recovery of world trade. The volume of world trade has doubled since before the war, and in recent years has grown faster than world production. The major currencies are, for all practical purposes, convertible into each other and discriminations have been very largely removed. International trade is now freer of restrictions and arbitrary controls than at any time in the last thirty years. In spite of all the difficulties, an expanding system of world trade has been re-established. In the field of industrial products, particularly capital goods, there are widening opportunities for those nations able to compete. In these categories, especially, performance and efficiency are once more the test of success.

However, there remain a number of important weaknesses. These relate mainly to agriculture and to the position of the underdeveloped countries. World trade in agricultural products has been in a straight-jacket for many years and has not benefited from the revival of world trade and production. Today agricultural protectionism is more widespread and more restrictive than it has ever been. Government intervention in the regulation and control of the agricultural industry is universal and the result has been a universal strangulation of trade. In this game there are no rules and no agreed principles of international conduct which individual governments will respect. This anarchy is maintained for the supposed purpose of enhancing the economic welfare of farmers, but the economic condition of agriculture has fallen progressively lower. It is an economist's nightmare from which there appears to be no escape.

The underdeveloped countries have not shared in the expansion of world trade to the same extent as the industrialized nations. There is a pronounced lag which is due in part to the disappointingly slow rate of economic progress in the underdeveloped countries, in part to their dependence on agriculture and on raw materials. Their continued failure to cope with inflation has been a factor which is also of considerable importance. I have already spoken of the handicaps which arise from a dependence on agriculture in the present-day world. Raw materials have not kept pace with the growth of manufactured goods in world trade. The raw material content of total economic output is declining. The trend is in the direction of higher degrees of fabrication and of services. In recent years capacities for the production of fuels and raw materials have tended to run ahead of demand. Furthermore countries which are heavily dependent on raw materials are affected by wider fluctuations in prices and consequently their economies are subject to greater instability.

The contrast between the favourable position of the highly industrialized nations and the less favourable position of the underdeveloped countries is a serious weakness in the present world situation. This weakness provides a most inviting opportunity to the Soviet Union with its growing economic power.

Against this background I now wish to discuss the developments in international trade policy during the post-war period. In the 1930's the situation had degenerated into a state of complete chaos. There were no broad international agreements respecting objectives, procedures, or rules of conduct. Individual countries tried to get along as best they could by using every available device of trade restriction and trade promotion, including deliberate exchange depreciation and the bilateral clearing of payments. Consequently the further cataclysm of the war provided a most opportune occasion to make an entirely new start.

The effort to make a new start began to take concrete form in the

Master Lend-Lease Agreements which the United States signed with its allies. Countries signing these agreements undertook to establish in the post-war period a system of multilateral trade without arbitrary restrictions and discriminations. The broad aims were translated into specific undertakings and specific arrangements in a series of international conferences, in particular the Bretton Woods Conference in 1944, and the GATT conference in 1946 and 1947. Out of these conferences there emerged three international agreements and three international institutions, namely the International Monetary Fund, the International Bank for Reconstruction and Development, and the General Agreement on Tariffs and Trade. Under the IMF and GATT agreements countries agreed to follow orderly exchange policies, to re-establish convertibility of currencies, to eliminate arbitrary restrictions and controls on exchange and trade, and to remove discriminations. In the conditions of the early post-war period these objectives could not be immediately realized, and hence exceptions were allowed until circumstances permitted the full implementation of the undertakings. The basic underlying principles consisted of the most-favoured-nation rule and the adherence to the free market or price system in the conduct of international trade. The most-favoured-nation rule required all countries to grant to each other equal treatment. Whenever one country gave a trade or tariff concession to another, it would have to be granted automatically to all the others.

Hence, it will be seen that the underlying principle of the IMF and the GATT was essentially a "one-world" concept—at least as far as the free world was concerned. In accordance with this concept all countries, large and small, weak or strong, were to have equal opportunity to participate in and to benefit from international trade according to their efforts, their efficiencies, and their resources. An aspect of this "one-world" or multilateral concept was the belief that it would facilitate the most rapid expansion of world production and incomes and would enable all countries to share in the benefits.

Whatever one thinks of the validity of these beliefs it can be said that the multilateral approach has made possible substantial progress in the reconstruction of world trade. Today, thirty-seven countries are members of the GATT and they comprise four-fifths of the total trade of the free world. Under the auspices of the GATT, three major tariff negotiations have been conducted which resulted in the reduction or binding against increase of some 57,000 tariff items. This is a gigantic accomplishment in the light of past history which we are now inclined to take for granted. We might well ask ourselves what would have happened in this disordered world if this degree of tariff stability had not existed. It is true that for much of the post-war period many of the tariff reductions were nullified by exchange and other restrictions. Also, there have been some lapses into unilateral protectionism. However, the main structure has stood and at the present time the exchange restrictions and discriminations in the principal industrial countries have nearly all disappeared. The tariff agreements are making possible a rapid expansion in the world trade of industrial products. Except for agriculture, the channels of world trade are now less restricted than at any time since the First World War. The deteriorating events of the 1920's and the 1930's stand in sharp contrast to this achievement.

However, there has not been a clear line of international policy in the post-war period. In spite of the formal emphasis on multilateralism there has been a dichotomy and some considerable inconsistency in policy. The consequences are now very apparent. While the most-favoured-nation rule was enshrined in international agreements, many particular problems and situations were approached on a regional, a bloc, or an otherwise limited basis. Thus in the Marshall Plan the United States deliberately encouraged a regional approach to the task of restoring trade inside Europe. Under the O.E.E.C. (Organization for European Economic Co-operation) trade and exchange restrictions were progressively removed within western Europe but were maintained against dollar countries. The Sterling Area was long maintained as a distinct trading bloc which discriminated against other parts of the world. The United Nations has encouraged the establishment of regional commissions in Asia, in South America, and in Africa to promote regional solutions to particular problems. The communist countries have from the beginning constituted a tight economic bloc. All these developments have in one way and another encouraged a regionalization of world trade, including the tendency toward a regionalization of trade in North America.

At present, the most prominent developments in this direction are taking place in Europe where six continental countries have established the European Common Market. Over the next ten to twelve years the six propose to adopt a common tariff against the rest of the world and to achieve free trade among themselves. This project has been officially encouraged by the United States. Here the trade bloc approach is being used as a means to closer political union for which the most-favoured-nation rule is inadequate. Recently seven other European countries, with Great Britain at the centre, have erected another trading bloc, namely the European Free Trade Association, which intends, over a period of years, to establish free trade within the group while maintaining separate national tariffs against the rest of the world. In many respects these two European blocs are the descendants of the O.E.E.C. and the Sterling Area. Indeed the seven are trying desperately to achieve an alignment with the six. The two groups together control about 40 per cent of the world trade, and the nature of the alignment, which will have to be worked out between them, is bound to have far-reaching effects upon the future of world trade.

Proposals for free trade areas are being considered in South America and in Africa. In North America there is already a high degree of regional interdependence between Canada and the United States.

These events have brought us to an important watershed. How should world trade be organized in the future? Should we try to maintain the multilateral principle as far as possible or should we go in the direction of increasing regionalism? Should we attempt to reconcile these two concepts and try to reap the advantages of both? Much will depend on the spirit of protectionism that will exist in the future. If the newly emerging blocs could be persuaded to adopt low tariff and liberal trading policies, then the universal advantages of the multilateral system could be very largely retained. If the regional groups seek to become more protectionist and self-sufficient, then the most-favoured-nation rule and the multilateral principles of international conduct would break down.

One of the more disturbing problems which arise from recent developments is the difficult choice which they pose for countries such as Canada, Japan, and many small nations around the world. Canada has built her post-war policy on the multilateral and most-favoured-nation principle. Should Canada now seek to align herself more closely with some regional groups, none of which could provide a satisfactory arrangement? Should it be toward Europe or toward the United States? Is it possible to build a wider Atlantic association into which Canada could fit? Or, failing this, should Canada seek to go it alone in the hope that reasonably liberal international policies can be made to prevail?

These are some of the questions which the changing objectives and changing trends in world trade pose for us today, and in the years to come.

The Royal Commission on Dominion-Provincial Relations

THE REPORT IN RETROSPECT

RONALD M. BURNS

Problems of jurisdiction and responsibility in government are almost as old as government itself, but they have been brought into sharper focus in modern times by the development of the federal state under the involved social and economic conditions of our age. Conditions were not ideally suited to complete objectivity when the members of the Rowell-Sirois Commission in the years from 1937 to 1940 undertook what was probably the most complete survey of an existing system of government ever attempted. But looking back over the twenty years that have elapsed since they first took up their task, years of depression, recovery, war and boom, it is to be wondered not that their plans achieved no early success but rather that so much that they foresaw as necessary has come to pass. It is in an attempt to provide some clearer understanding and appreciation of their aims and accomplishments that this paper is written.

Canada has probably gained much, even if she has suffered somewhat in the process, from the sporadic attacks of investigators regally blessed and otherwise, upon her body politic. From the first days of Confederation the terms of union have been tinkered with in the fervent if short-lived hope that each adventure was the final one. In earlier years conferences were concerned principally with specific grievances of specific provinces and the efforts were largely the prerogative of the politicians. Developments in the economic and social structure of Canada following the First World War coupled with the paralysis of the 1930's made some deeper approach to the broad problem inevitable and it may be that it was the lack of permanent results from the former method coupled with these greater urgencies that led in more recent years to the use of the agency of the royal commission.

The years have dulled our memories, but to anyone who lived and tried to work through the years of depression, the circumstances that made the more decisive action necessary are only too clear. Perhaps it should suffice here to say that changing social concepts with their attendant responsibilities had led and continued to lead to a greater lack of balance between income and outgo in the various jurisdictions and this, coupled with the social urgencies of the economic collapse, made something more than political palliatives necessary. Possibly the rapid growth in the fields of provincial and municipal responsibilities that was characteristic in the 1920's could have been cared for by the traditional adjustments. The collapse of economic life in parts of Canada with the resultant burden of unemployment and agricultural relief was the decisive factor in requiring some more permanent treatment.

Prior to the 1930's relief in Canada had been a local and often a family responsibility. No matter how inadequate it was, the system had general acceptance and therefore worked reasonably well. But with the full force of depression unemployment the system collapsed. A normal family or municipal responsibility became a provincial one and soon, by the very size of the problem, the federal government became inextricably involved. The areas of responsibility became so tangled that drastic surgery was called for before the nation strangled itself in its own red tape.

These various factors could not help but lead to some very earnest thoughts on our constitutional problems. Where federal-provincial relations had been a mere question of soothing local sores, they now became an essential feature in the struggle for survival.

It was in this atmosphere that Mr. King called the 1935 Dominion-Provincial Conference, the most elaborate to that time. While much was discussed, little was accomplished and soon, spurred by the recommendations of the Bank of Canada among others, the Government approached the problems that had been brought to fruition by the economic climate of the previous seven years.

The depression by this time was showing signs of abating, although with some reluctance, but the long-term questions of our intergovernmental relationships remained unsolved. Obviously the causes were too deep and the problems too involved to be satisfactorily dealt with by any governmental inquiry or political conference. Neither of these methods under existing conditions could be expected to produce the independent analysis of the problems that seemed so necessary. A royal commission, then as always, was the obvious and in this case the logical answer.

Whether in its original concept the Commission was intended to cover the all-embracing field of enquiry it eventually was authorized to is open for speculation, but certainly by the time its terms of reference were drawn up its actions were limited only by its own discretion and the essential basic requirements of a framework of federalism. Following upon other royal commissions and commissions of inquiry, federal and provincial, it went further than any in the scope of its studies and in the all-embracing nature of its report. The Commissioners by their terms of reference were empowered to make "a re-examination of the economic and financial basis of Confederation and of the legislative powers in the light of the economic and social developments of the last seventy years" and "to express what in their opinion, subject to the retention of the proper distribution of legislative powers essential to a proper carrying out of the federal system in harmony with national needs and the promotion of national unity, will best effect a balanced relationship between the financial powers and the obligations and functions of each governing body, and conduce to a more efficient, independent and economical discharge of governmental responsibilities in Canada."[1]

When late in 1937 the Commissioners commenced their public hearings, it was in the atmosphere of a country just beginning to come out of the economic slough of despond and one in which the great agricultural areas of the Prairies were still bowed down under the double burden of depression and drought. In most instances the ability of the provinces to deal with their problems had been seriously affected and many local governments had been forced to abdicate their traditional duties and responsibilities and in some cases accept bankruptcy. Only the Dominion government had displayed the financial capacity to deal with the pressing problems of the times, unsatisfactory as its efforts may have been in some respects.

Important in any evaluation of the work of the Commission and essential to an understanding of its recommendations are these basic economic facts. Under the circumstances it is not to be wondered that the necessity of heavy reliance upon the central government in times of economic crisis stamped itself indelibly upon the minds of these

[1]Royal Commission on Dominion-Provincial Relations, *Report* (1940), Terms of Reference, I, p. 9.

men. It is hard to see how they could have reacted other than the way they did and much of their apparent predilection for greater centralism must be attributed to the facts with which they were faced. That this predilection was not confined to the Commission and its staff is well remembered, for the feeling was widespread in Canada at that time (even among many of the provincial ministers and their advisers) that greater control at the centre was essential to meet the complexities in the modern world.

Some further understanding of the nature of the *Report* of the Commission is given by a consideration of its members. That it was essentially a report of professional economists and political scientists, and not of professional politicians or jurists, is obvious at first reading. Probably more weight was given in the assessment of qualifications to the ability to make economic judgments than to the ability to sift legal evidence and draw conclusions therefrom, as had been customary in such appointments. While Mr. Justice Rowell, Mr. Sirois, and Mr. Angus all had legal training, it does not seem that they were chosen on this account. Certainly Mr. Rowell for his political knowledge and Mr. Angus for his economic experience were to be valued. Mr. Sirois as a representative of standing in his native province was an essential part of the Commission's composition. These were all men of accepted worth and unquestioned (except by Mr. Hepburn) integrity and it seems clear that although they were certainly all liberals in the philosophical sense they gave themselves to their task with open and questioning minds.

Much has been made in some quarters of the enforced retirement of Mr. Justice Rowell from active participation in May, 1938, before the Commission had started writing its report or for that matter completed its public hearings. That the Commission was weakened by his absence it would be idle to deny, but there is no body of evidence to indicate that there would have been any basic change in the tenor of the *Report* had he participated in its final judgments. The Commissioners in the main had a considerable affinity of outlook and with this to assist them, unanimity was no doubt of high priority. Under the circumstances it could be expected at the most that with Mr. Rowell's guidance the *Report* would in some respects have been a more realistic document insofar as some of its principal recommendations were concerned, and might well therefore have had a better reception at the hands of the dissentients. The lack of a clear appreciation of the political implications was, I believe, probably the only noticeable result of his unfortunate retirement.

The Commission made many recommendations; in fact it is in several of its less prominent observations that the more far-reaching suggestions are contained. It must, however, for purposes of judgment stand or fall on its main financial proposals known as Plan I. Two different approaches were in fact made. Plan I called for radical fiscal changes—for major surgery. Plan II was a palliative that now seems somewhat out of place in the *Report*. For our brief purposes here there seems little profit in dwelling other than upon the major proposals as contained in Plan I. The essence of these can be given as follows:

(1) Provincial debts were to be assumed by the Dominion with adjustment for assets represented by the debt. Special provision would be made in Quebec to cover the provincial-municipal debt situation. Provinces and municipalities were to retain their borrowing authority, but if any borrowings were undertaken without approval of the Finance Commission, which was to be appointed to review financial terms, the debt costs could not be considered for purposes of future adjustment grants.

(2) The Dominion was to assume the full burden of the relief of unemployed employables.

(3) The provinces and municipalities were to retire from the fields of personal and corporation income taxes and succession duties.

(4) While the Dominion would retain the right to unlimited taxing powers, it would recognize an obligation to respect the revenue sources remaining to the provinces and in addition would pay over to each province an amount equal to a tax of 10 per cent on the net income derived from mining, smelting, and refining of ores and oil produced in the province.

(5) The Dominion would pay to a province, as financial circumstances required, an annual adjustment grant determined by an independent but federally appointed Finance Commission. This grant would be of a size to enable a province to provide adequate social, educational, and developmental services without resort to taxation heavier than the Canadian average. Emergency grants would also be payable where abnormal economic conditions dictated the immediate need.

(6) Control of its expenditure would be a prerogative of each individual province.

Looking at the concrete results of these recommendations following the consideration of the *Report*, one might be excused for thinking that they suffered from severe malnutrition, but this is not a judgment that can be supported by facts. Certainly there was a noticeable lack of immediate success in that the recommendations were not nourished forthwith, but this was at least in part a result of the rapidly changing times. How many commissioners can look to early and full acceptance of their ideas, particularly if they are made without acceptability as a prime motivation? But the Commission had done something bigger than putting forward specific proposals, it had laid down the pattern for fiscal co-operation between the federal and provincial governments which was so necessary in the years of emergency and reconstruction. The Wartime Tax Agreements, the Green Book proposals of 1945–6, the rental agreements of 1947 and 1952, and the current fiscal arrangements all owe something of their respectability to the background laid for them in this *Report*. Had the way not been thus prepared provincial co-operation, readily given in 1941 and less readily later, might have been exacted only at some considerably greater effort.

In studying the recommendations of the *Report*, one of the first questions that comes to mind is whether some of them, in particular the adjustment grants, the emergency grants, and the debt controls, are entirely consistent with the full maintenance of the federal system which was a prime condition of the terms of reference. These were to be determinable by a Finance Commission which, subject to federal appointment, could not be more than quasi-independent. The proposals could, in fact, be said to have the effect of placing an important part of provincial financial policy outside of provincial control. That the Commission did not apparently look for the heavy weather in this connection that they eventually ran into is something that is a little hard to understand.

As mentioned, the actual implementation of the specific proposals was somewhat slower and often under different guises and auspices than would have been originally hoped for. A great deal was, however, achieved and it was really only in the field of debt consolidation and control that success was completely lacking. This is not surprising, for it was probably the least well-thought-out of the proposals, even if apparently supported by the extremities of the times. It left itself vulnerable on too many points, particularly as the control of debt policy is a very important prerogative of any political power that lays claim to a measure of independence. Even the provinces have shown considerable political delicacy on occasion in dealing with their creature municipalities in this field. Possibly the influence of Australian experiments was strongly affecting the Commissioners at this stage and these ideas were adopted without sufficient consideration of the differences in the political climate. Influenced by the existing circumstances, the Commission seems in large measure to have disregarded the fact that much development in the country must perforce take place at the provincial level even if only by reason of the provinces' responsibility for natural resources under the British North America Act, and centralized control could well have resulted in the restriction of much that has been done. It is not easy to accept the premise that the Finance Commission could have risked its reputation in approving many of the projects on which provincial politicians have gambled (often so successfully) in the recent years of expansion. Alternatively, if such approval had not been forthcoming, it is likely that its recommendations would have been disregarded and the whole carefully planned fiscal system would have been ignored and eventually would have collapsed from neglect.

The recommendation for assumption by the Dominion of unemployment responsibility was inevitable in view of the conditions which the Commission investigated. The logic of the arguments that this responsibility was a national one was accepted even by the stoutest defenders of provincial rights, who have never been slow to recognize when a provincial right becomes a provincial liability. The recommendation very soon became largely effective by the Unemployment Insurance Act in 1940, but it has only been fairly recently that the federal co-responsibility for uninsured unemployed has been conceded. It is likely, however, that this time-lag was more a by-product of the full employment of the period from 1941 to 1954 which made the whole problem a fairly academic one. It was only the anticipation of recession in the winter of 1954 which stimulated action that has resulted in a status of equal federal-provincial responsibility for relief of both employables and unemployables.

If one had to select one particular facet of the *Report* on which to base a judgment of the Commission's place in Canadian history, it would logically be the section on taxation policy. It contained the most important and far-reaching of all the proposals made. Welcomed by some, spurned by others, it was not long before the essence of it was incorporated into the Wartime Tax Agreements of 1942. This centralized control of the income tax system of the country has continued with some exceptions and with some variations in degree ever since, especially in the personal income tax field.

While the war was the immediate force that put into practical operation the Commission's ideas on taxation, most people will agree that the Commissioners are entitled to considerable credit for preparing the ground for the subsequent action under the rental agreements which eliminated much of the chaos and confusion that had grown up in our tax system in the pre-war years. As a result of these developments, the Canadian tax system is a reasonably neat package (although the seams are a bit sprung here and there) and if the principles involved are not so widely accepted as once they were, in the context of the times they played an indispensable part in the fiscal management of the Canadian economy. If the Commission had contributed nothing else, their efforts in this respect would have justified their existence.

The idea that the Dominion should respect the rights of the provinces in the tax fields remaining to them means different things to different men depending partly on where they live and which newspapers they read. Whether the Commissioners' views on this point had any influence on the Dominion action in the post-war years in withdrawing from the use of various consumption taxes such as gasoline, retail sales, and amusements and the stock transfer tax is hard to say. At any rate these fields are now cultivated free of federal interference with a degree of assiduity by most provinces which might even be said to encroach on the federal domain of indirect taxation in some degree.

The Commissioners' recommendation on natural resource taxation, which would have provided for a special interest of the provinces in profits from mineral and oil production, seems to have been based on a rather sketchy consideration of the problems involved. It was an attempt to recognize by special treatment the development costs and depletion factors of these two resources, by allocating part of the profits to the provinces, not just from the basic production but from the processing and refining also. At the same time, in those resources such as forestry and fishing where governmental interest in development and rehabilitation costs is much more noticeable than in mineral and oil production, no such concession was recommended. Insufficient regard seems to have been given to the existing facilities for recovering such costs through royalties, rentals, and so on, which could have been utilized without the introduction of the more complex and somewhat artificial method proposed.

This recommendation was not followed in subsequent federal-provincial agreements, but there is no doubt that it had an influence upon future policy. The present special provisions for logging and mining taxes, which recognize a provincial priority that in many cases has already been alienated, are the complicated and controversial result of a general idea tossed off by the Commission, apparently without the extensive research and consideration that was given so adequately to most of the other problems faced.

I have speculated previously on the possible influence of the Australian experiment. This is worthy of a little more attention. It is true there is no great documentary evidence in the *Report* of any such influence, but the Commissioners did have the benefit of special evidence from a former member of the Commonwealth Grants Commission of Australia, Professor Giblin, and in view of the fiscal recommendations it is hard to escape the feeling that the influence was fairly important. If so, it is perhaps unfortunate that an experiment which was in little more than its infancy should have been applied if only in principle to a country with so many different problems. The results in Australia certainly have confirmed, in my mind at least, the belief that fiscal need subsidies and centralized control of debt adjusted by a quasi-independent body can have no practical application in our present political and economic climate. The differences of race, religion, and social and political philosophies are too broad for any general acceptance at this time of this centralized control of fiscal policy.

Now it can be argued that awareness of the practical unacceptability of a principle should not be a reason to turn away from it. But royal commissions are not as a rule set up to write treatises on political science or any other subject, but to mark out the path of practical approach to the solution of the problem which they were set up to study. A recommendation doomed to failure from the start can well be worse than no recommendation at all, for, in the field of government at least, unacceptability only generates ill-will and argument—of which we have had more than enough in our short national life. It is really somewhat surprising that a man of Mr. Dafoe's experience and the two "Respectable Professors of the Dismal Science" should have fallen into this trap. However, we should honour them for their apparent detachment.

It has been with the main fiscal proposals of the *Report* that assessments of the Commission's work have generally and properly been concerned. But the doubting ones who have used the lack of immediate positive results to illustrate their views on the impotency of royal commissions generally, and this one in particular, seem to have stopped at this preliminary judgment and never explored below the surface. Perhaps on a box-score basis the Commissioners do not fare well, but investigations of this nature and scope cannot be dismissed so superficially. In a study of the broad vistas of the economic and political life of a complex federation, as developed over a period of seventy years in the aftermath of world depression, knowledge and direction rather than specific guidance are probably the most we should expect or even hope for. We should take into account not just what was immediately achieved but rather the atmosphere for change and development created through both the recommendations themselves and the vast background of information assembled in the course of the enquiry.

It is a truism to say that Canada became a federation only because of its problems. The questions that existed in 1867 have continued to plague us in different magnitudes and ways. Inequality of wealth and resources has always existed and no doubt always will. Probably recognized from the beginning, it never received formal recognition until the *Report* brought official standing to what has become one of the basic principles of inter-governmental relations—fiscal need. Undoubtedly the idea was an influence in the several adjustments in terms of union made from time to time, but it was never formally recognized even though Nova Scotia in 1934 specifically advanced fiscal need as a basis for adjustment in its submissions to the White Commission. It was only six years later that this idea became basic in the recommendations of the Rowell-Sirois Commission. Subsequently it took actual form as it was incorporated into the Tax-Rental Agreements of 1947 and 1952 and the Federal-Provincial Tax-Sharing Arrangements Act of 1956. Further acceptance of special need is contained in the policy of providing special grants to the Atlantic Provinces, where economic conditions have been constantly below the national level over a prolonged period.

As has been said, the need for positive action in overcoming abnormal regional differences in standards of public services and economic wealth has long been recognized by those intimately concerned in such matters. But the acceptance of this need was not general, and it was in the bringing of this need into the open that the Commissioners made an important contribution. The open recognition of these inequalities and the need for readjustment have become a prime feature of Dominion-provincial negotiation of recent years.

There still remains even today some remnant of what we might call the "to him that hath" attitude. To the extent that this has become increasingly rare it has contributed to the better fiscal relationships that have developed in the domestic inter-governmental field in Canada over these past few years.

One of the inevitable features of a report of this scope and length is that some of its most important contributions do not lend themselves to summary and the easily scanned headline. Unfortunately, there does not seem to be any ready remedy for this—certainly experience seems to indicate that the solution is not in the official summary unsupported by its basic arguments. In their exposition of the functioning of the federal state, the Commissioners put forward certain fundamental ideas and principles which if read and assimilated might well have gone far to discredit some of the more irresponsible and parochial views that unfortunately for our national interests are still held widely and used to practical political effect.

In these and many other ways the Commissioners made their voices heard—perhaps distantly and through the haze of the years, but in the growing-up of a nation and the development of its constitution ten years, or twenty, is no time at all. To the extent that they did fail it was perhaps that in facing the results of years of temporizing they did not understand that in many ways federalism and temporizing are inevitably linked and this must be allowed for.

In a very real sense the *Report* was a casualty of war but it may be wondered why, despite this, more was not achieved in concrete form. To this many answers might be given depending on the personal bias of the answerer, for the field of political science is more given over to subjective judgments than most. Some obvious points come to notice, however, some related to subjects within the scope of the enquiry and others to the nature of our changing times.

It is somewhat surprising, in view of the broad concept of the whole investigation, that in their analysis of the economic and social problems facing Canada in many ways the Commissioners seem to have taken a surprisingly short-term view. Perhaps this is understandable under the conditions in which they worked, for ten years of depression, four of which were those of impending war, cannot be said to be the atmosphere for secular thinking on the buoyant approach. It is probable that even the Gordon Commission might have found its enthusiasms seriously restrained by like circumstances.

This preoccupation of the Commissioners with the short-term outlook, while understandable, proved a serious fault. It was the job of the Commission to be concerned with re-plotting the course of Confederation and their failure to rise above their environment was probably the most serious shortcoming with which they can be reproached. Not to have seen that the 1930's could not be typical if our system was to survive, and not, in this realization, to have made some attempt to apply their findings to future conditions of a much different kind, is a failing that seems now to be incomprehensible in men of so many talents. Political and economic sciences being the lively arts that they are the Commissioners might well have been excused some wide margins for error in their ideas of future trends and events. But it was in the general recasting of our political life in the economic terms of the 1930's under the presumption that this was good for the long term that the main weakness lay.

The political innocence of the Commissioners, too, is difficult to understand. As was previously noted, it was in the matter of political implications that Rowell's guidance was probably missed the most. Gifted as we are with hindsight, that most widely held of political senses, it seems obvious to us now that it should have been accepted as a stark reality that recommendations which would have had such centralizing effects could never have been acceptable to many of the provincial governments under any conditions and would be much less so in view of some of the provincial personalities upon whom so much depended.

While we can admire them all for the objectivity, an acknowledgment by the Commissioners that "the better part of valour is discretion" might have been in order. How great the influence towards centralization of some of the prominent staff members was could form an interesting part of a study on the problems of indirect influences on national history.

The Commissioners in some ways rather neglected the opportunities they were given, by interpreting the broad terms of reference somewhat more narrowly than appears to have been necessary. For while it is undoubtedly correct constitutionally and practically for the federal government to take the unvarying position that municipal problems are only part of the provincial, a royal commission of this scope might have been justified in dealing with this intrinsic part of the problem in a more positive manner than it did.

To some degree at least, they seem to have appreciated the dilemma encountered when a body, no matter how respected, appointed by one power attempts to deal with mutual problems involving other jurisdictions that to a considerable extent are sovereign within their own orbit. This recognition may account in some degree for the attention the Commission paid to the need for more consistent and continued federal-provincial co-operation such as is now just beginning to be achieved in some measure at least. In the light of all this it might be well in future to give serious consideration to the idea of having royal commissions in the field of inter-governmental relations examine and report without recommending specific approaches, leaving the working out of the ultimate detailed financial and constitutional solutions to the instruments of inter-governmental co-operation at the policy and administrative level that the Commissioners apparently considered so necessary. While the expert must prepare the way, in the final test the success will be with the politicians. In the continuing give and take of inter-governmental negotiations, national as well as international, they must of necessity have the active roles. They cannot wait in the wings merely to take the bows.

As has been pointed out on more than one occasion, the *Report* and its supplementary studies laid the groundwork and prepared the way for many of the far-reaching developments in federal-provincial relations that have taken place since 1941. The Wartime Tax Agreements, the 1945 Reconstruction Proposals, the Tax-Rental Agreements, the current equalization provisions, and now the special Atlantic Provinces grants all owe in a substantial degree a debt to the *Report* for their basic principles. True, there were variations in degree and method but the primary philosophy of trying to preserve the whole by maintaining and strengthening the parts has prevailed.

In view of all this, to try to judge how the Commission would have in its turn assessed the tax-rental proposals and the arrangements that took effect in 1957 is of more than casual interest. Conceived in different economic circumstances, nevertheless they follow many of the same principles. It is in the application that the differences are found. The fiscal need payments to the less wealthy provinces to enable them to provide a reasonable standard of services have been provided in some measure at least in the new equalization proposals. Perhaps the methods employed have not been as direct or as theoretically precise as the National Adjustment Grants, but at least they have the real merit of political practicability and have provided one more step along the way.

It is in fact only in the recommendations leading to centralization of fiscal control that some concern would now still be felt. Many of these fiscal theories received wide acceptance and were in fact an essential part of the federal system in Canada in the war and post-war years. Of late, however, stronger provincial pressures have reasserted themselves and the practicalities of control seem somewhat more open to question in this atmosphere.

The recommendations for the centralization of debt control received no recognition, then or now. Probably this was originally owing to changes in conditions that made any action superfluous, soon after the *Report* was made public. In this connection it is interesting to wonder on the Commissioners' reaction to the many pleas now being made for federal assistance in provincial and municipal capital projects. It would seem that they might well have been sympathetic, but it seems probable, too, that some form of debt control would have been considered a necessary part of any such proposals, a suggestion that would not be likely to receive wide provincial enthusiasm.

In two of its judgments we could, I think, expect some change in point of view in line with the times. Very strong reservations were expressed on the value of indirect taxes, especially the manufacturers' sales tax, and a very high regard was expressed for the personal income tax. It is questionable if today this attitude would have been maintained in view of the changes in thinking on the place of taxation in the welfare state, with the greater consideration for the application of funds as well as the source in the assessment of their social and economic desirability.

The other field of development in inter-governmental relations which has been contrary to the terms of the *Report* has been that of conditional grants. This system did not on the whole meet with the approval of the Commissioners, but developments of the past few years have been in the opposite direction and new programmes have been developed and old ones extended. There is a continuing acceptance of the trend in this field, and it is perhaps a product of the increasing complexity of our modern system and the continuing difficulties of adjusting to changing needs in the face of our constitutional rigidities.

The Commissioners took three main volumes and many subsidiary works to put their views before the Government and the country. There is here a great storehouse of information for future study and action. They saw many things needing attention even if they did not always know exactly what remedies were required.

Some criticism has been passed on the timing of the *Report* in view of the coming of war, but any other course would not have been practicable, for recasting would not have been possible at that late stage. Whether the *Report* should have been presented to the provinces by the Government of Canada when it was is a moot point, however. Even if the timing of the release was acceptable the method of calling a conference to consider the adoption of the *Report* now seems to have been curiously inept. But this was a political decision and not a matter in the control of the Commissioners.

Wherever they may have erred, I think we would all be willing to accept the judgment that the Commission, nevertheless, laid the groundwork for developments in government in Canada for many years to come—not only by its Report but indirectly through the influence ultimately exerted by the many men who were brought to prominence through their work for the Commission. To these men we owe the fact that inter-governmental negotiations in Canada are gradually assuming something of the nature of a branch of political science, to the extent that this can be possible, rather than continuing purely as an adjunct of regional politics.

In times like these as we again face the formal negotiations that will decide the inter-governmental fiscal relationships for another period, we may hope that those whose responsibility these now are will bring to the task the same intensity of purpose and understanding as did Rowell, Sirois, Dafoe, Mackay, and Angus. If they do, their names, too, will be well remembered.

Government Policy and the Public Lands

ANTHONY D. SCOTT

The achievements of the Rowell-Sirois Commissioners can now be examined with the maturity of twenty-one years of progress and experience. In view of the events of the past ten years it cannot be said to have settled with finality any of the great questions of federal finance. As this paper is being prepared for press, the Canadian Government has proposed scrapping the tax rental agreements and returning to provincial direct taxation. Conditional and unconditional grants are made and modified, the terms of Confederation with Newfoundland are reopened, and new expenditures are allocated to province or Dominion on seemingly arbitrary principles.

One of the great contributions of the Rowell-Sirois Commission, indeed, may now be said to have been its pioneering refusal to regard any part of the fiscal structure of the federation as unalterable. Every part of the structure, every need and opportunity, every principle and statute, was examined pragmatically. By asking what would be best, instead of stressing what the Fathers of Confederation had planned, the Commission established a new approach that is today in marked contrast with the older "disabilities-of-Confederation," "unkept-promises" recriminations. For the American necessity to bend forcibly their great Constitution to meet new situations was substituted a Canadian willingness to keep the federal furnace warm, ready always to melt down and remould the Dominion-provincial economic framework.

An important exception to this general rule is the distribution of powers over and revenues from natural resources, only briefly mentioned in the British North America Act. The general principles laid down then have been surprisingly durable. In spite of puzzles and litigation arising when powers were jointly held, there has emerged a reasonably harmonious division of jurisdiction over the farming and extractive industries. The reason for this harmony is undoubtedly the strong constitutional position of the provinces over resources, in marked contrast with that in other federations. The chief anchor for this constitutional position is an unusual quasi-proprietorial interest in land, an explanation for which is suggested by Dean Angus in the selection quoted below.

So strong has been this proprietorial interest in certain provinces that all provinces are now treated as though each had some special right over all the landed wealth within its borders. Thus the Maritime Provinces are as free as Ontario to levy logging taxes, though little of their forest is now in public ownership. For the same reason, the Prairie Provinces had their resources "restored" to them in 1930. The Americans had long firmly denied to the newer states the public lands within their boundaries, but in Canada the provinces were by now identified with their public lands. It is true that the provinces have acquiesced in federal participation in a number of large-scale resource projects such as dams, waterways, and roads, and have agreed to the encroachments of the Canada Forest Act and the newer Department of Forests. These transgressions have been on the expenditure side, however—no one has yet dared to challenge the provinces on the "right" to the resource revenues. Indeed, scarcely anyone has even discussed these rights since the Rowell-Sirois Commission's occasional references to the adequacy of the provincial stewardship over resources. Even there, however, while the whole revenue and expenditure pattern of federalism was brought under the microscope, "rent," "resources," and "the public domain" were allowed to be a purely provincial matter.

In his searching 1953 paper, "An Echo of the Past—The Rowell-Sirois Commission," however, Dean Angus did examine the matter.

> Provincial "ownership" of natural resources is basic to the problems of federal finance, for it is largely the difference in resources that accounts for the differences in per capita income. It is usually taken for granted and is less frequently challenged than the unequal operation of national policies of which it is the condition.
>
> A colonizing country is apt to begin by considering that it is the beneficial owner of the land and other resources of territory which it has acquired for settlement. Often absentee estates are created. But there comes a time when the colonists insist that it is they, and they alone, who are entitled to the national

> wealth, which they consider a heritage for their children. The same considerations apply within a federation if new territories are acquired and settled. The older provinces may expect to recoup their developmental costs, but sooner or later the settlers will establish a good claim. In Canada this particular issue arose with the purchase of the Hudson's Bay Company's territory and had been settled before the Royal Commission on Dominion-Provincial Relations was appointed.
>
> If countries with mature economies federate, the problem is somewhat different. Rights over natural resources are rarely, if ever, transferred to the federal government. Freedom of trade and freedom of movement may assure access to resources by individuals from all provinces, but the right to get revenue from resources is strictly provincial. Revenue from the public domain, or from the taxation of resource use, may enable a province to supply the social and educational services which its people demand without resort to heavy taxation. The only form which equalization [as between provinces] is likely to take is aid for a province which is lacking in resources. Otherwise each province makes the most of what it has and experiences no sense of guilt if its forests, its mines, its fisheries and its lands enable its people to enjoy a superior standard of living. The [Rowell-Sirois]Report recognized this quasi-proprietary interest by allowing a province to share in the corporate income tax on incomes derived from the depletion of natural resources.[1]

It will be seen that Dean Angus does not defend the quasi-proprietary situation, but merely attempts to account for it as a social phenomenon. It certainly is not universal, as the American federal retention of the western lands demonstrates.

In the following pages, I should like to resist this social pressure, asking instead whether it is desirable that resources should be provincially controlled and taxed. Because my space is limited I must omit references to business-cycle problems, though it should be pointed out that land taxes and conservation expenditures must be thoroughly considered in designing a stabilizing policy. I will also refrain from labouring the obvious point that when resources (such as river basins)

[1]H. F. Angus, "An Echo of the Past—The Rowell-Sirois Commission," *Canadian Tax Journal*, I (1953), pp. 445–6.

refuse to stay within provincial boundaries, the co-operation of the federal government in their development is essential. Finally, I will spare the reader an amateur's efforts to discuss the administrative and legal aspects of a possible transfer of natural resources to federal control, pausing only to admit that attempting to rationalize ten different methods of taxing and regulating resource industries *might* be like unscrambling an omelette. One of the points I wish to make is that the provinces have not yet made a very large omelette.

Omitting these topics, therefore, let us proceed to the question. What arguments might be heard by some future royal commission considering a proposal to transfer the taxation, regulation, and ownership of the provincial natural resources to the federal government?

They might well begin by examining the tendencies Dean Angus has described in the paragraphs above. What moral claims can new arrivals in a new land establish to their natural resources? It is apparently a "natural" assumption that the rent of the land belongs to the people. The worldwide popularity of Henry George's single-taxing doctrines suggests the same consensus. And it is certainly widely accepted in Canada that most property taxes, most public domain revenues, and a good part of the corporation tax revenue "may be considered a levy on the rental values arising from scarcity of land and other resources . . . the transfer to society of the increase in incomes which has been created in large part by the development and expenditure of organized society," as the Rowell-Sirois *Report* put it.[2] But of course it does not follow that the "society" said to be entitled to this transfer of income is to be represented by the provincial government.

The missing link in the argument appears to be supplied by the widespread tendency to apportion to the smallest government units the revenue sources that are local, or localized, in nature. To confine the effects of the taxes of provincial and municipal governments to their own territories, it is usual to search for taxable objects that are confined within that territory. Hence local government revenues almost everywhere are dominated by the taxation of real estate and the use of natural resources. Consequently it is not surprising that Canadians frequently associate the public "right" to the rent of land with the taxation of that rent by local and provincial governments. Resources "belong to" the people living in the same region. It goes

[2]*Report*, I, p. 213.

without saying, however, that this vague association of physiocratic and tax-collecting principles produces a very weak argument for provincial control over natural resources. At the very best it suggests merely that those who control the taxation or exploitation of natural resources should have a jurisdiction *at least* as large as the territorial extent of each resource. A right of property taxation over only a portion of an oil field, or the duty of preventing fires on part of a forest, is likely to produce unfortunate results if neighbouring governments pursue different policies.

Furthermore, there is a strong ethical argument against local claims to resources. Professor Angus reminds us of it when he tells us the resource-wealthy province experiences no "sense of guilt" if "its" resources give it a superior standard of living. Professor D. C. Corbett cites Rousseau's expression of the principles that might inspire a little guilt in the wealthier regions: "How can a man or a people seize an immense territory and keep it from the rest of the world except by a punishable usurpation, since all others are being robbed, by such an act, of the places of habitation and the means of subsistence which nature gave them in common?"[3]

It would be better, perhaps, to leave the ethical battle unresolved. Any federation is a compromise between a union and a Balkanization of economic regions. There is no agreement on the degree of income equalization that is to be sought in this compromise. In the present context it may be more useful to query the social usefulness of the idea that the people, as represented by the province, have inherited a sort of feudal overlordship. The frequent use of the phrase "public domain" to describe the Crown lands seems to carry over from Europe this idea of the sovereign's revenues from his private domain. Should this domain remain the property of the provincial Crown? It may once have seemed reasonable to make the political powers and the landed estates of the barons coterminous. But today there seems nothing particularly "natural" about continuing this arrangement.

Rights of private property are granted on principles that promote social goals. The enrichment of local landlords is certainly not a prominent goal today. Private title to resources is awarded as an incentive to prospecting; as a reward for conservation of forests; in accordance with prevailing notions of the rural community's social structure; to prevent competitive depletion of oil fields and fisheries;

[3]Cited in David Corbett, *Canada's Immigration Policy* (Toronto, 1957), p. xi.

to make the best use of rivers; and so forth. This plethora of principles reflects the variety of problems posed by the difficult forms and locations of natural resources. The notion of private property itself, as a "natural" right, was rejected by the Benthamites, but then defended by them on the utilitarian ground that it was a precondition for capital accumulation and hence for economic progress. In the same way any system of property rights ought to be defensible on the grounds of its social desirability. Can the endowment of the provinces with rights over the natural resources in their own jurisdictions stand this test?

It would have to be conceded that, other things being the same, there is a *prima facie* case for having local rather than remote landlords. Of course, much of the traditional antipathy to the owner who accepts the rents while living elsewhere is irrelevant here. The analogue is the taxpayer who benefits from the bonus on Alberta oil lands. Is a taxpayer in Calgary any less an absentee than one living in Toronto?

The essence of the attack on the absentee landlord is, however, not merely jealousy of a remote *rentier*. Rather it is that in his absence the landlord does not apply himself to making the best use of his property. He has not actively sought the best tenants; he has not known of new opportunities for investing his own capital or attracting others'; in brief, he has not regarded his holdings as a potentially profitable enterprise, but merely as a portfolio asset.

Active ownership, even without investment of capital by the owner, may be a full-time occupation. The landlord cannot instruct his steward merely to collect the rents and audit the accounts. Instead, there must be a constant search for better-paying uses for the land. Rents may be bettered, for example, by finding a more efficient tenant, either to carry on the prevailing practices, or, more important, to change the practices, harvest new crops, or search for new minerals. Often the relative merits of competing proposals for tenancy are not clear. The terms of payment, the length of the tenure, the subsequent value of the property, and the need for complementary social capital may differ as between the contenders. Further, there may be no proposals actively pushed for certain tenure possibilities. Then the active landlord must himself canvass the possibilities and find investors and users.

It is not obvious that the best uses for particular lands and resources will be contrived by landlords who live near at hand. The vehemence of the criticism, from the French Revolution onwards, suggests only that absentee landlords have often been found wanting in enterprise and discrimination. Today, infuriated or frustrated users of national park lands, national forests, government cattle ranges, fishing and hunting areas, and mineral and oil fields rain showers of addresses, proposals, and protests on the remote administrators at the seat of government. "Theorists" and "bureaucrats" are the mildest terms of abuse. Anyone who has listened to the complaints from Alaska about the control over its resources exercised by the Forest Service, the Fish and Wildlife Service, and the Department of the Interior will realize how keen these United States authorities must have been to further proposals that Alaska be free to take its own resource decisions. And in Canada members of Parliament from remote constituencies and touring royal commissions hear a great deal about the local distrust of centralized resource administration.

It might be argued, therefore, that control by Ottawa would be absentee ownership to an extreme degree. With the best will in the world, administrators faced with all Canada's resources could not conceivably become "active" landlords. The strength of this argument, however, is weakened by the suggestion that administration from the provincial capitals is already tarred with the same brush. The provincial governments are frequently, both in miles and in spirit, as far from the local scene as Ottawa is. At the same time, they may be more vulnerable to the immediate political consequences of their lands policies. Indeed, they may be said to be often too remote for immediate knowledge yet too close for detached policy-making—the worst of both worlds.

It would be easy to draw up a strong indictment of the provincial policies toward their resources. In the first place, to make the best use of their resources they must make heavy investments in perpetuating the returns from wasting assets. Although there has been some progress in this respect, it is remarkable how little of it has been undertaken by the provincial governments themselves. In forestry, for example, the chief initiative in making forest inventories has been that of the federal government, under the Canada Forest Act. Responsibility for the regeneration of cut-over land has, wherever possible, been turned over to private exploiting companies in return for further cutting privileges. There is no harm in this, but any good results are then little to the credit of the governments concerned. Almost everywhere in Canada the public forests which are under the direct care of the forest services receive significantly less expenditure than the privately preserved tracts or than the American national forests.

The largest part of primary geological surveying in the provinces is still carried out by the Geological Survey of Canada, at national expense. Those who believe the gold-mining and the coal-mining subsidies to have been helpful should be reminded that these have been national policies—even in oil-rich Alberta. The building of mining access roads, the subsidization of prospectors, and endowment of geological and metallurgical research, all of these provincial programmes are maintained on a minimum scale. It is a striking fact that the Borden Commission's estimates of the possible or ultimate oil reserves of western Canada were not obtained from the governments concerned but from the industry being investigated.

Provincial water and hydro-electric administrations are usually much more elaborate. Probably this is because the resources serve a local market, and are therefore politically significant. Further, the firms are often publicly owned. Even then, however, the provinces have willingly accepted federal leadership in the planning of extensive projects.

The fisheries, of course, are constitutionally a federal responsibility. No one would claim that the federal Fisheries Department is without fault; but the care with which Ottawa tends this minor and highly localized industry and its resource provides a thought-provoking contrast with the casual provincial standard in other resources.

This review of the various resources suggests that the provinces have not much to boast of in their performance as active landlords of wasting resources. There are, of course, bright spots; standards differ from province to province and department to department. Everywhere dedicated officials are struggling with enormous loads of unfinished business, and with impressive-sounding projects financed by inadequate budget votes. It has long been this way. Conceding the justice of the provinces' claims that much of the revenue from certain taxes represented profits from the depletion of wasting assets, and urging that the provinces needed to amortize provincial expenditure on new development, to prepare for the expenditures necessary when the resources are depleted, and to undertake conservation measures for the continuance of reproducible resources, the Rowell-Sirois *Report* suggests in several places that such amortization and conservation were not in fact being undertaken by the provinces.[4] Nor is it today —by the provinces.

There is a second respect in which the provinces are not particularly successful as active landlords. To play this role it is necessary for them

[4]*Report*, I, p. 243; II, pp. 125, 129–30, 181.

actively to seek the best uses of land, both by setting resource prices which will exclude second-rate resource development projects, and by adjusting tenure arrangements to encourage land uses made possible by new market demands for raw materials, new exploitive techniques, and new transportation methods. I have suggested elsewhere, writing in another context, that their performance in doing this has not been satisfactory.[5]

Third, and perhaps most important, is the *increasing* need for active development of the resource industries. The world's primary-producing countries seem only slowly to be recognizing that the great tide of scientific progress that is already changing much of the world's technology is running adversely to their interests.

Not long ago most of the great extractive industries could be said to be "at the mercy of nature." They had no control over the extent or the quality of the material which they exploited. They took their deposits and forests as and where they were revealed, making the best of technical difficulties by applying enormous amounts of capital, fuel, and power. So great was the demand for certain scarce minerals and for wood that heavy expenditures on transportation facilities and pipelines and on more or less random exploratory techniques could easily be justified. The exploiting firms shipped to distant markets roughly milled raw materials little different in composition from their occurrence in nature: these were the so-called "staples" of the extractive industries.

Today the raw-material industries and the consuming industries that they supply are moving rapidly out of this highly capitalized, extractive phase. One of two things is happening. First, the techniques of discovery are becoming much more certain, making the industry more able to predict the chances of success, more able to find resources close to markets, in desired grades and qualities. The reproducible resources are being farmed and harvested in convenient locations. The stress on finding *any* supply of certain scarce minerals and energy has been replaced by an ever more intensive search for low-cost sources. No longer are international development firms so willing to go anywhere in the world, investing large funds in new locations, in the effort to acquire assured supplies of these materials. In brief, many of the resources are coming "under control," in the sense that agriculture

[5]"Resourcefulness and Responsibility," *Canadian Journal of Economics and Political Science*, XXIV (1958), p. 213. See also Bertil Ohlin, *Interregional and International Trade* (Cambridge, Mass., 1933), pp. 184–5.

and the manufacturing industries have already brought their processes and products under control.

It is necessary, however, to recognize that many resources cannot be brought under control in this way. It is unlikely that science can ever devise techniques that will make forests as easy and cheap to manage as annual crops; that certain minerals will ever be found close to their markets; or more generally that certain staples can ever be produced in standardized qualities and quantities that are really convenient for the consuming industries to use. In these cases the technical revolution is simply sweeping such raw materials aside. When variations in quality and quantity make them costly for certain uses, they are simply replaced by substitutes. So whale oil is supplanted by agriculturally produced fats and oils; coal by petroleum, gas, atomic, and perhaps nuclear or solar energy; wood by steel, glass, aluminum, concrete, and agriculturally produced cellulose; and so forth. It is also evident that substitution takes place in the final product: television commercials replace advertisements printed on newsprint; heated buildings replace fur coats; rubber-tyred cars replace leather-soled shoes; and bottled foods replace tin-covered cans.

With such extensive technical possibilities, the owners of raw material deposits and resources can no longer rely on business capital venturing far from the market to develop resources. More and more it will instead be necessary for private and public resource owners to develop their own properties, to attract extractive industries to known resources, and to install social overhead capital similar to that in competitive resource locations in other countries. In the same way, it will be increasingly necessary for resource *owners* to establish marketing services so as to maintain demand for their raw materials over actual and potential substitutes. Similarly, they will need to maintain laboratories to adapt the quality of their raw materials, as delivered, to the requirements of the increasingly fastidious consuming industries. No longer can unassorted "staples" be dumped at the delivery dock of secondary industry. Requirements of each buying industry as to chemical composition, grade, and physical characteristics must be carefully studied by laboratories serving the materials industries, and the requirements transmitted back to the mills and smelters.

As "proprietors of their own natural resources," these tasks begin to fall to the provincial governments. In the past they have confined their activities to collecting revenue from and granting tenure to eager mineral and forest industries, while eagerly catering to the needs of secondary manufacturing industries for good locations, market statistics, skilled workers, and overhead capital. In the future, however, they must transfer much of this solicitude to their "own" resource industries. In this respect, and in other ways, the resource industries will increasingly resemble manufacturing and farming sectors: stable in location, vulnerable to keen competition from other regions, buying as well as selling raw materials. Unless the resource industries are thus assisted, the flood of technical change may irreversibly pass them by, draining the value from previously promising ores and resources.

This is perhaps the most important reason for distrusting the "natural" allocation of resource revenues and powers to the Canadian provinces. Their failure to carry out alone the relatively simple tasks sketched by the Rowell-Sirois Commission had already induced the federal government to interest itself increasingly in resource matters. But the problem of maintaining intact a *physical* resource capital stock was relatively simple in comparison with the new problem: to maintain the value of resource stocks in the face of increasing competition from other regions and increasing substitution of products made more cheaply from other raw materials.

In earlier discussions of the role of natural resources in the determination of incomes and revenues in federal countries, it was taken as axiomatic that the rich resources of wealthy regions caused their high per capita incomes. It was recognized that it was actually the location of the primary and secondary processing establishments that was the direct determinant of population and income, but the processing, if done at all in Canada, tended to be located in the same province. In such circumstances the rich provinces could afford passively to allow the world's great resource industries to explore, develop, transport, and market their resources. Paradoxically, it was the poor provinces that struggled most actively to encourage more mining, logging, or exploration. Soon, however, the challenge will be thrown to the land-rich provinces to conserve the value of their resources.

It is disquieting that their past performance suggests that they may fail to respond to this challenge. Perhaps, as with the social welfare functions, Ottawa can take a lead in resource-product development without actually assuming the provincial powers. If not, to reassign these powers to the federal government might well be preferable to permitting the resource-rich provinces to fall behind in the forthcoming international materials struggle for markets.

Some Contrasts and Similarities in Canadian, American, and British Procedures for the Examination of Monopolistic Situations

ALBERT S. WHITELEY

In a number of western industrial countries the post-war period has been marked by significant developments in public policy toward restrictive business arrangements.[1] In the case of Canada and the United States the developments, in large measure, have been the extension of policies whose origins lie a considerable distance back in industrial and political history. In the case of the United Kingdom, however, the framing of public policy into legislative enactments has been a distinctly new development, which has been described as "a break with tradition."[2] The most recent enactment, the Restrictive Trade Practices Act,[3] was passed in August, 1956, and the first decision of the special court set up under that legislation, the Restrictive Practices Court, was given on November 3, 1958. On the other hand, the Parliament of Canada in 1889 passed "An Act for the Prevention

[1]See *Report of the Ad Hoc Committee on Restrictive Business Practices*, United Nations Economic and Social Council, Official Records, Sixteenth Session, Supplements nos. 11A and 11B (New York, 1953); European Productivity Agency (E.P.A.), of the Organisation for European Economic Co-operation, *Guide to Legislation on Restrictive Business Practices* (Paris, 1960); *Proceedings, International Conference on Control of Restrictive Business Practices* (Chicago, 1960).

[2]E.P.A., *Guide*, vol. II, United Kingdom, 0:3.

[3]Restrictive Trade Practices Act, 1956 (4 & 5 Eliz. II, c. 68).

and Suppression of Combinations formed in restraint of Trade," which was incorporated in the Criminal Code in 1892 and persists in much the same form in present legislation. The Canadian statute thus preceded by a year the Sherman Act of the United States, which was passed in 1890 "to protect trade and commerce against unlawful restraints and monopolies."

In spite of the difference in legislative approach, particularly between the recent British legislation, on the one hand, and the older Canadian and American on the other, the concern in all three countries is to secure more effective competition among business enterprises. In the 1956 debate in the British House of Commons during the passage of the Restrictive Trade Practices Act, the President of the Board of Trade said that the purpose of the measure was to secure that the virtues of free enterprise "are not throttled by restrictions imposed by industry upon itself."[4] It has long been held by the courts that the purpose of Canadian legislation in this field has been to protect the public interest in free competition and similar interpretation has been given to legislation in the United States by the courts in that country.

Although the procedures and scope of remedies differ among Canada, the United States, and the United Kingdom, there is an element of similarity in the reliance which all three place upon the judiciary in determining the public interest. Constitutional interpretation in Canada has so far led to measures relying principally on the federal authority in criminal law. In the United States judicial interpretation has confirmed the federal power over interstate commerce, and legislation has been adopted which provides for both civil and criminal proceedings in federal courts in antitrust actions. In addition, supervision of this field is also entrusted to a regulatory body. The United States Federal Trade Commission was established in 1914 as a regulatory agency to control unfair competitive practices, including restraints on competition. In carrying out its functions, particularly in antimonopoly cases, it has operated largely as a court of law.[5] As its decisions have been appealable to the courts its findings have followed the interpretations which the courts have given to the antitrust laws.

[4]*Hansard*, March 6, 1956, col. 1955.

[5]*Antitrust Law Enforcement by the Federal Trade Commission and the Antitrust Division, Department of Justice—A Preliminary Report*, Select Committee on Small Business, House of Representatives, 81st Congress, 2nd sess., 1951.

In the debate on the 1956 legislation the British Labour party suggested an administrative tribunal instead of the Restrictive Practices Court, but this was not accepted and the Government's proposal for a judicial body to appraise agreements was incorporated in the legislation. The Court was to be composed of both judges and lay members.

NATURE OF ORGANIZATION FOR MAKING INQUIRIES

Canada

Canadian anti-combines legislation, as already indicated, has been based primarily on federal jurisdiction in the field of criminal law. Unlike the United States, where a system of federal courts administers federal legislation, the administration of criminal law, in its ordinary course, is not a federal responsibility in Canada but, along with other phases of the administration of justice, is placed by the constitution in the hands of the provinces, although judicial appointments are made by the federal government. From an early period in Canadian experience with anti-combines legislation it has been felt that special measures should be provided for the investigation of restrictive practices or arrangements, as the regular machinery of criminal investigation did not seem to be well adapted for such purposes. Over the years various legislative changes have been made to supplement and extend the basic law. These have been directed to ensuring more complete methods of inquiry and appraisal as well as strengthening the methods of court proceedings. In the process the responsibility of initiating court actions for alleged offences against the anti-combines laws has been increasingly assumed by the Minister of Justice. The present legislation embodies recommendations made in 1951 and 1952 by the Committee to Study Combines Legislation, often referred to as the MacQuarrie Committee.[6] The present Combines Investigation Act, which was originally enacted in 1923,[7] provides for two agencies

[6]The members of the Committee were the Honourable Mr. Justice J. H. MacQuarrie of the Supreme Court of Nova Scotia, Dr. W. A. Mackintosh, Principal of Queen's University, Professor Maurice Lamontagne, then Assistant Director of the Department of Economics, Laval University, and Mr. George F. Curtis, Dean of the University of British Columbia Law School.

[7]The first Combines Investigation Act was passed in 1910 and provided for preliminary inquiry by a judge who might issue an order for a full investigation to be made by an *ad hoc* board of three persons appointed by the Minister of Labour. This Act was superseded in 1919 by the Combines

reporting to the Minister of Justice. The Director of Investigation and Research, who is a permanent civil servant appointed by the Governor in Council, is charged with the duty of investigating combines and other restrictive trade practices. The Director makes an annual report of proceedings under the Act to the Minister of Justice, who submits the report to Parliament. The other agency provided in the present legislation is the Restrictive Trade Practices Commission, consisting of three members appointed by the Governor in Council for terms of ten years, with one member appointed as chairman. Members of the Commission are eligible for reappointment on expiration of their terms. The Commission is responsible for appraising the evidence submitted to it by the Director and by the parties concerned in an inquiry and for making a report in each inquiry to the Minister of Justice. The Act does not contain specific qualifications for members of the Commission. The first appointments went to two lawyers, including the chairman, and an economist. The latter had been previously on the staff of the former Combines Investigation Commission.

The separation of the functions of collecting information about and making inquiry into monopolistic situations, and of appraising and reporting upon the evidence presented, which is made in the Canadian legislation, is reflected in the organization of the two divisions. In June, 1960, the staff of the Director of Investigation and Research consisted of forty-five persons, including the Director and sixteen investigation officers. The latter are usually persons trained in law, economics, or commerce. The regular staff of the Restrictive Trade Practices Commission, on the other hand, embraced one economist and four secretarial positions. Both the Director and the Commission may, with the approval of the Governor in Council, employ temporary special assistants, and university professors or other consultants may be engaged for some particular research or analysis in connection with an inquiry. The Minister of Justice may also appoint special counsel to assist in an inquiry. These provisions enable the small permanent staff of the Director or the Commission to be supplemented whenever necessary.

In considering the staffs of the investigating agencies in the respective countries one should have in mind the relative populations. In

---

and Fair Prices Act and the Board of Commerce Act. Under this legislation the Board of Commerce was authorized to conduct inquiries and enjoin the continuance of designated practices. The legislation was held *ultra vires* by the Privy Council in 1922.

1959 the population of Canada was approaching 18 million. In the same year the estimated population of the United States was 178 million and that of the United Kingdom approaching 52 million.

United States

The investigation of monopolistic situations in the United States is divided between the Antitrust Division of the Department of Justice and the Federal Trade Commission. The Antitrust Division was established in 1903 and remained a relatively small division until the mid-1930's with never more than twenty-five attorneys on its staff. There was a considerable expansion in staff after 1935, and by 1942 the professional staff of the Antitrust Division, largely attorneys, numbered about 280. There was some contraction during the Second World War, but in recent years the total staff has been about 475, including about 250 attorneys and 25 economists.[8]

The Antitrust Division forms part of the executive branch of the American government and is under the charge of an Assistant Attorney General. The headquarters of the Antitrust Division are in Washington. There are also field offices, in recent years usually eight, at which about 180 of the total staff of 475 are stationed. In addition to its own staff the Antitrust Division has the assistance of the Federal Bureau of Investigation in conducting investigations, the majority of the Bureau investigators being either graduates in law or accountants. F.B.I. investigators are assigned to antitrust investigations from regional offices in the territory in which the inquiry is carried on. Prosecution for violation of the federal antitrust laws is conducted by the Department of Justice.

The Federal Trade Commission is an investigatory and administrative agency which is empowered to issue cease and desist orders to prevent violations of statutes which it administers. As well the Commission may seek to secure voluntary compliance with the laws through less formal procedures.

The Federal Trade Commission consists of five members appointed by the President of the United States with the consent of the Senate. One of the members is appointed by the President to serve as chairman of the Commission. The Federal Trade Commission Act provides that not more than three of the commissioners can belong to the same political party. Commissioners are appointed for a term of seven years and each commissioner's term of office expires in a different year, but

[8]E. P. A., *Guide*, vol. II, United States, 0:10.

a commissioner continues to hold office at the expiration of his term until a successor is appointed and has qualified. In the event of a commissioner's office becoming vacant before the expiration of his term a person is appointed for the unexpired term. All the present members of the Commission have had legal training. Three were members of the federal civil service at the time of their appointment, two being senior officials on the staff of the Federal Trade Commission.

The functions of the Federal Trade Commission extend into a number of fields in addition to its antitrust activities; consequently no precise statement can be made as to the portion of its work which consists of what are described as antimonopoly activities. Other major fields of activity in which the Commission is engaged are concerned with false advertising and other deceptive practices, the labelling of wool and fur articles, the distribution of flammable fabrics, and the business of insurance not regulated by state law. The principal office of the Commission is in Washington, where a branch office is also maintained, and there are branches in seven other cities.

The total staff of the Commission reached a peak of 694 in 1941 and then declined during the war years. The staff fluctuated around 600 in the post-war period until 1957 when an increase to more than 700 was made possible by larger appropriations. In recent years the total staff of the Commission has been about 740, including about 190 at branch offices. The Commission has on its staff about 325 lawyers, 25 economists, 20 accountants and 5 statisticians.[9]

According to the *Annual Report of the Federal Trade Commission* for the fiscal year 1959, about 52 per cent of the appropriations of the Commission was devoted to antimonopoly activities, including investigation and litigation and economic and financial reports.

United Kingdom

The first step taken in the United Kingdom to set up an agency for the investigation of monopolistic situations was the passage of the Monopolies and Restrictive Practices (Inquiry and Control) Act in 1948. This Act provided for the Monopolies and Restrictive Practices Commission of not less than four nor more than ten members, including the chairman, to be appointed by the Board of Trade. By an amending Act in 1953 the maximum number of members was increased to twenty-five and authority was given for the functions of the Commission to be exercised by separate groups, of not less than five

[9]*Ibid.*, 0:10.

members, selected by the chairman. The structure of the Commission was again altered by the Restrictive Trade Practices Act of 1956, which reduced the maximum number of members to ten and changed its name to the Monopolies Commission. The provisions for groups of members to conduct investigations were also withdrawn.

As we have seen, there are two agencies in the United States, one executive and one regulatory, with responsibility for conducting investigations into monopolistic situations. While the functions of the two agencies differ, there is some overlapping of their respective fields and co-operative arrangements are maintained between them to avoid duplication. Since the passage of the Restrictive Trade Practices Act in the United Kingdom two organizations to deal with monopolistic situations, both statutory agencies, have existed, but overlapping has been avoided by withdrawing from the jurisdiction of the Monopolies Commission matters which will be within the purview of the Restrictive Practices Court established by the Act of 1956. In a general sense it may be said that the Monopolies Commission henceforth will be concerned with investigating and reporting upon cases involving single-firm monopolies, arrangements relating to export trade, or policies restrictive of competition among a group of dominant firms which are not the result of agreement, while the Restrictive Practices Court will be concerned with agreements or arrangements among two or more firms in the domestic market, what, in Canadian parlance, might be called "combinations." The types of agreements which will be reviewed by the Restrictive Practices Court are described as follows in the 1956 *Annual Report on the Monopolies and Restrictive Practices Acts, 1948 and 1953*, made by the Board of Trade to Parliament: "collective agreements on prices or other terms or conditions, and collective agreements which involve discrimination between persons, the sharing of markets or restrictions on production or processing. They include agreements which have come to be known as 'Common Price', 'Agreed Tendering' and 'Collective Discrimination' agreements."

In the case of the Monopolies Commission, it appears to have been the intention from the outset to have a commission consisting largely of part-time members drawn from various spheres of activity with a full-time chairman. Members are appointed to the Commission for terms of not less than three nor more than seven years, as specified by the Board of Trade at the time of appointment, and are not eligible for reappointment. These provisions do not apply to the chairman, who may hold office until the age of seventy-two years, and in the case of other members the Board of Trade may extend from time to time the term of office, but not for a period exceeding twelve years. Following the reconstitution of the Commission in October, 1956, the membership consisted of a full-time chairman, who had previously been an active member of the bar, four industrialists, one of whom had been a member of a firm of solicitors before the war, one university economist, one trade union official, one accountant, who had been engaged with a public authority, and one former civil servant with legal experience.

During the period when the Monopolies Commission was the only agency for investigation its staff grew from about thirty-seven persons in 1949 to about a hundred in 1955. It would appear from a report of the Select Committee on Estimates of the House of Commons made in 1953 that about one-half of the persons on the staff would rank in the administrative class of the British civil service, and the proportion was equivalent, roughly, to that formed by the professional classes in the agencies in Canada and the United States. By the end of 1959 the total staff of the Monopolies Commission had been reduced to thirty-five.[10]

The Act of 1956 provides for the registration and judicial investigation of restrictive trade agreements of the nature previously described. A system of registration as a prior stage to investigation has no close parallel in procedures in Canada or the United States, but examples of registration may be found in some European countries.

An office of Registrar of Restrictive Trading Agreements is established by the Act of 1956. The Registrar is given the duty of maintaining a register of such agreements and of instituting proceedings before the Restrictive Practices Court with respect to such agreements in such order as the Board of Trade may direct. When the Act of 1956 came into force the Board of Trade, without limiting the Registrar in taking other proceedings, issued directions as to the classes of agreements to be first brought before the Restrictive Practices Court. The first direction was made in April, 1957, and subsequent directions were issued in September, 1957, March, 1958, and October, 1958, which brought the total number of agreements to which the Registrar was to give priority to about 450.[11] Since 1958 the Board of Trade has not exercised the power to direct the Registrar on the order

[10]*Annual Report by the Board of Trade, Monopolies and Restrictive Practices Acts, 1948 and 1953, for the Year Ending 31st December, 1959* (London, 1960), p. 2.

[11]*Board of Trade Journal*, Oct. 10, 1958, p. 731.

in which proceedings shall be taken. The register is open to public inspection on the payment of a fee, except for particulars of agreements which, on the direction of the Board of Trade, are to be kept in a special section because their publication would be contrary to the public interest or would reveal details of secret processes to the damage of legitimate business interests.

The Registrar is appointed by the Crown and is not responsible to any Minister. The person appointed to the office had previously held the position of Treasury Solicitor. The Registrar is given considerable powers to obtain information both for the purpose of securing the registration of an agreement and for securing further information in connection with the registration of an agreement. The staff of the Registrar has remained at about 120,[12] which is the number for which provision was made when the office was established according to the following details published in the *Manchester Guardian* of April 17, 1957:

> A total of £110,853 is to be provided in 1957–8 for the work of the new registry. Of this £103,003 will be paid in salaries and £6,150 in travelling and incidental expenses. There will be a staff of 122 including 21 executive officers, 53 clerks and typists and 23 messengers. The registrar is to be paid £4,250 a year, and his principal assistant £3,250. In addition, there will be three assistant registrars, two senior legal assistants, three temporary legal assistants, five principals, one chief executive officer, one senior executive officer, and eight higher executive officers. These details were given in a Civil Estimate published yesterday.

All the staff of the Registrar are seconded civil servants. The work of the Registrar's office is carried on in separate divisions dealing with registration and with the preparation of cases for the Restrictive Practices Court. Legal work in connection with the cases is handled by a special branch of the Treasury Solicitors Department to which the cases are referred after being prepared in the Registrar's office.

The Restrictive Practices Court is a superior court of record consisting of five judges, one of whom is selected by the Lord Chancellor to be President of the Court, and not more than ten other members appointed by the Queen on the recommendation of the Lord Chan-

[12]E.P.A., *Guide*, United Kingdom, 0:5.

cellor from persons having knowledge of or experience in industry, commerce, or public affairs. The lay members are to hold office for such period not less than three years as may be determined at the time of appointment and are eligible for reappointment. Three of the judicial members are to be puisne judges of the High Court nominated from time to time by the Lord Chancellor, one is to be a judge of the Court of Session in Scotland nominated by the Lord President of that Court, and one is to be a judge of the Supreme Court of Northern Ireland nominated by the Lord Chief Justice of Northern Ireland. Provision is also made for increases in the number of members of the Court and for the appointment of temporary members when an appointed member is unable to act. Under the Act of 1956 the Court may sit as a single court or in two or more divisions. For the hearing of any proceedings the Court shall consist of a presiding judge and at least two other members.The judges nominated to the Court are to give priority to their attendance on the Restrictive Practices Court, but the Act does not make it mandatory that lay members should be engaged full time on their court work. In addition to removal for inability or misbehaviour, the Lord Chancellor may remove a lay member on the ground of any employment or interest which appears to him to be incompatible with his duties as a member.

The appointment of five judges and eight lay members to the Restrictive Practices Court was announced in May, 1957. Three retired business men, one accountant, two civil servants, one chairman of a public authority, and one trade union official were appointed as the lay members. Five were appointed as full-time and three as part-time members.

INITIATION OF INVESTIGATIONS

Canada

The Canadian Combines Investigation Act, since 1952, has provided for two classes of inquiries. The first embraces situations alleged to be forbidden by the anti-combines legislation, and the second embraces conditions or practices which, while not alleged to be within the first class, are related to monopolistic situations or restraint of trade. The latter are sometimes referred to as "general" inquiries. General inquiries may be initiated by the Director of Investigation and Research on his own motion or on direction of the Minister of Justice or the Restrictive Trade Practices Commission.

Inquiries into alleged violations of anti-combines legislation may be undertaken by the Director in one of three ways, namely, (*a*) on formal application by six citizens, (*b*) on direction from the Minister of Justice, or (*c*) when the Director "has reason to believe" that a violation has occurred or is about to occur. The experience since the original Act was passed is that a formal application for an inquiry or a direction by the Minister is rarely made. This outcome is not surprising when it is considered that any person may bring any information he possesses to the attention of the Director in an informal way, and that if information comes to the attention of the Minister he may be expected to refer it to the Director for examination. However, in the various revisions which have been made in the legislation the right of six citizens to make formal application and the authority of the Minister to direct an inquiry to be undertaken have been maintained.

Informal complaints and requests for investigation are made to the Director by consumers, business men, and associations representing various interests. The attention of the Director may also be directed to a particular matter because of reports in the press or other publications or because of information received in other ways.

The large majority of complaints and inquiries received by the Director of Investigation and Research do not lead to formal inquiry and report. Many of them are disposed of on first examination in the Combines Branch because they obviously do not come within the provisions of the Act. After further examination of others it may be found that continued investigation would not be justified. The attention which may be given to various matters which do not result in a full investigation may range, therefore, from brief study to quite extensive examination. The legislation does not define the stages of an inquiry, but it does require the Director to secure the written concurrence of the Restrictive Trade Practices Commission to discontinue an inquiry in which any evidence has been brought before the Commission. Although no reports are published in connection with discontinued inquiries, it has been the practice of the Director to make reference to the fields of the more important of such inquiries in his annual report and to indicate the nature of the practices involved.

For these reasons it is very difficult for any statistics to be compiled which would give any accurate indication of the activities of the Combines Branch. In recent years the Director of Investigation and Research has included in his annual report a table showing the number of inquiries during the year. The figures in Table I are taken from recent annual reports and are subject to the qualifications already mentioned.

TABLE I

NUMBER OF INQUIRIES UNDER COMBINES INVESTIGATION ACT

	Fiscal years			
	1955–6	1956–7	1957–8	1958–9
Number of files opened on receipt of complaints or inquiries of the nature of complaints	91	48	77[a]	127[a]
Number of formal directions from the Minister for inquiries	0	0	0	0
Number of formal applications from citizens for inquiries	1	0	1	0
Situations examined extensively on the initiative of the Director	8	7	5	[b]
Number of formal investigations of possible contraventions in progress at end of year	17	20	30	31
Number of general inquiries under section 42 in progress at end of year	3	3	4	3
Number of investigations disposed of by preliminary reports during year	2	2	4	3
Number of reports made to the Minister by Restrictive Trade Practices Commission	6	3	3	10

SOURCE: annual reports of the Director of Investigation and Research.

[a]This does not include a large number of complaints on the subject of loss-leader selling, some of which were in general terms.

[b]This classification was not made in the years prior to 1954–5 and has been discontinued. Inquiries of this class have been included in other items since 1958–9.

United States

Complaints by consumers and business men also play a large part in the initiation of investigations by the Antitrust Division of the Department of Justice in the United States. In an address to the New York State Bar Association in January, 1954, Hon. Stanley N. Barnes, then in charge of the Antitrust Division, said:

> We are developing economic surveys of large industrial concentrations, designated originally by our lawyers. These economic surveys may point up those areas where action by the Division is warranted. Combined with the leads developed through Congressional hearings and complaints by businessmen and consumers, these surveys should give us a well balanced enforcement program.[13]

Referring in the same address to concurrent work of the Antitrust Division and the Federal Trade Commission, Judge Barnes said that

[13]Stanley N. Barnes, "Theory and Practices of Antitrust Administration," in J. E. Van Cise and C. W. Dunn (eds.), *How to Comply with the Antitrust Laws* (Chicago, 1954), p. 38.

there had been very little duplication in enforcement activities and practically no duplication in investigations. Co-operative arrangements are maintained between the two agencies so that a proposed investigation by either is first cleared with the other. The experience in the United States also appears to have been that many complaints may be disposed of on initial examination.[14] The Antitrust Division receives a thousand or more complaints during the course of a year and apparently less than one-fifth results in an investigation. The following summary of investigations is given in the annual report of the Antitrust Division for 1957:

> A steady increase in the number of investigations being handled by the Division brought the number to a ten-year high of 293 pending as the year opened and 302 as it closed. During the year, 139 new investigations were opened and 130 closed. In addition, the Division reviewed 1400 suspected interlocking directorate situations and studied 202 mergers for possible violation of the Clayton Act. Over 1394 complaints of possible antitrust violations were received and processed by the Division. This number is higher than any year since 1950.[15]

Table II gives some statistics relating to activities of the Antitrust Division in recent years.

TABLE II
ACTIVITIES OF THE ANTITRUST DIVISION

	Fiscal year ended June 30			
	1956	1957	1958	1959
Number of complaints processed	1185	1394	[a]	[a]
Number of investigations opened	143	139	144	124
Number of investigations closed	130	130	131	126
Number of investigations pending, end of year	293	302	315	313
Number of cases filed				
Civil	25	37	32	21
Criminal	23	18	21	41
Number of cases pending, end of year				
Civil	62	72 }	103 (Civil and Criminal)	99 (Civil and Criminal)
Criminal	35	30 }		

SOURCE: annual reports of the Attorney General of the United States.
[a]Figures not available.

[14]See Marcus A. Hollabaugh, "Development of an Antitrust Case," in American Bar Association, Section of Antitrust Law, *Proceedings at the Spring Meeting, Washington, D.C., April 1–2, 1954* (Washington, 1954), pp. 14–26.

[15]*Annual Report of the Attorney General of the United States for the Fiscal Year ended June 30, 1957* (Washington, 1957), p. 172.

In somewhat the same way as in Canada investigations of the Federal Trade Commission fall into two classes, those involving general or industry-wide inquiries and those related to a specific question of violation of the laws enforced by the Commission. General inquiries may originate with the President or with Congress, or may be initiated by the Commission on its own motion. The initiation of antimonopoly investigation was described in the following way in the *Annual Report* of the Commission for 1953:

> Generally, most antimonopoly investigations are the result of complaints received from businessmen, trade groups, consumers and consumer organizations, members of Congress, congressional committees, and Federal, State, and municipal governments. Many are instituted, however, on the Commission's own initiative, particularly cases involving corporate mergers or acquisitions questioned under section 7 of the Clayton Act.
>
> In fiscal 1953, 704 applications for complaint were received, 225 of which were docketed for field investigation.[16]

Statistics of activities of the Federal Trade Commission in connection with antimonopoly investigations in recent years are given in Table III.

TABLE III

ANTIMONOPOLY ACTIVITIES OF THE FEDERAL TRADE COMMISSION

	Fiscal year ended June 30			
	1956	1957	1958	1959
Number of complaints or inquiries entered for investigation	590	822	814	884
Number of investigations completed	[a]	277	[a]	270
Number of investigations pending	455	440	485	449
Number of formal complaints issued	42	55	86	79[b]
Number of findings and orders	37	31	45	64[c]

SOURCE: annual reports of the Federal Trade Commission.

[a]Figures not available.

[b]In addition, there was an antimonopoly charge included in a deceptive practice complaint.

[c]In addition, there were 5 orders partially disposing of cases.

Like the Antitrust Division, the Federal Trade Commission has followed a policy of keeping the identity of complainants confidential. The same course has usually been followed in Canada.

[16]*Annual Report of the Federal Trade Commission for the Fiscal Year ended June* 30, *1953* (Washington, 1953), p. 16.

It has also been the experience in the work of the Federal Trade Commission that the great majority of the cases do not proceed beyond the informal stage in Commission proceedings.[17] Included in this stage, however, are voluntary stipulations by the parties under investigation to cease and desist from the practice complained of.

In connection with an inquiry by a Congressional Committee into the operation of the antitrust laws the following summary was made of the activities of the Federal Trade Commission in the period 1915 to 1946:

> From 1915 to date the Federal Trade Commission handled approximately 22,000 cases, of which roughly—
> 40 per cent were either dismissed or closed without further proceedings;
> 35 per cent resulted in stipulations to cease and desist; and
> 25 per cent resulted in complaints being issued by the Commissioners.
>
> Only about 15 per cent of all formal cases (those in which FTC issued complaints) were antitrust cases.[18]

In addition to specific investigations the Federal Trade Commission also carries on each year a limited number of general inquiries. In recent years a major field for such inquiries has been the study of industrial concentration.

United Kingdom

The procedure for the initiation of investigations under the British legislation of 1948 and 1956 differs markedly from that followed under Canadian and American legislation. Under the 1948 legislation the Monopolies Commission has no authority to initiate inquiries on complaints or on its own motion, but is restricted to references made to it by the Board of Trade. The latter has power to refer matters to the Commission when "conditions to which this Act applies" prevail with respect to the supply, processing, or export of goods. The "conditions," as defined, include a situation in which at least one-third of the supply is controlled by a single firm or by two or more firms acting

[17] *Antitrust Law Enforcement by the Federal Trade Commission and the Antitrust Division*, p. 10.

[18] *United States Versus Economic Concentration and Monopoly*, Staff Report to the Monopoly Subcommittee of the Committee on Small Business, House of Representatives, 79th Congress, 2nd sess., 1946, p. 20.

so as to restrain competition. It has already been noted that since the passage of the 1956 Act the scope of references will no longer extend to agreements which are required to be registered. The references are made by the Board of Trade with respect to particular classes of goods or processes and not to individual concerns. References may be of two types. They may be restricted to the finding of facts, that is, whether there is a monopolistic situation and if so, what practices are involved in it. Or the Commission may be directed to ascertain the facts and also to report whether any of the practices operate or may be expected to operate against the public interest. The Board of Trade is given authority to vary a reference before a report is made by the Commission, but it has no power to restrict an inquiry to the "facts" if the Commission has been directed to express an opinion as to the "public interest." The Commission may, however, be directed to extend a "fact-finding" reference to embrace consideration of the public interest. Provision is also made in the legislation for the Board of Trade to direct the Commission to report on the general effect on the public interest of practices of a specified class which are related to monopolistic situations. These have usually been called general references. The Commission made one report of this type, that on collective discrimination, which preceded the legislation of 1956, and a second reference on common prices and agreed tendering was allowed to lapse after the adoption of the Act of 1956.

Under the Act of 1948 the Board of Trade is required to make an annual report to Parliament on the operations of the legislation, and to include a review of suggestions and requests received by the Board of Trade for investigations by the Commission. Such annual reports do not indicate the number of representations received each year but list the classes of goods and the type of restriction mentioned. The number of products listed in the annual report for 1955 in the various classifications totalled seventy, including a number of goods which had been listed in earlier reports. In the annual report for 1956 it was stated that many of the suggestions and requests made in that year related to restrictive agreements which became subject to registration under the Act of 1956. The report then listed eighteen products which it had been suggested were affected by monopoly or other conditions within the purview of the reconstituted Monopolies Commission. In succeeding annual reports the number of commodities so listed has tended to decline. Table IV gives the number of references made in each year by the Board of Trade to the Monopolies Commission and the number of inquiries completed. The number of products listed by the Board of Trade each year as being the subject of representations is also included.

TABLE IV

ACTIVITIES UNDER THE ACT OF 1948

Year	Number of references from Board of Trade during year	Number of references pending at end of year	Number of reports made by Monopolies Commission	Number of products listed by Board of Trade as the subject of representations
1949	6	6	0	36
1950	2	7	1	29
1951	2	7	2	38
1952	3[a]	6	3[b]	38
1953	5[c]	8	3[c]	41
1954	4	11	1	26
1955	6[a]	12	5	70
1956	3	4	7[d]	18
1957	1[e]	5	0	13
1958	0	4	1	10
1959	0	3	1	10

[a]Including one requirement for a general study.

[b]Two references were covered by one report.

[c]A report was completed in one reference as to the facts and the reference was then varied to include consideration of the public interest. The matter is included in the above tables as two references and two reports.

[d]Before its reconstitution on October 31, 1956, the Commission completed reports on all references previously made to it with the exception of one matter which was continued and one general reference and three specific references which were allowed to lapse. Three new matters were referred to the reconstituted Commission late in 1956.

[e]A reference under section 12 of the Act of 1948 requiring the Commission to report whether and to what extent the parties concerned have complied with the recommendation in the Commission's report on the supply of imported timber (July, 1953).

With the work of the Monopolies Commission now confined largely to the defined field of monopoly and export arrangements, the judicial review of agreements by the Restrictive Practices Court has become the most important feature of the control of restrictive arrangements in the United Kingdom. Under the Act of 1956 the registration of restrictive agreements of the kinds defined in the legislation was to proceed in accordance with orders issued by the Board of Trade and confirmed by Parliament. The first order of the Board of Trade came into operation on November 30, 1956, and required registration of certain classes of agreement within the following three months. In general, the order embraced agreements affecting prices, terms or conditions of sale or purchase, and discrimination as to supply or purchase of goods. In the main, therefore, the order included practices which had been referred to in the report of the Monopolies Commission on collective discrimination and also those relating to the fixing of common prices. As previously mentioned, the latter practice had been the subject of a reference to the Monopolies Commission which was withdrawn on the enactment of the new legislation.

When the public register was opened in April, 1957, about 1,000 agreements were on file out of about 1,400 which had been submitted up to that time. By the end of 1957 there were about 1,550 agreements on the register and an additional 300 or so were being examined to see if they were registrable. A second registration order was approved by Parliament on December 2, 1957, and required registration by March 31, 1958, of all other classes of agreements covered by the Act. These consist mainly of market-sharing agreements and agreements imposing restrictions on types or quantities of goods to be produced.[19] The addition of agreements registered as a result of the second registration order and the filing of new agreements brought the total number of agreements entered on the register to 2,200.[20]

The principle in the Restrictive Trade Practices Act is that all agreements entered on the public register should be examined by the Restrictive Practices Court, which will decide on the grounds set out in the Act whether all or any of the restrictive features of the agreements are in the public interest. Until the Court has decided that an agreement is not in the public interest it may remain in force.

As previously mentioned, when the Restrictive Trade Practices Act first came into force the Board of Trade exercised its authority to direct the Registrar as to the first cases to be brought before the Restrictive Practices Court. In July, 1957, the Attorney-General, in answer to a question in the House of Commons, stated that proceedings had been started by the Registrar in connection with twenty agreements listed in the first direction given by the Board of Trade.[21] When the Restrictive Practices Court sat for the first time in April, 1958, counsel for the Registrar informed the Court that thirty-nine cases were in preparation to come before the Court.[22]

[19]Rupert L. Sich, "Current Legislation in the United Kingdom Dealing with Restrictive Business Agreements," in *Proceedings, International Conference*, p. 14.

[20]E. P. A., *Guide*, United Kingdom, 2:10.

[21]*Hansard*, July 23, 1957, col. 191.

[22]*The Times*, April 23, 1958.

CONDUCT OF INQUIRIES

Canada

When the Director of Investigation and Research under Canadian legislation is put upon inquiry in any of the ways already described, he usually proceeds by having brought together information which is readily available in regard to the matter. The files of the Combines Branch may contain some information, and other government departments may be able to provide relevant statistics or other general information. Additional information may also be secured informally by correspondence or interviews with those who may be engaged in the particular line of commerce or who may have knowledge of its practices. Only when such information justifies more extensive inquiry is an investigation carried further and, as already mentioned, only a small proportion of the files opened in the Combines Branch is carried beyond this stage.

When it becomes necessary to proceed more formally the Director may secure from a member of the Restrictive Trade Practices Commission authorization to have combines officers visit the premises of those engaged in the trade and examine their records for documentary evidence. In the same way the Director may also have witnesses called to give evidence or may secure authority to require written returns of information. Documents taken away for examination or copying by representatives of the Director must be returned within forty days unless the time is extended by the Commission.

Canadian legislation provides that all inquiries are to be conducted in private, although the chairman of the Commission may order that all or part of any proceedings shall be conducted in public. Persons who are called to give evidence in an inquiry are usually examined before a member of the Commission, but the Combines Investigation Act provides that a member may direct witnesses to appear before another person named in the order.

A witness called to give evidence in an inquiry is permitted to be represented by counsel and a member of the Commission may permit a person whose conduct is being inquired into to be represented by counsel. In view of the requirement that proceedings are to be conducted in private the evidence of witnesses from one company is usually taken without other persons being present. However, when there is no objection and the progress of the inquiry would be aided, counsel for other parties may be permitted to attend. Although at this stage witnesses are called to assist the Director in securing information, there is opportunity for a witness to present information he considers relevant to the inquiry either by oral statement or by filing documentary evidence.

At any stage of an inquiry the Director is empowered to discontinue further inquiry if he concludes that the matter does not justify further action, but if evidence has been brought before the Commission its concurrence is required. On discontinuing an inquiry the Director must report the matter to the Minister of Justice, who has authority to instruct the Director to continue the inquiry.

When the Director is of the opinion that the evidence in an inquiry discloses a situation contrary to the legislation, he prepares a statement of the evidence for submission to the Commission and to parties against whom allegations are made as being responsible for the alleged violation. This statement is a comprehensive review of all the information obtained in the inquiry relating to the practice or situation which is called into question. The following view as to the nature of the statement was given by the MacQuarrie Committee in its report:

> We are of opinion that, save in the exceptional cases where, for the protection of legitimate trade interests or for similar reason it is necessary to withhold evidence, the parties should be furnished in the allegations with the material and controversial evidence against them so that they may have opportunity to be heard with respect to it. No evidence should be used to substantiate a charge of misconduct alleged against any person unless that person shall first have had such opportunity. We understand that this is, in fact, the present practice.[23]

The statement of evidence usually contains a description of the industry as well as of the individual companies in it. Where relevant statistics are available from the Dominion Bureau of Statistics or from returns made to the Director, such information is also included in the statement. In an extensive inquiry the statement of evidence is a document of considerable length, and in addition to a review of the evidence contains the Director's allegation as to the nature and effects of the practices or situation disclosed. In view of the fact that proceedings in the inquiry are conducted in private the statement of evidence does not become a public document, although extensive

[23]*Report of the Committee to Study Combines Legislation and Interim Report on Resale Price Maintenance* (Ottawa: Department of Justice, 1955), p. 33.

references may be made to it in the published report of the Commission.

Unless the Commission requests the Director to supplement the statement of evidence by additional information, this concludes the Director's work in so far as the conduct of the inquiry is concerned, and the Commission then undertakes its functions of hearing argument by the Director and the parties, reviewing the evidence and representations, and making a report to the Minister.

In the case of "general inquiries" in which no specific allegations are made by the Director against any parties, the matter of privacy does not have the same significance. In such general inquiries the Commission may hold public hearings to secure as wide an expression of views as possible on the practices under inquiry and may make the Director's statement available to anyone interested.

United States

The Antitrust Division of the Department of Justice does not possess any compulsory powers of investigation which can be used without the contemplation or initiation of criminal or civil proceedings.[24] The initial stage of an investigation by the Antitrust Division is sometimes described as a "preliminary inquiry."[25] At this stage an attorney to whom a particular case has been assigned collects available information to see whether there are grounds for proceeding with a more complete investigation. This preliminary inquiry, which proceeds on a voluntary basis in securing information, may be made by the antitrust attorney himself or with the assistance of the F.B.I.

When the Assistant Attorney General in charge of the Antitrust Division approves a recommendation that a full investigation should be undertaken, the usual course is to prepare a detailed description of the type of information required and the most likely persons or places for its procurement for the guidance of F.B.I. agents. The investigation may still be conducted on a voluntary basis if the parties concerned are willing to co-operate by furnishing information and making their business records available for examination. This method of investigation is often sufficient.[26] If the investigation cannot be made adequately in this way and the Antitrust Division has to use com-

[24]See *Report of the Attorney General's National Committee to Study the Antitrust Laws* (Washington, 1955), p. 344.

[25]See Hollabaugh, "Development of an Antitrust Case," p. 17.

[26]*Report of the Attorney General's Committee*, p. 344.

pulsory means, a decision must be made whether to invoke the powers of a federal grand jury who can compel the attendance of witnesses and the production of documents, or to file a civil complaint which would permit the use of compulsory discovery processes. The latter procedure, however, contemplates that the Antitrust Division is already in possession of information which establishes the existence of a situation contrary to law, and the courts frown upon the bringing of an action in order that further investigation may be carried on to discover whether the action should be pursued. There may also be criticism if a grand jury investigation is used for the purpose of a civil complaint. Various proposals have been made to give the Antitrust Division some process of civil discovery before the filing of a complaint for use when voluntary co-operation cannot be secured, but legislation along such lines has not yet been adopted.[27]

The commencement of an antimonopoly investigation by the Federal Trade Commission is very similar to that by the Antitrust Division and by the Canadian Combines Branch. Examination is first made of the hundreds of informal complaints which are received each year by the Bureau of Investigation of the Commission to select those which relate to matters within the Commission's jurisdiction, and which indicate a matter of sufficient importance to justify further inquiry. The first step is to assign the matter to a project attorney who pursues the inquiry by correspondence in a simple case. If the matter is complex it is referred to the appropriate field office, where it is assigned to an attorney examiner. The investigation then usually proceeds by the attorney examiner visiting the parties complained against to indicate the substance of the complaint and to request relevant information. Competitors and consumers may also be interviewed and information sought from them. The Federal Trade Commission endeavours at this stage to carry on the investigation without resorting to compulsory powers for the examination and copying of documents, the calling of witnesses, or the production of documents at an investigation hearing. The following description has been given of the Commission's procedure in an investigation:

> Important antimonopoly cases require complete and prompt development of all relevant facts. This should be fully performed prior to complaint. Where the parties refuse to co-operate during an investigation, the Commission's process will

[27] *Ibid.*, pp. 345–6.

> generally take the form of a subpoena returnable at an investigational hearing as provided in the Commission's Rules of Practice, Rule III (b). As a general rule, the Commission employs this method only where it has been impossible to arrange a co-operative examination of records at the offices of the parties.[28]

When the attorney examiner completes the preliminary investigation, he prepares a report summarizing the information obtained and recommending the course of action he thinks the Commission should take. This report is reviewed by the branch manager and then forwarded to the Bureau of Investigation for consideration. If the Bureau decides that a case should be closed the matter is reviewed by the Commission's secretary and then by the Commission itself. If the recommendation is for the issuance of a complaint the matter is transferred to the Bureau of Litigation.

In the Bureau of Litigation attorneys are assigned to study the investigational files and recommend the form of complaint to be issued. The draft complaint is considered by the Commission itself and a decision made whether a formal complaint should be issued. If a formal complaint is issued, the subsequent proceedings are conducted as in a trial with attorneys of the Bureau of Litigation presenting oral testimony of witnesses, introducing documentary evidence to support the complaint, and rebutting the evidence which may be offered by the defence.

The formal complaint is drawn up as a legal document containing brief descriptions of the respondents and their business, followed by a recital of alleged violations of the law. In a complex case the documents may run to twenty or more pages. There is no detailed review of the evidence obtained during the investigation except to support the offences charged in the complaint.

United Kingdom

Under the Act of 1948 the Monopolies Commission was given power to summon witnesses to give evidence under oath, to require the production of documents and the furnishing of returns or information by any person carrying on a trade or business. The Commission was not given power to enter premises and inspect records. It appears,

[28]Harry A. Babcock, "Legal Investigation," in American Bar Association, Section of Antitrust Law, *Proceedings, April 1–2, 1954*, p. 164.

however, that the Commission in collecting information has proceeded largely on a co-operative basis with the parties concerned and has not found it necessary to rely on its compulsory powers to any great extent.[29]

On receiving a reference from the Board of Trade the Commission has advertised its readiness to receive written submissions from anyone interested in the inquiry. Only scant information has been volunteered in response to such general invitations and the Commission has sought the views of users and consumers by means of questionnaires.[30] At a preliminary stage of the investigation when the staff of the Commission is engaged in compiling general information about the industry, the Commission invites the parties concerned to an informal meeting at which the procedure of the Commission is explained. Various questionnaires may be sent to the trade associations and members of the industry. If an association is involved in an inquiry its records are examined in detail by the Commission's staff on a voluntary basis and summaries or extracts prepared from them. In completing the compilation of the factual information the Commission may hold an oral hearing to clarify any matters of fact left doubtful by the written evidence. While the inquiry has been proceeding along the two lines mentioned the Commission may also have undertaken an accounting investigation, which covers such matters as turnover, costs, prices, and profits as well as the extent of the trade controlled by the group.[31]

When the Commission has ascertained the facts by these means of investigation, it informs the parties of its provisional conclusions on the facts, and if these are critical the Commission usually indicates some ways in which the practices questioned may be held to be against the public interest. At the same time the parties are invited to attend a hearing before the Commission to present their views. The proceedings at this stage will be described in the next section.

Under the Restrictive Trade Practices Act the field of investigation is established by the fact that, in principle, all registered agreements are to be brought by the Registrar before the Restrictive Practices Court for examination. The Registrar must determine the order in which cases are to be prepared for examination by the Court and this

[29]See Dame Alix Kilroy, "The Task and Methods of the Monopolies Commission," *Progress*, Summer, 1953, p. 129. Reprinted from *Transactions of the Manchester Statistical Society*, March, 1953.

[30]*Ibid.*, p. 129.

[31]See E.P.A., *Guide*, United Kingdom, 2:12.

has been left to his discretion apart from the general directions given by the Board of Trade when the Act came into force.

The Registrar has power to give notice to persons he believes are parties to registrable agreements which have not been registered to furnish him with particulars of such agreements. The Registrar also has the same powers to secure supplemental information in regard to an agreement which has been registered. In exercising this authority the Registrar may apply to the High Court, not the Restrictive Practices Court, for an order for a person to be examined on oath and to produce documents or information. An alternative procedure is also provided, in the case of default in furnishing particulars for registration, for the Registrar to apply to the High Court for an order requiring the furnishing of particulars within such time as the Court may specify. The High Court is also given jurisdiction to receive an application from any person party to an agreement for a declaration that the agreement is not registrable. One of the first proceedings under the new legislation involved the question whether a certain type of agreement between automobile dealers and the manufacturer was required to be registered. The Court decided that the particular agreements were excepted from the Act of 1956.[32]

The following comment on the duties of the Registrar was made in the *Board of Trade Journal* when notice was given of the first group of agreements on which proceedings would be taken:

> In each case the Court has to decide whether the restrictions contained in any agreement by virtue of which it is registrable are contrary to the public interest or not. The duty of the Registrar is to give the Court all possible assistance in reaching its decision, and in everyday terms this means he must try to ensure that all the cards are on the table. He will therefore be getting in touch very shortly with anyone he believes to be able to assist the Court with evidence about the agreements listed above.
>
> Anyone else who may be able to provide evidence from his own experience of results of any of these agreements which he thinks affect the public interest is asked to communicate as early as possible with the Solicitor to the Registrar. . . .[33]

It would appear that under the Act of 1956 the Registrar could

[32]*In re Austin Motor Company Ltd.'s Agreements*, [1957] L.R. 1 R.P. 6.
[33]*Board of Trade Journal*, April 27, 1957, p. 946.

exercise the powers for the examination of witnesses and for the production of documentary evidence in gathering information for use in proceedings before the Restrictive Practices Court. Proceedings taken under the Act so far indicate that the Registrar will proceed as far as possible on a voluntary basis and make infrequent use of the compulsory powers.

Proceedings in connection with cases brought before the Restrictive Practices Court are governed by rules of procedure made for the Court by the Lord Chancellor, who is authorized by the Act of 1956 to make rules "for securing, by means of preliminary statements of facts and contentions, and by the production of documents, the administration of interrogatories and other methods of discovery, that all material facts and considerations are brought before the Court by all parties to any proceedings, including the Registrar."[34] The Court Rules provide that the institution of proceedings shall be by a notice of reference made by the Registrar stating the agreement or agreements which are referred to the Court. Before the formal commencement of proceedings it is the practice of the Registrar to send out a preliminary warning letter to the parties to an agreement informing them that it is proposed to refer the agreement to the Court.

When the Restrictive Trade Practices Act was adopted there appears to have been expectation that registration in itself would lead to the abandonment or modification of restrictive agreements in a considerable number of cases where the parties to them would not wish to have the agreements subjected to the examination of the Court in the form in which they had previously been operative. It also appears to have been expected that if the Court in early cases found agreements of certain types to be against the public interest this would lead to the cancellation or alteration of other agreements registered of similar effect without formal proceedings being taken in connection with them. Both expectations have been borne out in the operation of the legislation so far. In an address to the Economics Section of the British Association in September, 1959, the Registrar said that up to August 7, 1959, preliminary warning letters had been sent in 380 cases and that parties to 250 agreements had responded that the agreements were abandoned or were being abandoned. In the same period parties to 350 other agreements had notified the Registrar that their

[34]The Restrictive Practices Court Rules, 1957, were made by statutory instrument laid before Parliament on April 11, 1957. See Andrew Martin, *Restrictive Trade Practices and Monopolies* (London, 1957), pp. 228–54.

agreements had been abandoned or were about to be abandoned.[85]

When an agreement is to be brought before the Restrictive Practices Court for examination the case must be prepared for trial by the Registrar and the parties to the agreement. The staff of the Registrar must consider the main lines of the case to be presented, including the witnesses to be called. When economic and financial analyses appear likely to be of assistance to the Court the Registrar may retain economists and accountants to appear as expert witnesses. The administrative staff of the Registrar prepares instructions for the Treasury Solicitor who acts for the Registrar in the proceedings and who is responsible for briefing the barristers who act as counsel for the Registrar before the Court.[86]

The evidence which the Registrar and the parties to an agreement intend to present to the Court is set out in pleadings which are filed with the Court in advance of the hearing and contain the "facts and matters" upon which each will rely.[87] In one of the first cases in which proceedings were taken the Restrictive Practices Court emphasized that "to save time and expense it is desirable that as much evidence as possible should be put into writing, and that statements of witnesses and memoranda be submitted to the court and shown to the other side in advance of the final hearing."[88] The directions of the Court thus require that the full case of the Registrar and of the parties to the agreement be put in written form before trial.

HEARINGS AND OPINIONS

Canada

When the Restrictive Trade Practices Commission receives a statement of evidence from the Director of Investigation and Research, it is required to fix a time and place so that persons against whom allegations are made in the statement will have full opportunity to be heard in person or by counsel. In giving notice of the hearing the Commission customarily advises the parties that they will have opportunity of re-examining any witness who gave evidence at the investigation stage or of calling additional witnesses or of submitting additional documentary evidence. Such evidence, which may also include the

85*Financial Times*, Sept. 4, 1959.

86E.P.A., *Guide*, United Kingdom, 2:9.

87*Ibid.*, 2:9.

88*In re Chemists' Federation Agreement*, [1958] L.R. 1 R.P. 43.

testimony of expert witnesses, such as engineers, economists, or accountants, is presented to the Commission during the first part of the hearing so that the Commission may hear argument based on all the evidence, including that presented by the industry as well as that previously obtained. The Director makes his argument as to the effect of the evidence and reply is then made by each of the parties represented at the hearing. A brief rebuttal may then be made by the Director and sometimes supplementary briefs or statements are filed after the hearing to clear up any factual points which may seem doubtful.

The Commission hearing in a major case is generally extensive and may require sessions of a week or more. In addition to considerable evidence which may be given by persons directly concerned in the industry, there may be voluminous special studies prepared by accountants or economists which may lead to considerable oral evidence as well. In the inquiry into the distribution of gasoline at retail in the Vancouver area[39] two economists were called to give evidence on behalf of the gasoline retailers. In the Commission's report of 128 pages, fifteen pages were devoted to a review of this evidence and a further fourteen pages to the Commission's appraisal of it. A large part of the report of the Commission dealing with the metal culvert industry[40] is devoted to the examination and appraisal of statistical and other evidence presented to the Commission by two economists retained by the leading manufacturer to make special studies of competitive conditions in the industry.

After concluding its hearing the Commission is required to make a report to the Minister of Justice which, in the words of the Act, "shall review the evidence and material, appraise the effect on the public interest of arrangements and practices disclosed in the evidence and contain recommendations as to the application of remedies provided in this Act or other remedies."[41] In arriving at its conclusions the Commission is directed by the Act to consider the statement of the Director "together with such further or other evidence or material as the Commission considers advisable."[42]

[39]*Report Concerning an Alleged Combine in the Distribution and Sale of Gasoline at Retail in the Vancouver Area* (Ottawa: Department of Justice, 1954).

[40]*Report Concerning the Manufacture, Distribution and Sale of Metal Culverts and Related Products* (Ottawa: Department of Justice, 1957).

[41]Combines Investigation Act, R.S.C. 1952, s. 19(1).

[42]*Ibid.*, s. 18(3).

A report of the Commission is required to be made public by the Minister of Justice within thirty days of its receipt, unless the Commission recommends against publication. In the latter case the Minister has authority to publish the report in whole or in part.

On receipt of the Commission's report the Minister considers whether in view of the situation disclosed any of the remedies provided by the legislation should be invoked. Although the report expresses the Commission's opinion as to whether there are restrictive practices operating or likely to operate against the public interest, the Commission has not followed a practice of recommending prosecution or non-prosecution, but may recommend that the parties be placed under a court order to restrain them from continuing the detrimental practices, or may recommend other remedies provided by the legislation such as modification of the customs tariff. If, after receipt of the Commission's report, the Minister considers court proceedings, the policy has generally been followed of first securing an opinion on the evidence from counsel retained for this purpose. The Act as amended in 1952 provides that the court, in the event of a conviction, may issue an order prohibiting the continuance or repetition of the offence. In the case of a conviction with respect to the formation or operation of a merger or monopoly, the court may order dissolution. The court may also order the parties convicted to make returns from time to time within a period of three years disclosing fully operations carried on since the date of the offence. Since the passage of the amendments in 1952 there have been no proceedings in which an order for dissolution has been sought, but there have been a number of cases in which a restraining order has been issued and the validity of such orders as an adjunct of criminal procedure has been upheld on appeal to the Supreme Court of Canada.[43]

The constitutional aspects which have led to reliance upon criminal proceedings under anti-combines legislation in Canada are described in the report of the MacQuarrie Committee as follows:

> . . . it must be pointed out that monopoly legislation raises intricate constitutional problems in Canada. Up to now, with few exceptions publicity and criminal prosecution have been the principal means used against monopolies, mainly because the legislation has been based on the federal power over criminal law, and has been upheld by the courts on this ground.

[43]*The Goodyear Tire & Rubber Company of Canada, Limited et al.* v. *The Queen*, [1956] S.C.R. 303–14.

> There has been a widely held view that the jurisdiction of the Federal Government did not extend beyond the criminal field. This partly explains why other types of action, which have been adopted in other countries, have not been used in Canada. On the other hand, there is another view to the effect that Parliament has under the trade and commerce head of the British North America Act complete jurisdiction in monopoly situations, at least in those involving international and interprovincial trade. However, neither of these views has been sanctioned by judicial decision so that they cannot be considered as settled.[44]

By amendments made to the Combines Investigation Act in 1960 provisions for the use of court orders of injunction or dissolution were widened to include them as an alternative to prosecution. Under the amendments made in 1952 application for such orders could be made by the Crown in the case of an incipient offence but there was some doubt whether the provisions would have embraced a situation in which an offence had been completed. In addition to providing an alternative to prosecution by way of a court injunction, the recent amendments to the Act confer upon the Exchequer Court concurrent jurisdiction with that of the superior courts of the provinces with respect to prosecutions for offences against the anti-combines legislation or to entertain applications for orders of injunction or dissolution. Applications for such orders may be made at the discretion of the Attorney-General in either the Exchequer Court or a superior court of criminal jurisdiction in the province, but proceedings by way of prosecution in the Exchequer Court may be taken by the Attorney-General only with the consent of all parties. Appeals from decisions or orders of the Exchequer Court would be taken directly to the Supreme Court of Canada. When the provisions giving jurisdiction to the Exchequer Court are proclaimed they will introduce an alternative procedure which has hitherto not been employed in Canada.

Other remedies, in addition to criminal proceedings, are provided in Canadian legislation. Action may be taken to prevent the improper use of patent or trade mark rights in connection with restrictive practices. If the Governor in Council is satisfied that the tariff is facilitating the operation of a combine, customs duties may be reduced or removed.

The first reports of the Commission, following the amendments made in 1952, were met with criticism in some quarters, apart from

[44]*Report of the Committee to Study Combines Legislation*, p. 7.

the industries directly involved, that the Commission was not exploring fully and taking into account in its reports all the "effects" which might have been brought about in an industry during the period when the restrictive practices and arrangements called in question had been operative.[45] As more reports of the Commission have been published some of the first critics have made revisions in their views, and other economists have pointed out that to attempt to explore fully all possible "effects" would not only be a task of such magnitude as to preclude effective administration, but would have to be attempted in the absence of any conclusive methods of testing the discernible consequences.[46]

United States

Following an investigation by the Antitrust Division a decision is made by the Attorney General of the United States on the recommendation of the Assistant Attorney General in charge of the Antitrust Division whether the matter should be pursued by criminal or civil proceedings. It has already been mentioned that if it were not found possible to complete the investigation on a voluntary basis a decision might be made at that stage to use the investigatory powers of a grand jury under federal criminal law.

The policy of the Department of Justice toward the use of criminal action in antitrust proceedings was stated by the Attorney General in 1954 as follows:

> . . . Criminal proceedings will be limited to the obvious form of *per se* illegality. Thus, of ten criminal actions instituted from May to the end of 1953, all but one involved practices which

[45]See V. W. Bladen and S. Stykolt, "Combines Policy and the Public Interest," in W. Friedmann (ed.), *Anti-Trust Laws: A Comparative Symposium* (Toronto, 1956), pp. 45–95. See also W. Friedmann, "Monopoly, Reasonableness and the Public Interest in the Canadian Anti-Combines Law," *Canadian Bar Review*, Feb., 1955, pp. 133–63.

[46]See S. Stykolt, "In Defence of the Canadian Consumer," *Business Quarterly*, University of Western Ontario, Summer, 1956, pp. 118–21; G. E. Britnell, V. C. Fowke, M. F. Timlin and K. A. H. Buckley, *Workable Competition and Monopoly*, A Submission presented to the Royal Commission on Canada's Economic Prospects at Public Hearings in Ottawa (Saskatoon, 1956); Robert Solo, "The U.S. Attorney General's Report on the Antitrust Laws," *Canadian Bar Review*, June–July, 1956, pp. 669–90; G. W. Wilson, "Anti-Combines and Injury to the Public," *Canadian Journal of Economics and Political Science*, Feb., 1957, pp. 121–7; J. N. Wolfe, "Some Empirical Issues in Canadian Combines Policy," *Canadian Journal of Economics and Political Science*, Feb., 1957, pp. 113–21.

> courts had persistently held to be *per se* violations. With one exception, these criminal cases struck at activities such as price-fixing, allocation of territories or customers, and boycotts. . . .[47]

If the evidence brought before the grand jury supports allegations of violation of the antitrust law the offences will be charged in the form of an indictment. This will describe the defendants, the nature of the trade and products involved, the particular offences which are alleged to have been committed, and the effects of the practices or arrangements. In addition to, or instead of a criminal indictment, the Antitrust Division may lay a civil complaint based on its investigation. This will also describe the defendants, the nature of the trade and products involved, and the offences charged. The complaint will also contain proposed remedies which the court will be asked to order. These may embrace such actions as the dissolution of an offending association and orders prohibiting the continuance or repetition of the offences or positive requirements as to future conduct. In the case of a monopoly brought about by merger or acquisition the court may be asked to order divestiture of particular assets or to prohibit future acquisitions. If patents are involved the court may be asked to order that the patents or future patent rights be made available for use by other parties. The proceedings, whether criminal or civil, are conducted in the regular federal courts in the usual way. While the indictments and complaints may contain, in major cases, a good deal of descriptive material about the operations of an industry, this is necessarily greatly abbreviated and does not present all the information which has been obtained by investigation.

More than 75 per cent of all civil antitrust actions instituted by the Antitrust Division are terminated by a consent judgment. This results when the government and defendants are able to reach agreement as to the form of remedy before trial, and the court is then asked to embody the settlement in a court order. In recent years there have been negotiations in some civil cases before the complaint has been laid, which have led in a few instances to the application for a consent judgment being made at the same time that the complaint is filed.[48]

[47]Herbert Brownell, Jr., "Economic Liberty under the Antitrust Laws," in Van Cise and Dunn (eds.), *How to Comply with the Antitrust Laws*; p. 23.

[48]See Stanley N. Barnes, "Settlement by Consent Judgment," in American Bar Association, Section of Antitrust Law, *Proceedings, April 1–2, 1954*, pp. 8–13.

Reference has already been made to formal proceedings under the Federal Trade Commission Act which begin with a complaint issued by the Commission alleging a violation of the laws within its jurisdiction. The matter is assigned to one of the group of hearing examiners on the Commission's staff. Procedure is governed by the Administrative Procedure Act which applies to federal agencies, and which requires that an examiner should take no part in investigatory activities or be assisted by investigative or prosecuting officials in reaching his decision. The hearing examiner conducts public hearings on the complaint, at which the Commission attorney supporting the complaint leads documentary and oral evidence and the respondents have the right to present evidence and cross-examine witnesses. After the reception of evidence the Commission attorney supporting the complaint may file proposed findings and conclusions to which oral argument may be addressed by attorneys on both sides. Within thirty days after the record is closed the hearing examiner is required to file an "initial decision" setting out his findings and conclusions and an appropriate cease and desist order if the complaint is sustained. The decision sets out findings on all material issues of fact and the reasons for the conclusions reached. Such initial decision, unless appealed by the attorney supporting the complaint or by a respondent, or stayed by the Commission itself, becomes the decision of the Commission. Orders of the Commission are appealable to a federal court of appeal which has power to affirm, modify, or set aside the Commission's order, but "the findings of the Commission as to the facts, if supported by evidence, shall be conclusive." The fact that the formal proceedings of the Commission are conducted as a trial means that the decisions must be made in legal form with due emphasis given to all points of legal argument. In recent years an effort has been made to have the findings assume more of a descriptive character, as indicated in the following statement made in 1954 by Edward F. Howrey, then chairman of the Commission:

> . . . the findings should include a specific statement of the salient facts, as well as the conclusions of fact. They should give a narrative and descriptive account of the controversy involved and the issues presented. In the recent Pillsbury opinion, an attempt was made to set forth the facts in a manner that may serve as a partial pattern for future findings.[49]

[49]Edward F. Howrey, "Federal Trade Commission and the Administrative Process," in Van Cise and Dunn (eds.), *How to Comply with the Antitrust Laws*, p. 35.

Since May, 1955, the use of consent orders has become more frequent in the disposition of complaints issued by the Federal Trade Commission. Under amendments to its rules made at that time, the Federal Trade Commission authorized hearing examiners to accept or reject as the basis for initial decisions stipulations containing proposed consent orders, and eliminated the previous requirement that consent settlements contain findings of fact and conclusion of law. A consent cease-and-desist order may be negotiated at any stage of the proceeding and before any evidence has been presented.

United Kingdom

The proceedings of the Monopolies Commission in the United Kingdom, like those of the Restrictive Trade Practices Commission in Canada, have been conducted in private. During the investigation stage witnesses are examined individually and there is no cross-examination except for questions by members of the Commission. There is usually no appearance by counsel at this stage.[50] At the final hearing, after notice has been given of the Commission's tentative conclusions, the parties are usually represented by counsel, who present their answers and deal with any additional points which may be raised by members of the Commission. Following the hearing the members of the Commission undertake the completion of the report. At this stage further information and comment may be sought from the parties concerned if some matters arise on which further explanation is desired.

The Monopolies Commission is required to include in its report "such a survey of the general position in respect of the subject matter of the investigation, and of the developments which have led to that position, as are in their opinion expedient for facilitating a proper understanding of the matter"[51] and where a reference includes the aspect of public interest the Commission is directed to consider whether any action could be taken to remedy the situation and may make recommendations as to the type of action.

The fulfilling of the first function has led the Monopolies Commission to gather information in each inquiry on the history of associations and on the development of restrictive practices under conditions prevailing in the past. The resulting report has, necessarily, been very extensive in character.

[50]See Kilroy, "Task and Methods of the Monopolies Commission," p. 129.

[51]Monopolies and Restrictive Trade Practices (Inquiry and Control) Act, 1948 (11 & 12 Geo. VI, c. 66), s. 7(1).

Reports of the Monopolies Commission dealing with the effects on the public interest as well as the "facts" are required to be laid before Parliament by the Board of Trade, except that the Board of Trade is authorized to withhold publication of a report or any part of it when publication is considered to be contrary to the public interest, and may omit particulars in any report which might reveal trade secrets in a way which would damage legitimate business interests. While not required to do so, the Board of Trade may also present to Parliament reports of the Commission on references restricting inquiry to the "facts."

Although the Act of 1948 did not attempt to define the public interest, it did indicate certain general conditions which "amongst other things" the Commission could take into account in appraising the effect of restrictive practices. These general conditions embrace the need for greater efficiency, the most effective use of labour and other resources, the development of technical improvement, and the adequate supply of goods at favourable prices. These directions are in very general terms and are not mutually exclusive, so that they have not been considered as affording any clear guidance as to where the balance of public interest lies but rather as indicating that all relevant factors must be taken into account.[52]

Although the Monopolies Commission was directed by the Act of 1948 to make recommendations for the correction of detrimental conditions which it considered resulted from the restrictive practices investigated, the continuation of the practices reported against was not made a legal offence. It appears to have been hoped that business firms would modify their practices voluntarily in the light of the findings of the Commission. Provision was made, however, for the appropriate Minister to take action, where he considered it desirable, by way of statutory order which would be effective when approved by Parliament. Such an order could require the termination of a restrictive agreement or make unlawful an act of discrimination. No authority is given to order the alteration of corporate structures or acquisitions. Under the amendments made in 1956 the scope of future statutory orders will not extend to agreements registrable under the Restrictive Trade Practices Act. Prior to 1956 only one statutory order was issued, but annual reports of the Board of Trade under the Act of 1948 describe a number of instances in which restrictions which had been found detrimental in reports of the Monopolies Commission had been

[52]Kilroy, "Task and Methods of the Monopolies Commission," pp. 127–8.

abandoned or modified. In a number of cases the action was taken after discussions between the Board of Trade and the parties concerned.

Under the Act of 1956 the Restrictive Practices Court is bound to conclude that an agreement brought before it by the Registrar is contrary to the public interest unless the parties to the agreement establish affirmatively that it comes within one or more of the exceptions specified in the Act and unless the Court is satisfied that benefits are not outweighed by detriment caused to others by the restrictions. The Act sets out seven conditions which the Court can take into consideration. These so-called "gateways" may be grouped as follows: (*a*) the restriction is necessary for public safety, (*b*) the removal of the restriction would deprive the public of specific and substantial advantages, (*c*) the restriction is necessary to offset monopolistic practices by others, (*d*) the removal of the restriction would have a serious effect on employment or export trade, (*e*) the restriction is necessary for the maintenance of another restriction not contrary to the public interest.

As the onus is placed on the parties to an agreement to satisfy the Court that the agreement meets one or more of the specified conditions a trial before the Court is opened by them, and they present their evidence first and after their presentation is concluded evidence is called on behalf of the Registrar. The extensive written pleadings which are exchanged between the parties and submitted to the Court before the trial do not become part of the public record except to the extent that witnesses present such evidence or portions of briefs are read to the Court.[53]

The part which he considers he should take in the examination of an agreement before the Court has been described by the Registrar as follows:

> It is the duty of the Registrar to assist the Court in reaching its decision by trying to secure that all relevant material is before it. We expect that the parties to the agreement will bring forward anything that can be said in its favor under the "benefits" provisions and the task of the Registrar is to test that case thoroughly, but I hope fairly, by cross-examination of the respondents' witnesses and by leading witnesses of his own. Naturally, however, the parties to the agreement are not likely to produce evidence about detriments caused thereby so that the Registrar will probably lead any evidence there may be

[53]*Cartel*, Jan., 1959, p. 33.

> about damage to consumers and also to the public, generally including the sort of considerations that are the field of study of the economist.[54]

The pre-trial preparation of evidence has apparently assisted in reducing the number of days which the Court devotes to the hearing of a case, although the trials of some major cases have run from ten to thirty days.

The Act of 1956 does not specify the form in which a decision is to be given by the Court, except that the decision is to be delivered by the presiding judge and that on a question of fact the judgment shall be final. On a question of law the opinion of the judge or judges on the Court shall prevail, but an appeal shall lie from any decision on a question of law.

An agreement found by the Court to be against the public interest is void, and on application of the Registrar the Court may issue an order restraining persons from giving effect to or enforcing the agreement, or from making any other agreement to like effect. No penalties are provided, but disregard of such an order would be punishable as contempt of court in the ordinary way.

In the first case decided by the Restrictive Practices Court the agreement was found to be against the public interest but the court refused the request of the Registrar that a restraining order should follow as a matter of course, after the parties had undertaken to keep the Registrar informed of the action taken as a result of the Court's declaration.[55] In subsequent cases the practice has been for the Court to accept undertakings from parties to an agreement found to be against the public interest that they will inform the Registrar if they intend to make a similar agreement so that he can apply for a restraining order before they do.

Up to January 1, 1960, the Court had held trials on nine agreements. In only one case[56] was the agreement found consistent with the conditions set out in the Act and in the case of one other agreement one restriction was so held.[57] In all other instances the parties failed to satisfy the Court and the agreements were held to be contrary to the public interest.[58] Thirty-four agreements were undefended after

[54]Sich, "Current Legislation in the United Kingdom," p. 15.
[55]*In re Chemists' Federation Agreement*, [1958] L.R. 1 R.P. 75.
[56]*In re Water-Tube Boilermakers' Agreement*, [1959] L.R. 1 R.P. 285.
[57]*In re Blanket Manufacturers' Agreement*, [1959] L.R. R.P. 271.
[58]Between January 1, 1960, and July 16, 1960, the Restrictive Practices

the Registrar had referred them to the Court and the parties to them consented to orders declaring the agreements void. In addition, 730 agreements had been abandoned or modified so as to remove restrictions covered by the Act of 1956. At the beginning of 1960, there were 120 agreements in preparation for trial before the Court and on the basis of previous experience under the legislation it would be expected that only a small number would actually be brought to trial.

CONCLUDING REMARKS

This brief and incomplete survey of the methods used in Canada, the United States, and the United Kingdom for inquiry into and dealing with trade situations involving monopoly or restrictive practices points up the varied nature of the approaches in the respective countries. The United Kingdom, having only recently adopted legislation in this field and thus having no strong precedents, has been experimenting with different methods. The aim in all three countries has been to prevent limitations on competition which operate to the detriment of the public. In Canada and the United States public policy as interpreted in judicial decisions is to prevent undue restraints of trade, which are considered as those restrictions which seriously affect the public interest in free competition. The recent legislation in the United Kingdom was also introduced with the purpose of reinforcing a "system of free and flexible competitive enterprise."[59] In the report of the Monopolies Commission on collective discrimination it was proposed by the majority signing the report that there should be a general prohibition of defined restrictive practices "for the great majority of agreements would be found not to be in the public interest"[60] and that provision should be made for exceptions on grounds which would be set out in the legislation. This recommenda-

---

Court delivered judgments in two defended cases. In the Phenol Producers' agreement the restrictions were found to be contrary to the public interest (*The Times*, April 8, 1960), and in the Black Bolt and Nut Association's agreement the Court held that the fixed price scheme, except for the provisions relating to special quantity discounts and orders obtained from government departments, was not contrary to the public interest (*The Times*, July 16, 1960).

[59]*Hansard*, March 6, 1956, col. 1955.

[60]*Collective Discrimination: A Report on Exclusive Dealing, Collective Boycotts, Aggregated Rebates and other Discriminatory Trade Practices* (London: H.M.S.O., 1955), p. 85.

tion was not embodied in the legislation subsequently adopted which, as already described, establishes a presumption that restrictive agreements are contrary to the public interest, which cannot be set aside unless the Restrictive Practices Court is satisfied that certain defined conditions are operative. Athough the Court would proceed to examine individual agreements, the Act of 1956 empowers the Court to deal in a summary way with classes of agreements which involve issues previously decided by the Court, so that a series of general judgments may in time be established. Although the procedure under the Act of 1956 falls short of the general prohibition recommended by the Monopolies Commission, it is rather the reverse of proposals sometimes made in Canada and the United States that the onus should be on the investigating agency not only to prove that there has been serious interference with free competition, but that this has produced specific ill effects.[61] Under the British legislation there is a presumption that restrictive agreements are contrary to the public interest, and the onus is placed on the parties to establish that because one or more of certain specified conditions exist an exception is justified.

[61]See Bladen and Stykolt, "Combines Policy and the Public Interest." See also Corwin D. Edwards, *Big Business and the Policy of Competition* (Cleveland, 1956).

Telephone Rates in Canada

ARCHIBALD W. CURRIE

In 1909 Alexander Graham Bell told an audience in Ottawa that "of this you may be sure, the telephone was invented in Canada . . . and the first actual use of telephone lines was in this country."[1] Nevertheless, "it was made in the United States"—made in both the physical and economic senses, for the technological problems were solved and the economics of telephone service worked out by Americans.

THEORY OF TELEPHONE RATES

Like many other enterprises, including universities as Dean Angus has made clear,[2] the telephone industry is one of joint costs. The same equipment produces a number of economic utilities, such as local and long distance calls, one- and two-party service, peak and off-peak communication. Except by use of more or less arbitrary methods, it is considered impossible to allocate correctly the total costs of operation among kinds of service or classes of users. Moreover, the demand of different people for service differs in intensity. A medical doctor absolutely needs a phone:[3] many farmers are in doubt whether it is worth what it costs. Consequently, the rate or selling price of each class of service depends not so much on the cost of service as on the

[1]Alexander Graham Bell, "Recent Developments in the Science of Aviation," in G. H. Brown (ed.), *Addresses Delivered before the Canadian Club of Ottawa* (Ottawa: Mortimer Press, 1910), p. 181.

[2]H. F. Angus, "Economic Theory of a State-Supported University," *Queen's Quarterly*, May, 1932, pp. 261–71.

[3]K. J. Dunstan, later Vice-president of Bell, took the first order for a phone from a doctor in Canada and claimed a "triumph of salesmanship." "Doctors were loath to subscribe, as they did not know how to charge patients for advice given by phone." "History and Development of the Telephone Business," in *Lectures on the Telephone Delivered at the University of Toronto* (The Company, 1927, mimeographed), p. 5.

willingness of the consumer to pay, that is, on what is called value of service.

Despite the importance of value of service, costs are still significant. The total revenue from all services should cover the total expenses of the company including interest and dividends. The price of a few special services is fairly closely related to cost. These include the extra charge for a private branch exchange, a weather-proof set, a loud-ringing bell, and a change in the location of the instrument within the subscriber's home or office. In some instances the relationship between the charge to the subscriber and the cost to the company of providing the service is only approximate. This applies to an additional listing in the directory which is the same for all directories, notwithstanding wide differences in number of pages, circulation, and costs of printing. In 1924 the charge for a hand (or cradle) set was 50 cents a month plus an initial or non-recurring charge of $3.00. Later, customers using desk and hand sets paid 20 and 35 cents a month more than subscribers with wall sets. The companies justified the differences by relative costs of manufacturing and maintaining the instruments and of keeping adequate inventories.[4] By 1950 the differential had been wiped out by improved design and construction of handsets. Cradle phones are preferred by subscribers and will eventually replace other kinds of instruments. Coloured phones which according to the advertisements are "streamlined sets in dark-velvet, cool moss-green, warm pink beige or rich old ivory" are more expensive to manufacture and store than black models. Coiled wire to connect handset and base is somewhat more costly than wire without built-in kinks. The one-time charge of $12 for a phone in pastel colours is also designed to cover extra costs of merchandising.

BUSINESS AND RESIDENCE RATES

The difference in monthly rates on telephone service to residences and businesses are quite pronounced. In Toronto the rates effective

[4]*B.C. Telephone* v. *Vancouver* (1949), Board of Transport Commissioners for Canada, *Judgments, Orders, Regulations, and Rulings* (hereafter cited as J.O.R.R.) vol. 40, p. 215, at p. 245: *Canadian Railway and Transport Cases* (hereafter cited as C.R.T.C.) vol. 66, p. 7, at pp. 54–5. Volumes of C.R.T.C. are numbered consecutively with *Canadian Railway Cases* (cited as C.R.C.). See also F. R. Simpson, "The Handset Telephone: A Problem in Public Utility Regulation," *Journal of Land and Public Utility Economics*, Nov., 1937, pp. 331–42.

November 1, 1958, were $16.25 a month for a business phone and $5.85 for a one-party line to a residence. Such differential pricing is based partly on differences in cost of service.[5] As a rule business phones are busy more often and more continuously than residential ones. Being in use only during business hours, they necessitate the purchase and maintenance of equipment for the heavy day-time peak. Business subscribers should pay for use of the additional equipment for which they are responsible. By comparison, residence phones are used mainly for social purposes, are idle much of the time, and are more likely to be used at off-peak periods, notably in the evening and at weekends. The length of wire or cable needed to connect business phones with each other is frequently shorter than connections between phones in residences, but this is not usually true when businesses locate in suburbs. Any savings on account of shorter milage between business phones are also offset by the higher cost of subterranean cable compared with pole lines, by the difficulty of preventing electrical interference in commercial and factory districts, and by the trouble of repairing "leads" in the walls and floors of office buildings.

Differences, if any, in the quality of service available to business and residence phones are said not to be significant in accounting for the difference in rates between them. Telephone companies try to give the same service to all customers and point out that on any given exchange the mechanism for handling business and other calls is identical. Businesses are not exclusively located in large cities where dial equipment is used. In Ontario a few quite small exchanges already have dial service and one large exchange in Metropolitan Toronto was manually operated until after the Second World War. In short, while admitting that the kind of equipment in the central exchange may affect speed of service, the companies state that all subscribers on any given exchange are treated alike. In fact, the important thing in determining rates by communities or rate groups is not the presence of dial or manual equipment but the number of people who may be called without payment of long distance tolls. The number of subscribers on each local exchange affects both value of service and the cost of making the interconnections. These factors, rather than the quality of service supplied to business and residence

[5]B. J. Sickler, "A Theory of Telephone Rates," *Journal of Land and Public Utility Economics*, May, 1928, pp. 175–88. See also E. Jones and T. C. Bigham, *Principles of Public Utilities* (New York: Macmillan, 1932), pp. 360–75: W. E. Mosher and F. G. Crawford, *Public Utility Regulation* (New York: Harper, 1933), pp. 286–97.

subscribers, determine the relationship between rates for the two classes of service in each rate group.

The explanation of differential pricing between classes of subscribers takes another form. Admittedly, the business rate is high, but if it were lowered, residential rates would have to be increased to provide the company with the same gross revenue which, let us assume, is absolutely essential if it is to meet its operating expenses, taxes, interest, and dividends. If their rates were raised, some occupiers of homes would presumably try to get along without phone service or use pay stations. If this happened, the company's gross revenue would be reduced. In order to provide for all its financial requirements, the company would have to raise its rates on the remaining phones. If this occurred, still more home-owners would have their phones disconnected. In the end, the rate on business phones would have to be raised. Thus, low rates on residential phones make it possible for the company to quote lower, not higher, rates to businesses than otherwise.

To the uninformed it may appear that a monopolistic telephone company overcharges business men and quotes preferential rates to householders. It "holds up" one class of subscribers because it knows that they must pay whatever it demands, since they cannot operate their businesses without a phone. It favours another class of subscribers because they have votes in elections, which have sometimes hinged on the question of public versus private ownership of public utilities. More careful analysis shows that businesses actually gain from the relatively low residential rates: their own rates are lowered because of the low charges quoted to people who cannot or will not pay higher rates. Furthermore, the scheme of differential pricing allows businesses to communicate with a larger number of customers than would be the case if uniform prices were charged to all telephone users. Subject to certain limitations some of which are briefly dealt with later, the difference between business and residence rates has a sound economic justification.

It must be admitted, of course, that the telephone is now so essential to social life that some families would pay a good deal more than they do rather than go without the convenience of a phone. At the same time there are many householders who, to judge by complaints in the press, are marginal users of telephone service. They are in doubt whether it is worthwhile to have a phone at all, and will discontinue service if rates are raised. Certainly if residence rates were set at the same high level as business rates, cancellations would be heavy. Some of the post-war rate increases in Ontario and Quebec were followed by the cancellations of from one to three per cent of the phones in use.

However, it is impossible to ascertain how many of the disconnections were caused by the rate increase as such and how many by deaths, removals from the city, loss of a job, and so on. Disconnections soon were outnumbered by restorations of service and by installations in newly built dwelling units.[6] The net effect of an increase in telephone rates is undoubtedly less when other prices are rising than during periods of general price stability or decline.[7] Moreover, there is a strong upward secular trend in the demand for phone service. In a word, though it is not easy to prove the elasticity of the demand for phone service from the over-all statistics which are published, it is certain that residence rates have to be much lower than business rates if the gross revenues of telephone companies are to be maximized and the optimum number of people given an opportunity to communicate with each other readily and cheaply.

The distinction between a business and a residence is the source of some difficulty. A clergyman is entitled to the residence rate for a phone in his home: a monastery or convent is charged the business toll.[8] A trained nurse used her phone for social calls regularly and got about one professional call a week. According to the Board of Transport Commissioners, which had jurisdiction in this case, a business phone does not become a non-business one because of infrequent use. One business man may use his phone fifty times a day: another only once a day but after all it is open to be used by him, if his business demands it, just as much as that of his neighbour. The nurse was in practically the same position as a dentist, medical doctor, or lawyer who had an office in his house and so she had to pay the business rate.[9] Later, an electrical contractor in Montreal argued that he used his phone almost exclusively for household purposes and rarely for

[6]The annual demand upon Bell Telephone for new phones increased from 80,800 in 1952 to 119,000 in 1957. Of all the households in the Company's territory, 85 per cent had phone service in 1956 and an estimated 89 per cent in 1958.

[7]In Ontario and Quebec the number of long distance calls per phone declined in 1957. This was partly the result of the elimination of long distance calling brought about by extended area service which is described later. The number of calls from public telephones declined considerably when the rate was increased from 5 to 10 cents.

[8]*Desroches* v. *Bell* (1915) 18 C.R.C. 322; *Noviciat de Notre Dame des Anges* v. *Bell* (1914) 17 C.R.C. 277.

[9]*Bayly* v. *Bell* (1910) 11 C.R.C. 190; *Medico-Chirurgical Society* v. *Bell* (1914) 16 C.R.C. 267.

business communications of any kind. He had no office, peddled goods from his car, did little business in Montreal, kept no books apart from a few sales records in the glove compartment of his car, and had discontinued having his home telephone number printed on his business card. Even so, he was obliged to pay the business rate.[10] His position resembled that of a market gardener in an earlier case[11] rather than a business man who had one phone in his office and another in his home and who occasionally received business calls on the latter.

These rulings of the Board often burdened small business subscribers, especially those in larger cities where the difference in the rates for business and residence service is considerable. For example, in the City of Toronto after November 1, 1958, business phone rates range from $8.10 to $16.25 a month compared with $4.50 to $5.85 for residence service. Hence in cities with more than 20,000 phones, Bell of Canada provides message rate service. It permits a specified number of calls per month (90 in Greater Toronto) at a given monthly rate ($9.05) with a charge of 5 cents per outgoing message on the excess above the minimum. This service was introduced to attract marginal business users, such as barbers and cobblers, who felt they could not afford a phone at the standard one-party business rate and who were hard to "pair" for two-party business service. At small exchanges pairing can usually be accomplished without an excessive milage of "leads" or undue deterioration in quality of service. It will be noted that message rate service places no special charge on incoming calls.

GROUPING

Differential pricing is not limited to business and residence phones. Bell of Canada divides the communities it serves into 10 basic groups according to the number of phones and it charges different rates for each group.[12] Group 1 takes in about 120 exchanges with up to 500 phones each. The upper limits of Groups 2 to 9 are (in thousands) 1, 2, 5, 10, 20, 50, 100, and 250 phones. Each of the two communities,

[10]*Mainville* v. *Bell* (1937) 27 J.O.R.R. 352; 47 C.R.C. 279.

[11]*Newman* v. *Bell* (1914) 17 C.R.C. 271.

[12]Until 1950 residence rates for Groups 1 and 2 were identical but business rates were somewhat higher for Group 2. In British Columbia rates were first arranged on a full group basis in 1950. The upper limits of the first nine groups are 250, 750, 1,500, 2,500, 5,000, 10,000, 20,000, 40,000, and 80,000 phones. Group 10 includes communities with over 80,000 phones each.

Greater Toronto and Montreal, has over 250,000 phones. The rates for a one-party residence phone in the different groups are in the approximate ratios of 60, 60, 64, 68, 72, 77, 81, 86, 92, and 100. In order to provide for "fringe" exchanges in Metropolitan Toronto, as described later, Group 10 is divided into three sub-groups with percentage rates for one-party residence phones of 100 for Group 10 (Montreal), 102 for Group 10A (Toronto, Scarborough, Don Mills, Willowdale, Weston, Islington, and New Toronto), and 110.5 for Group 10B (Agincourt, Thornhill, etc.).

Subscribers in Metropolitan Toronto and Montreal pay the highest rates because they can, without paying a long distance toll, talk with a very large number of subscribers over a wide area. It is both difficult and expensive to interconnect about 650,000 phones in the more than 400 square miles included in the Toronto exchange area. It is far less costly to interconnect 200 phones in the single square mile of a town or village. The use of manually operated switchboards and magneto telephones, where one has to turn a crank to ring central or call another subscriber on the same line, keeps down capital investment but involves relatively higher expenses per call for operator's wages than in large automatic or dial exchanges. All things considered, costs of telephone service in small towns are less than in cities.

Differences in value of service between cities are as real as differences in cost. No subscriber in Toronto wants to talk with each of the roughly 649,999 other subscribers in the metropolitan area. At four minutes per call, he would be occupied for over 5,000 eight-hour days or at least 20 years. Still, he has this opportunity, and the willingness of the Company to give such a large number of connections at a flat rate per month should be worth a great deal. Certainly, the potential value of the service to Torontonians is worth much more than the amount of service available at the monthly rate to subscribers in villages and towns. What is more, people in Toronto and Montreal are generally more prosperous than those in rural areas. They are able to pay more: experience proves they are willing to pay more: and so, like the business man, they are charged more. The low rates which are given to subscribers in small communities, who would have their phones disconnected if they were asked to pay more, adds to the gross revenues of the Company. On the assumption that Bell must have a given *quantum* of revenue, low rates to subscribers in Groups 1 and 2 actually reduce the rates of subscribers in Group 10. Besides, these low rates add to the value of service available to subscribers in Toronto, at least potentially. For upon payment of a long distance toll, they are able to communicate with every town, village, and hamlet and with most farms throughout two provinces.[13]

Setting the boundaries of exchange areas has proved troublesome whenever the result has been increased rates or less satisfactory service to some subscribers. Up to 1938 the Board of Transport Commissioners, which has jurisdiction over most of the operations of Bell and of the British Columbia Telephone System, lacked legal power to interfere with exchange boundaries, except where the resultant rates were unreasonable, unjustly discriminatory, unduly preferential, or otherwise contrary to law.[14] In other words, until 1938 the establishment and alteration of exchange boundaries was a matter of internal management for a telephone company except where unjust discrimination resulted.

The problem of rates in neighbouring exchanges can be illustrated by reference to Metropolitan Toronto. Originally all subscribers in Toronto and Leaside (except for Centre Island) had the same monthly rate and they had to pay long distance tolls to subscribers outside this area. People in Weston, then a small town, paid the rates applicable to a relatively small exchange. In time, people moved from Toronto to this and other suburbs. Naturally, they resented being asked to pay long distance charges when they called friends in the city or down-

[13]H. C. Goldenberg, *Report of Government Commercial Enterprise Survey* (Winnipeg: King's Printer, 1940), emphasizes this point in connection with complaints by Winnipeg subscribers of their high rates relative to those on farms and in small villages throughout the province.

[14]*Toronto* v. *Bell* (1913) 15 C.R.C. 142: reheard and reaffirmed in *ibid.*, (1914) 17 C.R.C. 263; *Tinkness* v. *Bell* (1916) 6 J.O.R.R. 100; 20 C.R.C. 249; *North Lancaster* v. *Bell* (1917) 7 J.O.R.R. 314; 21 C.R.C. 220; *Dundas* v. *Bell* (1921) 11 J.O.R.R. 83; 31 C.R.C. 352; *Union of B.C. Municipalities* v. *B.C. Telephone* (1921) 11 J.O.R.R. 325; 27 C.R.C. 381; *Saanich* v. *B.C. Telephone* (1925) 15 J.O.R.R. 63; 31 C.R.C. 364; *Point Grey* v. *B.C. Telephone* (1926) 16 J.O.R.R. 37; 31 C.R.C. 387; *ibid.*, (1928) 18 J.O.R.R. 72; 34 C.R.C. 170; *Quebec-Montmorency Chamber of Commerce* v. *Bell* (1937) 26 J.O.R.R. 423; 46 C.R.C. 203; *Weston* v. *Bell* (1938) 28 J.O.R.R. 179; 48 C.R.C. 145; *Mimico* v. *Bell* (1938) 28 J.O.R.R. 247; 48 C.R.C. 180; *Etobicoke* v. *Bell* (1938) 28 J.O.R.R. 258; 48 C.R.C. 222; *Phillips* v. *Bell* (1940) 30 J.O.R.R. 405; 52 C.R.T.C. 49; *Kohen* v. *Bell* (1940) 30 J.O.R.R. 409; 52 C.R.T.C. 3; *St. Dunstan* v. *Bell* (1948) 38 J.O.R.R. 111; 62 C.R.T.C. 188. The Board apparently lacks the legal power to order Bell to construct lines in order to remove discrimination between a patron whom it serves and one who is served by a competing company. *Lachance* v. *Bell* (1958) 48 J.O.R.R. 291.

town department stores or husbands while at work. These views were shared by some business men in Weston who had frequent dealings with customers and suppliers in Toronto proper. All these patrons were prepared to pay higher monthly basic charges if they could have the same calling privileges as subscribers in Toronto and Leaside. But other residents of Weston, those whose cultural, social, and economic roots remained in what had been an agricultural community, objected to heavier charges for a service to Toronto which they would rarely use.

A compromise was arrived at by allowing subscribers just outside Toronto and Leaside to be served by a city exchange if they wished.[15] These so-called "foreign exchange" subscribers paid more per month than subscribers on the Weston exchange because, of course, they could get in touch with a much larger number of people without calling long distance. They also paid slightly more than subscribers in Toronto because of their distance from the city exchange. The chief drawback of this arrangement was that the foreign exchange subscriber, like anyone else with a city number, had to pay long distance charges to get in touch with other subscribers in Weston even though in his case they might be only a few doors away. Meanwhile, suburban monthly rates were raised because of the steady growth of the number of subscribers listed under the Weston exchange. When most of the patrons in Weston and other communities near Toronto favoured the change, they were given the same service and charged the same rates as Toronto and Leaside.[16]

By 1955 many residents in West Hill, Agincourt, Thornhill, Woodbridge, Malton, Cooksville, and Port Credit, the so-called "second fringe" communities, also wanted to have the same calling privileges as Toronto, Weston, and so on. The second-fringe communities were becoming "dormitory" towns for people who worked in Toronto, and industries were locating away from the heart of the city. Inevitably, long-established subscribers in the second-fringe, who customarily called only nearby neighbours and local merchants, preferred the low monthly rates, relative to Toronto, which they had always enjoyed. In the boundary cases brought before it, the Board of Transport Commissioners had consistently refused to approve higher tolls if their

[15]See *Weston* and *Mimico* cases, *supra*.

[16]*Metropolitan Area Service, Toronto* (1951) 41 J.O.R.R. 1, 209; 67 C.R.T.C. 1, 99; *ibid.*, (1955) 45 J.O.R.R. 1; 72 C.R.T.C. 112; *Extended Area Service, Montreal* (1954) 44 J.O.R.R. 33; 71 C.R.T.C. 318; *ibid.*, *Hamilton* (1955) 43 J.O.R.R. 223; 70 C.R.C. 168.

effect was to benefit only a few subscribers. For instance, the application of the Toronto rates to the Agincourt exchange would benefit those who frequently telephoned Toronto and would hurt those who were content with more limited phoning privileges. Up to 1953 Bell had followed the practice of having its subscribers who were affected vote on the question of amalgamation with a larger exchange area. In 1955, however, Company officials explained their proposal for what they called extended area telephone service to editors of urban and suburban newspapers, to service clubs, and to municipal councils. Although Bell's officials stated they would welcome criticisms and explained the inexpensive process of filing a formal complaint with the Board, the number of objections to the scheme was trifling.

In working out the plan[17] both Board and Company agreed that subscribers in the second-fringe should pay a higher flat monthly rate than patrons at the Toronto, Weston, and other first-fringe exchanges. More poles, wire, and cable were needed to serve them, and thicker wire is required for clear transmission of sound over long distances than over short ones, unless the voltage is stepped up which also causes extra expense. Moreover, it would be very expensive to provide equipment so that every subscriber in the northeast portion of Greater Toronto (Agincourt) could personally dial any phone in the southwest section (Port Credit) which is about 25 air-miles distant. The number of such calls is far too small to justify the high capital cost of interconnecting every phone so that two subscribers could communicate with each other without the intervention of an operator at a central exchange. Therefore, subscribers listed under exchanges in both the first- and second-fringe of suburbs continue to pay long distance tolls to non-adjoining exchanges. Their basic monthly rate entitles them to make as many calls as they like within their own exchange, to adjoining exchanges, and to Toronto and Leaside.

The situation may be illustrated by the accompanying table.

		RATES*		
		1954	*1955*	*1958***
Second-fringe exchanges in	A B C D E F G***	$3.90–$4.15	$5.95	$6.35
First-fringe exchanges in	H J K L	5.35	5.45	5.85
Base area exchanges in	Toronto and Leaside	5.35	5.45	5.75

*Residence rates per month, one-party service.
**After November 1, 1958.
***Second-fringe exchanges are more numerous than first-fringe ones because population is more scattered. The boundaries of exchanges and of municipalities do not always coincide.

[17]*Extended Area Service, Toronto* (1955) 45 J.O.R.R. 1; 72 C.R.T.C. 112.

Any subscriber in Toronto and Leaside may call anywhere throughout the entire area without payment of long distance tolls. Under the plan his monthly rate was slightly raised because he received the right to communicate with a somewhat larger number of phones than before. Since December 1, 1958, a subscriber at a first-fringe exchange, such as J, pays a little higher monthly rate than a patron in Toronto and may call any phone in Toronto or Leaside or H, C, D, E, and K without extra payment. A person listed under a second-fringe exchange, for example F, pays 50 cents a month more than subscribers attached to exchanges in the first-fringe and 60 cents more than those in the base area. By virtue of his monthly rate, he may call any phone in the base area or in E, K, L, and G. In some instances, where a community of interests has existed among groups of subscribers, he may, without extra charge, also call one adjoining exchange outside Greater Toronto, such as Markham or Richmond Hill, not otherwise covered by the plan. Callers between all other areas shown in the table, for example from J to A, B, F, G, and L, or from F to A, B, C, D, H, and J, must dial long distance and pay the appropriate long distance toll. It will be noted that the increase in rates in the second-fringe exchanges following promulgation of the plan was substantial, though quite in line with the huge increase in the number of subscribers in adjoining exchanges and in Toronto and Leaside which they might now dial directly. This metropolitan or extended area service has been or is shortly to be applied to Toronto, Montreal, Quebec, Ottawa, Hamilton, and Windsor, as well as to Vancouver and Victoria.[18] Bell also provides "authorized locality rates," a modified form of extended area service, for suburban areas near smaller cities such as Arvida, Kingston, and Sudbury.[19]

Segregation of exchanges into groups has created another problem. The number of phones in a given community may increase or decline because of changes in population and industrial development. In the 1930's these changes were rarely large enough to necessitate transferring a town from one group to another. During the war any increase in tolls brought about by regrouping required the approval of the Wartime Prices and Trade Board. Some shifts in population resulting from the establishment of war industries and military camps were considered temporary. For these reasons between 1927 and 1950 only 18 communities served by Bell of Canada were transferred to their

[18]*Extended Service, Vancouver & Victoria* (1952) 42 J.O.R.R. 69; 69 C.R.T.C. 65, 223.

[19]*Bell* v. *Municipalities* (1958) 47 J.O.R.R. 439, 474–81.

appropriate rate group and over 200 others which should have been changed were left undisturbed.

Transfers require the Board's approval because rates to some subscribers are altered. The Board dealt with each transfer *ad hoc* and had developed no precise formula for automatically shifting a community from one group to another. In the general rate case of 1950 the Board authorized the transfer to the appropriate group of 209 exchanges which were above or below the prescribed limits. The City of Quebec felt particularly aggrieved by this part of the Board's Order, because it jumped from Group 6 to Group 8 notwithstanding that it had only 800 telephones more than the minimum for Group 8.[20] The city also objected because Bell in its advertisements urged patrons to add extensions to their phones. Then it counted each of these extensions as a separate phone for rate-making purposes, and even added extensions located in offices of the provincial government. On the other hand, when they were faced with the application for a general increase in tolls, some communities which remained in the same group in 1950 as in 1927 thought the Company was remiss for not regrouping communities earlier. If it had not neglected to collect all the revenue (about $250,000 in 1949) to which it was entitled under correct grouping, it would not have needed such a large general increase in tolls which obviously had to be borne by all patrons wherever located. To cover this situation the Board ruled, in 1951, that a community might be regrouped whenever the number of its phones varied from the limit of the group in which it was currently placed by ±5 per cent.[21] Under this rule, which is partly designed to prevent too frequent movement of places between groups, the Board has authorized the regrouping of about 50 exchanges which has resulted, in every instance, in higher rates.[22]

PARTY LINES

Still another application of the principles of cost of service and of value of service relates to party and rural lines. Some telephone costs

[20]*Bell* v. *Toronto* (1950) 40 J.O.R.R. No. 17A, 1, 54–6; 67 C.R.T.C. 1, 78–80 (Deputy Chief Commissioner Armand Sylvestre). In the general rate case of 1958 Bell proposed that about 20 places should be transferred to more expensive groups and that Group 1 be consolidated with Group 2. See also fn. 25.

[21]*Circular* 267, dated Oct. 18, 1951.

[22]*Re-Grouping of Exchanges, Bell* (1952) 41 J.O.R.R. 393; 71 C.R.T.C. 280; *Bell* v. *Riverside* (1954) 44 J.O.R.R. 175; 71 C.R.T.C. 286. See also

vary directly with the number of customers, for example, billing and collecting accounts, listing in the directory, and dealing with complaints. Some other expenses, such as poles, wire, and switching equipment, can be shared by two or more parties on the same line. At the same time the company incurs a few extra expenses for two-party service in addition to those of one-party service. These include two "leads" from the pole line instead of one, a device which may be used for ringing only one of the parties instead of both, and so on. As the cost of extra poles and wire needed to connect subscribers having two-party service is likely to be higher in villages than in densely populated cities, the two-party rate in small places (Group 1) is more, relative to the one-party rate in the same communities, than is the case in Montreal (Group 10). Specifically, the two-party rate for residence service is 17 per cent lower than the one-party rate in Groups 1 and 2 whereas it is 22 per cent less in Group 10. If the relationship were the same in Group 10 as in Group 1, the two-party rate in Group 10 would be so high that some of the present subscribers would presumably be discouraged from having a phone. In order to add to its revenues and broaden the use of its service, Bell feels that the two-party rate in large cities should be cheaper, relative to the one-party rate, than is the case in small towns.[23] Apparently subscribers in small communities do not object to this arrangement. Although their two-party service is not as cheap, relative to the rates paid by their neighbours who have one-party service, they pay roughly two-thirds of the rate charged two-party subscribers in downtown Toronto and Montreal. Furthermore, it is probable that the two-party rate in Group 1 is set so close to out-of-pocket cost of giving service to these subscribers that any lower rate would actually reduce the Company's net revenue.

There is no reason for believing that two-party service in small towns is any less satisfactory, merely because two parties share the line, than two-party service in cities. The critical factor in determining rates by groups is value of service to subscribers as measured by the number of other subscribers who may be called under the basic monthly rate. Incidentally, complaints of an inconsiderate or even obnoxious "other party on the line" are ticklish and expensive for

---

Vancouver Federated Ratepayers v. *B.C. Telephone* (1937) 27 J.O.R.R. 452; 47 C.R.C. 294.

[23]This feeling apparently explains why Bell proposed that the difference between rates for two-party and one-party service which had been roughly 11 and 21 per cent in 1950 should become 17 and 24 per cent in 1958.

a telephone company to handle. Sometimes it can add to its revenue by selling one or even both of the disgruntled subscribers the more expensive one-party service.

CRITICISM OF LOCAL RATES

The system of differential pricing is not without some theoretical blemishes and practical shortcomings. First, it does not make allowance for frequency of use or for length or timing of calls. The gossipy or socially ambitious housewife who is "on the phone the whole day long" and the talkative teenage girl should obviously be charged more than the business girl who uses the phone in her apartment only occasionally, and at times (in the evening and at weekends) when the physical facilities of the Company are not being used nearly to capacity. Formerly in some American cities, telephone operators manually recorded every call made on each phone and the subscriber was charged for the excess above a certain minimum. This arrangement was expensive, though it did reduce congestion and the capital investment which had to be made. Because of the possibility of error, disputes often arose between patron and Company. Telechronometers, which are mechanical devices for recording calls,[24] are too expensive for general use, but are authorized in message rate service as described above and in long distance direct dialing now being introduced.

A second criticism of the Board's method of setting local rates is that it refuses to take into consideration comparisons between rates in various parts of Canada and the United States. Legally the Board's position is unassailable, for it is obliged to deal only with companies within its jurisdiction. Besides, the difficulties of securing truly comparable statistics are greater than appear on the surface. As matters stand, however, people rely on hearsay, differences are exaggerated and telephone companies come in for unjustified criticism.

Finally, it is often alleged that rates in various groups, and indeed for other services, should be more closely related to costs than they are at present. It is all very well to say that tolls should be based mainly on value of service. The trouble is that if rates in any one group fail to cover the out-of-pocket costs for that group, then other subscribers are actually burdened by the unprofitable service. Instead of gaining by the extension of service at low rates to people who cannot pay higher rates, which is what the theory assumes, subscribers

[24] J. K. Hall, "Intra-Exchange Telephone Rates—The Telechronometer," *Journal of Land and Public Utility Economics*, Nov., 1932, pp. 378–95.

who now pay high rates would enjoy lower rates if non-paying services were abandoned. In 1950 the City Council of London, Ontario, alleged that it was inequitable for urban users to subsidize suburban rates.[25] In general, the Board supports Bell which insists that it should not undertake cost studies similar to those made in the United States.[26] The theory of differential rates is basically sound, but telephone companies and regulatory authorities in Canada may not have been sufficiently aggressive in applying the principles of cost accounting to the problems of rate-making. It is only fair to add that the same sluggishness is apparent in railroading and other public utilities, at least until recently.[27]

LONG DISTANCE

Every long distance call involves terminal expenses such as getting instructions from the caller, contacting the recipient, billing, and asking the party called if he will accept responsibility for the charges if they are to be reversed. A long distance call also gives rise to line charges which vary with distance, duration of call, and kind of service. As terminal expenses are presumably the same regardless of the distance over which the message is carried, the total charge does not increase in direct proportion to distance. Furthermore, high charges per call tend to discourage use, so that value of service holds down rates over longer distances. In 1958 on "anyone" daytime service for 100, 200, 400, and 800 miles Bell proposed charging 80 cents, $1.20, $1.90 and $2.60. It will be observed that for each increase of 100 per cent in the distance, rates were to rise by only 50, 58, and 37 per cent. Long

[25] *Exchange Re-Grouping, London and Trois Rivières* (1956) 45 J.O.R.R. 241; 74 C.R.T.C. 53, 54. In 1958 the Company proposed making slight readjustments in the rate relationships of the various groups. The ratio of charges for one-party residence phones in the various groups which had been 61, 64, 68, 74, 79, 84, 90, 95, and 100 would become 61 (Groups 1 and 2 consolidated), 65, 68, 73, 77, 81, 86, 92, and 100.

[26] *Bell* v. *Toronto* (1950) J.O.R.R. at pp. 37–8; C.R.T.C. at p. 60 which confirmed *Bell* v. *Montreal* (1927) 16 J.O.R.R. 229, 253; 34 C.R.T.C. 1, 34.

[27] Ford K. Edwards, "Cost Analysis in Transportation," *American Economic Review*, 1947, pp. 441–61; Interstate Commerce Commission, Bureau of Accounts and Cost Finding, *Explanation of Rail Cost Finding Procedures and Principles Relating to the Use of Costs* (Washington, 1948, 1954); D. R. Ladd, *Cost Data for the Management of Railroad Passenger Service* (Cambridge, Mass.: Harvard University, 1957).

distance rates are computed by air-miles between cities, not by the milage of the route taken by the message.

Long distance rates are higher when the caller asks to speak with a particular person than they are when he is prepared to talk with anyone at the number called. On person-to-person calls the operator must hold the line until the individual who is called gets to the phone. If he is not immediately available, she must either call later or cancel the call. In one case the Company is put to some extra expense: in the other it collects no revenue. Up to 1941 Bell made a "report" charge on person-to-person calls when the party called could not come to the phone. This charge, which varied with the basic rate subject to a 10 cent minimum, was voluntarily eliminated because of public objection. In 1958 Bell began making a flat charge of 10 cents per message on each station-to-station call billed to a telephone other than that from which the call was made, unless advance credit arrangements had been made in writing with the Company. This charge recognizes the additional cost to the Company of handling such calls.

Lines which are held open until the particular person called gets to the phone are sometimes the immediate cause of poor service. This was especially true in the 1940's when, because of the war, the number of circuits in operation was often inadequate for prompt completion of all long distance calls which were placed. "Held" lines cannot be used for other revenue calls and so are unproductive from the telephone company's standpoint. Therefore, the charge for a person-to-person call should be higher than for an "anyone will do" message. In addition, the caller should pay something for the satisfaction of being able to talk with the desired person for the full three minutes which is allowed on long distance calls without extra charge. He also gains in that he avoids the risk on station-to-station calls that the person best qualified to take the message may not be at hand and that the actual recipient may so garble the message that eventually a person-to-person call is necessary anyway. Finally, most person-to-person calls, especially those made during the day, are paid for by businesses and governments which commonly do not watch expenses as carefully as individuals. In 1955 Bell widened the spread between person-to-person and station-to-station calls in order to encourage more "anyone" service. In this way it hoped to reduce holding time, effect operating economies, and make better use of circuits.[28]

Lines could be used more effectively and capital expenditures cut

[28]*Bell* v. *Toronto* (1950) J.O.R.R. at p. 44; C.R.T.C. at p. 71.

down if unnecessarily lengthy calls could be eliminated, especially at periods of peak business. One way of doing this would be to make the rate per minute of overtime much higher than the rate per minute for the initial period. In fact, the overtime rate per minute is about one-third of the station-to-station rate and usually less than one-fifth of the person-to-person rate for the initial three-minute period. This is no penalty on loquacity. Yet another scheme might tempt a long-winded but astute caller to place two successive calls and thus defeat the purpose of the disproportionately high overtime rates. During the war when telephone companies found it impossible to add to the number of long distance circuits, they asked the public to talk briefly in order that others might share the facilities. With plenty of circuits now in operation, telephone companies consider that overtime is, in fact, more remunerative than the initial period since the cost of establishing the connection has been met. Direct distance dialing, which is currently being introduced, should reduce the length of time needed to make a long distance connection.

Another feature of long distance tolls is that rates on calls made at night and on Sunday are less than on daytime calls. The purpose of this differentiation is the same as in other instances, to add to the Company's revenue by popularizing use. By 1918 Bell was charging half the corresponding day rate on long distance calls made between 6 P.M. and 6 A.M.[29] In 1919 its long distance tolls between 8.30 P.M. and 11.30 P.M. became 60 per cent of the corresponding day rates and between 11.30 P.M. and 6 A.M. they were 40 per cent of the day rate. These reductions pleased the public so much that huge operating peaks developed just after 8.30 and particularly after 11.30. Bell found it hard to get enough operators to deal with these peaks, had to pay them at higher rates for working awkward hours, and even had to install extra circuits for the peak loads. Patrons were often annoyed by delays in the completion of calls which were placed just after the reduced rates went into effect. Consequently, in 1926 the discount on calls after midnight was made 50 per cent and rates on long distance calls made between 7 P.M. and 8.30 P.M. were set at 80 per cent of the corresponding day rate. This discount of 20 per cent was not sufficiently enticing to patrons to have much effect on reducing the peak after 8.30. Beginning in 1935 a reduction of 50 per cent below day rates became effective at 7 P.M. and continued to 4.30 A.M. Still later, the reduced rates took effect at 6 P.M. and were good all day

[29]*Re Bell's Application* (1919) 9 J.O.R.R. 63, 64; 25 C.R.C. 1, 2–3.

Sunday. A peak still occurs after night rates become available but it is not as pronounced as formerly. Since there is more time to get in touch with the recipient before he goes out for the evening, calls are spread over a longer period of time. Expiration of night rates at 4.30 A.M. effectively prevents an early morning peak.

Under the tariffs of Bell Telephone there is no difference between day and night rates for distances up to 35 air-miles. The Company cannot afford to cut rates which, in view of the heavy terminal expenses, are already so low that apparently they barely cover out-of-pocket costs. A reduction of 10 cents on a day rate of 40 cents would probably not lead many people to call in the evening instead of during the day. If it did, their calls might add to the peak which occurs just after night rates take effect, and which the companies wish to avoid as far as they can.

It is quite clear, however, that people tend to refrain from making calls during the day if, by waiting until after 6 P.M., they can save a tolerable amount. Up to a point this is precisely what the Company wants. The trouble is that if too many calls are held until the evening, they accentuate the peak in traffic which is so undesirable for the Company. The fundamental purpose of low rates at night is not deferment of calls from business hours but expansion of revenues by getting people who cannot afford the day rate to use the cheaper night and Sunday service. If the effect of the reductions is merely to take business from the day and transfer it to the evening, then the Company is deprived of revenue which it would otherwise have got. While some shifting is inevitable and perhaps desirable, the Company wants to avoid an excessive number of postponements.

The temptation for a patron to withhold calls becomes greater as rates increase. Most people pay more attention to savings in dollars and cents than in percentages. A reduction of 40 per cent in rates on person-to-person calls and for 2,500 miles will induce the deferment of relatively more calls than the same percentage reduction on "any-one" calls for the same distance and on calls between places which are only 300 miles apart. In the general rate case of 1950, Bell did not ask for authority to increase day rates for distances beyond 240 miles because it wanted to prevent patrons from withholding their calls until the evening and thereby throwing an undue burden on the Company immediately after 6 P.M. For most intermediate distances the discount on night and Sunday station-to-station calls is now 40 per cent and on similar calls person-to-person roughly 30 per cent. If it is assumed that most person-to-person calls are for business purposes and most "anyone" calls are for social reasons, willingness or ability to pay is a factor in this differentiation.

On long distance calls over several hundred miles, another element enters. The time which is in effect where the call originates determines the rate which applies. A Torontonian who places a call to Vancouver shortly after 6 P.M. in Toronto, will pay night rates but talk with his party during business hours at destination. He gets most of the advantages of a day call at night rates. This is unfair to patrons who call people within the same time zone and to those who place a call just before 6 P.M. local time to a more easterly time zone rather than to a western one. The call from Toronto to the Pacific Coast adds to the early evening peak in Toronto and the afternoon peak in Vancouver. It raises the cost of operation, helps create congestion, and prevents lines being used by other subscribers in both places. To cover this situation, the difference between day and night rates over long distances is relatively less attractive to the patron than on intermediate distances. On station-to-station calls from Toronto to Vancouver day and night rates differ by 30 per cent compared with 40 per cent on the same kind of service between Toronto and Montreal. The corresponding percentages on person-to-person calls are 22 and 30.

For long distance communication, telephone companies compete with telegraph and air mail. Use of the phone permits discussion and provides friendly contact between caller and recipient. On the other hand it does not supply a written record of decisions or give as great an opportunity for deliberation as do letters and telegrams.[30] Tape recordings of conversations may be made with the knowledge of both parties and permission of the telephone company which will supply a device for automatically interjecting "beep" signals over the telephone circuit and on the tape.

Until recently, telegraph rates in Canada were, broadly speaking, blanketed by provinces. More zones were introduced in 1957 and now telegraph rates bear a reasonably close relation to distance.[31] As a result, the discrepancies which formerly existed between telephone and telegraph rates to and from points near provincial boundaries have tended to disappear. Telegraph companies differentiate rates by

[30]Short period private line service is a form of long distance service which is provided on a contract basis for a specified period of time each day. Rates for this service, which is used by stock brokers and other businesses, are somewhat lower than ordinary long distance message rates.

[31]*Re Telegraph Tolls* (1957) 47 J.O.R.R. 253.

time of day and priority of use of facilities. A message may be sent day expedited, day letter, night message, and night letter. The sender of a message has to choose between various classes of service by both telegraph and telephone, and the charge made by each. These relationships are too complicated for brief summary. The increase in Canadian telegraph tolls made late in 1957 just after an application for higher telephone rates had been launched suggests that the two methods of communication keep their price level more or less in line with each other.

JURISDICTION OVER TELEPHONE RATES

Canadians are served by numerous telephone companies. In Nova Scotia, the Maritime Telegraph and Telephone Company owns about 95 per cent of the roughly 159,000 phones but 4,600 homes and businesses are served by approximately 200 mutual and other privately owned systems. In Newfoundland, New Brunswick, and Prince Edward Island the dominant concerns are Avalon, New Brunswick Telephones, and the Island Telephone Company, a subsidiary of Maritime T. & T. In Ontario and Quebec, Bell has upwards of 3,000,000 phones and connects with about 600 local companies having a total of about 300,000 phones. In the three Prairie provinces substantially all phone service is provided by the provincial governments while the British Columbia Telephone Company operates west of the Rockies.

In 1904 Sir Wilfrid Laurier appointed a committee to collect evidence on the advisability of government ownership of all telephone companies, as in Britain.[32] The committee failed to bring down a report partly because of the resignation of the Postmaster General, Sir William Mulock, who was active in getting the committee set up. The only result of the committee's work was that in 1908 Bell and the British Columbia Telephone Company were put under the Board of Railway (now Transport) Commissioners. By virtue of section 92 of the British North America Act, Parliament can declare any telephone or other company to be a work "for the public advantage of Canada" and thereby bring it within federal jurisdiction.

Although the Dominion has the legal power to bring other companies besides Bell and British Columbia Telephones under its control, it has, for obvious reasons, left the smaller privately owned systems

[32]Canada, House of Commons, Select Committee on Telephone Systems, *Proceedings* (Ottawa: King's Printer, 1905).

and the provincially owned companies under provincial control. Nevertheless, rates set by the Board of Transport Commissioners for the two major concerns in the three most populous provinces have a powerful effect on rates elsewhere in Canada. As a rule, Bell's rates are increased earlier than those of any other Canadian company. Consequently, no serious opposition is apparently aroused when rates are finally raised by the Department of Telephones in Manitoba, Saskatchewan, and Alberta, or by the Public Utility Commission or Municipal Board in other provinces. In Nova Scotia, however, the Public Utilities Commission conducts full-scale investigations.[33] In Ontario the Municipal Board has from time to time been zealous in examining the telephone rates of the so-called farmers' lines.

FINANCIALLY WEAK COMPANIES

One of the most serious problems facing the telephone industry in Canada is the poor quality of service provided by impoverished rural telephone systems.[34] Subscribers can rarely use the line when they want to, because it is out of order so often and serves so many patrons. They refuse to pay even the low annual charge for service. They have their phones disconnected, thereby reducing the corporation's revenue and aggravating the entire problem. Often they clamour for the construction of parallel lines either by a different local company or by Bell. Regulatory authorities are reluctant to authorize duplication of facilities and the economic wastes which they involve, although the alternative is often progressive deterioration in rural telephone service.

Up to a point this situation is effectively dealt with by the major companies. From time to time they buy up the smaller concerns or purchase part of their common stock and mortgages.[35] Even where it has no financial control, Bell takes paternalistic interest in the independents. It hopes that revenue from long distance calls inter-

[33]See particularly Nova Scotia, Public Utilities Commission, *Annual Report*, 1946, pp. 188, 211 (Maritime Telephone & Telegraph).

[34]For example, Ontario Railway & Municipal Board, *Annual Report*, 1928, p. 100 (Parkhill-Arkona Telephone); Nova Scotia, Public Utilities Commission, *Annual Report*, 1945, p. 182 (Cumberland Rural Telephone).

[35]For instance, in 1952–4 B.C. Telephone acquired the Mission, Kootenay, and Chilliwack telephone companies and the telephone portion of the Dominion Government Telephone & Telegraph Service west of the Rocky Mountains.

changed with the independents will increase. Chiefly, Bell wants to avoid the capital expenditures and operating difficulties which it might have to take on if the independents completely collapsed. At all events, it gives much free advice to the numerous small companies with which it connects.

Although the Board of Transport Commissioners has no power to set the rates of the independents, it may legally determine what Bell charges for its connections with them. Local calls between subscribers on independent and Bell lines, for example between farms and a nearby town, are handled in one of two different ways. If the independent operates its own exchange, the number of calls interchanged between the two companies is counted and the difference is paid for at an agreed rate. This rate takes into account the proportion of the line connecting the two exchanges which is owned by the two companies. Sometimes, the charge per message is commuted into an annual payment per rural subscriber.[36] This arrangement, though common at one time, has generally been superseded by the Service Station System. The independent has no switchboard of its own, and Bell does all the operating besides listing subscribers of the independent company in its own directory. The charges for this service are partly based on cost but mainly on value of service. The number of Bell phones which the subscribers of the independent company may call without extra charge determines the monthly rate which they pay in addition to the charge levied by the independent for constructing and maintaining the rural line. As most independents pay no dividends and fail to make adequate provision for depreciation and sometimes not even for repairs, in 80 per cent of the cases their charges are 50 per cent lower than those of Bell for similar service.[37]

On long distance calls, independents formerly collected at least 10

[36]*General Order 114*, dated Nov. 12, 1913: *General Order 149*, dated Sept. 14, 1915. See also *Byron Telephone* v. *Bell* (1911) 11 C.R.C. 433; *People's Telephone* v. *Bell* (1911) 12 C.R.C. 319; *Ernestown* v. *Bell* (1915) 18 C.R.C. 325; *Bell* v. *Falkirk Telephone* (1916) 6 J.O.R.R. 260; 20 C.R.C. 256; *Joliette* v. *Bell* (1918) 7 J.O.R.R. 35; 21 C.R.C. 443; *Lemieux* v. *Bell* (1918) 8 J.O.R.R. 179; 23 C.R.C. 141; *La Ligne Téléphonique des Cultivateurs* v. *Bell* (1946) 36 J.O.R.R. 273; 60 C.R.T.C. 227. At one time Bell was reluctant to interchange long distance messages with companies which competed with it for local business. See *Ingersoll Telephone* v. *Bell* (1911) 53 Supreme Court Reports 583; 31 Dominion Law Reports 49; 22 C.R.C. 135; *Port Hope* v. *Bell* (1914) 17 C.R.C. 343.

[37]*Bell* v. *Toronto* (1950) J.O.R.R. at p. 43; C.R.T.C. at pp. 69–70.

cents more than Bell charged from junction point to destination. This extra charge covered cost of billing, collection, and possible loss by bad debts. The larger independents also charged for their own lines when used for a long distance call. Later, Bell and the independents divided joint long distance revenue in agreed proportions, having regard to the costs of originating the call, putting it through to destination, and the comparative expenses of operating the lines connecting origin and destination of the call. In other words, after deduction of certain terminal expenses, the remainder of the toll was divided in accordance with the relative milages of the lines of the companies concerned in handling the message. In 1944 the pro-rate or division of joint revenue which Bell paid to the connecting companies was increased by 10 per cent. In 1951 a scheme of weighting by the number of telephones on the independent system was introduced. "By applying the weighting factor to the milage of the connecting company, and maintaining the Bell milage at actual distance, a greater percentage of the line haul revenue accrues to the connecting company."[38] The revised method of divisions costs Bell about $250,000 per annum more than the previous scheme of pro-rating.

The purpose of weighting was to add to the revenues of small, poverty-stricken concerns without unduly benefiting the Québec Téléphone of Rimouski which has 40,000 phones in 17 counties and the Ontario Northland System which is owned by the province. The Board of Transport Commissioners declared that it was not responsible for the financial welfare of the connecting companies. It also pointed out that weighting had been agreed upon by the companies concerned. It said the only alternative method of bolstering gross revenues of hard-up independents was the imposition of combination rates, usually called "other line charges." The Board asserted that it had no thought that it "should ameliorate the connecting companies' position at the expense of Bell."[39] It could, however, confirm the new scheme without fear of having to get more money from Bell's subscribers since the principle of weighting had already been applied to international traffic. Increased revenue to Bell from this source more than offset the higher pro-rate or division of long distance tolls which it would pay to connecting companies on calls between subscribers on different systems within Canada. The Board's decision seems to be sounder in economics than in law.

[38] *Joint Telephone Service & Tolls* (1951) 41 J.O.R.R. 247; 68 C.R.T.C. 23.

[39] *Ibid.*, J.O.R.R. at p. 253; C.R.T.C. at p. 32.

BELL AND BRITISH COLUMBIA TELEPHONE COMPANIES

In 1880–1, shortly after Bell started operations, its charges in Montreal, which then had about 1,000 subscribers, were $50 a year for business and $30 a year for residence service. It used Blake transmitters in which the return circuit was through the ground. The Company soon discovered that, especially for long distance connections and for ringing central, it needed a complete metallic circuit with central station energy. Its early charge of $70 a year for all-wire circuits proved higher than the public was then prepared to pay. By 1912 phones with all-wire circuits cost only $5 a year more than Blake transmitters, but a few of the older type phones were still in use.[40]

Though assuming jurisdiction over Bell's rates in 1908, the Board was not presented with a general rate case until 1912. In that year Bell asked for an increase in tolls generally and for permission to make rates on Blake transmitters the same as on all-wire circuits in order to discourage their use. The City of Montreal demanded reductions of $5 per annum in both business and residence rates. It contended that Bell was clearly in a satisfactory financial position, and that it had not proven its contention that subscribers in Montreal were not contributing their fair share to the general revenues of the Company. The city also argued that the existing 35,000 subscribers should not be required to pay interest and dividends on a plant built for 50,000 customers. In its judgment the Board stated that a public utility should not allow demands for service to accumulate until they could not be quickly satisfied. Within limits, piece-meal construction of plant only increased costs. Further, every additional subscriber who could get a phone installed quickly added to the value of service enjoyed by present users. The Board refused to make any general changes in rates, though it did make some adjustments to eliminate unjust discrimination.[41] It also recommended that depreciation charges be based on book value of assets rather than a fixed annual amount per phone in service.

Toward the end of the First World War, telephone companies began to feel the effect of rising costs. In October, 1918, Bell applied for an increase of 20 per cent in most of its charges. The Board examined such questions as wage rates, prices of materials, taxes, depreciation, obsolescence, and yields on securities. With minor changes, it allowed the application "so that the company may be able to meet increasing operating costs, meet its service requirements, and

[40]*Montreal* v. *Bell* (1912) 15 C.R.C. 118, 121–3.
[41]*Ibid.*, at pp. 137–41.

be in such a position as will enable the necessary reconstruction and extension to be made."[42]

In July, 1920, when the Company asked for a further 20 per cent, depreciation was more fully discussed and the relation between Bell and Northern Electric was studied. The Board confirmed the grouping principle, rejected a proposal for measured rate service in Montreal, Toronto, Ottawa, Hamilton, and Quebec City, and authorized payment of bills monthly instead of quarterly. Effective April 1, 1921, the Board allowed an increase of 10 per cent, or half the amount requested.[43] Ten days later the percentage was changed to 12 to correct an error in the estimates of revenue to be secured in Toronto. To get identity of rates in Toronto and Montreal under the grouping plan, all subscribers in Toronto had to pay an additional $5 a year whereas the business rate in Montreal was slightly lowered. The City of Toronto exercised its legal right to appeal to the Governor-in-Council (the federal Cabinet) for redress. The appeal was argued, judgment was reserved, and finally the case was referred back to the Board for consideration along with another application.

In the new case the Company proposed a revised schedule of rates and not merely a uniform percentage addition to current rates. It alleged that it had had but indifferent success in a recent attempt to sell securities and argued that inadequacy of net earnings was the basic cause of its inability to raise new capital as quickly as required. The majority of the Board believed that the efforts of the Company to sell stock were neither very insistent nor very thorough. As the comparative failure of the issue

> might possibly justify an immediate return to the Board for an increase in rates, it could be borne with serenity as being not without its compensations. . . . The company did not, before launching this application, so readjust its business and institute proper and reasonable economies as would in their result have shown that the [previous] . . . increase . . . was sufficient to enable it to carry on until a stable [revised] rate structure could be prepared. . . . [Bell had not tried] to adjust rates in any scientific way to value of telephone service to subscribers, having regard to the population of the telephone area, . . . or the cost therein. . . . The grouping of towns is not brought

[42]*Re Bell's Application* (1919), *supra.*
[43]*Bell* v. *Toronto* (1921) 11 J.O.R.R. 35; 27 C.R.C. 231.

> about upon any satisfactory basis. The proposed tariff is not reasonable *as a whole* as regards the company nor reasonable from the point of view of the people who have to pay.[44]

The decision of three Commissioners, and therefore of the Board, that no increase in tolls be permitted, was not concurred in by Chief Commissioner F. B. Carwell or Assistant Chief Commissioner S. J. McLean. The former emphasized the Company's operating efficiency, the necessity for higher wages, and the need for capital. He felt that officials of Bell were better qualified than outsiders to judge of suitable methods of finance. Dr. McLean was impressed by the need for higher dividends in the sale of securities. While thoroughly cognizant of discriminations and disparities in the existing system of rates, Dr. McLean felt that an emergency existed and that the application should be allowed.

Meanwhile, the British Columbia Telephone Company was also experiencing the effects of war and post-war inflation. It argued in favour of a fair return on the replacement cost of physical assets. This method would give the Company a higher valuation and therefore a larger amount of net earnings for division among shareholders than would rates based on original cost of assets. The Board reaffirmed the view it expressed in the Montreal case of 1912: neither book value nor replacement cost was of primary importance. What a telephone company was entitled to was a set of rates which would bring in enough revenue so that it could meet all its reasonable operating expenses, taxes, interest, dividends, and a small surplus. In short, the Board would use the so-called financial requirements method to arrive at the appropriate rate level.[45]

As in the Bell cases, depreciation got a good deal of attention. Some witnesses wanted rates for each locality to be directly related to the local investment in plant. As no valuation by areas had ever been made, the Board did not deal at length with this point. Although the Company wanted to raise rates in Vancouver, North Vancouver, New Westminster, Victoria, and Nanaimo by 15 per cent, the Board allowed only 10 per cent. No change was made in rates elsewhere.

Following the post-war collapse in prices, telephone companies were able to keep expenditures within the revenues which were produced

[44]*Bell* v. *Ontario* (1922) 11 J.O.R.R. 440; 27 C.R.C. 277.

[45]*B.C. Telephone Exchange Rentals & Charges for Service* (1921) 11 J.O.R.R. 216; 27 C.R.C. 259.

by the rates set in 1921. By 1926–7, however, Bell found it necessary not only to provide increased facilities for the conduct of an ever expanding business but also for the necessary alteration of its system from manual to automatic or dial operation. Thus there was not only normal expansion but an obsolescence factor as well. In view of the importance of obsolescence, the Board examined depreciation policies with the greatest care.[46]

The Board also scrutinized contracts made by Bell with its subsidiary, Northern Electric, for equipment and with American Telephone and Telegraph for the use of patents, "plans, methods, systems, and ideas, designed to promote the safety, economy, and efficiency in the equipment, construction, and operation of telephone plants." It reaffirmed the use of the financial requirements method and stated that value of service should be the basis of rates by areas. With minor exceptions, it approved the application *in toto*, the over-all increase in rates being between 5 and 6 per cent.

Widespread complaints in the 1930's that telephone rates should be reduced like other prices came to a head in a formal complaint by Wilfred Lacroix, M.P. (Ind. Lib., Quebec-Montmorency).[47] He had four main arguments: (*a*) between 1930 and 1937 rates were so high that out of earnings Bell was able to meet all operating expenses and taxes, pay generous dividends, spend $103 million on renewals, and add nearly $33 million to investment in new assets; (*b*) despite the general decline in interest rates, the Company paid annual dividends of 8 per cent in 1930–2, 6 per cent in 1933–5, and 7½ per cent in 1937; (*c*) the reserve fund of about $8 million should be used to reduce rates; (*d*) depreciation was not needed because the plant was well maintained. Lack of space prevents analysis of these contentions and of the implicit assumption in Lacroix's arguments that all prices should either fall or be forced down in a depression.[48] At all events, the Board dismissed the case.

From 1939 to 1941 Bell met the demand for telephones chiefly by putting into service the unused plant which existed at the outbreak of

[46]*Bell* v. *Montreal* (1927) 16 J.O.R.R. 229; 34 C.R.C. 1.

[47]*Lacroix* v. *Bell* (1940) 30 J.O.R.R. 43; 51 C.R.T.C. 1.

[48]For discussions of public utility rates and the business cycle, see B. W. Lewis, "Public Pricing of Electric Power," in Temporary National Economic Committee, *Economic Standards of Government Price Control* (Washington: Government Printing Office, 1941), pp. 1–54; D. H. Wallace, "A Critical Review of Some Instances of Government Price Control," *ibid.*, pp. 397–431.

hostilities. After 1941 the Company had to refuse service to non-essential users. In the four years after 1945 Bell added 545,000 phones, an increase of 50 per cent. Although it had spent $232 million on construction, it was unable to make much impression on the back-log of orders for service. Meanwhile, its revenues from monthly rates for local service doubled in the years 1939–49, revenues from long distance tolls nearly trebled, and miscellaneous operating revenues such as rentals of private wires to stockbrokers and other businesses, moving and connecting telephones, and charges for private exchanges in hotels and business offices, more than trebled. But while total operating revenues rose 153 per cent, total operating expenses includ-ing taxes increased 201 per cent. Net operating income remained comparatively constant but was insufficient for interest, dividends, and surplus, especially in view of the increased capital investment which it was necessary to make. Consequently, in October, 1949, Bell applied for an increase of about 20 per cent in tolls, the percentage varying from one service to another.

The broad principle to be followed in general rate cases is simple enough.

> Under efficient management tolls and charges should be such that they would normally provide all reasonable and normal expenses including taxes and also a sufficient amount for reasonable dividends and surplus to maintain the credit of the Company so that as and when advisable new capital can be attracted to meet new demands for service and for the moder-nizing of existing facilities. The interest of management and subscribers run parallel to this point and beyond this the sub-scriber should not be asked to contribute. With this in view it is incumbent upon the Board in its regulatory capacity to give careful scrutiny to all items of expense . . . and other matters which might reflect themselves in unjust or unreason-able or unjustly discriminatory impositions on . . . subscribers. But at the same time to recognize also that there is a "reason-able zone" wherein the functions of management should not be usurped.[49]

It is in applying these principles that controversy develops. Deter-mination of rates of depreciation gives a chance for expert accountants

[49] *Bell* v. *Toronto* (1950) J.O.R.R. at p. 5; C.R.T.C. at p. 7. See also *Bell* v. *Montreal* (1927) J.O.R.R. at p. 231; C.R.C. at p. 3.

and engineers to present a mass of detailed and often conflicting testimony. Telephone companies, like other public utilities, require enormous investment in plant. Consequently, their annual depreciation charges are heavy. In 1949 they equalled nearly 18 per cent of Bell's total operating expenses or about $10 per telephone. Though past experience can be used to forecast future life of assets and rates of depreciation, data are sometimes not available and technological changes confound predictions. "The factors which one person may consider as being important in the future may tend to be discounted by another. Yet each may express his honest and sincere conviction."[50] Though witnesses appearing on behalf of 24 city councils and boards of trade in opposition to the application claimed that depreciation charges might safely be reduced by 10 per cent, the Board accepted Bell's figures without qualification. Similarly, the Board concluded that, notwithstanding vigorous criticism by experts engaged by the cities concerned, assets were not being extravagantly maintained.

The service contract between Bell and the American Telephone and Telegraph Company was complicated by three factors. First, in 1949 A.T. & T. owned about 12 per cent of the common stock of Bell. Though its proportion has been declining since the early 1920's when it was as high as 48 per cent, it is claimed that negotiations between the two concerns are not conducted at arm's length. The two parties do not act in a truly independent manner in arriving at the terms of the agreement. Second, payment for services is based on the gross revenues of Bell (one per cent since January, 1929). When Bell's revenues grow, it has to pay more to A.T. & T. even though it may not receive services of any higher value than before and indeed may receive less. Third, the contract was improvident because it was not based on actual costs of A.T. & T. Unfortunately, neither the Board of Transport Commissioners nor any regulatory body in the United States has jurisdiction over how A.T. & T. uses the funds which it gets from its American subsidiaries and from Bell.

In 1927 and again in 1950 the Board recognized that

> to place precise values on the services rendered under the contract is impossible. It would certainly be more helpful if this could be done. Failing this it is bound to be always open to suspicion and attack. . . . On the other hand no evidence is before the Board that better and fairer arrangements could

[50]*Bell* v. *Toronto* (1950) J.O.R.R. at p. 15; C.R.T.C. at p. 23.

> satisfactorily and less expensively and with the equivalent or better advantages to the Company and Subscriber be made. Undoubtedly, . . . it would be an exceedingly difficult matter to ascertain with any degree of exactitude the value of royalties, patent rights, new technology and the multitude of benefits obtained by the [Bell] Company under the contract.[51]

The Board accepted the statements of Company officials that Bell could not carry out its own research on the same scale, with the same benefits, or at the same cost, as A.T. & T. "The function of the Board is one of corrective regulation, not of business arrangement."[52] The Board felt it must be careful not to try to replace efficient management and so it refused to interfere unless management was indiscreet or improvident. Besides, regulatory commissions in the United States, "while at times condemning the principle of payment not founded on ascertainable costs, have allowed it in full."[53]

The Board found it easier to examine the contract between Bell and Northern Electric, because the latter manufactures and sells the same equipment to other purchasers as to Bell. A comparative study of prices on ten different kinds of equipment was made by Bell's auditors. It showed a distinct margin in favour of Bell. Despite the smallness of the sample and the possibility of bias in the selection of items, the Board concluded that the prices paid by Bell were not unreasonable. The Board denied an application of counsel for the cities to enquire into the finances and costs of Northern Electric. Its jurisdiction did not extend to the accounts of that concern.

Inasmuch as one of the basic arguments of the Company was that it needed higher rates to provide stable dividends in order that it might raise new capital economically, capital financing formed an important part of the case. Witnesses for the cities which opposed the application claimed that Bell could safely raise half or even 60 per cent of its capital by means of bonds. On the other hand Company executives stated that a prudent debt-to-common-stock ratio was one-third. As the Board's calculations of the significance of this ratio were garbled, it is necessary to re-compute the figures. In 1950 Bell paid about 3.3 per cent on bonds and estimated that it should earn a dividend of $2 plus a surplus of 43 cents per share of $25 par value. Its common

[51] *Ibid.*, J.O.R.R. at p. 18; C.R.T.C. at p. 28.
[52] *Ibid.*, J.O.R.R. at p. 18; C.R.T.C. at p. 29.
[53] *Ibid.*, J.O.R.R. at p. 18; C.R.T.C. at p. 28.

stock was selling at about $40 per share. Thus the net return on the market value of stock was 6.1 per cent. Corporation income tax, which was 51 per cent in 1950, is payable after interest and before dividends. Hence, to earn 6.1 per cent on the market value of its common stock, Bell must earn 12.45 per cent after interest but before income tax. If the Company's capitalization is one-third bonds and two-thirds common stock, on each $100 of capital (bonds plus stock) it must earn $1.10 on the bonds and $8.30 on the common stock before taxes, or a total of $9.40. If its capitalization is half bonds and half common stock, the corresponding figures are $1.65 and $6.22 or a total of $7.87. In short, an increase in the bond-to-common-stock ratio of from one-third to one-half reduces the requirements for interest and dividends by more than 16 per cent.

The Board's conclusions on the debt-to-common-stock ratio were not very consistent. "It is to the interest of subscribers that the capital structure be constituted of the greatest possible proportion of debt capital and the least possible proportion of equity. . . . The question of what may or not be an appropriate debt ratio is, in itself, largely academic."[54] No one could tell what the Company would do after a year or two. Nevertheless, the Board was satisfied that a debt ratio of 40 per cent which existed in 1950 and which "has resulted from the free determination of the Company's management . . . would not be detrimental to the Company's undertaking."[55]

On the rate of dividend, the Company advanced several points. Securities of utility companies have little or no growth possibilities. Therefore, the companies seek to substitute stability of dividends for capital gains as a means of attracting new investment. The stock of Bell was purchased because of its past dividend record and because investors expected the traditional rate of 8 per cent of par value to continue. Inadequate dividends would lower the price at which new issues could be put on the market and thereby add to the number of shares which would have to be sold to raise a given capital sum. Thus, the ultimate effect of any reduction in the rate of dividend allowed by the Board would make matters worse for the telephone patron. Then, too, over the years money which might legally have been paid out as dividends had been reinvested in the Company and stock had been sold at a premium. The equity per share ($31.47 in 1949) exceeded the par value ($25) per share because of plowed-back earnings and especially because of premiums on the sale of stock. The share-

[54]*Ibid.*, J.O.R.R. at pp. 30, 32; C.R.T.C. at pp. 49, 51.
[55]*Ibid.*, J.O.R.R. at p. 32; C.R.T.C. at p. 51.

holder who got an annual dividend of $2 or 8 per cent of par value received only 6.26 per cent on his equity. This yield compared with 7.12 per cent in 1926. The decline in yield was even greater if the purchasing power of the dollar is taken into account.

Witnesses for the cities pointed out several differences between financial conditions prevailing in 1926 and 1949, particularly changes in the going rate of interest and the dividend tax credit of 20 per cent which reduced the amount of personal income tax otherwise payable by shareholders. These witnesses further testified that the Company over-stressed the importance of stability of dividends. No reference seems to have been made, at least in the printed judgment of the Board, either to the valuable stock rights received by shareholders or to the yield on other securities of comparable risk to those of Bell. The Board admitted that it was difficult to decide with precision "where the border line should be drawn without on the one hand creating financial hazards and on the other being unfair to the subscriber."[56] Apparently it believed that nearly a quarter century earlier a Board had been competent to draw such a line, for in 1950 it refused to disturb the rate of dividends allowed in 1927.

The Board, the Company, and the representatives of the cities all agreed that Bell was entitled to a surplus after it had paid its operating expenses, taxes, interest, and dividends. Counsel for the cities pointed out that the over-all surplus from 1927 to 1949 amounted to less than 20 cents a share and that on such a surplus the Company successfully financed sales of stock. Therefore, it was unreasonable for Bell to ask for rates high enough to provide for a surplus of 43 cents a share in 1950. Where rates are regulated and the Company enjoys a monopoly, the surplus need not be large. The primary reason for a surplus was to permit a stable rate of dividends in years of lower-than-average earnings. According to counsel for the cities, subscribers should not be asked, by means of the surplus, permanently to contribute to the capital funds of the corporation. But Bell's position, which the Board accepted, was that a surplus of 43 cents per share was a fair measure of what was necessary in 1950 to ensure the raising of more capital from the public.

In its judgment the Board discussed several other matters—pension scheme, cost of handling accounts of subscribers, the commission (15 per cent) paid to owners of drug stores and other establishments where pay phones are located and to hotels (15 per cent if the hotel makes a surcharge above Bell's rates, otherwise 10 per cent) on long distance

[56]*Ibid.*, J.O.R.R. at p. 35; C.R.T.C. at p. 57.

calls to and from hotel rooms, Company advertising via press, radio, and television, the telephone directory, wage rates, and the construction programme. The Board stated that some other topics raised in the hearings but not discussed in the judgment had also got consideration. Taking everything into account the Board gave the Company all that it asked for.[57] It allowed further increases in 1951 and 1952 because of rising wages, charges for pensions, and income tax.[58]

In the meantime the British Columbia Telephone Company was faced with the same conditions as Bell. Its operating costs were rising faster than gross revenues. Its plant was inadequate because of rapid growth of population and demands for service, and it urgently needed new capital. In 1950 it was earning 2.84 per cent on total investment under existing rates and would get 4.44 per cent if its application for higher tolls were allowed in full. Although witnesses discussed various rate bases, the Board relied on financial requirements. Other topics dealt with were the service contract between the British Columbia and its parent, Anglo-Canadian Telephone which is part of the General Telephone System, the advisability of having advertising in phone directories and the supply of equipment handled by two other subsidiaries of Anglo-Canadian, capital structure, quality of service, wage rates, and the proper differentials in the rates paid by subscribers in towns of various sizes. As in the Bell case, the Board approved the Company's application in full. Within less than three years, it allowed two further increases.[59]

By 1957, inflation had again caught up with the telephone companies and Bell applied for another increase. Broadly speaking, the evidence of the 1950 case was repeated. The Company was fearful that, because of its vulnerable long distance business and its rigid costs, it would be badly hurt by a serious business recession. It felt that its ability to raise capital was being impaired both by the adverse trend in earnings per share and by the size and frequency of its new issues of stock and bonds.

Representatives of the municipalities who appeared in opposition

[57]The increase allowed by the Board in 1950 took place in two stages: an interim increase effective July 7, 1950, of roughly half the amount applied for (40 J.O.R.R. 289); and the remainder effective Jan. 1, 1951.

[58]*Re Bell Telephone* (1951) 41 J.O.R.R. 289; 68 C.R.T.C. 127; *ibid.*, (1952) 42 J.O.R.R. 1; 68 C.R.T.C. 359.

[59]*B.C. Telephone Case* (1950) 40 J.O.R.R. 215; 66 C.R.T.C. 7. Supplementary increases were allowed in *ibid.*, (1951) 41 J.O.R.R. 351; 68 C.R.T.C. 15; *ibid.*, (1952) 42 J.O.R.R. 251; 68 C.R.T.C. 261; *ibid.*, (1958) 48 J.O.R.R. 225

to the application believed that the common stock of the Company had achieved the status of a bond or at least of a preferred stock. Therefore, they seriously questioned whether the Company needed as much surplus per share (43 cents) as the Board had customarily allowed. They reiterated that the purpose of a surplus was to equalize dividends, and so it need not be large where rates are regulated.

Counsel for the municipalities described the evidence submitted by the Company on the relative prices charged by Northern Electric to Bell and to other customers as irrelevant and inconclusive. No proof was given of the cost and earnings of Northern Electric sales to Bell and to the public, or of the prices of other manufacturers of telephone equipment. Municipal witnesses also asserted that the earned surplus of Northern Electric was excessive and should be taken into account in assessing the financial needs of Bell. Northern had paid out 54 per cent of its earnings as dividends in 1957 and 26 per cent in previous years. If its "payout ratio" had been higher, Bell's needs would have been reduced. The Board agreed with counsel for Bell that it had no direct jurisdiction over Northern Electric, but considered that in discharging its statutory duty to fix just and reasonable rates for Bell it was entitled to take into account all relevant factors. The applicant's case for a higher level of earnings was based to a considerable extent on the necessity for maintaining investors' confidence in Bell's corporate securities. This confidence was bound to be influenced not only by the credit of the telephone business as such but also by all other assets and financial resources available to Bell. This part of the Board's judgment is significant because it went beyond what it had previously held to be its legal functions with regard to Northern Electric.

In its application Bell had included the effect of a possible increase in wage rates. The Board did not consider it proper to allow as an expense for rate-making purposes a sum which would be the subject of future collective bargaining and which, even if it did become payable, might be offset, as in the past, by economies, by greater efficiency, or by increased revenue from the extension of telephone service. The Board excluded this item and it also re-calculated the estimated deficiency in the applicant's revenue using a debt-to-common-stock ratio of 40 per cent instead of 37.8 per cent as assumed by the Company.

One of the most controversial issues in this case was the question of deferred taxes. Briefly, in 1954 the Government changed the basis for depreciation for income tax purposes by allowing companies to choose between straight line and diminishing balance. To illustrate the point at issue, let us take an asset costing $100 without any salvage value and with a serviceable life of 20 years. The annual rate of straight line depreciation would be 5 per cent or $5. Under the diminishing balance method, the same asset would be depreciated 10 per cent of its original cost ($100) in the first year, 10 per cent of its depreciated value ($90) in the second year, 10 per cent of $81 in the third year, and so on. For approximately the first 8 years of the asset's life, the depreciation charges, or capital cost allowances as they are now called, are heavier under diminishing balance than under straight line. As a result, operating expenses are higher and payments for income taxes less. After 8 years, provided income tax rates and certain other factors remain unchanged, the diminishing balance method results in lower depreciation charges, higher taxable income, and higher taxes than straight line. To take account of this situation, Bell set up a reserve to cover the difference between the tax actually paid under the diminishing balance method during the first 8 years of the asset's life and the tax which would have been payable under straight line. This reserve, which amounted to nearly $48 million on December 31, 1957, was to be available to meet the higher income taxes which might result after 8 years.

Counsel for the municipalities argued that just and reasonable rates should be fixed on actual costs and, as the deferred tax reserve had not been paid to the Department of National Revenue, it was not a cost for rate-making purposes. The reserve was a means of forcing customers to make an involuntary contribution to capital. In other words, the case should be decided on existing conditions and, if these conditions changed at some future date, then future customers would have to take the risk of higher income taxes, as they did other kinds of risks. A possible increase in tax payments some years hence had no relationship to current income and should be excluded from consideration by the Board. Professional accountants and provincial public utility commissions differ in their views on deferred tax credits. Pending further investigation, the Board decided to allow the deferred tax credit in the Bell Telephone case as it had already done for the Canadian Pacific in a railway rate case. The net result of the Board's decision was that it allowed an increase in tolls of less than half the amount requested by the Company.[60]

In accordance with procedure laid down in the Railway Act, the municipalities appealed this decision to the Cabinet which already had before it an appeal on railway rates. In both cases the Cabinet ruled that the Board should have excluded the item for deferred taxes from operating expenses. Had it done this, no deficiency in revenue would

[60]*Bell* v. *Municipalities* (1958) 47 J.O.R.R. 439.

have existed and no increase in rates would have been necessary. In short, on April 29, 1958, the Cabinet set aside the Board's judgment of the previous January authorizing the increase of 3.9 per cent.[61]

Higher wage rates, which the Company had foreseen in making its initial application to the Board, became actually payable in May and June, 1958, with the result that it soon re-applied for higher tolls. The Board re-examined such familiar themes as maintenance, long distance tolls, and rate groupings. Inevitably, it had to pay particular attention to the deferred tax reserve. After the Cabinet's decision, the Company could have adopted one of three policies: (*a*) claim maximum capital cost allowances for income tax purposes and claim a lesser amount as depreciation on the Company's books, that is, use the diminishing balance method for income tax but use straight line depreciation for its own accounts and for rate-making; (*b*) continue to claim the maximum capital cost allowances for income tax purposes and charge the same amount on its own books; (*c*) revert to its earlier practice which it had followed to the end of 1953 whereby only the amount charged as depreciation in the Company's books (that is, straight line depreciation) was charged for income tax. Under neither of the first two alternatives would Bell be able to earn its current dividend of $2.00 per share of common stock. Under the third alternative, however, earnings would be barely adequate to cover the dividend. Institutional investors, notably insurance companies, pension funds, and investment trusts, were the chief purchasers of new bond issues of the Company. New issues of Bell must be competitive not only with other new issues but also with securities already on the market. Unless earnings on Bell's common stock were sufficient to provide an adequate margin of safety for bond interest, Bell's programme of capital expansion would have to be drastically curtailed to the ultimate detriment of users of its service.

Bell's application for higher tolls was opposed by 35 municipalities in Ontario and 25 in Quebec but not by the governments of these two provinces. Counsel for the municipalities argued that the Cabinet, in deciding against the deferred tax credit, had obviously intended that the other alternatives mentioned above should be similarly disallowed. According to the municipalities, the Company was obliged under the Order-in-Council to charge capital cost allowances but not the deferred tax reserve.

An interesting feature of the case was that the governments of all the provinces except Ontario and Quebec got the Board's permission

[61]P.C. 1958–602 reprinted in (1958) 48 J.O.R.R. 95.

to intervene whereas the two provinces in which Bell's operations were conducted decided to stand aside. Moreover, the two major railways submitted that the Board should refuse to permit the eight governments to intervene. The explanation for those anomalies is that the Board's decision in the Bell case with respect to the tax equalization reserve would presumably bind it in a pending application on freight rates dealing in part with the same question. When all was said and done, the Board allowed Bell to adopt the third alternative it proposed. New and higher tolls became effective not earlier than November 1, 1958.[62]

CRITICISMS OF THE RATE-MAKING PROCESS

A striking feature of the history of the general level of telephone rates in Canada is the willingness of the Board to grant telephone companies substantially all they requested up to 1950 (with the exception of 1921), and its refusal to grant more than 42½ per cent of the amount applied for in 1958. The Board's generous treatment of general increase applications in earlier years has left it open to the charge that it is somehow or other under the thumb of big business. This is patently false and in its defence, the Board could argue that it is compelled to ride along with conditions which are not of its making. Higher rates are forced upon the companies and the Board by inflation of wages and the prices of supplies, the growth and relocation of population, the persistent secular trend in the demand for phones, technological progress, rising interest rates, and the necessity for telephone companies successfully bidding for funds in a highly competitive capital market. Rate cases are only superficially conflicts between company and users. Basically, they involve users of telephone service on the one hand and suppliers of labour, capital, equipment, and expert advice on the other. The applicant must prove to the satisfaction of the Board that he has bargained as hard as he possibly could with all these suppliers. The processes and results of these negotiations are patiently probed and alternative procedures are suggested by counsel and witnesses for the patrons. The Board will not interfere unless, as it says, "there is ample justification through proof of indiscreet or improvident use of management's discretionary powers."[63] Substantially, the Board uses the same approach toward the two large telephone concerns under its jurisdiction as the Supreme

[62] *Bell* v. *Municipalities* (1958) 48 J.O.R.R. 391.
[63] *Bell* v. *Toronto* (1950) J.O.R.R. at p. 18; C.R.T.C. at p. 29.

Court of Canada has adopted toward the Board itself. "A practice has grown up not to interfere with an order of the Board unless it seems manifest that the Board has proceeded upon some wrong principle, or that it has been otherwise subject to error."[64]

In 1958, however, the Board departed from the doctrines of "compelling circumstances" and "managerial discretion." In turning down most of Bell's application, the Board properly excluded the effect of an increase in wages which was not yet payable. Its allowance of the deferred tax reserve was excusable because expert opinions differ and higher judicial or semi-judicial authorities had not ruled on the matter. But by adhering to a permissive level of earnings of $2.43 a share instead of $2.65 as requested by the Company, the Board took a debatable position. Company officials feel that, while the demand for residence and business service will be relatively stable in the event of a decline in gross national product, long distance revenue, which currently provides one-third of Bell's gross operating revenues, will be vulnerable. In March, 1958, Bell's accumulated earned surplus was only $1.95 a share or 6 per cent of the equity. This figure compares with 73 per cent for 22 large Canadian industrial companies and 29 per cent for 8 important Canadian electric utilities. Obviously, if Bell's revenues fall, it will have to cut its rate of dividends, unless it can reduce wages promptly and drastically, which appears unlikely.

Any reduction in the rate of dividend might shake public confidence in Bell stock. Even as matters stand, professional investors, such as managers of investment funds and insurance companies who are in control of a growing proportion of investment in Canada, are not buying nearly as much Bell stock, relative to their total portfolios, as in the past. On the other hand it is undeniably true that Bell has thrived under the rates heretofore allowed by the Board. Apparently, it assumes that Bell's stock will remain popular with individual investors even on a "bare-bones" rate of return. It may also believe that it is human nature for executives of telephone companies, like professors at universities, to think they are doing a much better job than they really are. Perhaps the relative ease with which, at least up to 1958, telephone companies have got authority from the Board of Transport Commissioners for higher rates has encouraged laxity in the performance of day-to-day operations. In other words, having in

[64]*Re Railway Freight Rates* [1933] 2 Dominion Law Reports 209; 40 C.R.C. 97. See also *Manitoba & Saskatchewan* v. *Railway Association* (1920) 26 C.R.C. 147: *C.P.R.* v. *Toronto Transportation Commission* [1930] Appeal Cases 686; 37 C.R.C. 203; 4 Dominion Law Reports 849.

the past been solicitous about the sensitiveness of investors to low corporate earnings, the Board may now be taking into account the effect of regulation on the psychology of management. At all events, the Board must be given full marks for its patience in hearing evidence and argument.[65]

It is obvious from its judgments that the Board has faced peculiar difficulties in its study of the relationships between Bell and American Telephone and Telegraph and between British Columbia Telephone and its parent, the General Telephone Company of Chicago which in 1957 sold its holdings to Anglo-Canadian which has its Head Office in Hawaii. In December, 1957, 98 per cent of Bell's 157,000 shareholders lived in Canada and they owned 92 per cent of its stock. Theoretically Canadians can easily outvote representatives of A.T. & T., which owns but 4.2 per cent of the shares. From this point of view Bell is controlled by Canadians. At the same time A.T. & T. has a representative on the Board of Directors in Montreal and, if Canadians do not vote *en bloc* or if most of them fail to attend the annual meetings, A.T. & T. can still run Bell. The American concern and its subsidiary, Bell Laboratories, provide Bell of Canada with a vast amount of business experience, operating methods, and patents. Canadian executives are free to accept or reject these ideas as they see fit, but inasmuch as Bell of Canada must pay one per cent of its gross revenues for these ideas whether it uses them or not, the assumption is that they are used. Certainly, they must be carried out without change insofar as Bell interchanges messages with sister companies south of the border. In many instances Bell adapts the ideas and equipment to meet what it regards as its own peculiar requirements. In a few cases, such as painting motor vehicles a distinctive shade of green to reduce non-company use especially after working hours, Bell of Canada contributed a money-saving innovation which was snapped up by other members of the "family." Bell passes on the experience it acquires to independents in Ontario and Quebec, to the Maritime and New Brunswick telephone companies in each of which it owns a block of shares, and to other concerns associated with it in the Trans-Canada Telephone Company which arranges for long distance service coast to coast in Canada. In short, it is impossible to ascertain the effect of the engineering and financial interrelationships between Bell and its numerous corporate brethren on the rates payable by Bell's subscribers.

[65]The hearings in Bell's 1950 case involved 50 days of sittings, 6586 pp. of transcript, and 147 exhibits. The B.C. Telephone case in the same year resulted in 1550 pp. of transcript and 82 exhibits.

The Board's judgments raise a few other matters. In telephone cases it keeps repeating its view of the importance of managerial discretion: in railway cases it rarely mentions this topic. For some reason which is not clear from the printed judgments, the Board is far more critical of British Columbia Telephone than it is of Bell. The Board should also have power to regulate the price of every service rendered by the telephone companies which come within its jurisdiction. At present it has no legal control over charges for the use of teletype machines, advertising in directories, and a few minor sources of revenue.[66] These charges may be quite reasonable and since they are determined mainly by competition with other suppliers of communication services and advertising, the Board's practical control over them might be small, even if it had the legal power to set them. On the other hand, exclusion of these prices from purview by the regulatory authority creates a feeling of uneasiness among well-informed telephone users and among competitors.[67] Most of all, the Board should have greater jurisdiction over Northern Electric.

SUMMARY

Although telephone companies provide a service which is vital to our business and social lives, the rates which they charge have attracted much less attention than railway freight rates. The principles on which telephone rates are based—value of service and cost of service—are the same as for telegraph companies, electric light and power concerns, gas companies, and all other public utilities. The comparative neglect of rates is in itself a tribute to the efficient yet unobtrusive service which is rendered at any hour of the day or night by our telephone companies. Among the marvels of the modern world is the quality of the service which one gets by holding a piece of plastic in one's left hand while making a few semi-circular motions with one's right forefinger.

[66]The Board has jurisdiction over general mobile service, e.g. the charge made to a business man who has a phone in his car or to a taxicab company where the Bell supplies service. It has no control where the taxicab company operates its own system. In all mobile services, the Department of Transport assigns wave-lengths.

[67]It would certainly be convenient if the Railway Act were divided into several pieces of legislation each dealing with a single topic such as the incorporation of railway companies, the Board of Transport Commissioners, the Railway Grade Crossing Fund, and telegraph and telephone tolls.

The Export of Electricity from Canada

A. E. DAL GRAUER[1]

Canadians are among the world's most prolific traders. Per capita, they export a greater volume of raw and semi-processed materials than any other people on the face of the globe. Theirs also is a country which is well endowed with water power resources. It may, therefore, seem strange that Canada's exports of electricity have, for many years, been limited to a comparatively small part of the nation's total output of hydro-electric energy. A study of the history of Canada's exports of electricity throws a good deal of light on this seeming paradox. While the following pages have been written with this in mind, they have also been prepared in the hope that a careful recounting of past events will be of some assistance to those who desire to obtain a better understanding of some of the issues which are currently affecting international relations between Canada and the United States.

Around the turn of the century, electricity was regarded in somewhat the same way as nuclear energy is today. It was only in the 1880's that it had been first generated on a commercial scale. Soon its advantages for lighting purposes and in driving industrial motors began to be recognized. Assured of a goodly supply of energy in this form, various electro-process industries began to be developed, and concerns using these techniques to manufacture carbide, abrasives, fertilizers, and aluminium began to locate close to water power sites such as those at Niagara Falls, which were also near to the continent's main transportation arteries. Pulpwood, metal ores, and industrial minerals like salt and limestone were also suited to this type of treatment. Canadians therefore saw in this industrial revolution a long-

[1]I wish to acknowledge the invaluable assistance of Dr. John Davis, Director of the Research and Planning Division of the British Columbia Electric Company Limited, without which I would have found it impossible to complete this study within the time allowed.

sought-after opportunity to process more of their own raw materials at home.

In those days power still could not be transmitted over more than a few dozen miles. Hence centres like Welland in southern Ontario and Buffalo in northern New York were favoured as sites for new manufacturing plants which required electricity in abundance. With the servicing of these needs in mind, various schemes were launched. By 1906 more than half of the water which could be readily diverted from the Niagara River had already been allocated to half a dozen newly formed metallurgical or other power-producing utilities. Plans were also being laid to acquire such additional flows as would not hinder the natural beauty of the Falls. Since most of this energy would be destined for consumption in the United States, opposition arose in Canada to the granting of exclusive licences to harness these resources. A dozen Ontario communities immediately banded together, their objective and that of later participants in the Hydro-Electric Power Commission of Ontario being to put more of this water power to work in Canada.

Some years were to pass before demands on Canada became, in any way, commensurate with the hydro-electric capabilities on the Canadian side of the Niagara and lower St. Lawrence rivers. The Ontario and Quebec governments were, therefore, tempted to commit a portion of these resources for export, because they would produce immediate tax and other revenue. On these grounds, charters were granted to several companies controlled in the United States, whose declared intention was to provide a continuous supply of electrical energy to their parent utilities domiciled in New York State.

These projects, involving a relatively large amount of energy, were expensive to construct. Their financing, therefore, had to be based on long-term sales contracts. One, negotiated by the Ontario Power Company in 1904, envisaged the export of 45,000 horsepower of electrical energy to the United States for a period of 99 years. Another, entered into by the Montreal Light, Heat and Power Corporation in 1912, provided for the sale of 75,000 horsepower in the United States for a term of 85 years. Similar capabilities were also committed to the Canadian export market by the Canadian Niagara Power Company and the Electrical Development Company, both of which were building generating plants on the Canadian side of the Niagara River in 1907 and 1908.[2]

[2]The Ontario Power Company first received a licence permitting it to carry out certain works in the Niagara Park area in 1900. It was constituted

So rapidly did the demand for electricity increase that by 1910 all of the electricity produced on the United States side and about two-thirds[3] of all the energy generated on the Niagara River in Canada was being consumed by industries and other customers in the general vicinity of Buffalo, New York. In total, Canadian exports had grown

---

primarily for the production in Canada of hydro-electric power and its transmission to the United States. The electricity which it exported was sold to the Niagara, Lockport and Ontario Power Company, the latter holding a controlling interest in the Ontario Power Company. The initial contract between the subsidiary and parent companies was dated July 16, 1904, and called for the delivery of 60,000 horsepower on or before January 1, 1907. The contract was to remain in force until April 1, 1950, with certain provisions for renewal. On April 12, 1917, all the assets in Canada of the Ontario Power Company were purchased by the Hydro-Electric Power Commission of Ontario.

The Canadian Niagara Power Company received a licence from the Ontario authorities to develop water power at Niagara Falls in 1892. Its main purpose was to export electrical energy to the United States. It was closely connected with the Niagara Falls Power Company, the latter incorporated and doing business in the state of New York. It was financed by the American company which owned practically all of its stock. Construction began in 1901 and first deliveries of power commenced in 1905.

The Electrical Development Company was incorporated in the province of Ontario by Sir William Mackenzie, Sir Henry Pellatt, and Sir Donald Mann. A licence was granted to them by the province of Ontario for a period of 50 years, running from February 1, 1903. This company was the only one of the three which had developed, in Ontario, a transmission system of any extent by 1917. Its line served Toronto and intermediate territories, being built by the affiliated company, the Toronto & Niagara Power Company. It first exported energy in 1908.

The Montreal Light, Heat & Power Corporation was constituted in the province of Quebec in 1901, its primary purpose being to serve the Montreal area. Its principal exports were to the Aluminum Company of America at Massena, New York. These commenced in 1912.

[3]In 1910, the total installed capacity of generating plants on the Canadian side of Niagara Falls was 142,800 h.p. Of this, 91,000 h.p. was committed for export. At that time, the Ontario Power Company had the right to develop 180,000 h.p. Of this, it had installed 52,000 h.p. and exported 35,000 h.p. to the United States. The Electrical Development Company had the right to develop 125,000 h.p. It was then producing 42,800 h.p. and exporting 10,000 h.p. The Canadian Niagara Power Company enjoyed the right to develop 100,000 h.p. on the Canadian side. Its plants were capable of producing 46,000 h.p., all of which was being exported.

to the point where they absorbed about one-third of the nation's production of electric power. Moves were being made, meanwhile, to divert the remaining surplus water on the Canadian side of the International Boundary by various utilities, some of which were already in business and others of which hoped to export this energy to new market areas in the United States.

The newly formed publicly owned Hydro-Electric Power Commission of Ontario expressed alarm. So did the National Commission of Conservation which had been set up by the Laurier Government in 1909, under the chairmanship of Sir Clifford Sifton. In his dual capacity as Minister of the Interior, Sir Clifford stated in the Commission's first annual report that "The suggestion that power can be generated on the Canadian side and exported to the United States and that, thereafter, when it is required in Canada, the Company can be ordered to deprive the United States customers of the power and deliver it in Canada, is entirely illusory." His Commission also reported to the effect that: "Should power be exported to the United States, the vested interests which it would create there would prevent its subsequent withdrawal to meet the future needs of Canadian industries."[4]

Even at this relatively early date, political complications of an international character seemed inevitable. Large investments were involved. Customers who were already well entrenched in the United States had no alternative sources of supply immediately available to them. Besides, continuity of service is an obligation characteristically assumed by electric power utilities. Dislocations are intolerable, not only because they will cause considerable inconvenience, but because they may render worthless previous outlays on a wealth of transmission, distributing, and consumer equipment. Buttressing these arguments was also the comparative size and influence of the United States. Having allowed export agreements to be made, the Ontario and Canadian government authorities were already finding themselves in a position where they were unable to repatriate firm power exported under them, that is, power available under all conditions, as contrasted with surplus power. As it turned out, the necessary legislative steps had been taken. Their administration, both at the provincial and federal levels, however, was found to be wanting.[5]

[4]Commission of Conservation, *Water Powers of Canada* (Ottawa: Mortimer Co. Ltd., 1911).

[5]Ontario permits (1904 and later) required that at least half of the power sold by each licensee should be marketed in Ontario. The federal

Interestingly enough, the first limitations on the movement of electricity across the International Boundary were imposed by the United States itself. Concerned with preserving the natural beauty of Niagara Falls, the International Waterways Commission had proposed, as early as 1905, that withdrawals of water for power-making purposes should be limited. Early the next year, and prompted by this Commission's recommendations, the United States Congress passed what was commonly referred to in succeeding years as the "Burton Bill." Officially, it was "an Act for the Control and Regulation of the Waters of the Niagara River and for the Preservation of Niagara Falls."[6]

The Burton Bill stipulated that it was illegal to transmit electrical power into the United States from the Niagara River except in accordance with a permit issued by the United States Secretary for War. The amount of water power which would normally be imported in this way was set at 160,000 horsepower. Under its provisions, supplementary permits could also be issued under the United States Secretary's authority. They were in no circumstances to exceed, when included with such electricity as was generated for use in Canada, the total figure of 350,000 horsepower. As some 170,000 horsepower could also be generated on the United States side, this prompted Sir Clifford Sifton to say: "If the United States can utilize the electrical energy from the Canadian side immediately or in the near future, it will absorb nearly all of Canada's share before we have developed sufficiently to form a market for it."[7]

In Ottawa, these and other rumblings soon led to the passing of "An Act to Regulate the Exportation of Electric Power and Certain Liquids and Gases." Enacted on April 27, 1907, it was essentially restrictive in character. This Canadian legislation prohibited the exportation of any power or fluid except under government permit, and the possibility of an export duty of up to $10.00 per horsepower year was also envisaged. Licences, thereafter, had to be secured from the Department of Inland Revenue, Ottawa, and were to be subject to review every twelve months.

---

export act (1907) allowed the sale in the United States of "surplus" energy under a licence which had to be renewed annually.

[6]Commission of Conservation, *Water Powers of Canada.* The International Waterways Commission was a creation of the Rivers and Harbours Act of the United States, 1902.

[7]Arthur V. White, *Memorandum Respecting Exportation of Electricity*, Commission of Conservation, May 5, 1914. Burton Bill, Ref. 11.

Supporting Regulations framed later in 1907 stated that:

> Any licence issued hereunder shall be revocable at will by the Governor-in-Council, if the licensee refuses or neglects to comply with any of the conditions from time to time imposed by the Governor-in-Council with regard to the supply and distribution of electrical energy, gas or fluid in Canada and moreover, whenever such electrical energy, gas or fluid is required for the use of purchasers in Canada, any such licence shall be revocable upon such notices to the licensee as the Governor-in-Council deems reasonable in each case.[8]

Another qualification was that such energy as was sold for export should under no circumstances be marketed outside of Canada at a price or prices less than those charged to similar consumers in Canada.[9] With minor modifications in 1925, and again in 1955, this Act governing the export of electricity has continued in force down to the present time.

The Burton Bill, passed by the United States Congress in 1906, had a limited life. Originally, it was to run for three years. Then its term was extended. Finally, it expired in 1913. With its termination in sight, the United States Secretary for War (through the Office of the United States Chief of Engineers) called for tenders on projects, the declared purpose of which was to harness the remaining 80,000 horsepower of undeveloped electrical potential on both sides of Niagara Falls.[10] Formal applications were received from the Niagara, Lockport and Ontario Power Company, the Niagara Falls Power Company, and the Federal Light and Power Company. All were owned and controlled in the United States.

Within twelve months the New York state legislature also appointed a Joint Committee, the primary objective of which was to investigate

[8]Sir Henry Drayton, *Report on Export of Electricity from Canada and Report of the Power Controller* (Ottawa, 1919), p. 15.

[9]The Regulations issued on November 7, 1907, under the Electricity and Fluid Exportation Act for the same year read in part: "Where a supply of electrical energy, gas or fluid is provided in any part of Canada by the contractor for export and home consumption, then the price charged to any person or company in Canada by the contractor shall not exceed the prices at which electrical energy, gas or fluid is sold by the contractor for export, in like quantities, under similar circumstances." Commission of Conservation, *Water Powers of Canada*, p. 345.

[10]White, *Memorandum Respecting Exportation of Electricity*.

water conditions and to allocate the remaining flow of the Niagara River for power-producing purposes. Early in 1914 it made its report. Among other things, it drew attention to two bills then before Congress in Washington. One, sponsored by Congressman Cline[11] and aimed at the "Control and Regulation of the Waters of the Niagara River," included the provision that: "The quantity of electrical power which may be transmitted from the Dominion of Canada into the United States under this Act shall not exceed 250,000 h.p." Another bill, introduced by Congressman Levy, was designed to restrict the right of the United States federal government to such matters as navigation, national defence, and the amount of water diverted from international rivers such as the St. Lawrence. The Levy Bill[12] differed from that advocated by Congressman Cline in that it would have given the state of New York exclusive control over the allotment, distribution, and sale of electricity produced at Niagara Falls.

While these developments were annoying to Canadians, the first really discordant note was struck by the Public Service Commission of the state of New York. In reviewing the application of a newly formed American-owned company, the Canadian-American Power Corporation, for permission to import 46,000 additional horsepower of electrical energy from Canada for thirty years, it dealt at some length with the claim of opponents to this scheme, who had been arguing that, as a result of existing legislation, Canada could unilaterally withdraw this energy. While recognizing this possibility, the New York Commission reported itself as being of the opinion that:

> We have nothing before us but the suggestion that the Dominion of Canada may, at some future time, forbid this

[11]Ref. 12(x) Cline Bill: A Bill for the Control and Regulation of the Waters of the Niagara River above the Falls of Niagara and for other purposes, April 14, 1914, 63rd Congress, 1st sess.

Had the provisions of the Cline Bill come into effect, it would have given the United States the benefit of power produced from a total of 48,000 cu. ft. of water per second, as compared with power consumed in Canada to the equivalent of a flow of some 18,000 cu. ft. This helps to explain the remark which appears in the Report of the International Waterways Commission of 1906, to the effect that: "In respect to the amount of water diverted on the Canadian side, Canada's advantage is more apparent than real." (Canada, Parliament, *Sessional Papers*, Nov. 19, 1907.)

[12]Ref. 13(x) Levy Bill: A Bill to give effect to the fifth article of the

> exportation. This Commission must assume that international relations affecting so important a subject as the means of continuing great industries which have grown up in reliance upon the use of this imported power, and as well the interests of the Canadian producing companies themselves, have become fixed and subject only to such changes as will fully protect the great commercial and industrial interests and rights now served by this power brought from Canada. The time has long since passed when governments proceed ruthlessly from pure national rashness or anger to destroy the settled accepted commercial relations and formally vested rights of persons and corporations.[13]

This interpretation raised a storm in Ottawa. A special committee of the Privy Council was convened for the purpose of dealing with this contentious matter. After due deliberation, the federal Cabinet issued instructions to the effect that a carefully worded minute outlining the laws and regulations of the Dominion of Canada should be "forwarded to His Majesty's Ambassador in Washington, with the request that he make representations to the United States Government in the sense thereof in order that the matter may properly be brought to the attention of whatever persons or interests are concerned."[14]

This Order-in-Council, passed when the Canadian House of Commons was in recess, confined itself to pointing out that: (*a*) licences issued under the Canadian Electricity and Fluid Exportation Act were, in effect, revocable; (*b*) each licence was valid for only one year at a time; and (*c*) the use of exported energy by industries outside of Canada could not "create a situation or status which in any way involved an obligation on the part of the Canadian Government to permit a permanent diversion of this natural resource." Ottawa did not threaten to cut off Canadian exports immediately. Indeed, the Privy Council minute went on to say that many consumers who had been using electrical energy exported from Canada "may have placed themselves and their business activities in such a relation to the supply

treaty between the United States and Great Britain signed January 11, 1909, 63rd Congress, 2nd sess.

[13]White, *Memorandum Respecting Exportation of Electricity*, p. 13.

[14]P.C. 2203, Order-in-Council for communication to the Government of the United States, August 25, 1914.

of energy that any sudden, complete cessation of it would entail great inconvenience and possible hardship. Licences shall be revocable only upon reasonable notice." It also noted that:

> In accordance with the spirit of this provision, . . . the most careful consideration is being given to the question of the terms and the notice on which the undoubted right of this government to terminate at any time the exportation of electrical energy may be best exercised so as to entail the least possible inconvenience to those concerned.

The real explosion, if it can be described as such, was heard in 1917. Canada was then well advanced in her plans for the large-scale production of certain electro-chemicals vital to the manufacturers of munitions. More power was needed and the attention of the federal authorities was soon attracted to Niagara Falls. However, when the Imperial Munitions Board consulted the producers there, it found that export commitments, together with the already inflated demands of industrial and other consumers in Canada, had absorbed practically all of their existing capacity. Alarmed by this situation, the Canadian Government appointed a one-man Royal Commission, the purpose of which was to investigate the uses to which this electricity was being put and, if desirable, to arrange for the repatriation of some of this exported energy from the United States. Sir Henry L. Drayton, then Chairman of the Board of Railway Commissioners, was nominated for this purpose. His report, issued by the King's Printer in 1919 and entitled *Report on Export of Electricity from Canada and Report of the Power Comptroller*, contains an account of his official efforts in this connection.

Before summarizing the conclusions reached by Sir Henry Drayton in 1919, it may be as well to review the trends in and administration of Canadian power production and exports in these early years. Table I shows that exports from Ontario to the United States rose steadily until 1914. They then began to level off. About the same time the movement of power out of Quebec was getting under way. Exports from the Cedars plant of the Montreal Light, Heat and Power Company rose from negligible proportions in 1914 to the equivalent of one-third of Canada's total exports three years later.

As Canada's total sales in New York State can be seen to have risen from the commencement of the First World War onwards, the question might well be asked: Why did Ottawa issue licences permitting the export of these increased amounts of energy? The eventual magnitude of Canada's war production could not have been anticipated. If it had, some, if not all, of Sir Henry Drayton's difficulties would have been avoided.

TABLE I

ANNUAL QUANTITY OF ELECTRICITY EXPORTED TO THE UNITED STATES, 1908–20
(volume in millions of kilowatt hours)

Year	From Ontario	From Quebec	From other provinces	Total exports	Total exports as percentage of total Canadian production*
1908	113	—	—	113	
1909	358	—	1	359	
1910	474	—	1	475	33
1911	536	—	2	538	
1912	536	—	2	538	
1913	656	—	6	662	
1914	746	—	27	773	
1915	605	29	22	656	
1916	647	359	16	1,022	
1917	779	429	17	1,225	
1918	730	381	16	1,127	
1919	731	396	16	1,143	21
1920	643	283	24	950	16

*No statistics relating to the output of Canadian central electric stations are available prior to 1919. Their production in 1910 was estimated from capacity data published by the Dominion Bureau of Statistics and involved the assumption that the average system load factor at that time was 30 per cent.

SOURCES: 1908–10, Canada, Department of Inland Revenue, Publications in Dominion Bureau of Statistics Library; 1911–20, *Canada Year Book.*

Late in 1917 Sir Henry Drayton, then Power Controller of Canada, notified the export companies that their licences might be curtailed or even permitted to lapse on April 1, 1918. He then entered into discussions with the American authorities as to how this energy might best be devoted to the furtherance of the Allied war effort. Sir Henry's negotiations with Ontario Hydro, the private utilities operating on the Canadian side at Niagara, and the United States Department of Defense were essentially oral in character and little documentary evidence is available. However, it is noteworthy that, in his *Report* of 1919, Sir Henry, on the one hand, expresses his appreciation for the promptness and consideration with which the United States Secretary of War and his representatives dealt with this question and, on the other, complains about the difficulties which he encountered in getting the Ontario utilities to work together in the common cause.

One of the origins of this latter difficulty was the public versus private power issue in Ontario. The publicly owned Ontario Hydro-

Electric Power Commission, it seems, had sparked the drive to recapture Canadian-produced electricity. Having recently taken over all of the assets of the formerly American-owned Ontario Power Company in 1917, the Hydro-Electric Power Commission was reluctant to terminate the export contracts which it had inherited in this way. Instead, it claimed that the remaining privately owned companies should reduce their exports, thereby making much of the energy that they produced available for distribution and resale by the Ontario Hydro-Electric Power Commission. Its privileged position, Ontario Hydro argued, stemmed from the fact that the export commitments of the Ontario Power Company pre-dated the passing of the Fluid and Electricity Export Act by Parliament in 1907. Hence, Ontario Hydro should be allowed to continue the sale of 60,000 horsepower in the United States. On the other hand, the first deliveries of the Canadian Niagara Power Company and the Electrical Development Company were made after the Act was passed. Therefore, they and they alone should be forced to curtail their exports.

These differences were only partially resolved by the federal Power Controller. A 10,000 horsepower limitation of exports was eventually made by Ontario Hydro. This, together with diversions of power to Canada by the privately owned companies operating in Quebec and Ontario, served to reduce Canada's total sales in the United States by nearly 20 per cent.[15] United States authorities, meanwhile, arranged for a sizable tonnage of United States coal to be made available for the production of 16,000 continuous horsepower of electrical energy by an old steam plant in Toronto. With this additional energy, it was possible to accelerate the Canadian war effort. Most of the steam power, it should be noted, was used for the manufacture of cyanamide chemicals at Welland, Ontario. Also, most of the production from these factories was on order with the United States Department of Defense.

The shortage period, which lasted approximately 18 months, came to an end with the termination of hostilities. Demand fell sharply, dropping down by as much as one-third between November and December, 1918. The emergency had passed and with it the need for priorities, which were cancelled.

[15]According to the Standards Division, Department of Trade and Commerce, Ottawa, Canada's total exports in the year 1917 amounted to 1,225 millions of kilowatt hours. In 1918, the corresponding figure was 1,041 millions of kilowatt hours, or down by nearly 20 per cent.

Sir Henry Drayton had been unable to reduce Canada's exports at Niagara by more than 50,000 horsepower, but he did not believe that larger amounts of electrical energy should have been repatriated to Canada at the time. In fact, he notes in his *Report* that:

> If the export of power were prohibited, undoubtedly more power would become available for munitions plants in Canada; but, on the other hand, important manufacturing carried on in the United States, on which the allies are dependent, would directly suffer. The output would be still further decreased and, in some instances, probably stopped. The over-riding Canadian interest, as I see it, is best served by insuring the continuous operation of munitions plants, both in Canada and the United States.[16]

Sir Henry Drayton later went so far as to say that, in his opinion, a substantially higher proportion of the electricity exported from Canadian plants was being used for essential war purposes in the United States than was the case in this country.

The challenge which had confronted Canada's wartime Power Controller was partially political in character. The Ontario Hydro, whose Chairman was that aggressive champion of public enterprise, Sir Adam Beck, was at daggers drawn with the two other principal utilities operating at the Niagara River. In this connection, Sir Henry Drayton wrote: "It is to be regretted that there is not more co-ordination and friendly co-operation between the Companies. If the Ontario districts were served by a combination of the Hydro and Toronto Power Systems, a better diversity and load factor could be obtained and more power thus rendered commercially available from the present plants."[17] Also he said: "The incorporation of the Toronto Power Plant into the Hydro System would to an appreciable extent help the Ontario situation. With the present mutual distrust and lack of confidence, there appears to be no room for the hope of proper co-operation, entailing as it of necessity would, an entirely unselfish attitude and mutual assistance and trust."[18]

A further complicating factor, and one which plagued industries on both sides of the International Boundary, was the general shortage of coal which persisted throughout the late war years. Rationing resulted in hardships. Real suffering occurred at all levels, and industrial plants making munitions of war, like home-owners and commercial establish-

[16]Drayton, *Report*, p. 22. [17]*Ibid.* [18]*Ibid.*, p. 23.

ments, had to get by as best they could. Editorially and otherwise, Canadian writers bemoaned the fact that central Canada was dependent upon foreign powers for its supplies for this vitally needed fuel. Yet, Sir Henry Drayton, who was much better informed on these matters, rarely complained about the manner in which United States coal was allotted for Canadian consumption. Apparently the American coal administrators were scrupulously fair and Canadians shared more or less proportionately with Americans when it came to parcelling out coal from the mines in Pennsylvania and West Virginia.

The 1917–18 power experience, though it involved a minimum of high-level international acrimony at the time, assumed greater significance with the passage of time. Utility executives, industrialists, and residential consumers alike began to argue that no further commitments involving the sale of electricity to the United States should be countenanced, either at Queen's Park, Quebec City, or Ottawa. The previously moderate Sir Henry Drayton was eventually heard to express openly in the House of Commons that "power exported is power lost." Others took up the cue. During sessions of the Canadian Parliament in 1925, 1927, 1928, 1929, 1933, and 1937, leading members of the Government and of the Opposition all spoke to much the same effect, namely, that Canada should never again export firm power. No long-term contracts should be countenanced and sales to the United States should be essentially interruptible in character.

In 1925 the possibility of exporting power from the Ottawa and lower St. Lawrence rivers was discussed. A provision for placing a duty of up to $10 per horsepower was also incorporated in the federal Export Act.[19] During the debate a resolution was advanced by the then Prime Minister, the Rt. Hon. W. L. Mackenzie King, which said:

> In the opinion of this House, the export of hydro-electric power from Canada should be permitted only on a yearly licence, and that hereafter no licences for the export of power beyond that already granted should be issued, except with the concurrence of the Province or Provinces in which it is proposed to generate such power, and of any other Province adjacent to such development and interested therein.[20]

[19]Under the existing Act the Governor in Council is still empowered to impose, by proclamation, export duties not exceeding $10 per horsepower year on energy exported from Canada. An export tax of 0.03¢ per kilowatt hour, or roughly $2 per horsepower year, has been in effect since 1925.

[20]Canada, House of Commons, *Official Report of Debates*, 1925, p. 4288.

About the same time, the Leader of the Opposition, the Rt. Hon. Arthur Meighen, said:

> Power is not something that is in the world market, that another country can substitute for if the first country withdraws. Power is something which, once exported, becomes the foundation of a great vested right and the withdrawal of it—however closely, however narrowly, and carefully, it may have been provided for—becomes a practical impossibility. We found ourselves in the position that when we needed the power badly, we could not withdraw it, and we found, as well, that although we applied the system of yearly licences, the Company undertook to give contracts extending over a period of time and we were bound, not only by the rights secured by the industries erected, but were also bound, in a measure, by the contract, although that contract had no warrant to be entered into.[21]

In 1928, the Rt. Hon. R. B. Bennett, as Leader of the Opposition, argued that a licence to export power should only be issued on the authority of Parliament; not merely at the discretion of the Cabinet. In this connection, he stated:

> There is, however, a general tendency toward believing that, with respect to the exportation of electric energy, Parliament should be consulted because of the unfortunate incidents that sometimes arise by reason of such licences being granted, and then when the power may be required for domestic purposes at home, it is found that there have been created abroad vested interests of such a character that the cancellation of the licence is regarded as an unfriendly act. Parliament, therefore, should consider these matters in every detail before a licence is granted.[22]

In 1929, the Rt. Hon. W. L. Mackenzie King was commenting on the possible export of electricity from the Beauharnois development in Montreal. *Hansard* reports him as follows:

> Our Government has repeatedly made clear its policy with regard to the exportation of power from Canada to the United

[21] *Ibid.*, p. 4282.
[22] *Ibid.*, 1928, p. 361.

> States. We have given it as our opinion that power should not be exported. That opinion was endorsed by the National Advisory Committee with respect to the power which might be generated in connection with the development of the St. Lawrence. Accordingly, in writing the United States with respect to any possible basis of negotiations, our position in this regard was made very clear. The exact statement made by our Government in correspondence which passed between the United States and Canada in 1928, contains these words: "Public opinion in Canada is opposed to the export of hydro-electric power, and is insistent that such power as may be rendered available on the St. Lawrence, whether from wholly Canadian section or, from the Canadian half of the international section, shall be utilized within the Dominion to stimulate Canadian industry and develop the natural resources. With this view, the National Advisory Committee expresses itself as in complete accord."[23]

In 1933 Mr. Maurice Duplessis, then in Opposition, criticized the lack of enforcement of the Quebec Act of 1926, which was aimed at limiting the export of electricity to the United States. He was reported as saying:

> Once power went to the United States, it would be impossible to recall it, and to seek to do so would be a cause of war, so it was apparent that the Government would not have control of the power to be exported. It meant a permanent alienation of 250,000 horsepower developed in Quebec. Already, there was export of power from Cedar Rapids by the Montreal Light, Heat and Power Company. Also, the Southern Canada Power Company exported power to the United States. Evidently, the law was being breached.[24]

The Rt. Hon. Sir George Perley, when speaking of Ontario Hydro's proposal to export energy in 1937, said in the House of Commons in Ottawa:

> As a matter of fact, we learned from sad experience that, when we gave authority to export power, we could not stop its ex-

[23]*Ibid.*, 1929, p. 415.
[24]*Montreal Gazette*, April 5, 1933.

portation when we wanted it. That happened many years ago. We went over the papers[25] very carefully and it was therein stated, as definitely as words could make it, that the export of power could be stopped on proper notice whenever the Government of Canada wished to do so, or whenever the power was required in this country. But when it came to the time when we wanted power, during the War, the United States took the view that the industries in that country had been built up through the use of power and that it would be an unfriendly act on our part to discontinue the export of it. I take it that from that time forward everybody was pretty well agreed that it was not in the interests of Canada to grant licences for the export of power, even if it was not required by us at that particular time.[26]

Twice during the inter-war period, the House of Commons passed a bill, the intent of which was to take the power to grant additional permits for the export of electrical energy away from the Government and invest it in Parliament. Had this legislation been approved by the Senate, additional sales in the United States would have required special legislation. Such a bill was introduced in 1927 by a Conservative member, H. A. Stewart of Leeds. The second time, it was proposed by Prime Minister Mackenzie King. On both occasions, the Commons passed the bill unanimously, but the Senate allowed it to die. After the second denouement, Prime Minister King issued a statement to the effect that, in his opinion, all future Canadian governments would consider themselves bound to consult Parliament before granting further permits. Any number of statements by persons of lesser rank can be quoted, but the foregoing will indicate the importance attached to this question and the unanimity of opinion in the Canadian House of Commons on this subject.

Whenever these issues have been raised in Canada, the tendency has been to bring them up for resolution in Parliament. In the United States, on the other hand, regulation has long been recognized as a complicated matter requiring the attention of specialists. For example,

[25]Presumably, Sir George Perley was referring to the federal export permits. The contracts between the companies involved ran for much longer periods of time.

[26]House of Commons, *Debates* 1937, p. 2724.

the United States Federal Power Commission was set up by an Act of Congress in 1920[27]:

a) To make investigations and collect data concerning the utilization of water resources, the water power industry and its relation to inter-state or foreign commerce;
b) To co-operate with other agencies of state or national governments in such investigations;
c) To make public, from time to time, the information secured hereunder;
d) To issue licences;
e) To prescribe a uniform system of accounts; and
f) To hold hearings in connection with applications for licences, or the regulation of rates, etc., as provided in this Act.

Since that time, its terms of reference have become more elaborate[28] and its staff has been much increased. At the same time, cost criteria have been developed and a body of knowledge concerning the optimum use of energy resources has been accumulated. This, together with numerous opportunities which have been afforded to producers

[27]See *Federal Power Commission Laws and Hydro-Electric Power Development Laws* (Washington: U.S. Government Printing Office, 1953). See also H.R. 3184: An Act to create a Federal Power Commission; to provide for the improvement of navigation; the development of water power; the use of the public lands in relation thereto; and to repeal Section 18 of the River and Harbour Appropriation Act, approved August 8, 1917; Public No. 280; 66th Congress, approved June 10, 1920.

[28]Congress passed acts in 1930, and again in 1935, to reorganize the Federal Power Commission and to amend the Federal Water Power Act (Public No. 412; 71st Congress, approved June 23, 1930, and Public No. 33; 74th Congress, approved August 26, 1935). The latter amendment includes: "For the purpose of assuring an abundant supply of electric energy, throughout the United States with the greatest possible economy, the Commission is empowered to divide the country into regional districts for the voluntary inter-connection and co-ordination of facilities for the generation, transmission and sale of electric energy." Also: "Whenever the Commission determines that an emergency exists, [it] shall have authority, with or without notice, hearing or report, to require such temporary connections of facilities and such generation, delivery, interchange or transmission of electric energy as will best meet the emergency and serve the public interest."

and consumers of electricity to have their cases heard and obtain facts, has doubtless helped to facilitate the growth of the electric power industry in the United States.

Cases must be heard and permission obtained from the United States Federal Power Commission prior to the export of power from the United States. This became obligatory as a result of an amendment to the United States Federal Power Act. Amended in the early 1930's, it now reads: "No person shall transmit any electrical energy to the United States or to a foreign country without first having secured an Order of the Commission authorizing it to do so."[29]

Final authority rests with the President of the United States. Presidential permits, of which there are as yet only a few in number, typically read: "That this Permit may be terminated at the will and pleasure of the President of the United States with or without cause"; also: "The facilities herein authorized shall not be operated so as to impair the sufficiency of supply within the United States."

From the mid-1920's onward debates in Canada have centred on future possibilities, rather than on difficult situations which existed at the time. One promotion which attracted considerable attention in 1925 is described in a statement by Sir Adam Beck, Chairman of the Ontario Hydro-Electric Power Commission, in which he protests against the exportation of electric power from the Carillon power site on the Ottawa River near Montreal. In a pamphlet bearing his own signature, Sir Adam said that the Quebec–New England Electric Corporation, though it was only applying for a licence to export 100,000 horsepower, was really in search of 400,000 horsepower of electrical energy. The smaller amount was substantially in excess of that which could be generated at Carillon. He, therefore, saw in this application an attempt by the American-owned and -controlled corporation to establish a foothold in eastern Canada from which it could later develop an export power to New York and other adjoining states.[30]

In opposing this project, Sir Adam Beck pointed out previous experience in eastern Ontario. He said that, even though communities in the Ontario Hydro franchise areas of eastern Ontario continued to

[29]Elmer A. Lewis, *Federal Power Commission Laws and Hydro-Electric Power Development Laws* (1953), p. 34.

[30]Sir Adam Beck, *A Statement Protesting against the Exportation of Electric Power, with Special Reference to the Proposed Lease of the "Carillon" Power Site* (Toronto, 1925).

be short of electricity, transmission lines from the Cedars plant near Montreal were allowed to carry some 80,000 horsepower of energy through these areas for ultimate consumption around Massena, New York. He claimed to have approached the United States company which controlled these operations. All Ontario Hydro had been able to obtain for its Canadian customers was some 5,000 horsepower of firm energy.

Sir Adam also referred to an article in the *New York Times* which described "a project to link resources across the Border."[31] The over-all plan, he said, envisaged the eventual development of some 4,000,000 horsepower to supply the rapidly expanding markets for electrical energy in the northeastern United States. The Hydro Chairman declared: "To thus subordinate the very lifeblood of Canadian industry —low-cost electric power—to the dictation of foreign interests forebodes an ultimate political subservience that no Canadian can or will tolerate." He also was of the opinion that: "To export power to the United States would foster and build up industries in the eastern United States at the expense of those in Canada. Canadian cities and rural communities would be deprived of further low-cost power."[32] Attacks of this kind had their desired effect and the idea of a great international power pool was abandoned.

During the boom years which characterized the later 1920's the possibility of Canada and the United States jointly building a deep waterway between Montreal and Lake Ontario was revived. Now, however, power was to be an important by-product of the over-all programme. Figures as high as 750,000 horsepower were mentioned. Still, Canada's immediate needs fell short of this amount. Numerous proposals were, therefore, made by the United States and other authorities that Canada's share of these water power resources be exported for a period of years. These suggestions, as one might expect, met with little enthusiasm in Ottawa. The attitude of Quebec was openly hostile. There the feeling stirred up during debates in Parliament was sufficient to put an end to any idea of selling this energy to customers other than those in Canada.

With the onset of the depression, the demand for power showed signs of lagging. Plans for new projects were shelved. For nearly a decade, idle capacity and contractual obligations to purchase in excess of power requirements continued to hound the power industry. So

[31]*Ibid.*, p. 6.
[32]*Ibid.*

heavy did the burden of carrying charges become that, by 1935, the possibility of selling energy to the United States began to look good. When the Montreal Light, Heat and Power Company was approached by the Aluminum Company of America with a view of obtaining an additional supply of electricity for its refinery at Massena, the company jumped at the opportunity. First, it had to obtain permission to export an additional 40,000 horsepower of firm energy from the Quebec Government. This was readily forthcoming. Then the company applied to Ottawa for a licence under the Fluid and Electricity Export Act. In 1937 the Ontario Government, appealing on behalf of the Ontario Hydro-Electric Power Commission, also requested permission to sell additional quantities of surplus energy into the United States. After various delays and another lengthy debate on the subject of exports, both of these submissions were withdrawn. Mounting Canadian demands eventually took up much of the slack and by 1941 most of this surplus capacity was producing energy for home consumption.

Table II indicates the over-all trend and amount of Canadian energy exported, by province, to the United States during the inter-

TABLE II

ANNUAL EXPORTS OF ELECTRICITY TO THE UNITED STATES, 1920–40
(volume in millions of kilowatt hours)

Year	From Ontario	From Quebec	From other provinces	Total Canada	Total exports as a percentage of Canadian production
1920	643	282	25	950	16
1921	619	365	36	1,020	18
1922	501	324	37	862	13
1923	653	357	44	1,054	13
1924	723	425	52	1,200	13
1925	809	379	51	1,239	12
1926	814	376	63	1,253	10
1927	1,202	390	17	1,609	11
1928	1,250	413	12	1,675	10
1929	1,144	444	16	1,604	9
1930	1,028	449	20	1,497	8
1931	1,206	522	22	1,750	11
1932	660	327	21	1,008	6
1933	444	188	20	652	4
1934	789	391	19	1,199	6
1935	959	337	21	1,317	6
1936	1,080	477	21	1,578	6
1937	1,253	571	23	1,847	7
1938	1,232	571	24	1,827	7
1939	1,290	597	26	1,913	7
1940	1,471	637	28	2,136	7

SOURCE: *Canada Year Book*, 1920–41.

war period. It is interesting to note that during the 1930's the province of Quebec had reversed its stand on the export of electricity. In 1937 it actually supported the Montreal Light, Heat and Power Company's application to dispose of 40,000 horsepower of electrical energy to the Aluminum Company of America for a term of five years.[33] Its reasons were essentially financial. Had the sale been approved by the federal authorities, the province of Quebec would have received a tax revenue of 50¢ per horsepower-year. The Montreal Light, Heat and Power Company's customers in the province of Quebec were supposed to benefit to an even greater extent. Translated into a reduction in rates, the resultant annual saving was estimated to be in the vicinity of $340,000.

Ontario Hydro's predicament was also one of an embarrassment of riches. Unable to obtain additional water by diversion from above Niagara in the early 1920's the Commission had turned to Quebec for its future supplies of energy. Supply contracts had thus been written with the Gatineau Power Company, the McLaren Power Company, the Ottawa Valley Company, and the Beauharnois Light, Heat and Power Company, for a total of 791,000 horsepower, to meet requirements to the year 1937. These utilities had then scheduled the construction of new generating facilities on the Gatineau, Lievre, and lower St. Lawrence rivers, in such a fashion as to bring them on to the line in step with Ontario Hydro's projected demand for power. Unfortunately, markets did not develop in the manner in which they had been forecast, and Ontario Hydro was eventually forced to either cancel or apply for a reduction in the contracted amounts. Following extended negotiations and, in one case, litigation in the courts, a reduced schedule of deliveries was agreed upon. Under these altered circumstances the Ontario Hydro-Electric Power Commission was still required to take a total of 566,000 horsepower from Quebec in 1938, supplementary amounts to be added each year to 1944 inclusive.

New loads had to be developed if costs were to remain under control. One of the possibilities considered by Ontario Hydro was the exportation of part of its surplus to the United States. After careful consideration, a request for permission to export 120,000 horsepower of interruptible energy was sent to Ottawa by the Premier of Ontario,

[33]At that time, Montreal Light, Heat and Power Company already held a permit for the exportation of 75,000 horsepower at $15 per horsepower year for a term of 85 years and a second agreement to export 41,500 horsepower at $15 per horsepower year for a term of 3 years.

the Hon. M. F. Hepburn.[34] Revenue from the sale of this energy in the United States was estimated to be in the order of $1,500,000 a year. The Premier's supporting memorandum also stressed that this was another case of at-will surplus energy which could be withdrawn immediately, or on short notice. No change in the existing export Act was therefore envisaged or deemed to be advisable at the time.

Various other arguments were employed in support of this proposal. They bear repetition in that they may also be made by present-day utilities whose desire is to limit their investment in generating facilities while at the same time maximizing their revenues through inter-connections with other systems.

> In the ordinary course of events, almost any large power system will have available, from time to time, power resources which may be sold to advantage on a short-term basis, an interruptible basis, or strictly on an at-will basis. These resources will arise from such circumstances as:
> a) The necessity of making firm power commitments a number of years in advance of expected requirements;
> b) The impossibility of accurately estimating future power needs. Any capacity provided to meet an expected load growth which does not materialize is available for short-term sales;
> c) The well-recognized fact that power reserves must be provided to take care of losses in capacity due to contingencies of various kinds. These reserves are available for sale on a basis which enables the power to be recovered at any instant to meet contingencies as they may arise; and
> d) Seasonal variations in demand. These variations make possible the sale of certain quantities of power during the seasons when the primary demand is not at its heaviest.[35]

The Commission's Brief then went on to say that:

> It has been the policy of the Hydro-Electric Power Commission of Ontario to sell any electrical energy which could be derived

[34]See *Correspondence and Documents Relating to St. Lawrence Deep Waterway Treaty, 1932 . . . and the Export of Electrical Power* (Ottawa: King's Printer, 1938).

[35]Statement made by Hon. M. F. Hepburn to Hon. W. D. Euler, Minister of Trade and Commerce, in *ibid.*, p. 78.

> from resources in excess of primary power demands, for the highest price that it would bring. Substantial quantities of reserve power and seasonal power have thus been sold as "surplus export" to the United States and during the Depression considerable quantities were sold in Canada for the generation of process steam. Since then, small quantities of seasonal power for steam electric generation have been sold each year up to the present. These various sales have materially augmented the Commission's revenue.

In his supporting letter dated January 21, 1938, Mr. Hepburn also stated that:

> There is no risk of American industries and American communities along the border of Ontario becoming dependent upon Canadian power; large American power interests with extensive water power and practically unlimited fuel resources stand ready to supply American demands. The question is not whether a certain American industry or territory shall be supplied with Canadian power or, alternatively, shall do without power, it is rather a question of whether certain American power demands shall be temporarily supplied from Canada's water power, which otherwise would waste, or from American coal. Canadian power is wanted only because it can be made available at an attractive price. In this case, it would be recallable in accordance with the terms of sale without the slightest protest from anyone. It is a matter of record that the Commission has already interrupted its export deliveries on occasions too numerous to mention.
>
> The exportation of raw materials, which is permitted in large quantities, affords an interesting and illuminating comparison with electric power. In this connection, it is important to note that, in general, raw materials are assets which diminish with use whereas electricity produced from water power is a continuing asset which does not diminish with use, in fact, it simply wastes if not used. Again, the availability of raw materials exercises an important influence upon the location of industries. Surely there can be no argument for prohibiting the export of hydraulic power which does not apply with equal or greater force to the export of raw materials and no argument for permitting the export of raw materials which is not at

> least equally applicable to the export of electricity produced from water power.
>
> In connection with the contention that the export of power will interfere with the establishment of American industries in Canada, I would point out that the comparatively small quantity of power which is under consideration would have no noticeable effect upon the cost of power supplied by the large power corporations in the United States, nor would it have the slightest effect upon the location of the one and only industry which is directly concerned as that industry already has a large branch in Canada. Unless the saving in the cost of power were very marked and unless power cost had an unusually great influence on overall manufacturing costs, it would not ordinarily exercise as great an influence on the location of an industry as other factors such as tariffs and the cost of raw materials.
>
> An incidental feature of the granting of this licence would be the establishment of physical means in eastern Ontario of interchanging power with a very large American Power Company. Interconnections such as these are rapidly being established on a large scale all over the United States and Canada. They are of permanent advantage to both parties as a means of obtaining assistance in emergencies, such assistance being given to whatever extent may be practicable, but without obligation. Interconnections also make possible the exchange of seasonal power and purely at-will power which is instantly recallable, and, in general, they make for economy and efficiency. In the Commission's case, after the termination of the agreements under consideration, it would no doubt be possible and certainly advantageous to continue, under an appropriate licence, to export small quantities of power on a purely at-will and instantly-recallable basis during such seasons and times as it might otherwise be unsaleable.[36]

During the war years, power shortages were general. It therefore seemed a pity to let water run to waste over the Commission's dams at night time and during the seasons of highest flow. Aware of the situation, the American authorities joined with Ontario Hydro in an attempt to convince Ottawa that there was much to be gained by

[36]See *ibid.*

running this Canadian water through the Commission's turbines and sending it across the line to New York State under annual permit. This reasoning apparently prevailed and maximum use was, therefore, made of these resources throughout the Second World War. Ontario Hydro's sales into the Buffalo area rose year after year from 1939 right through until 1945.

With the termination of hostilities exports from Ontario fell off. They reached their post-war low in 1949, only to rise again to an all-time high in 1956. The signing of the Niagara Treaty between Canada and the United States in 1950, and an arrangement whereby Ontario Hydro can make use of water which will eventually be withdrawn on the American side above Niagara Falls, have been contributing factors in recent years.

As far as electric power is concerned, the Niagara Treaty of 1950 did two things. It (*a*) permitted both countries to withdraw additional amounts of water for power generating purposes; and (*b*) provided that henceforth the two countries should share equally in the total flow diverted above the falls. Once it was signed, Ontario Hydro acted promptly. By 1955 it had installed an additional 1,200,000 horsepower of generating capacity in the Niagara Gorge.[37] Some of this additional energy is being exported to the United States on an annual basis, the United States having agreed that Canada could make use of unappropriated American water until American installations are rebuilt in the vicinity of Niagara Falls.

Ontario Hydro first imported electric energy from the United States following the placing in service of high-voltage interconnection facilities with the Detroit Edison Company in 1953. These interconnections were established following the parties' desire to:

a) Render mutual assistance during emergencies affecting defence or war production in either or both of their service areas.
b) Render mutual assistance during emergencies affecting peacetime service to customers in either or both of their service areas.
c) Provide means for possible economy by the exchange of any surplus electric energy which may from time to time be available from either system beyond the needs of its own area.

[37]The completion of the Sir Adam Beck No. 2 Hydro-Electric Station on the Niagara River was carried out on the following schedule: 700,000

The agreements and obligations expressed in the interconnection agreement between the Detroit Edison Company and Ontario Hydro are subject to:

a) The initial and continuing governmental permission to both parties to establish and maintain the connections and to export electric energy under the terms of the agreement.
b) The granting and continuation of such grant of authority by the Department of the Army of the United States of America to maintain the suspension of wires across the Detroit and St. Clair Rivers.
c) The condition that the Detroit Edison Company shall not, under the terms of any existent or subsequent legislation by the United States Congress or by reason of rules and regulations of the Federal Power Commission, become subject to the jurisdiction of the Federal Power Commission in any respect other than that relating to the grant by the Federal Power Commission of a licence to export electric energy.

Such international connections have been of great benefit to Ontario Hydro. In 1954, for example, the Commission's new R. L. Hearn steam plant at Toronto was closed down in early April following the mechanical failure of two of the units and subsequent damage by fire. Every effort was, of course, made to meet local demands from other generating plants in Canada. However, a shortage of peaking capacity still threatened to cause "brown-outs" during the Ontario Hydro's hours of greatest demand. Certain power systems in the United States offered assistance in the form of steam power. Immediate application was made to the United States Federal Power Commission for authority to export electricity from the United States in the vicinity of Niagara Falls. Within 24 hours the Federal Power Commission granted the necessary authority to Niagara-Mohawk Power Corporation, to enable them to assist in making up the deficit. This temporary permit remained in effect until the following year when a new one was issued.

A new 230-kilovolt, 60-cycle interconnection across the Niagara

---

h.p. in 1954, 500,000 h.p. in 1955, and 400,000 h.p. in the main plant plus 228,000 h.p. in its associated pumping-generating stations in 1957 and 1958. The hydro-electric installation on the Canadian side of the Niagara is now completed and has a total installed capacity of 2,786,000 h.p.

River was placed in service in May, 1955, providing an additional link between Ontario Hydro and the Niagara-Mohawk Power Corporation. Present facilities permit Ontario Hydro to operate for extended periods in parallel not only with Niagara-Mohawk and other systems in the eastern United States but also with the Detroit Edison Company. In this way and with improved interconnections within its own service area Ontario Hydro is able to make the most economical use of such surplus energy it may have available from time to time.

The interconnection agreement between Ontario Hydro and Niagara-Mohawk is similar in scope to that with Detroit Edison Company in that its prime purpose is to render mutual assistance during emergencies and provide for possible economy by the exchange of electric energy which may be available from time to time on either system beyond the needs of its own service area. The agreements and obligations expressed in the Niagara-Mohawk and Ontario Hydro interconnection agreement are subject to the initial and continuing governmental permission to both parties to establish, operate, and maintain the interconnection specified and to export electric energy under the terms of the agreement.

Since the international interconnections were first established in 1953, Ontario Hydro has continued to export and import electric energy to and from the United States.

Before shifting our discussion to other parts of Canada, we will do well to put these happenings in Ontario into their long-run perspective. Prior to the First World War, the insistent demands on the American side of the International Boundary had brought about the appropriation for export, by American-owned and -controlled utilities, of a goodly part of the firm hydro-electric energy generated in Canadian plants. After 1914 further exports from Ontario were limited to interruptible loads. Canadian requirements increased steadily and, though the total amount of electricity exported from Niagara edged steadily upward, it, at the same time, lagged progressively behind Ontario Hydro's sales in Canada.

By 1950 the long-term contracts which caused so much concern during the First World War had run their course. Also, as a result of the Niagara Treaty of the same year, and the negotiations with the United States over the construction of the St. Lawrence Deep Waterway, the waters of the Niagara and lower St. Lawrence rivers were once and for all allocated in equal proportions to the state of New York, on the one hand, and to Ontario on the other. At long last, the objective of "Canadian resources for Canadians" has been attained.

Meanwhile, Ontario's exports of surplus water power are being offset, to an increasing extent, by imports of electricity produced from coal. Obviously, consumers in the industrial heartland of Canada are deriving some of the benefits of scale and interconnection that have been characteristic of system integration in many parts of the world.

Canada's trade in power has, by no means, been confined to southern Ontario. Electricity generated in Quebec has also been moving into northern New York State. Sales have also been made both ways across the New Brunswick–Maine boundary and to and from British Columbia and the Pacific Northwest States. While Quebec's exports have remained comparatively static, those emanating from other parts of Canada have, generally, tended to increase. Immediately prior to the Second World War, two-thirds of Canada's export sales originated in Ontario. Over 30 per cent came from Quebec. The latest information (1958) suggests that Ontario's exports now account for about 85 per cent of the Canadian total. Quebec's contribution is down to around 13 per cent. New Brunswick and British Columbia together account for the remaining one per cent.

Table III outlines the amounts of electrical energy exported to the

TABLE III

ANNUAL EXPORTS OF ELECTRICITY TO THE UNITED STATES 1940–58
(volume in millions of kilowatt hours)

Year	From Ontario	From Quebec	Other	Total Canada	Total exports as percentage of Canadian production
1940	1,471	637	28	2,136	7.1
1941	1,090	638	32	2,360	7.1
1942	1,767	655	32	2,454	6.6
1943	1,860	646	39	2,545	6.3
1944	1,919	629	37	2,585	6.4
1945	1,976	617	49	2,642	6.6
1946	1,824	618	40	2,482	5.9
1947	1,386	639	41	2,066	4.8
1948	1,041	653	49	1,743	4.1
1949	966	651	140	1,757	4.0
1950	1,046	642	238	1,926	4.0
1951	1,491	647	238	2,376	4.3
1952	1,577	665	251	2,493	4.2
1953	1,399	678	347	2,424	3.9
1954	1,847	659	212	2,718	4.1
1955	3,588	666	179	4,433	6.1
1956	4,384	675	45	5,104	5.8
1957	4,222	549	59	4,830	5.3
1958	3,404	526	145	4,075	4.2

SOURCES: 1940–52, *Canada Year Book*; 1953–8, Dominion Bureau of Statistics, Central Electric Stations.

United States, by province, and under annual permits, during the period from 1940 to 1958.

While small amounts of power have been exported from New Brunswick since 1908, an application of the New Brunswick Electric Power Commission to harness Grand Falls on the St. John River is of some historical significance. In 1925 the International Joint Commission heard evidence and listened to the claims of the United States authorities in this connection. It appeared that the dam would raise the waters at the International Boundary to a level of about 16 feet above the natural minimum (though about 4 feet below the natural maximum) water level. Some 400 acres of land were thereby affected in Maine. During the course of the hearings, the Attorney General for Maine laid claim to a portion of the power which, he said, was to be delivered to the United States as "reasonable compensation" for the resources involved. Mr. G. H. Hackworth, later President of the International Court of Justice at The Hague, speaking on behalf of the Government of the United States, said: "that pool . . . is a part of our property for which we are entitled to compensation," and "we are entitled to be considered and come in on the benefits."[38] Major Young, Corps of Engineers, United States Army, also said:

> The United States has the right to claim half a share in the amount of power corresponding to the flow past the International Boundary times the fall along the international section. That claim, of course, as I understand, would be on the basis that we would have the right to import at a fair price on the same basis that other customers are charged for power.[39]

As it happened, the New Brunswick Electric Power Commission had already made provision for the export of some 2,000 horsepower of electrical energy to consumers in Maine. As this amount was then deemed to be appropriate to the American resources involved, the over-all project was approved. A reservation to the effect that "The Commission . . . reserves the right of the parties to reopen the question . . . should . . . 2,000 horsepower cease to be available for use in the United States," was, however, attached to the final Statement of Opinion issued by the two sections of the International Joint Commission. The 90,000 horsepower Grand Falls project was approved in

[38]*Papers Relating to the Work of the International Joint Commission* (1929).

[39]*Ibid.*

1926 and was completed a few years later by the St. John River Power Company.

In subsequent years larger amounts of electricity have been permitted by the Canadian authorities to be sold in Maine. At times power has also been flowing in the opposite direction. As a result of these arrangements, approved both by the Canadian Government and the United States Federal Power Commission, utilities on both sides of the International Boundary have been able to keep their investments in reserve capacity to a minimum and, at times, to obtain revenue from generating facilities which otherwise would have remained idle.[40]

On the West Coast Canada's international trade in electricity has been more of the nature of an exchange of surplus capacity. Though small amounts of electricity were exported to the Pacific Northwest and Alaska prior to the Second World War, the volume moving either way across the International Boundary did not reach significant proportions until after 1945. Then, as the demand for power increased in the lower mainland area, the British Columbia Electric Company sought for and obtained authority to bring in an interim supply from the United States. Deliveries were made during the latter part of 1947, and during 1948 over a 230-kilovolt interconnection was built in British Columbia by the British Columbia Electric Company, and in the state of Washington by the Bonneville Power Administration. In 1949 when the first of British Columbia Electric's post-war hydroelectric projects provided a reserve of power in British Columbia, the situation was reversed and as there was a shortage of power in the Northwest States, power was exported under contract that was extended to August of 1955. This contract with private utilities in the Northwest Power Pool for 30,000 kilowatts at 70 per cent monthly

[40]In 1957, the United States Federal Power Commission granted authority to the Maine Public Service Company to export 27,000 horsepower of electrical energy across the International Boundary to its subsidiary, the New Brunswick Electric Power Company. The over-all agreement between the Canadian and American utilities provides for the curtailment of delivery in the event that such would impair the supply of energy in Maine. Under agreement with the New Brunswick Commission, each party would make available to the other, during such times of emergency, electrical energy in excess of their load requirements. Each party would also make available to the other such surplus energy as each may wish to purchase, the sale of surplus electrical energy being optional at all times.

load factor was subject to interruption under the terms of the export licence if there had been need for it in British Columbia. During 1956 power exchanges were relatively limited. In 1957 substantial amounts of surplus power were imported to British Columbia as a result of low precipitation and a part of this import was on behalf of the British Columbia Power Commission for use on the Commission's Vancouver Island system.

In the latter half of 1957 some steam power also from various sources in the Northwest States was imported for the same reason and for use on both the British Columbia Electric system and British Columbia Power Commission's Vancouver Island system. Exchanges in 1958 and 1959 have been of only minor proportions.

As a result of these various exchanges of energy in southern Ontario and British Columbia and a continuation of exports from southern Quebec and New Brunswick, Canada's trade in electricity has risen both in volume and dollar terms. In 1956, some 5 billion kilowatt hours were sold in the United States. This was about three times the amount exported from Canada in the late 1930's. As this lines up roughly with production, the percentage of the industry's total output sold outside of Canada (6 per cent) is about the same as it was twenty years ago. Imports, meanwhile, have risen from around 4 million kilowatt hours in 1938 to close to 120 million kilowatt hours in 1956. Even at that, United States sources are currently supplying only about 0.1 per cent of Canada's total electricity requirements. These trends are outlined in greater detail in Tables IV and V.

TABLE IV

EXPORTS OF CANADIAN-PRODUCED ELECTRICITY AS A PERCENTAGE OF THE OUTPUT OF ALL CENTRAL ELECTRIC STATIONS IN CANADA
(5-year averages)*

Year	Total production (millions KWH)	Total exports (millions KWH)	Exports as percentage of total production
1920–24	7,133	1,017	14.3
1925–29	14,211	1,476	10.4
1930–34	17,803	1,221	6.9
1935–39	26,173	1,696	6.5
1940–44	36,372	2,416	6.6
1945–49	42,420	2,138	5.0
1950–54	58,310	2,387	4.1
1955–58	87,451	4,611	5.4

SOURCES: 1920–52, *Canada Year Book*; 1953–8, Dominion Bureau of Statistics, Central Electric Stations.

*By comparison, exports as a percentage of total production in 1910 were 30 per cent and in 1919, 21 per cent.

TABLE V

VOLUME OF CANADIAN PRODUCTION AND TRADE IN ELECTRICITY, 1938–56
(quantity in millions of kilowatt hours)

Year	Production	Exports	Imports	Apparent consumption in Canada
1938	26,154	1,827	4	24,331
1939	28,338	1,913	4	26,429
1940	30,109	2,136	4	27,977
1941	33,318	2,360	8	30,966
1942	37,355	2,454	5	34,906
1943	40,480	2,545	6	37,941
1944	40,599	2,585	24	38,038
1945	40,130	2,642	9	37,497
1946	41,737	2,482	11	39,266
1947	43,425	2,066	9	41,368
1948	42,390	1,743	11	40,658
1949	44,419	1,757	66	42,728
1950	48,494	1,926	121	46,689
1951	54,852	2,376	10	52,486
1952	59,409	2,493	9	56,925
1953	62,861	2,424	51	60,488
1954	65,936	2,718	239	63,457
1955	72,911	4,433	146	68,624
1956	88,383	5,104	117	83,396
1957	91,042	4,830	283	86,495

SOURCES: 1938–52, *Canada Year Book*; 1938–57, Dominion Bureau of Statistics, Central Electric Stations, and *Trade of Canada 1938–52.*

What of the future? Both Liberals and Conservatives, when in office, have adhered to the view that to export electricity in substantial quantitites might get Canada into difficulties. They have, therefore, agreed that no electrical energy should be committed for sale in the United States on a firm or long-term basis. This conviction was put to test as recently as 1953. In that year the Department of Trade and Commerce turned down an application by the Consolidated Mining and Smelting Company to export approximately 100,000 horsepower of surplus electrical energy to the Washington Water Power Company in the Pacific Northwest. No doubt the Rt. Hon. C. D. Howe had this export proposal in mind when he said: "The only licences that are given for [the export of] electricity are for surplus interruptible power. And the fact that it is interruptible is pinned to the licence. Therefore, if at any time the power is no longer surplus, the export can be cut off and the customer will have no recourse whatsoever."[41]

Established Canadian policy respecting the export of electricity,

[41]See *Hansard*, Feb. 25, 1955, re proposed amendments to the "Exportation of Power and Fluids and the Importation of Gas" Act.

therefore, embraces two comparatively simple propositions, namely, that (1) no export licence shall be issued for a period of more than twelve months, although such licences may be issued year after year if the supply of electricity in question is deemed to be surplus to Canadian requirements; and (2) such authorized amounts are released only on an interruptible basis; that is, they can be reduced or cut off without notice if Canadian requirements so dictate.

While these are stringent conditions, the fact remains that Canada has been, and probably will continue to be, a substantial exporter of electric power. Not only have deliveries continued from one year to the next, but they have also increased in volume. Meanwhile regional shortages in Canada have recently been relieved by imports from the United States. This and other evidence of the advantages to be gained by system interconnections, therefore, continue to raise the question: Will some modification of the present Canadian export policy be desirable?

Some, like myself, who favour a change in attitude agree with past policy, but feel that some of the basic facts that justified past policy have so materially changed that strictly defined export of hydro-electricity can safely be allowed in those few big river developments where such relatively short-term export is needed to make the developments economically feasible.

The basic facts that have changed are these. First, hydro-electricity no longer has a big price advantage over steam-generated electricity. Electricity generated from coal, oil, or natural gas has become steadily lower cost per kilowatt hour, while hydro-electricity has tended to become higher cost per kilowatt hour because of increasing construction costs and longer transmission lines as more distant generating sites are being exploited. Second, reasonably priced electricity is now abundant as a result of great improvements in steam generation. No longer can an importing country realistically claim that the withdrawal of a block of power on due notice would upset its economy. Third, reasonably priced nuclear power is a practical matter for the near future. As nuclear power is relatively unlimited and can be generated anywhere, it not only greatly enhances the "abundant" outlook for electricity, but it also is quite possible that an importing area would be glad to have hydro on a relatively short-term contract to bridge it over the interim early period of high-cost nuclear electricity per kilowatt hour. Fourth, the consumption of electricity has increased enormously both in Canada and in the United States. The only areas in the United States where the question of importing electricity on an interim basis is a practical possibility have now such large electrical consumption that possible Canadian exports would be a relatively insignificant part of the whole.

The present-day situation therefore appears to be a far cry from the days when imports of hydro formed a large part of the total power consumed in the importing area, and when there appeared to be no reasonably priced alternative source of electricity either actual or prospective.

Indeed the shoe may now well be on the other foot. Nations with large undeveloped water power resources may find that if they are not developed quickly, their competitive advantage will be lost. This would be an extension of a trend that has been under way for some time. It arises from what appears to be the practical certainty of reasonably priced nuclear power in the near future, and the possibility of very cheap electricity from the fusion process applied to the hydrogen atom in the intermediate or more distant future. Under these circumstances it may be the course of wisdom for areas with large-scale hydro potentials to develop them as quickly as possible and in the most efficient manner possible while hydro still has a competitive advantage, so that a substantial part of the investment could be written off, if necessary through interim exports of electricity.

The granting of licences and the administration of our international trade in power would, of course, have to be improved as compared with earlier days. Then, no attempt was made to ensure that the contracts between the Canadian and United States utilities were compatible with, or even recognized the existence of the annual export permits issued in Ottawa. Licences for more than one year should only be granted in circumstances where the contractual obligations between seller and buyer cover an identical period of time and incorporate all the other terms and conditions contained in the relevant Export Act. Under such a policy certain large new water power developments could be partially financed by sales of power to the United States, and economically taken through the expensive "lag" period between the completion of a very large hydro project and the building up of Canadian consumption to utilize the full output. Cut off at the end of a stated period of years, or progressively reduced on an annual basis, arrangements of this kind might, under certain circumstances, be conducive to the early construction of one or more of our larger and potentially lower-cost hydro-electric developments.

The report of the Royal Commission on Canada's Economic Prospects had this possibility in mind when it concluded that:

> In some parts of the country, the efficient development of a large new project may require that it be designed to produce much more power than can be used immediately in the area of economic power transmission although the general growth of the area will require all the output over a period of years. Under these circumstances one possibility is to try, by low rates, to induce one of the relatively few industries that use very large amounts of power and for which power costs are therefore a very important factor, to locate in the area. The difficulty here, in settled or rapidly growing regions, is that such industries typically add relatively little to the diversified economic strength or to the employment opportunities of the region and permanently appropriate a large amount of power which a growing area will need for its own general expansion. In these circumstances there seems to be merit in permitting some part of the power from such a large new project to be exported where possible at economic rates for stated periods of years, after which it would be made available in the area for Canadian use. In this way, the interests of Canadian consumers, immediate and long term, would be properly protected. This would mean cheaper electricity to the general body of consumers immediately and a safeguarding of future electrical supply for the diversified requirements of the region. This policy would not, of course, apply to areas remote from settled centres where the development of hydro-electricity for industries requiring very large amounts of power seems to be desirable, from every point of view, or to areas far from the United States border.[42]

This recommendation has relevance in British Columbia. Two major rivers, the Peace and the Columbia, are capable of development as soon as financing and, in the case of the Columbia, international arrangements are worked out. A third great river, the Fraser, awaits the solution of the fish-power problem. More distant potentially large hydro rivers, like the Liard, may well become economic with expected

[42]Royal Commission on Canada's Economic Prospects, *Final Report*, p. 142.

improvements in long-distance, high-voltage transmission. New possibilities for large-scale generation of electricity, such as the Hat Creek coal field recently proven by the British Columbia Electric Company Limited, may arise from time to time.

There seems to be a surplus of generating potential to British Columbia's needs for many years to come. On the other hand, the Pacific Northwest in the United States is nearing the full utilization of its efficient hydro resources. It would appear to be to the interests of all concerned to speed up the development of British Columbia's generating possibilities by the export of surplus power to the United States subject to recapture after a stated number of years. This would have the additional advantage of making the financing of these huge projects easier because a certain proportion of senior securities could be offered with provisions for payment in American funds, and thus open up wider sources of capital funds. The result would be cheaper power for British Columbians both in the present, as a result of the economies of faster large-scale development, and in the future. In the future, the power recaptured would represent today's presumably lower costs and, further, the plant would have been substantially depreciated under the American export contracts.

In sum, none of the historic reasons against export seems to exist in the British Columbian case while there are weighty arguments in favour of such a policy. One caveat should be uttered, however. The potential power in British Columbia is from a number of sources and will therefore be at differing costs. It would seem to be sound public policy to keep the cheapest power for British Columbian use and to stimulate economic development here, rather than to export the least expensive power. This point seems to have particular relevance because the cheapest future power seems undoubtedly to be the downstream benefits of the Columbia River, and there might be some pressure from the United States to buy Canada's share at the American generating plants where it is produced, rather than returning it to Canada. To succumb to such pressure would, in my opinion, be a tragedy because most of British Columbia, unlike the states of the Pacific Northwest, has never had the stimulus of really cheap power. Now that the wheel of fortune in this respect is at last spinning in our direction, we should make every effort to take advantage of it.

Along with some export contracts or as an alternative to such, there is the interesting possibility of forming a fully integrated Pacific Northwest Power Pool comprising the electrical utilities, public and private, on both sides of the border. In layman's language, the aim of this Pool would be to use the huge potential for storage on the Peace River and the lesser, but still important, storages of the high dams on the Columbia in such an integrated way that no water would be spilled (that is, wasted) anywhere in the Pacific Northwest. Stated another way, the facilities of hydro and steam generation, transmission, and storage of all the electrical utilities in the Pacific Northwest would be used to their maximum, integrated efficiency. The resulting economies, increases in total electrical output, and benefits from the timing of such output throughout the year would be shared by all the member utilities to the advantage of the respective areas they serve.

A considerable amount of such integration is already in effect between utilities in the Pacific Northwest, and there is no doubt about its benefits. The bringing into being of large storage areas on the British Columbian rivers and the "firming up" possibilities of the big new Burrard Steam Plant, now under construction by the British Columbia Electric Company, add tremendously to the possibilities for integration and the advantages to be gained from it.

There is one danger, however, that Canadians need to guard against. The United States side of the Pacific Northwest Power Pool—comprising Washington, Oregon, Idaho, western Montana, and part of Utah—has a much larger annual increase in demand for electricity than has British Columbia. Furthermore, their hydro potential is almost fully developed, while we are just entering into our big river phase. Unless British Columbians are careful, therefore, they could find that such a wholly integrated Pacific Northwest Power Pool was a deceptive way of allowing most of British Columbia's power potential to go to the benefit of the United States. For a variety of reasons, it is my opinion that British Columbia can guard itself against this danger, and that there are common benefits to both sides of the border that can be achieved from such a Pool. Nevertheless, the Canadians involved have to know what they are doing.

It follows that if either properly guarded export contracts are permitted or an integrated Pacific Northwest Power Pool developed or a combination of the two allowed, the present export tax on electricity levied by the Canadian government is an anomaly. There is no similar tax in any comparable field; for instance, the export of natural gas. Applied to electricity, it is obviously a hold-over from the historic Canadian policy of discouraging its export. With a properly constituted National Energy Board, Canada is now equipped to deal with applications for the export of electrical energy on their merits. If they are contrary to public policy, they should be disallowed; if they are in the public interest, they should be permitted and encouraged; but in neither case is a tax on export relevant, and in the latter case it is unreasonable. Particularly if, as seems sensible, British Columbia were to keep its lower-cost energy for itself and export its higher-cost energy, the export tax could be the margin that made an export contract impossible, even though it was considered to be in the public interest.

As far as the export of electricity is concerned, the following principles seem to have proved acceptable to most Canadians: (1) export licences for electric power should be confined to amounts which are surplus to Canada's foreseeable needs; (2) interconnections between utilities on either side of the International Boundary should be facilitated in order to take full advantage of exchanges of off-peak and other interruptible energy; (3) there should continue to be a time limit on the export of firm power; (4) permits for the export of electricity should continue to be limited to such arrangements as will make energy available at lower prices and under more favourable conditions in Canada.

It seems reasonable to expect that, within this framework and subject to review by the National Energy Board, a programme will soon be put into effect for the hydro development of British Columbia's big rivers which will protect the public interest in Canada, while taking advantage of the impending favourable period for export before nuclear power becomes competitively priced.

The Shrinkage in the Value of Money

JOSEPH A. CRUMB

As most of us have come to expect, recent extensions of official indexes of prices and costs reveal that many of the world's leading currencies continue to record new lows in the generally downward trend in purchasing power which, so far as this generation is concerned, began with the Second World War and, with only an occasional levelling off such as we are now experiencing, has since continued. Relatively few of them still retain much more than one-third of their pre-war worth in goods and services and nearly all of them have already lost relatively more of their post-war values than was sacrificed during the war itself.[1] In Canada dollars spent on the necessities and conveniences of living had by 1946 lost 19 per cent of their 1939 value; and by 1960, 40 per cent of the remainder.[2] In the United States dollars similarly spent had by 1946 lost 29 per cent of their 1939 value; and by 1960, 34 per cent of the remainder.[3] In the United Kingdom the comparable losses in pounds were 23 per cent for the war period; and since that time, 41 per cent of the remainder.[4]

[1]See "The Cost of Depreciating Money," *First National Bank City of New York Monthly Letter* for Dec., 1956, reprinted under title of "Ten Years of Creeping Inflation in Sixteen Countries" in C. Lowell Harris, *Selected Readings in Economics* (Inglewood Cliffs, N.J.), pp. 292–4.

[2]Computed from Dominion Bureau of Statistics consumer price index as reported in annual supplements and monthly editions of *Canadian Statistical Review.*

[3]Computed from consumer price index of Bureau of Labor Statistics as reported in United States *Statistical Abstract* and Federal Reserve System *Bulletin.* Also available in *Canadian Statistical Review.*

[4]The 23 per cent loss for the war period is that revealed by the official cost of living index used during the war and undoubtedly contains a strong downward bias due to the operation of the war controls. The 38 per cent

Had the cost of luxuries and the services of skilled workmen—both of which provide some of our more conspicuous examples of shrinkage in the purchasing power of money—been included in the comparisons, the indicated losses would have been even greater.

Apart from concern for those least able to protect themselves against it, one of the really disquieting things about this continuing monetary disaster—and it is surely no less than that—is the widely held conviction that it is the price we must pay in order to avoid a major depression; that the twin goals of sound money and full employment have somehow become incompatible. However, such a conviction jibes neither with orthodox price and employment theory nor with plain common sense. When all of the more important forces and circumstances which have regulated the value of money during and since the war have been reviewed, it will be realized that the only novel element among them was the downward rigidity of prices and costs. For the first time on record, a period marked on the whole by balanced budgets and generally conservative fiscal policies failed to produce a general price level or purchasing power norm which would permit *downward* as well as upward variations.

Before attempting to bring to light the several causes of this phenomenon, a cursory review of the several price "plateaus" and purchasing power "landings" which have marked the course of the official indexes in Canada, the United States, and the United Kingdom during the past two decades would appear to be in order.

I. THE PRICE "PLATEAUS" AND PURCHASING POWER "LANDINGS"

Although the price and cost controls instituted by most of the belligerents at the outset of the Second World War limited the outward manifestations of the inflationary fiscal devices with which a considerable part of the war expenditures were met, they neither eliminated the inflationary fuel itself, nor did they provide any permanent solution to the problem of maintaining the purchasing power of money. The pent-up spending power which was freed when, at the end of the conflict, these controls were relaxed or set aside, was not completely exhausted until prices and costs had all but doubled and

loss for the subsequent period was obtained by linking the discontinued cost of living index to the interim retail price index which was compiled from 1948 onward. For the earlier period see *Statistical Digest of the War* (London: H.M.S.O.), p. 205; for the subsequent period see editions of the *Annual Abstract of Statistics* and *Monthly Digest of Statistics* (London: H.M.S.O.).

the price plateaus and purchasing power landings of 1947–9 had been reached. As shown by the accompanying charts the Canadian cost of living index then stood at approximately 158 per cent of its 1939 level; that of the United States, at 171 per cent of its 1939 level. The comparable United Kingdom index stood at 142 per cent. When wholesale prices are used as a yardstick the 1947–8 plateaus take on considerably more altitude. On a 1939 base the 1949 levels in the three countries were as follows: Canada, 200 per cent; the United States, 198 per cent; the United Kingdom, 224 per cent.[5]

In terms of purchasing power residues or "landings" dollars spent on consumer goods in Canada had by this time shrunk to approximately 63 per cent of their pre-war worth; and in the United States to 58 per cent. Because of the extension of the wartime controls pounds and shillings spent at retail in the United Kingdom "officially" still retained some 70 per cent of their pre-war worth; yet it must be remembered that some of the products were subsidized, and moreover that people were not at complete liberty to spend the means at their disposal. When money spent in the wholesale markets is considered the approximate retained real values in the three countries were: Canada, 50 per cent; the United States, 51 per cent; the United Kingdom, 45 per cent.

Inasmuch as no appreciable upward pressures were exerted on prices and costs during the two years of relatively subdued economic activity which followed upon the attainment of the 1947–9 plateaus, it appeared, for the time being at least, that a new post-war price and purchasing power plain finally had been discovered. In fact this period was adopted as the new and presumably tenable base for the projection of most of our post-war price and cost comparisons. However, subsequent events in the form of the Korean War and the 1955 "boom" not only conspired to make the selection of these new bases appear to have been premature but have raised grave doubt of the ultimate discovery of any standard capable of indefinite retention.

The outbreak of the Korean conflict ushered in a second period of war-born scarcities which by 1951 had driven wholesale prices in Canada to what is still an all-time high of 242 per cent of their 1939

[5]Computed from the wholesale price indexes of the D.B.S., the United States Bureau of Labor Statistics, and the United Kingdom Board of Trade. See *Canadian Statistical Review*, U.S. *Statistical Abstract*, and U.K. *Annual Abstract of Statistics*. All three series are available in the *Canadian Statistical Review*.

level; and to comparable levels of 229 per cent and 297 per cent respectively in the United States and the United Kingdom. Even though some of this new high ground was subsequently surrendered, the indexes eventually levelled off on a second group of plateaus well above those of 1949. On a 1949 base the new Canadian wholesale price plateau was about 112 per cent. The comparable approximations for the United States and the United Kingdom were 111 per cent and 126 per cent respectively. Meanwhile, with hardly any discernible lag, retail prices and costs also rose rapidly in all three countries. In Canada and the United States they levelled off on fairly well-defined 1952–4 plateaus which were about 116 per cent and 113 per cent respectively of those of 1947–9. In the United Kingdom there was no perceptible halt in the upward movement but by 1954 a comparable level of 128 per cent had been recorded.

Neither the stalemating of the Korean conflict nor the recession which followed appear to have exerted more than temporary restraints on the forces at work to drive up prices in Canada and the United States and none whatever in the United Kingdom. Along with the 1955 recovery and subsequent boom the indexes began another rapid ascent to their present levels or to what may well prove to be the plateaus of the early sixties. In Canada wholesale prices now stand at approximately 116 per cent of their 1949 level and retail prices at about 127 per cent. In the United States the comparable figures are 123 per cent and 120 per cent. In the United Kingdom wholesale prices have reached about 140 per cent of their 1949 level and retail prices, about 149 per cent.

By way of concluding the descriptive part of the analysis it may be noted that, when the 1939 levels are used as a base, wholesale prices are revealed to have considerably more than doubled in Canada and the United States, and to have considerably more than trebled in the United Kingdom. The comparable 1958 figures are: Canada, 232 per cent; the United States, 237 per cent; the United Kingdom, 314 per cent. Meantime, living costs almost exactly doubled in all three countries. The comparable 1958 figures are: Canada, 201 per cent; the United States, 211 per cent; the United Kingdom, 213 per cent.[6]

[6]The 213 per cent is intended to be only indicative of the rise in living costs in the United Kingdom. It was obtained by linking the discontinued cost of living index used during the war with the interim retail price indexes since released by the United Kingdom Statistical Bureau. For sources see footnotes 4 and 5 above.

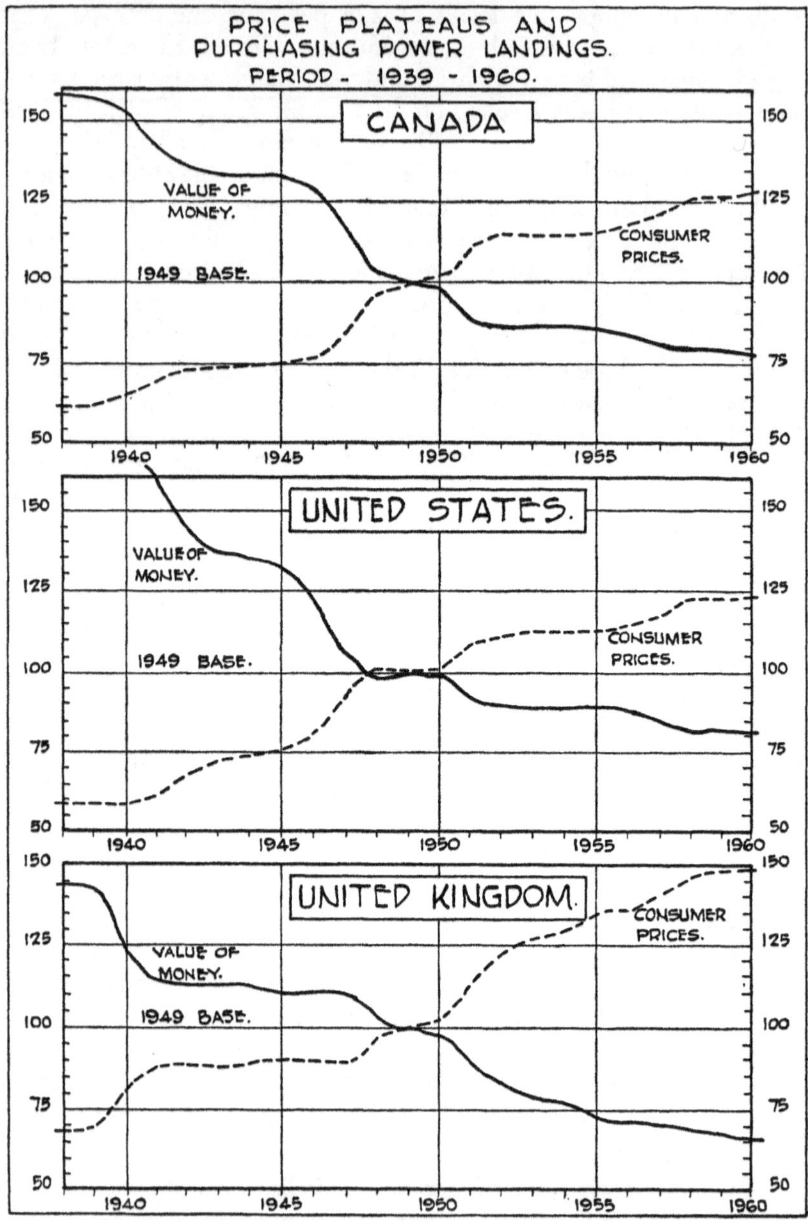
PRICE PLATEAUS AND
PURCHASING POWER LANDINGS.
PERIOD - 1939 - 1960.
CANADA
VALUE OF
MONEY.
1949 BASE.
CONSUMER
PRICES.
150
125
100
75
50
1940
1945
1950
1955
1960
UNITED STATES.
VALUE OF
MONEY.
1949 BASE.
CONSUMER
PRICES.
UNITED KINGDOM.
VALUE OF
MONEY.
1949 BASE.
CONSUMER
PRICES.

In terms of retained purchasing power consumer dollars and pounds have thus lost more than half of their pre-war worth and wholesale dollars and pounds even more. Worst of all, the debauchery still continues with each new landing providing a take-off for the next.

II. THE SEARCH FOR CAUSES

It is one thing to recite the rather foreboding story of the succession of reductions in the value of money during and since the Second World War; quite another to accompany it with a logical and convincing explanation of why it has happened and may go on happening. Many people would subscribe to the belief that the continued emphasis on military pursuits occasioned by the "cold" war has prolonged the "hot" war inflation by limiting the output of the civilian goods and services on which incomes are ordinarily spent. In the United Kingdom this problem has been further complicated by a heavy burden of social services and the overriding necessity of obtaining through merchandise and service exports the external income formerly received from investments made abroad.[7] The latter, as we all know, were among the war casualties.

Some expositors, apparently more intent on blaming than explaining, stress what has been called the "cost push" effect of organized labour's unrelenting pursuit of higher wages and fringe benefits, particularly since the end of the armed conflict. Their opposite numbers stress the "price pull" effect of the employers' presumed equally unrelenting pursuit of the higher prices necessary to preserve existing profit margins. The new phenomena of price "plateaus" and purchasing power "landings" are held to be the product of downward rigidities in both prices and costs, and to come into being when the chase is temporarily halted by a decline in consumer demand.

Apologists for the undeniably active roles played by both organized labour and employer groups in the continuing inflation emphasize the generally well-sustained or "excessive" demand for goods and services during the period under review. They contend that the resulting tendencies to over-employment, over-investment, and over-spending were themselves prerequisites of the cost-price chase. The fact that proponents of this thesis do not bother to enquire into the somewhat mysterious circumstances under which the implied general scarcity

[7]See Harry G. Johnson, *The Overloaded Economy* (Toronto: University of Toronto Press, 1952), particularly parts I and II.

could create generally higher prices and costs appears, unfortunately, to add rather than to detract from its general appeal. There is, however, considerable authoritative support for the contention that over-investment has contributed to the price-cost and money-value problem.

Finally, there are the monetary theorists, including the author himself, who contend that a profoundly important contributing factor if not the primary cause of this continued dissipation of the value of money was the easy money and credit policies pursued until quite recently by our central banks and primary lenders. Low interest rates made possible by arbitrarily increasing an already more than ample money supply, and failure to limit plant and improvement loans, as well as the acquisition of investments to available *voluntary* savings, not only provided the fuel for the inflation but considerably enhanced the competitive position of the nominally commercial institutions. Without this fuel prices could not have continued to climb beyond the plateaus of 1947–9; and while employment opportunities would not have been so plentiful they would not have been promoted by cheapening or adulterating the incomes of those already employed. Moreover, bankers themselves would have continued in their traditional roles as guardians of the integrity of money—the latter a long-run economic stabilizer of no less importance than reasonably full employment itself.

After analysing these several contentions we shall, I believe, be forced to conclude that none of them, acting alone, could have accounted for the continuance of the inflation; also, that the absence of any one of them would have made the others inoperative. Hence, it was both a joint and several undertaking with the illusion of wealth and prosperity created by plentiful money in the role of principal transgressor. Let us begin our analysis by reviewing the by no means well-understood relationship between the provision of money, the output of goods and services, and the prices at which the goods and services will be sold. Without this knowledge no rational explanation of the nature and causes of the downward trend in the value of money could be given, much less fully appreciated.

At the expense of appearing pedantic it may be instructive to repeat the basic truism that the general level of prices or its reciprocal, the purchasing power of money, is established by the money incomes which as business men, professionals, and workers we receive for the goods and services we produce and offer for sale; and which as users and final consumers we spend on these goods and services. It may also be stated that the method of financing the production and sale of goods and services is implicitly if not consciously designed to keep the total amount of money in process of being received or spent in constant relationship with the total amount of goods and services in process of being produced and consumed. When this design is or can be carried out without obstruction prices and the purchasing power of money remain stable. If there were a visible secular trend, it would likely be toward lower prices and higher money values because of technological improvements in the production process.

As every professional banker knows, commercial banks in the English-speaking world provide, primarily through deposit grants or money obligations assumed on behalf of their borrowers, the bulk of all money required in financing the economy's current output of goods and services. The banks are relieved of these deposit obligations as the goods and services are sold and the borrowers make good their loans. The central banks carry out the basic function of providing, through open market operations and rediscounting, whatever cash or lawful money may be required to meet the reserve needs of the banks and mercantile establishments and the pocket needs of individuals. Hence, in any economy functioning in an orderly fashion bank and cash balances rise as employment, real output, and consumption rise; and decline as employment, real output, and consumption fall. The general price level tends to remain stable, at least not to rise or to decline indefinitely, because almost without exception the original credit grants are made in keeping with the cardinal banking principle that they should not exceed the expected costs of the product at the prevailing level of prices. To grant the borrower more would jeopardize the repayment of the loan; to grant him less would unduly restrict his operations.

In a freely functioning economy where demand and supply govern individual prices there are thus no built-in "cost-push" and "price-led" inflators; and no built-in deflators save possibly that of technological progress itself. Long-term upward and downward movements in the general level of prices and costs could come about only as a result of changes in the terms of credit or in the average productivity of labour and invested capital. Neither a general scarcity of the agents of production nor an over-abundance of them could, acting alone, cause price and cost changes; for in the nature of things the *relationship* between levels of employment and output on the one hand, and levels of income and expenditure on the other, remains *constant* regardless of the volume of economic activity undertaken.

With this frame of reference in mind we may, I trust, take a critical look at the several explanations and apologies given for the creeping inflation with the idea of finding out just who or what may be held responsible for it. We shall begin with the war itself which provides the classic explanation of the forces and circumstances which almost inevitably lead to the debauchery of money.

III. SECOND WORLD WAR INFLATION AND ITS AFTERMATH

During and as a result of the war all of the affected governments had to call upon their industrialists and non-military personnel to produce war goods as well as peacetime goods, and to devise ways and means of meeting the mounting war obligations without reducing the work incentives necessary to a maximum war effort. While in theory at least the task could have been accomplished without resort to unorthodox fiscal devices, human nature being what it is, no democratically elected government could have survived while attempting to do so. After raising as much revenue as was deemed politically possible from ordinary forms of taxation and the sale of war bonds to the general public, whatever was needed to balance the budget was obtained, as a rule, by resort to what is technically known as inflationary forced savings. By this device purchasing power is transferred from the general public to the treasury by leaving the government war credits more or less permanently in the stream of money payments; or what amounts to the same thing, real incomes are reduced by multiplying the claims outstanding against them.

During both the French and American revolutions, also the American Civil War, forced saving was accomplished by the direct issuance of treasury notes or currency in the amount of the budgetary deficits. While the process nowadays is a bit more complicated, one might even say a bit more subtle, it accomplishes the same general result. The budget is balanced by selling bonds to investors who, having already exhausted their capacity to save voluntarily, eventually surrender them to the banks through which their purchase was financed; and by discounting increasing amounts of short-term notes with the central banks and commercial institutions. Hence, in the final analysis, what otherwise might have appeared as mounting issues of Exchequer, Dominion, or United States notes reveals itself in the somewhat less obvious inflationary expansion of bank deposits and central bank notes secured by government obligations.

Forced saving of this character—the "watering down" of the purchasing power of existing money media—provided anywhere from

10 to 50 per cent or more of the wartime revenues of the belligerents and no inconsiderable part of the revenues spent on defence measures by the non-belligerents.[8] Between 1939 and 1946 the outstanding note issue of the Bank of Canada rose from $185 million to $1,126 million wholly as the result of either direct or indirect extensions of credit based on government and treasury obligations. Similar extensions added $1.506 billion to the deposit liabilities of the chartered banks.[9] During the same period and for the same reasons the outstanding note issue of the Federal Reserve Banks rose from $5.163 billion to $23.651 billion and a staggering $81.871 billion was added to the deposit liabilities of the member banks.[10] Meantime, the outstanding note issue of the Bank of England rose from £635 million to £1,625 million and acquisitions of government bonds and treasury notes added £885 million to the deposit liabilities of the London clearing banks.[11] When it is realized that the increase in central bank currency alone was approximately sixfold in Canada, fourfold in the United States, and threefold in the United Kingdom; that in all three countries active deposit balances had increased by more than threefold; one does not have to search further for either the principal cause or the mechanism of the war-born inflation. By no stretch of the imagination could such increases have been absorbed in the growing need for cash balances resulting from the war activity.

It is interesting to note that, while the systems of price control and rationing adopted by most of the belligerents undoubtedly slowed down the tempo of the resulting rise in prices and made it less difficult to sell bonds and to collect taxes, these restrictions did not as popularly supposed halt the inflationary process itself. They merely stopped its outward manifestations. Budgets were still balanced by leaving government credit in the stream of money payments and not without some interesting consequences. Pressures built up by arbitrarily holding

[8]Estimates indicate that Canada covered about 15 per cent of her budgetary needs in this manner; the United States, a slightly larger proportion; the United Kingdom, about 20 per cent.

[9]Bank of Canada, *Statistical Summary*, Supplement for 1950. The figure used for the increase in deposit liabilities was that indicated by the increase in holdings of government securities and short-term notes.

[10]U.S. *Statistical Abstract* for 1950; also F. R. S. *Bulletin(s)*. The increase in member bank holdings of government bonds and short-term notes provided the basis for this estimate.

[11]U.K. *Abstract of Statistics* for 1950 (London: H.M.S.O.); also *Barclay's Bank Review*.

prices down while money incomes continued to rise were released in black markets where undeclared output and stolen merchandise were sold for what the traffic would bear. They were also released in the fantastic prices often paid for second-hand goods when new stocks were in short supply, as well as in traffic in the ration cards by means of which clothing and food were evenly distributed. The latter, to all intents and purposes, took on all the attributes of a primary currency —media which had to be obtained before ordinary money could be spent. Had the ration cards themselves been over-issued or "counterfeited" in a final desperate attempt to command a greater share of the national product for the war effort, one would have witnessed an inflation of the second degree not unlike that caused by the unsubstantiated expansion of the original currency. Then, no doubt, someone would have suggested a rationing of the existing ration cards with a second qualifying issue!

Regardless of how facetious the latter suggestion may appear, it does reveal the true nature of wartime inflation. The "ration cards" against available goods and services were over-issued to satisfy war needs that otherwise would have increased the direct tax burden. Where these redundant "ration cards" are not arbitrarily limited by a second qualifying issue, their purchasing power can be, and in many notorious cases has been, completely dissipated. The hyper-inflation in Germany and Austria during and after the First World War are cases in point.[12] After prices had reached astronomical proportions—even postage stamps were sold in denominations of hundred thousand marks—both currencies were repudiated.

We may now enquire into the extent, if any, to which the continuing burden of military activities occasioned by the "cold" war has been financed by an increase in the public obligations held by the banking system or, what amounts to the same thing, unsubstantiated increases in the supply of money. If this process of forced saving—more realistically, forced surrender—of a part of the purchasing power of existing incomes has been continued, then both the basic cause and the method of the post-war inflation are to be found in our systems of public finance. However, before testing this assumption it should be pointed out that relief from the burdens of actual war and a return to peacetime pursuits ordinarily bring war inflation to a halt. In fact,

[12]For an account of the hyper-inflation in Germany after the First World War see among others Frank D. Graham, *Prices and Production in Hyper-Inflation Germany, 1920–1923* (Princeton, 1930).

historical precedents generally reveal an immediate downward re-adjustment to price plains somewhat below the peak levels reached during wars, yet substantially above the plains of the pre-war periods. This comes about because post-war budgets balanced in orthodox fashion remove the upward pressure on prices but, as a rule, not their new higher foundations. The latter are sustained by the generally expanded money supply and the vested interest which meantime has been acquired in the higher level of incomes by the producing and income-receiving public.

It so transpires that both Canada and the United States were able to balance their budgets in orthodox fashion immediately after the war. So it cannot be maintained that fiscal policies *per se* were at work to prolong the inflations in these countries. The first, though not necessarily the only, "push" which carried them up to the 1947–9 plateaus—we have not yet considered rising labour costs and the easy money policies followed by the banks—was the pent-up buying power which was suddenly released when the wartime controls were set aside and accumulated cash balances, savings, and in many cases "cashed in" war bonds finally could be spent. During the first post-war years Canadian purchases of consumer goods in the United States alone are estimated to have approached the then unheard of total of two billion dollars. Only by the near exhaustion of the country's equalization fund and the reimposition of exchange controls were they brought back to manageable proportions.

The charts in part II above show the immediate response of prices to this unexpected wave of spending. However, as explained more fully later on, not all of the rise was due to trying to spend a second time money which had in effect already been spent on the war effort.

In the United States, quixotically, the failure to hold prices down, in spite of the war controls, appears to have lessened the urge to over-spend once these restraints were officially set aside. Nevertheless, both prices and costs moved on up to their 1947–9 plateaus before surplus means could be absorbed in the concomitant need for reserves and cash balances. By that time prices were at about the same level in the United States as they were in Canada.

While we may thus conclude that the "hot" war itself, rather than its "cold" war continuation, supplied much of the fuel for the post-war inflations in both Canada and the United States, one may not draw a similar conclusion in the case of the United Kingdom. In that country there was no immediate setting aside of the wartime controls on spending and no justification, in the form of a budget balanced in orthodox fashion, for doing so. The almost intolerable post-war burden placed upon the Treasury, including the continued support of large military establishments both at home and abroad, made it politically expedient if not absolutely necessary to continue to rely on the facilities for credit expansion provided by the Bank of England and the London money market. To whatever extent this was occasioned by war burdens *per se*—there were many other demands on the British Treasury, including a greatly expanded programme of social welfare[13]—the cold war itself may be said to constitute a cause of the continuing decline in the value of the pound sterling. In this connection it may be pointed out that between 1945 and 1950 the Treasury note holdings of the London clearinghouse banks rose from £188 million to £1,200 million and, of course, the deposit currency credited to the public, by a similar amount.[14]

As already noted, the outbreak of the Korean conflict caused immediate and decisive price rises in all three countries; and while one might say that these rises helped to promote the case for higher wages and costs generally they could hardly be said to have otherwise made any permanent contribution to a long-term inflationary trend. In the main they were the immediate result of material scarcities and in the ordinary course of events would have been driven down to normal levels by the natural reaction of supply. Furthermore, in the case of Canada and the United States at least, the Korean War was not in part financed by adding government credits to the stream of money payments. We must therefore look elsewhere for the cause of the continuing rise in prices and costs, particularly that which took place after 1949.

IV. THE PURSUIT OF HIGHER WAGES AND GREATER PROFITS

It would be absurd even to attempt to argue, as some apologists appear to, that either the continued pursuit of higher wages, the granting of higher salaries, or the pricing of output to include, where possible, profits in excess of a fair return on the investment required to produce it, were not major contributors to the post-war decline in the value of money or the inflationary rise in prices and costs in which the decline has been manifested. As a rule the resulting additions to

[13]See Johnson, *The Overloaded Economy*, part III, "The Attrition of the Welfare State."

[14]*Annual Abstract of Statistics* for 1950, Table 314 (London: H.M.S.O.).

the stream of money incomes were not substantiated by comparable additions to the stream of goods and services; hence higher prices and costs, or cheaper money, were the inevitable if unwanted consequence, despite the fact that many of the unsubstantiated increases may have been justified. While this conclusion will be more or less obvious to those who are well versed in monetary theory, the fact that it may not be fully grasped by the many others to whom this essay is addressed suggests some further elaboration. We will concentrate on the wage and salary pursuit first.

As already explained in section III above, the basic relationship between money received and goods produced, which dictates the general price level and the value of money, was distorted during the war by the necessity of putting men and capital to work on war goods for which there was no consumer demand; then failing to recover their entire cost through orthodox forms of taxation and voluntary thrift. However, meeting the uncovered balance in the budget with the proceeds of credit grants from the banks was not the only force at work to raise prices and cheapen money. The costs of both civilian goods and war goods were being driven up by the necessity of replacing experienced employees who had joined the armed forces with personnel who in ordinary circumstances would not have qualified for the tasks to which they were assigned. The resulting shrinkage in output per man-hour coupled with a downward rigidity in hourly rates of pay was quite as much a contributor to the war inflation as the credit grants by means of which the war budgets were balanced. The latter drove up prices and costs by making money relatively plentiful in terms of goods and services; the former further complicated the problem by making those goods and services relatively scarce.

It need hardly be added that the payment of cost of living bonuses to keep the rank and file of hourly rates workers abreast of the rising prices only served to make these prices just that much higher. It also initiated the generally futile, but still rapid, wage-price pursuit which has since recruited all income receivers—not just the more aggressive groups in the labour movement. Though it may be properly contended that such a pursuit was the only way by which wage and salary workers and even investors could shift a part of the burden of the postponed war inflation onto those who cashed in their war savings, there was little if any basis for this contention after 1949. By that time the full force of the war inflation had been spent and a new one in the form of continued requests for additional welfare grants and status gains had to all intents and purposes taken its place.

This latter force, unlike the former, provided its own means of propulsion. The status and welfare grants won by the stronger and more aggressive groups in organized labour, and the very considerable additions made to executive and staff salaries, immediately created a demand for comparable concessions to rank-and-file organizations and, belatedly, to unorganized white-collared, salaried, and professional personnel as well. By the time all of these claims had been dealt with, or the first round of grants had been completed, all of the contemplated *real* gains, save those from technological improvements, had been washed away by the inevitable resultant rise in prices, including of course the original gains made by the leaders in the chase.

Thus the so-called price-cost "spiral" may be more realistically visualized as a wage-chase-wage pursuit in which the vanguard of the labour movement, including teachers and other professional groups, must keep puffing along behind the more self-willed leaders in order to protect themselves from the consequences, in part at least, of their own collective acts. The argument that higher rates of pay increase buying power, and hence employment, when rates already reflect the earning power of the workers, is just so much wishful thinking and would hardly warrant a reply if it were not so often expressed. In slack times such increases inhibit employment because they make it just that much harder to sell the product of labour. In these circumstances a decrease in wage rates would be more likely to increase the *volume* of wage payments and consumer buying power than would an increase, however "reactionary" the suggestion may appear.

The mischievous illusion that substantial wage increases can be paid out of profits without marking up prices should also be given a proper airing. It arises from the erroneous assumption that the earning of a given rate of profit on the proprietors' investment in a business would involve a sufficient sum of net earnings to grant, in extremity, a similar rate of increase in the annual wage bill. Only in the exceptional case where the proprietory investment approached the annual wage bill would this be possible. Even then there would not necessarily be any justification for granting such a request, for the proprietors are entitled to as fair a return on their capital investment as are the workers on their time and energy. Take, for example, an undertaking where the proprietory investment equals one-tenth of the annual wage bill and the firm earns a 20 per cent profit before income tax. A 10 per cent increase in the wage bill in one year alone would not only wipe out all profits but involve the business in an 80 per cent loss.

Without any out-of-pocket loss the wages bill could be increased by only 2 per cent, the percentage relationship between annual profits and annual wages.

As in the case of unsubstantiated increases in wages and salaries, there can be no gainsaying the fact that mark-ups in prices to provide excessive profit margins are at once contributors to and manifestations of inflation or shrinkage in the value of money. In common with unsubstantiated wage increases such mark-ups have cumulative effects which, while stimulating the wage race, also keep the "profiteer" on the run. Yet even so, one would be unrealistic to assume that the price of any good or service can be marked up at will without impairing its market. In many cases the consumer may pick and choose and producers can and have priced themselves out of their markets quite as recklessly as have some of the labour unions. The coal and to some extent the lumber industry are cases in point. Marketings appear to be unduly depressed because the prices at which the products are offered appear to be unduly high where feasible substitutes are taking their places.

Perhaps the greatest offenders from the point of view of value of money are found in the construction industry where not entirely by coincidence we also find the most aggressive unions. Here for more than a decade the demand for new housing, industrial and commercial buildings, pipelines, bridges, and highways has continued, on the whole, to exceed the immediately available supply not only of contractors but of workers and materials as well. As a consequence tenders have moved radically upward in a cost-chase-profit spiral unparalleled anywhere else in the economy. In some areas it has been as much as fivefold. While it is true that much of the anticipated profit may have been dissipated by retroactive wage grants and by income taxes, the very fact that each succeeding tender for substantially the same amount of work brings forth still higher estimates is evidence enough of the trend.

Finally, it may also be pointed out that, notwithstanding the persistence of arguments in favour of keeping profits sufficiently high to compensate for income tax levies, a measure of success in doing so would be no less inflationary than a wage increase granted for the same purpose. The resulting increase in the price of the product or service offered for sale adds nothing whatever to its real value. Moreover, such practices may be criticized as attempts to shift legitimate tax burdens onto the consuming public in the form of higher living costs. As every accountant knows, however, such practices tend to defeat their own ends by increasing the profits base upon which the tax itself is computed.

V. THE RISING DEMAND, OVER-EMPLOYMENT, OVER-INVESTMENT AND OVER-SPENDING THEORIES

Inasmuch as they provided climates in which resistance to wage and other cost and price increases was relatively low, the generally rising demand for the agents of production and the resulting tendencies to over-employment, over-investment, and over-spending which characterize the period under review undoubtedly contributed to the decline in the value of money. Yet one could not assign originating roles to any one of these conditions without presuming upon the existence of other more fundamental ones, such as the wage and profit races which we have just looked into, and monetary policy which is still to be considered. To do so would be to yield to a temptation to substitute apologies for basic causes and to shy away from the indicated cures for the *malaise* itself.

To begin with, a continually rising demand for the agents of production, nurtured by a large backlog of unsatisfied wants and the resulting favourable business expectations, could not of itself cause wages and other costs to *continue* to rise, in spite of the semblance of scarcity which such circumstances create. Where the rise resulted from the employment of formerly idle labour and plant, the balance between income and output, upon which the price level and the purchasing power of money depends, would not be disturbed unless the additional employment added relatively more to the stream of income payments than it did to the stream of goods and services. And this is tantamount to saying that the latter disturbance caused the rise in prices, not the increase in demand *per se*.

If after reasonably full employment were achieved, the momentum of the antecedent rise in the demand for the agents led some business men to plan outputs in excess of existing capacity, both agent prices and unit costs in the over-worked establishments would rise and the groundwork would be laid for an incipient inflation. But a general inflation could neither be initiated nor sustained, unless organized labour or some other agent were able to extend ephemeral increases in the demand for its services into a fairly general increase in the whole cost structure; and what is equally important, unless the business men persisted in executing plans which in the nature of things would be destined to involve them in continued short-term losses. Both assumptions, it will be noted, presume upon the willingness of the banking system to ease the terms of credit sufficiently to make these questionable ventures possible. Here again the original favourable climate does not prove to be a basic *desideratum*, although it admittedly does encourage the pursuit of policies which are inflationary.

The tendency to over-investment, that is, the provision of additional plant and public improvements at the expense of additional current output from existing facilities which was apparent during most of this period, may account for some heightening of levels of costs and prices. Yet when taken alone such a tendency could hardly cause an enduring inflation. Under orthodox conceptions of the investment process, plant extensions and public improvements, while originally projected on bank credit, are ultimately financed by voluntary savings obtained through the sale of securities to individuals, corporate investors, insurance companies, and ordinary savings banks. Hence in theory at least there could be no long-run change in the available means–available goods relationships arising from over-investment. The latter would be held in check by natural limitations on the supply of voluntary savings.

When, however, the economy is expanding its frontiers very rapidly—Canada is a case in point—this conclusion may have to be modified. In these circumstances the continued sacrifice of current output in favour of new plant and public improvements eventually manifests itself in rising living costs, and workers have, to that extent at least, a legitimate claim for cost of living grants. And it goes without saying that, as these claims are met, primary costs rise and with them the final costs, not only of newly planned facilities but of consumer goods as well. The same conclusion can be reached by emphasizing the fact that when an economy is expanding at the base the payments received by the agents of production will continue to exceed the output of goods and services upon which those payments will ultimately be spent. Were it not for the brake provided by the supply of voluntary savings, a rapidly expanding peacetime economy could literally explode pricewise, as indeed a wartime economy does, from adding to the stream of money payments incomes which do not find their way into savings and investment, but instead are spent on a relatively dwindling supply of consumer goods and services. Our concluding discussion on banking policy will show that this has been quite as decisive a factor in the post-war inflation as it was during the war itself.

Some authorities attach considerable importance to the over-spending which takes place when, by virtue of better than average employment and income opportunities, buyers reduce their customary cash and deposit balances and add to their current debts. This is known as the *velocity* theory and its adherents claim, logically enough, that the resulting disproportionate increase in expenditure—the rate of output is presumed to be unaffected—brings with it a rise in prices. A decline occurs when the prompting conditions are reversed and, for the moment, expenditure fails to keep pace with output. Once started, the process is said to be self-generating; for losses in real income due to rising prices may be minimized by further reducing cash balances and incurring additional debts. Conversely, gains in real income due to declining prices may be maximized by building up cash balances and reducing debts.

Here again, though, caution should be exercised lest a short-run phenomenon be cast in the role of a long-term force. In the first place, there would be no original inducement to go into debt or to reduce existing cash balances unless inflationary forces of a more fundamental nature were already at work in the economy. And in the second place, even if there were such forces, current balances would soon be entirely exhausted; money receipts would then be the regulator of money expenditure and the velocity factor would cease to operate. Finally, it should be pointed out that the rates at which income is received and output is produced are not independent variables; that long-run changes in the velocity or rate of turnover of money would be accompanied by compensating changes in the rate of turnover of goods and services.

Before moving on to the final section on banking policy, it should perhaps be noted that if individuals and firms threw caution to the winds and converted their more or less permanent savings accounts and security holdings into cash, or were permitted to do so by the banks; then proceeded to spend the cash quite recklessly; there would be not only continuing inflation but hyper-inflation of a sort that would indeed make money quite worthless. Still, it will bear repeating that this could happen only when the original savings or their investment counterparts were realizable in cash *without* penalty; and when the aggregate of savings held by potential spenders was substantially greater than the cash and current deposit balances originally outstanding.

VI. THE CONTRIBUTIONS OF THE EASY MONEY AND CREDIT POLICIES

Without doubt, the easy money and credit policies followed by both central banks and commercial institutions since the war have had a great deal more to do with the continuing decline in the value of money than is generally assumed to have been the case. Not only did low interest rates and liberal credit grants encourage the over-employment, over-investment, and over-spending to which we have already alluded; these inducements cast the private banks, if not the public ones, in the role of providing the means which made such extravagances possible and, incidentally, of achieving a very considerable prosperity while doing so. Many banks more than quadrupled their holdings of earning assets between 1940 and 1960 and more than kept abreast of their increased capital needs from the resulting improvement in the amount of their net earnings. Hence, many bank owners and managers have not been immune to the seductive appeal which easy money makes to most of us, and to the best of my knowledge none of them has expressed disapproval of the continuation of the policy. A monetary theorist is indeed alone in a wilderness when he must plead with the money providers themselves to resist the temptation to cheapen their own merchandise.

As already noted, none of the central banks undertook to curb the inflationary pressures let loose when the wartime price controls were finally eliminated. In fact, their continued support of the government bond market and, *ipso facto*, low interest rates unquestionably hastened the process by which the war bonds were converted into inflationary cash and current deposit balances. Though it is granted that a complete withdrawal of this support would have created chaos in the bond and money markets as they were then organized, a backward glance does reveal that neither artificially high bond prices nor their equally artificially low earning rates are prerequisites of a sound money policy. In other words, the continuance of cheap money policies must continually cheapen money itself. Save for a short period after the outbreak of the Korean War, during which the Bank of Canada advertised a mildly restrictive rate and announcement was made of the famous *concordat* between the Federal Reserve Board and the Secretary of the Treasury,[15] this policy remained substantially unchanged

[15]The *concordat* of 1951 relieved the Reserve Banks of any further presumptive responsibility for supporting the market for United States government securities. This did not mean, however, that Federal Reserve Board policy had ceased to be a factor in the market.

from the beginning of the Second World War until the now well-known decisive reversals of 1955. Meanwhile, as we have already seen, enough new and unsubstantiated cash and deposits had been poured into the money stream to double the general price level and to cut its purchasing power in half. The Bank of England has not since reverted to the easy money policy but both the Bank of Canada and the Federal Reserve Banks were driven to do so during the 1958–9 recession by the persistence of the illusion that full employment can neither be achieved nor maintained under a policy sufficiently hard to maintain money values.

In addition to having encouraged inflationary undertakings, this easy—one could almost say loose—money policy removed the fear of cash and reserve shortages which ordinarily exerts a restraining influence on the lending activities of commercial banks and, indeed, of grantors of credit generally. Moreover, it made possible the acquisition of reserves through open market operations initiated without penalty by the primary lenders themselves, thus reducing the central banks to a purely subordinate position as policy executing agencies. The latter institutions could not possibly limit the creation of cash while maintaining a seller's market for bonds. While no one would insist that legitimate demands for credit be denied to anyone capable of adding to the level of employment and output in the country, it does not follow that this cannot be accomplished without impairing the central bank's power to regulate the value of money; much less without nullifying the restraints which promote sound lending policies on the part of the commercial banks.

In addition to the encouragement given to borderline lending activities, this unrestricted privilege of converting investments into cash also relieved the banks of the necessity of following the well-tested rules of prudence in granting long-term loans and acquiring long-term investments. Whereas earning assets of this character are presumed to provide the normal outlet for voluntary savings either left with or solicited by the bank, it is quite obvious that deposit advances have been used increasingly for this purpose. It need hardly be said that when either bonds, real estate mortgages, or any long-term "frozen" loan is acquired in this manner the stream of money payments rises without a comparable *immediate* rise in the stream of goods and services: the inevitable consequence, a rise in prices. If it is contended, as some social creditors may contend, that the earning assets made possible by this particular variety of forced saving ultimately justify the process, one need but reply that meanwhile prices will have been driven up; and a vested interest will have been acquired in holding them there.

This "mixing up" or failure to discriminate between newly created deposits and voluntary savings was noted by Governor Coyne of the Bank of Canada in his 1956 Report.[16] It is also implied in a recent statement of a leading New York banker to the effect that "the dynamic factor in the supply of investment funds is the transformation of commercial banks into aggressive buyers of securities and aggressive mortgage lenders."[17] Such aggressiveness may help to keep interest rates down, but when it is made possible by forced saving or abuse of the privilege of issue it necessarily must increase building costs by as much as or more than the nominal saving in interest.

Although the effects are not of a long-term nature it may also be observed that deposit advances made either directly or indirectly on instalment paper when the amount outstanding is increasing are definitely inflationary. Voluntary savings brought into the banks or procured from the sale of debentures in the investment market should be used for this purpose, if forced saving as well as over-selling is to be avoided. The not too obvious reason for this conclusion is that the costs of the instalment goods are already in the money stream when the instalment loan is made.

VII. CONCLUSIONS

When all the presumed forces and circumstances are brought together and subjected to even a cursory analysis, it appears that there is no single cause for the continued decline in the value of money. Nevertheless, it is quite clear that the latent ones are: the easy money and credit policies pursued by the central banks and the commercial institutions, including the funding of both public and private investment through money creation or forced saving; the opportunities for profit afforded by the post-war expansion, particularly in the construction industry; and the successful attempts of the more aggressive groups in organized labour to improve their economic status at the expense of other workers and income receivers in general. Without in any way

[16]*Annual Report of the Governor to the Minister of Finance for the Year 1956*, pp. 27–36.

[17]Alfred J. Cassaza of the Savings Bank and Trust Company of New York as reported by Albert L. Kraus in the *New York Times*, March 16, 1958, Financial Section, pp. 1, 12.

indicting those immediately responsible for them, one should, I believe, place monetary policy in the role of the first prompting agent and the unsubstantiated demands of labour in that of the predominant force. Cheap money is the *condicio sine qua non* of inflation, and excessively low interest rates not only increase the inducement to over-investment and over-spending; they lower the barrier which a sound money policy provides against attempts by either organized labour or industrialists to obtain status gains at the expense of other members of society, and thus assist in keeping the inflationary price-cost chase in motion. Meanwhile, it would appear that nearly everyone, not just labour leaders, bankers, and industrialists, has lost sight of the fact that the only source of the enduring status gains in which all of us may share is the continued pursuit of lower costs. To pursue them through higher prices merely continues the age-old illusion that we can all become wealthier by increasing the number of claims on our common product.

Trade Unions and Inflation

UNITED STATES AND CANADA

STUART M. JAMIESON

One of the most controversial questions in economics for many years has been the degree to which trade unionism and collective bargaining can be held primarily responsible for the problem of inflation. A considerable number of reputable economists on the one hand seem to enjoy widespread popular support in their contention that the upward pressure that trade unions in the aggregate exert upon wages (or their dollar equivalent in fringe benefits) is the most important single factor contributing to the almost uninterrupted rise in the price level since the Second World War. Some economists even argue that, with labour now well organized in key sectors of the economy, we are in a new era of "permanent inflation." An equally respectable but apparently less numerous and less popular group of economists hold to a quite different view. They maintain that trade unionism has little or no effect on general wage and price levels, and that inflation and recession develop from forces quite independent of the collective bargaining activities of organized labour. The two schools of thought each present a convincingly logical framework of analysis, supported by a formidable mass of historical facts and statistical evidence to support their views.

This controversy has been raging in the United States for more than a decade, in books, articles, and monographs, senate and congressional investigations, official reports, and the like that now number in the hundreds.[1] Recently a number of ingenious experiments have been

[1]See, for instance, the bibliography for George H. Hildebrand's survey, "The Economic Effects of Trade Unionism," in N. W. Chamberlain, F. C. Pierson, and T. Wolfsan (eds.), *A Decade of Industrial Relations Research, 1946–56* (New York: Harper and Bros., 1958).

made to use refined mathematical analysis to test various hypotheses concerning the impact of unions on prices.[2]

No attempt will be made in this paper to assess, evaluate, or summarize this vast body of data, or to present the main arguments of the more outstanding contributors. This has already been done in a number of excellent critical surveys.[3] Nor will any detailed statistical analysis be undertaken here. All that is proposed is to present a rather broad outline of the main hypotheses that have been formulated about the question of trade unionism and inflation in the United States, and to broadly test such hypotheses for Canada, in the light of several well-known but special features of this country's economy.

In dealing with this question it might be well at the outset to attempt some clarification of the term "inflation." Broadly speaking, it may be defined as any situation in which the general price level of a country rises to a significant degree in any given period. Inflation in this general sense of the term can occur, however, from widely different causes and under widely differing circumstances.

The traditional or classical type of inflation is one in which the general level of prices in a country rises, during any given period, because total money supply, income, and demand increase more rapidly than the total output of goods and services. It is associated with "full," or nearly full, employment (in Sir William Beveridge's sense of the term, in which total job openings exceed in number total job applicants) and over-all *shortages* of productive capacity and output in relation to over-all demand. This is the only sort of concept of inflation that seems meaningful in terms of long-run trends.

The general price level in a country may also rise, of course, as in Canada and the United States during 1957–8, in the midst of a "recession" characterized in its early stages by "tight" money and credit restrictions, stable or declining national income, excess plant capacity and shutdowns, rising unemployment, and unsold surpluses. Some observers have called this a "new kind of inflation," or "cost-push" inflation, to distinguish it from "fiscal," "monetary," or "demand-pull" inflation of the classical kind. A rising price level under such circumstances presents a quite separate problem in some respects from that occasioned primarily by excessive currency and credit expansion and, in the short run, would call for different corrective measures.

[2]Cf. F. D. Holzman, "Inflation: Cost-Push and Demand Pull," *American Economic Review*, L, no. 1 (1960), pp. 20–42.

[3]Hildebrand, *v. supra.*

Perhaps, however, it would be misleading to consider these as two different kinds, or causes, of inflation. Rather would it appear that, in the modern economy of large-scale organizations and "administered" prices, "cost-push" inflation represents a periodic and more or less brief cyclical interruption to the longer-term trend of inflation arising out of fiscal or monetary expansion. Rising wages, costs, and prices may make a recession more severe and prolonged, and perhaps make inflationary monetary and credit expansion more likely as a recovery measure. A long-term trend of higher wage and price levels, in a context of continually shrinking output and rising unemployment, would be difficult to visualize.

But, in any case, the special combination of circumstances that developed in the United States and in Canada during 1957–8 cannot, in itself, be accepted as evidence that the upward pressure of unions on wage levels has been the main factor accounting for the almost uninterrupted rise in prices that has gone on since the Second World War.

The inflation that has occurred on this continent since the war has had a variety of causes. At least two of these clearly were not attributable mainly to union wage pressure, though this may have aggravated them once they got under way. The immediate post-war inflation of 1946–9, of course, arose essentially from the excess of government expenditures over revenues during the war, and the consequent huge accumulation of bonds and liquid assets bidding for goods that were in short supply as a result of wartime scarcities. Along with this there was a rapid increase in velocity of circulation for several years immediately after the war. Again, the sudden rise of prices from mid-1950 to mid-1951 was generated after the outbreak of the Korean War by sudden speculative increases in the demand for raw materials and finished goods, coupled with a rapid increase in defence expenditures. The third distinct period, and type of inflation was that which (except for the brief recession of late 1953–4) applied from early 1952 to mid-1957. Prices of non-agricultural goods and services in both Canada and the United States continued to climb year by year during this period. This occurred despite the absence of any major war or any large new additions to defence expenditures (except for the Korean War, the main inflationary impact of which had begun to wear off by late 1951). The consumer price index remained practically unchanged only because the decline in prices of agricultural products and certain other raw materials from the 1951 peak compensated for price increases in the non-agricultural sectors. The fact that wages generally continued to rise each year by more than increases in average productivity has been widely interpreted as being clear proof that union pressure for higher earnings was largely responsible for the inflation of that period. The case, however, is far from clear.

Rational analysis of the question is made all the more difficult in Canada because numerous economists as well as spokesmen of organized labour and management in this country tend to base their arguments on assumptions that are valid for the most part only in the United States. Wage and price changes and monetary and fiscal policies in that country, of course, have significant effects on the Canadian economy because of Canada's extreme dependence upon the United States as a major market for her exports, a major source of imports, and a major supplier of investment capital. But the impact of changes in wage, price, and income levels, and the forces that bring these changes about, tend to be markedly dissimilar in the two countries because of their quite different economic structure, particularly as regards dependence upon foreign trade.

As regards the controversy itself, there is a remarkable lack of agreement, among Canadian and American economists alike, not only about the ultimate effect of union wage policies on the level of prices and incomes, but also about the basic assumptions upon which their reasoning is built. To take one of the most fundamental questions: Do unions, or union leaders, arouse bigger wage expectations or demands among workers than would occur if the latter were unorganized? Or are unions merely agencies through which workers articulate their demands and attempt to achieve the wage increases and other benefits that they aspire to? Popular impressions seem to be in line with the first view. Union leaders are often pictured essentially as agitators who are continually engaged in arousing otherwise contented workers to demand, and periodically strike for, wage increases or bigger "fringe" benefits. At a somewhat higher level of discussion, a sizable body of literature in economic theory pictures the trade union in the typical collective bargaining negotiations as a more or less conventional type of sellers' monopoly that attempts to maximize the gains of its members by charging what the traffic will bear. A quite different view, however, is presented by A. M. Ross in his *Trade Union Wage Policy*,[4] and by a number of authors who have done intensive studies of collective bargaining in particular industries. They present the picture

[4]A. M. Ross, *Trade Union Wage Policy* (Berkeley: University of California Press, 1948).

of rank-and-file union members with exaggerated wage expectations, who periodically force their more cautious and realistic leaders to press for sizable wage increases. The higher union officials tend to exert a moderating influence on their followers.[5] Their main preoccupation is not to gain the largest possible wage increases or other dollar gains for their members at the expense of employers. Rather is it a "political" settlement that they seek, one that will keep the majority of members reasonably satisfied for the time being without provoking open conflict with employers. Year by year many such wage settlements are made, at levels that employers would be willing and able to pay if greater force were used against them.

In practice, of course, both types of situations are found, among the thousands of collective bargaining negotiations that occur each year or two. In some cases the main stimulus for new wage or other demands comes primarily from the union leadership, in others primarily from the membership. The number and proportion of unions in each category and the net effect of union policies upon members' attitudes and expectations concerning wages and fringe benefits, industry by industry, would be extremely difficult to assess at all accurately.

The relationships and interactions between union bargaining and the wage expectations or demands of workers over the economy as a whole, of course, may be different from those in particular industries. The publicity given to a large increase in wages or fringe benefits won by members of an important union in a major industry or business firm generates new demands among workers in other industries, particularly those which are most closely comparable in job content or status. Competition among union officials for higher status and prestige in the complex hierarchy of organized labour, coupled with invidious comparisons of wages and living standards among union and non-union workers in the community, tend to transmit new wage expectations and pressures over the whole economy every year or two and thus, in effect, shift the labour supply curve continually upward.

It is very difficult if not impossible, however, to isolate and measure the *specific* impact of union policies on workers' satisfaction or dissatis-

[5]Ross appears to have modified his reviews recently on this point somewhat, as a result of more extensive research. See A. M. Ross and P. T. Hartman, *Changing Patterns of Industrial Conflict* (New York: Wiley & Sons, 1960), pp. 42–5.

faction with their wages. Union wage gains in particular industries are only one, and not necessarily the most important by any means, among the forces that tend to create new and constantly higher wage demands. The various accoutrements or by-products of post-war inflation and economic expansion—the highly publicized profits of major business concerns, spectacular "killings" in real estate and the stock market, conspicuous expenditures of the newly rich or well-to-do, and above all, the unprecedented effort and outlays of money by business firms generally for high-pressure advertising and salesmanship, using the most up-to-date media of mass communication—all of these forces would tend to have the same effect of upward wage pressure even if unions were non-existent. The demand for higher wages, in other words, expresses the aspirations of workers (or their wives!) as *consumers* rather than as producers and union members. If union leaders are, as Wright Mills defines them, the "managers of discontent," employers, salesmen, advertisers, and those who control the main media of mass communications are the more important instigators of that discontent.

There is still greater disagreement among economists over another crucial question: Given the fact that there are continually rising wage expectations among workers, are unions able, and have they been able, actually to achieve bigger wage increases or other benefits than workers could have won if they had been unorganized? Here again is a question that defies accurate and conclusive analysis, and one that tends to involve misleading comparisons. In studying the problem in terms of any one industry, the answer is likely to depend upon such variables as: type of market; elasticity of demand for labour and for the end product; degree of competition among employers, in both the labour and the product markets; militancy and bargaining-power of workers; and so on.

It seems obvious, on the face of it, that a strong union could win larger wage increases than could unorganized workers in an industry in which production is concentrated in a few large firms that are free, within the limits of market demand, to set their own prices for their output. Employers in these circumstances may be able to grant large wage increases or other concessions to their workers, and pass these increases on to the consumers or buyers through higher prices, with little or no reduction in their net profits. Indeed, a case could be made for the argument that unions on occasion may enable employers to make larger profits than they otherwise could in a buoyant sellers' market. Prominent business firms may be inhibited from "charging what the traffic will bear" for fear of hurting their "public relations," or of being investigated by the government for monopolistic price fixing. Union pressure for higher wages or fringe benefits may "get them off the hook" and enable them to raise prices by more than enough to cover the higher labour costs.

Much the same result may occur in highly competitive industries that have inelastic demands for their products, such as building construction and some local service industries in major metropolitan centres, if the employers all simultaneously grant uniform wage increases under "master" agreements with unions and raise their prices accordingly.

It is possible, on the other hand, that wage increases achieved through collective bargaining in highly competitive industries, particularly in periods of rapid economic expansion, may average out to less than would be paid if the labour were unorganized. In the latter case, competition among employers in a period of labour shortage tends to lead not only to rapid wage increases, but also to unequal wage rates among competing firms due to "imperfections" in the labour market. Wage differentials among them, it may be assumed, will be based primarily on unequal ability to pay. Under collective bargaining unions tend to be preoccupied with ironing out such differentials and achieving uniform rates for workers in comparable occupations throughout the industry. As Kerr and Fisher[6] point out, unions (or union officials) tend to give greater priority to the "political" objective of achieving greater unity and harmony within the ranks than they do to the purely economic objective of getting the highest possible wages for their members. At the same time employers, acting in concert when dealing with unions, are likely to resist wage increases which some or most of them would have been willing and able to pay if they had had to bid competitively for workers in a tight labour market.

It is even more difficult to estimate with any degree of accuracy what the impact of unionism has been on the *general* level of wages over the national economy as a whole. For this involves trying to compare what is and has been, on the one hand, with what might have been, under purely hypothetical circumstances, on the other. In attempting to get an answer of some sort to this question, several

[6]C. Kerr and L. Fisher, "Multi-Employer Bargaining: The San Francisco Experience," in R. Lester and L. Shister (eds.), *Insights into Labor Issues* (New York, 1948).

economists at one time or another have made lengthy and detailed historical and statistical analyses comparing the relative wage increases enjoyed over a long period by union and non-union workers in different industries and occupations. The results have been generally inconclusive and contradictory. Paul Douglas in his *Theory of Wages*[7] came to the conclusion that, from the 1890's to the end of the 1920's, unorganized workers in general gained relatively larger wage increases than did unionized workers. The validity of these findings was challenged by A. M. Ross,[8] who found that the more highly unionized workers generally won greater wage increases, in dollars-and-cents terms, than did unorganized or poorly organized workers. The wage increases of the former were smaller in *percentage* terms, as Douglas found, only because they were based on the generally higher wage levels of unionized as compared to non-union workers. The question of which index is the most significant—gains in terms of percentages, or of dollars-and-cents—remains a source of controversy. Furthermore, wage increases among unorganized workers have been due to a considerable degree to the "demonstration effect" of gains negotiated by unions through collective bargaining, particularly in highly publicized negotiations in major mass production industries. To just what degree this applies, however, has long been a matter of intense controversy.

These basic differences in underlying assumptions regarding the power of unions to force up the general wage level lead to divergent conclusions regarding the responsibility of trade unions, in the aggregate, for inflation.

One school of thought maintains that inflation develops quite independently of trade union wage policies. It is a diverse group that includes such outstanding economists as F. H. Knight, Milton Friedman, Kenneth Boulding,[9] and, by implication, the late Lord Keynes, as well as a number of neo-Keynesian labour economists such as L. G. Reynolds.[10] Inflation, according to this group, can develop only when fiscal and monetary policies lead to expansion of money and credit in sufficient volume to maintain higher price levels. These arise essen-

[7]Paul C. Douglas, *The Theory of Wages* (Chicago, 1930).

[8]A. M. Ross, "The Influence of Unionism upon Earnings," in *Trade Union Wage Policy*.

[9]D. McC. Wright (ed.), *The Impact of the Union* (New York: Harcourt Brace, 1951).

[10]L. G. Reynolds, "The General Level of Wages," in G. W. Taylor and F. C. Pierson (eds.), *New Concepts in Wage Determination* (New York: McGraw-Hill, 1957).

tially from forces that stimulate large new investments and a subsequent "multiplier effect" on national income, such as: excessive government expenditures for public works or military facilities; widespread anticipation of long-run increases in consumer demand; excessive credit expansion from instalment loans to consumers; and so on. Without the underlying expansion in money, credit, and national income from such causes as these, there would obviously be upper limits to the over-all wage increases that unions could achieve directly for their own members, and indirectly for other workers. For, to the extent that wage increases exceeded increases in productivity, costs would rise. Attempts to raise prices generally to cover the higher costs would, in the face of limited aggregate money income and demand, lead to decreased output and sales, and shrinking employment. Widespread union pressure might continue to force up wages and prices for a while (as during the recession of 1957–8), but sooner or later unemployment and falling sales would strengthen the resistance of employers, undermine the bargaining power of unions, and reduce or eliminate the wage increases that unions seek to attain.

It is implicitly assumed in this argument that union wage demands and wage increases have no effect (or if anything, have a *negative* effect) upon the expectations and consequent actions of business men and consumers with regard to income, demand, and prices. The expectation, or actuality, of higher wages, costs, and prices, that is to say, would discourage monetary and credit expansion because, without the kinds of outside stimuli mentioned earlier, higher costs would induce business men to cut back their outputs and investments, and consumers their purchases.

Those who hold trade unions mainly, or to a large degree, responsible for the inflation of recent years include, among others, such prominent economists as John Dunlop,[11] Sumner Slichter,[12] John Galbraith,[13] Lloyd Ulman,[14] and others. The new factor that has to be taken into account in economic analysis of business cycles and long-term price trends, this group emphasizes, is the rise of strong unions in the major capital goods and mass production industries,

[11]John Dunlop, *The Secular Outlook: Wages and Prices* (Berkeley: University of California, 1957).

[12]S. Slichter, "The Problem of Inflation," *Review of Economics and Statistics*, XXX (Feb., 1948).

[13]J. Galbraith, "Are Living Costs Out of Control?" *Atlantic*, Feb., 1957.

[14]Lloyd Ulman, "Collective Bargaining and Inflation," *California Management Review*, II, no. 3 (Spring, 1960).

such as steel, automobiles, rubber, oil, chemicals, and electrical products. These industries are monopolistic or oligopolistic in structure, and are thus able to pass on wage and price increases to their customers, and ultimately the consuming public. They are also undergoing rapid increases in productivity which help pay for large wage increases or other dollar benefits every year or so. These industries tend to be the "pace-setters" in collective bargaining, and create pressure for comparable wage increases in less productive sectors of the economy, which necessarily involve bigger cost and price increases.

In examining this question it might clarify matters to distinguish the effects of wage, cost, and price increases upon (1) monetary and credit policy; and (2) fiscal policy. In practice, of course, the two have been closely interrelated since the war, but conceptually there may be some advantage in considering the two separately for purposes of analysis.

The argument that wage and price increases due to trade union pressure in "key sectors" of the economy would lead to an inflationary expansion in money and credit is based on quite different assumptions from those outlined above, as regards public expectations and reactions. Barring adverse "exogenous" developments, or governmental restrictions like those of "tight money," it is assumed that widely publicized wage increases in major industries on balance induce business men and consumers to borrow and dishoard, invest and spend *more* than they otherwise would, in anticipation of higher costs and higher prices in the near future. They tend to react positively in this manner to anticipated wage and price increases, it is assumed, partly because of past experience with inflation since the 1930's. In the eyes of most business men and consumers alike, substantial wage increases by major trade unions are associated with or accompanied by rapid economic expansion rather than contraction. If and when large numbers of consumers and investors act accordingly, expectation becomes reality and, in a predominantly "closed economy" like that of the United States, the larger money income and aggregate demand generated by increased business and consumer expenditures (financed in part by credit expansion) maintain the same (or greater) volume of output, sales, and employment than before, and at a higher level of wages, costs, and prices. Thus, it is argued, wage increases brought about by unions through bargaining pressure in key sectors of the United States economy tend to induce continued inflation year by year. This could happen even if the federal government were to maintain a balanced budget or a moderate surplus each year if, on the basis of rising prices and expanding national income, government revenues from taxation continue to equal or to exceed expenditures.

In practice, it is pointed out, the fiscal policies of the federal government in the United States have served to reinforce such inflationary tendencies in a number of ways. Fear of mass unemployment, as a sure road to political ruin, together with the fact that "full" employment has been legislated into existence as a public duty, require that the federal government be ready at all times to incur substantial deficits by cutting taxes and/or increasing public expenditures in order to sustain aggregate demand and prevent unemployment reaching politically dangerous proportions. Over the long pull this means, in effect, underwriting union wage increases and consequent price increases. This tendency is reinforced by the pressures exerted upon the government by various interest groups—farmers, business men, army veterans, and other recipients of public welfare benefits, and local and state governments—to increase expenditures without raising taxes in proportion. Even more directly contributing to budgetary deficits and inflation have been the huge commitments for defence production, foreign aid, and numerous public works projects that are fixed in *real* terms—that is, in physical units rather than merely in dollar outlays. In the aggregate these mean, in effect, that over a considerable range of prices there is a highly inelastic demand for a large volume and variety of goods and services. Production of such items, furthermore, is concentrated to a high degree in large firms in the strongly unionized "heavy" goods and mass production industries. Wage, cost, and price increases in such cases may therefore pay for themselves directly through inflation, by forcing the government to incur budgetary deficits in order to finance the larger dollar outlays required to meet its fixed commitments.

In general, then, a plausible case can be made for the assertion that trade union wage pressure in "key sectors" of the economy tends to create a continually inflationary trend in the United States. Official statistics on wages, productivity and prices, while they do not *prove* any close causal sequence emanating from union wage pressure, do none the less present a concatenation in which the latter seems to be one of the most important elements. A survey by the United States Bureau of Labor Statistics in 1957 concluded:

> . . . the figures indicate that average hourly compensation in current dollars increased much more than productivity in the postwar period. The former increased by about 61 per cent,

> the latter by 26 per cent, leading to an increase in employee compensation per dollar of real product of about 28 per cent.

The study pointed out that this 28 per cent was "almost identical with the increase in prices between 1947 and 1956."[15]

J. Galbraith pinpoints the argument further:

> . . . The inflation of recent years has been marked in those parts of the economy that are subject to the [wage-price] spiral. Thus in the steel industry, where the spiral works relentlessly and where wage advances are invariably the occasion for even larger price increases, the prices of most products are now between 70 and 80 per cent above their 1947–49 average. At present rates prices of steel products are doubling themselves approximately every ten years. To take a random selection of other relatively well-organized industries where prices are also subject to considerable control, machine tools are up about 60 per cent since 1947–49; aluminum ingot is up 70 per cent; bulldozers are up between 50 and 60 per cent; tractor tires are up 61 per cent; mining machinery on the average is up about 75 per cent. . . .
>
> Where the spiral does not operate the behavior of prices is very different. In the cotton textile industry—an industry of weak unions and fairly numerous manufacturers—prices are now on the average between 8 and 9 per cent *below* the 1947–49 level. In the apparel industry, where unions are strong but the manufacturers are not, prices are now about the same as in the late forties. Prices of farm products, where there are no unions and where all producers are relatively small, are about 10 per cent below the level of the late forties.[16]

One might expect, on the face of it, that much the same pattern of inflation induced by union wage pressure would apply in Canada as in the United States. The vast majority of unions in Canada are affiliated to more than one hundred so-called "international" unions, the membership and top executive personnel of which are overwhelmingly American. There tends to be a parallel relationship between Canadian and American industry. As special studies by the

[15]Dunlop, *v. supra.*
[16]Galbraith, *v. supra.*

Gordon Commission[17] brought out, non-resident (predominantly American) capital accounts for well over one-half of the total investment in manufacturing, and more than two-thirds of the total in mining and smelting and in petroleum exploration and development. While no exact statistical estimate has been made of the question, it is safe to estimate that a large fraction if not a majority of all organized wage-earners in Canada are employed in the nearly 4,000 firms that are subsidiaries of American parent companies. This includes some of the largest and most influential firms on the continent, in such fields as automobiles, rubber, chemicals, electrical equipment, pulp and paper. And, as brought out in a comprehensive study by Gideon Rosenbluth a few years ago,[18] there is an even greater degree of monopolistic or oligopolistic concentration in industry in Canada than in the United States. In the broader picture there are such factors as rapidly improved transportation and communication, high-pressure advertising and salesmanship by American firms or subsidiaries in the Canadian market, highly publicized industrial disputes and collective bargaining gains of unions in the United States—the rapid Americanization of Canadian life generally.

All such developments tend to inculcate Canadian workers with higher wage and living standards (as distinct from actual *levels* prevailing) in line with their higher income counterparts in the United States. These in turn tend to generate continual pressure upon Canadian unions to win greater wage and other concessions from employers in this country. One might therefore be led to conclude that union wage pressure would be even more inflationary in effect in Canada than in the United States, in view of the generally lower levels of productivity and real income of Canadian as compared to American workers. This does not appear to have been the case, however. For a number of reasons there has not been a very appreciable narrowing of United States–Canadian differentials in wages and fringe benefits in any but a few fields of employment since the war.

By and large, the convincing case outlined above in support of the wage-push inflation thesis would appear to have only limited validity in Canada. For self-perpetuating inflation along the lines portrayed

[17]J. Brecher and S. S. Reisman, *Canada–United States Economic Relations* (Royal Commission on Canada's Economic Prospects, Ottawa, 1957).

[18]Gideon Rosenbluth, *Concentration in Canadian Manufacturing Industries* (Princeton, 1957).

depends upon a number of conditions more or less peculiar to the American economy. Among the more important of these are the following:

(1) A "self-contained" economy, in which (*a*) only a small fraction of any additional income generated in inflationary policies is lost through import "leakages"; and (*b*) any reduction of exports due to domestic inflation and higher costs would have only a minor impact on total employment and output. Only under these conditions could it be argued that (i) higher wages, costs, and prices for capital goods and materials (for example, steel, chemicals, rubber, electrical products) would directly raise costs of production and prices in all other industries using these products; and (ii) monetary and credit expansion induced initially by higher wages and material costs could generate enough additional money income and demand to maintain or increase output and employment at the higher wage, cost, and price levels.

(2) The most influential or powerful interest groups in the nation directly or indirectly press for fiscal and credit policies that are inflationary in effect, and the federal government, on balance, is responsive to such pressures.

The Canadian economy differs markedly from the American model in both respects. Consequently, inflation in Canada, during the 1950's at least, appears to have developed from quite different causes initially, followed a different sequence, and had different effects.

(1) Canada is far from being a "self-contained economy" along the lines of the American model. On the contrary, as every schoolboy should know, Canada depends upon foreign trade for 20 to 25 per cent of her national income. In such an economy various exigencies of foreign trade and exchange tend to set very clear limits to any sort of self-perpetuating inflation of the American type arising from trade union wage demands or other internal pressures. A large and growing part of any additional income generated by internal inflation tends to be lost through import "leakages" for two main reasons: (*a*) the high "propensity to import" among Canadians, such that the *proportion* as well as the absolute amount of income spent on imports, rises as *per capita* incomes increase; and (*b*) growing competition from lower-cost imports when the domestic level of cost and prices rises. At the same time, higher wages and costs of production, if out of line with those in other countries, would tend to reduce exports and generate unemployment, trade deficits, and depreciation of the Canadian dollar in relation to foreign currencies. Currency depreciation arising from domestic inflation and growing trade deficits would, in turn, tend to

discourage foreign investment in Canada (and, if severe enough, would cause a "flight of capital"), reduce domestic savings and capital formation, and generally slow down the rate of economic growth. In brief, "wage-push" inflation would tend to "price labour out of employment" more than to raise the general level of prices above those of the United States and other major industrial trading nations.

(2) Because of this dependence upon foreign trade, federal government policy in Canada cannot be said to be, or to have been, responsive primarily to domestic inflationary pressures. Thus, in contrast to the United States, the federal government in Canada has had budgetary surpluses in each fiscal year since the Second World War except 1946, 1955–6, and 1958–60.

If unions were to push wage, cost, and price levels in Canada too far out of line with those in the United States and overseas markets, of course, falling exports, rising trade deficits, unemployment, and currency depreciation might occur even if the government and the banking system were to keep a tight checkrein on monetary and credit inflation.

So far none of these developments have occurred to any significant degree since the Second World War (except perhaps during the current recession of 1957–8 and the partial recovery of 1959–60), and even here the case is far from clear. The inflationary spurts and trade difficulties of 1946–9 and later in 1950–1, as noted before, clearly arose from causes other than excessive wage and cost-price increases. From 1949 through 1956 Canada underwent one of the most rapid rates of economic expansion of any country. Employment generally increased by about 22 per cent (including the net absorption of more than one million immigrants), gross national product (in real terms) grew by 44.4 per cent, and exports by more than 60 per cent. The annual volume of domestic savings as well as foreign capital investment in Canada both *doubled* during this period. The Canadian dollar, far from depreciating, has consistently maintained a premium above the American dollar and other foreign currencies during this period (except for a short period of speculative inflation after the outbreak of the Korean War in mid-1950).

Clearly, then, unions in Canada did not, as is so frequently alleged, "price labour out of the market." The price level (as measured by the consumer price index of the Dominion Bureau of Statistics) increased by 18.1 per cent between 1949 and the end of 1956, while average weekly earnings increased by 51.2 per cent. But in view of the other major economic developments in Canada during this period, as outlined above, the wage increases brought about by union pressure do not appear to have been mainly responsible for the inflation that took place in this country. The main factors were high export sales and prices, and the tremendous level of investment, from domestic savings and credit expansion as well as from the huge inflows of capital from the United States, to expand productive capacity to take advantage of the greatly increased foreign and domestic demand for Canadian output. The weight of evidence, therefore, seems to indicate that inflation in Canada, up to mid-1957 at least, was of the "demand-pull" rather than "wage-push" variety. It appears to have been primarily a by-product of, and response to, inflation in the United States and abroad, rather than a self-generating phenomenon originating from union wage demands or other internal pressures in Canada itself.

The picture appears to have changed considerably during the past three years. There is some evidence that wage-push inflation has been one operating factor, though it is difficult to distinguish in its effects from the inflationary deficit financing of the Dominion government. The momentum of rapid wage increases and other cost factors that developed during the unprecedented expansion of 1955–7 carried over into the subsequent period of contraction. Wages and other major cost items, and the general level of prices, continued to rise in Canada during the recession of late 1957–8, when the effects of earlier monetary and credit restrictions, coupled with slackening demand for Canadian-produced output at home and abroad, were bringing rising unemployment, unsold surpluses, and cutbacks in production. This combination of circumstances may well have contributed to the persistence of serious unemployment during the limited recovery of 1959–60. While Canada's total exports reached a record level during 1959, industries selling mainly in the domestic market experienced greater competition from lower-cost or more efficient foreign producers. Canada's deficits in trade and current accounts also reached a record level during 1959 and, at the time of writing (early 1960) the Canadian dollar appears to be declining in value in foreign exchange. It remains to be seen whether these various developments since mid-1957 are merely part of a relatively brief cycle of recession and recovery, or whether they represent persistent, long-term tendencies that will require serious readjustments in various sectors of the Canadian economy. In any case, the role and impact of trade union wage policy in Canada seems far more difficult to analyse and identify during this latter period than in the previous era of expansion.

Some Reflections on Economic Security for the Aged in Canada

ROBERT M. CLARK

Future historians will regard the second half of the twentieth century as one in which governments in the western world made very important changes in welfare legislation for the aged. Great Britain in 1959 enacted legislation to provide a contributory pension programme with small graduated benefits, to supplement the contributory pensions programme with flat benefits established as part of a comprehensive social insurance system in 1946. The United States in the same decade added disability benefits to its Old-Age and Survivors Insurance programme, and has extended the coverage of this programme to include about 90 per cent of the American population. The Government of Canada, with the support of all the political parties in the House of Commons, introduced in 1952 a flat pension for all persons age 70 and over who could meet the residence requirement of 20 years. In each of these three countries the benefits have been increased, both in the above-mentioned programmes, and in the older means- or needs-test assistance programmes which supplement them.[1] During the last two decades employee pension plans in these countries have grown impressively in coverage and in benefits.

That we live in an era of rising public expectations in regard to pensions, as in other fields, is recognized by the public generally, and by all the political parties who seek their support. This is true in Canada, as well as in other nations of the western world.

The extraordinary increase in average life expectancy in Canada in the twentieth century has had the natural consequence of increasing

[1]The West German legislation of 1957 and the Swedish legislation of 1959 provided even more extensive government pension benefits for the aged than are found in the United Kingdom, the United States, or Canada.

the importance of making financial provision for income in old age. In the absence of satisfactory Canadian statistics relating to the beginning of this century, it is useful to consider statistics for the United States. Average life expectancy at birth in 1901 was 48 years for white males and 51 years for white females.[2] Life expectancy figures for the United States were probably slightly higher than the corresponding Canadian figures. The typical American or Canadian adult did not live long enough to retire because of old age.

The average life expectancy at birth for Canadians in 1956 was 67.6 years for men and 72.9 years for women.[3] In the 25 years between 1931 and 1956 the percentage of male babies born in Canada expected to reach age 70 increased from 48.9 to 56.5. For female babies the corresponding increase was from 52.6 to 70.3 per cent.[4] In 1956 the average life expectancy for men at age 70 was 10.5 years, and for women, 12.2 years.[5] Average life expectancies of women at all ages from birth to age 70 and beyond have been increasing in the twentieth century at a faster rate than average life expectancies for men. The widespread demands for pensions from private employers and from government are thus seen to arise from a need which affects a much larger proportion of the population than were concerned with pensions in the nineteenth century.

Private pension plans have grown remarkably in the past quarter of a century, and are continuing to grow in coverage and in benefits provided. The Dominion Bureau of Statistics undertook its first survey of employee pension plans in 1936. This was a survey of 615 firms,

[2]Communication to the author from Mr. H. G. Page, Chief, Vital Statistics Section, Health and Welfare Division, Dominion Bureau of Statistics, September 8, 1960.

About 31 per cent of men and 35 per cent of women born in the United States in 1901 were expected to reach age 70.

[3]Canada, Dominion Bureau of Statistics, *Canadian Life Tables 1950–1952–1955–1957* (Ottawa: Queen's Printer, 1960), pp. 10 and 12.

[4]*Ibid.*, pp. 11 and 13; and Canada, Dominion Bureau of Statistics, *Life Tables for Canada and Regions 1941 and 1931* (Ottawa: King's Printer, 1947), pp. 43 and 46. The corresponding percentages for the male and female population in the United States born in 1956 expected to reach age 70 were 67.7 and 78.8 (H. G. Page, communication of September 8, 1960).

[5]The increase in average life expectancy between 1931 and 1956 for persons at age 70 has been from 10.1 years to 10.5 years for men, and from 10.6 to 12.2 years for women.

each of which had 15 or more employees, and all of which had 1,028,750 employees; 35 per cent of these employees worked for firms with pension plans.[6] The latest published survey by the Dominion Bureau of Statistics was made in 1957. It covered 1,854,086 employees in 11,304 firms or establishments, each of which had at least 15 non-office employees; 78 per cent of the employees worked for firms with pension plans.[7] The proportion of employees covered by pension plans in Canada has been much lower than these figures might suggest. This is partly because a significant but unknown proportion of employee pension plans are voluntary, and many persons exercise their option not to join a pension plan. Apart from this factor, many employees are excluded from coverage by a minimum waiting period or by an age requirement.[8] In 1957 approximately 29 to 33 per cent of the civilian labour force plus the Canadian armed forces were protected by employee pension plans.[9]

[6]Robert M. Clark, *Economic Security for the Aged in the United States and Canada* (Ottawa: Queen's Printer, 1960), II, para. 1532, 1548–9.

[7]*Ibid.*, para. 1542, 1548–9.

[8]Pension plans may be classified as contributory or non-contributory. The great majority of these plans in Canada are contributory (*ibid.*, para. 1453). Generally speaking, membership in non-contributory plans is automatic, except for casual employees. A majority of contributory plans are voluntary.

Contributory pension plans administered by insurance companies are much more likely to be voluntary than contributory plans administered by trust companies. The National Trust Company in 1960 published a study of 117 pension plans, a majority of which were administered by trust companies. Of the 117 plans, 92 were contributory. Of these contributory plans, 18 were compulsory for all members, 26 were voluntary for existing members but compulsory for new members, 34 were voluntary for all members, and the information was inadequate for the remaining 11. (Pension Division, National Trust Company Limited, *A Study of Canadian Pension Plans* (Toronto, 1960), Table II, pages not numbered; communication from Mr. Lawrence Baldwin, Pension Trust Officer, National Trust Company, Toronto.) For business firms with contributory pension plans it is broadly true that the larger the firm the more likely it is that membership in the plan is compulsory.

For age and service eligibility requirements in employee pension plans see Clark, *Economic Security*, para. 1454–5, and National Trust Company, *Study of Canadian Pension Plans*, Table II.

[9]Clark, *Economic Security*, para. 1555.

The Old Age Pensions Act of 1927 authorized the Government of Canada to pay to provincial governments half the cost of old age assistance payable to persons age 70 and over. This means-test programme was improved from time to time by increasing the benefits and by making the means test less severe.[10] Under the Old Age Assistance Act of 1951 the federal Government offered to pay half the cost of Old Age Assistance payments to persons age 65 and over.[11] Old Age Assistance payments were in effect limited to persons aged 65 to 69 by the passing of the Old Age Security Act in the same year. This act provided pensions without a means test to all applicants age 70 and over who had resided in Canada for the last 20 years. The four political parties represented in the House of Commons all supported the act.[12] The Old Age Security pension was raised to $46 a month by the Liberal Government shortly before the 1957 election, and to $55 a month by the victorious Conservatives soon after the election. The latter have reduced the minimum residence requirement to 10 years, and, subject to certain restrictions, allow Canadian residents who have become eligible for this pension to receive it while living outside Canada.[13] The federal Government in 1952 passed the Blind Persons Act and in 1954 the Disabled Persons Act to share in the cost of means-test programmes administered by the provincial governments to assist persons who are blind or totally and permanently disabled.[14] The income of certain categories of needy recipients of Old Age Security or of assistance under one of the three mentioned means-test programmes is augmented by supplementary allowance in the four western provinces and Ontario.[15]

[10]*Ibid.*, I, para. 897; II, appendix VI.

[11]*Ibid.*, I, para. 1009–10.

[12]*Ibid.*, para. 929 and 981.

[13]*Ibid.*, para. 926 and 927. The latter paragraph explains how the residence requirement is applied in the case of persons who have resided in Canada for more than ten years but not for the ten years immediately preceding the day on which their application for the pension is approved.

A person who wishes to take up residence outside Canada and to continue receiving Old Age Security abroad must have lived in Canada for 25 years. If an individual has never received Old Age Security, and is living outside Canada when he applies for it, he must fulfil an additional condition in order to qualify for it: he must live for a further year in Canada (1960, c. 34, s. 3).

[14]Clark, *Economic Security*, I, para. 1144 and 1159.

[15]*Ibid.*, para. 1173–1209.

These various acts represent a fundamental advance in providing greater security for the Canadian people. In the remainder of this article I wish to suggest some of the ways in which I believe they could be improved. The approach chosen is to ask what are the most significant gaps or anomalies in existing legislation, and then to consider what, if anything, should be done about them. Limitations of space prevent my commenting on government regulation of employee pension plans, and lack of knowledge precludes me from making suggestions for the provision of medical services for the aged.

At the outset, an emphatic warning is necessary. The study of one field of government expenditures does not entitle an economist—or anyone else—to say that his field of interest is the most urgent priority for increased government spending. Those whose principal concern is with unemployment or education are likely to believe that their favourite projects should have the highest priority. The federal Government, struggling with the problem of persistent unemployment, the perplexities of national defence, and the perpetual demands from the provinces for a greater share of the nation's tax revenues, obviously could not carry out all the spending proposals made to it by well-intentioned persons at a level of taxation acceptable to a majority of the public.

I believe that in the field of economic security for the aged, the following are problems especially deserving consideration as soon as possible having regard to the other commitments the federal Government will be making. In selecting these problems and in suggesting possible solutions, I am not attempting to state what problems are politically most significant, or what solutions to them have the most political appeal.

(1) The lack of survivor benefits.
(2) The illogical basis of financing Old Age Security.
(3) The hardships created for some persons who do not quite qualify for Old Age Assistance by the fact that Old Age Security is not payable until age 70.
(4) The discrimination against single persons in relation to married persons under the Old Age Security and the Old Age Assistance Acts.
(5) The discrimination against those in receipt of Old Age Security or of means-test benefits who live in relatively high cost areas.
(6) The undesirable equating of the maximum amount of

Old Age Security and Old Age Assistance, and the limitation of Old Age Assistance to those between the ages of 65 and 69. (7) The unnecessary distinction between Social Assistance and Old Age Assistance.

Items (1) to (3) relate solely to Old Age Security, items (4) to (6) relate to both Old Age Security and Old Age Assistance.

Before considering these seven items, I wish to deal briefly with a query which may occur to some readers. Would you, they may ask, regard these items as having about the same significance or priority whether or not the federal Government were to modify its Old Age Security programme by adding graduated pension benefits, and changing the financial basis of the programme to require graduated contributions to which the graduated benefits were related? The answer is yes. Each of these seven problems should be solved whether or not a contributory pension programme with graduated benefits is introduced.

In this connection it is desirable to point out that the existing Canadian Old Age Security programme is not contributory in the sense in which the British National Insurance programme and the American Social Security programme are contributory. I suggest that it is useful to define a government social security programme as contributory if the benefits are only available to persons or their dependents who have paid identifiable contributions either of a specified amount or at a specified rate or rates on covered income. Under this definition the present Canadian Old Age Security programme, unlike the corresponding British and American programmes, is not contributory, since persons can qualify for Old Age Security in Canada without having paid any of the personal income tax in Canada designated for Old Age Security.[16]

A contributory government pension programme usually has two additional characteristics. Receipt of pension benefits is conditional upon a specified minimum contribution record. The relationship of pension benefits to contributions is positive and sufficiently marked to justify the cost of maintaining records of contributions by individuals. These two characteristics do not need to form part of the definition, as it would be possible to pay for a flat pension programme out of an earmarked tax on earnings without any exemptions and without any need to keep a record of contributions by individuals

[16]*Ibid.*, para. 187–96.

over their working lives. Such a programme would be contributory in the sense in which I have defined it.

In the limited space available I do not wish to repeat the arguments for and against a contributory government pension programme with graduated benefits contained in *Economic Security for the Aged in the United States and Canada*.[17] There is a very strong case both for and against introducing such a programme. Although I am not opposed in principle to limited graduated benefits, my own preference for Canada is a flat benefit programme financed by graduated contributions. This is what we have now, although, for reasons I shall indicate later, I feel strongly that our system of raising revenue to pay for Old Age Security should be reformed.

The logic of a flat-benefit programme lies in the belief that a government programme to provide pension and survivor benefits should be regarded essentially as a social service device to transfer from the working population a minimum income to the aged and certain categories of survivors. The prime concern of the Canadian Government in such legislation should be the needs of those below an average income, since, generally speaking, those farther up the income scale are in a better position to provide for themselves.[18] While a contributory pension programme with graduated benefits presumably would be weighted on the benefit side in favour of the lower income groups, such a programme must exhibit significant positive correlation between contributions and benefits. Otherwise there is little justification for the administrative costs to employers and the Government in keeping the record of contributions for each individual covered by the programme. For the same amount of expenditure a flat benefit programme is likely to do more to help those who are in greater need than is a contributory programme with graduated benefits. This is obviously true in the short run, since under a contributory programme with graduated benefits, the latter benefits inevitably build up slowly. I expect that it is also true in the long run.

If the Government of Canada were starting now to draft legisla-

[17]*Ibid.*, II, chaps. XIX and XX.

[18]If the Government's sole concern was need, it would make the receipt of an old age pension subject to a means test. This policy would do most for those in greatest need, while avoiding making any payments to those obviously not in need. The Canadian people through their representatives in Parliament clearly have rejected the means-test approach, as the main approach to be used in social security legislation, while retaining it for important subsidiary programmes.

tion to supplement the Old Age Security pension and to introduce survivor benefits, and if employee pension plans were no further developed than they were in the United States when the Social Security Act was passed in 1935, I believe that the balance of advantages would lie in working towards a government programme closely similar in many respects to the American programme.

Our circumstances, however, are different, and because of this I think the most advantageous path lies in the direction of improving benefits within the framework of an expanded flat-benefit programme. Wherein are our circumstances different? In at least two important respects.

The payment of an Old Age Security pension of $55 a month is substantially higher than the American minimum Old-Age benefit of $33, a minimum achieved after contributions have been collected for the programme from 1937 to the present.[19] The average personal income in Canada is about 30 per cent below that of the United States.[20] A consequence of these facts is that the range of graduated benefits would have to be much smaller than in the United States, for at least a few decades, even if Canadians were prepared to pay as much per capita in contributions as is paid in the United States.

Private pension plans in the United States covered about 7 per cent of the civilian labour force in 1935. Employee pension plans, both private and government as indicated earlier, are now much more widespread in their coverage in Canada, as indeed they are in the United States.[21] The growth of these plans increases economic security in old age for those covered by them, provides a valuable addition to the nation's savings, and reduces the need for the Government to provide a pension programme with graduated benefits.

From the general viewpoint of the public interest that as many as possible of the aged should have an adequate income, and not merely a subsistence income, employee pension plans have two disadvantages, apart from the limitations of coverage referred to earlier. Under the majority of pension plans in Canada, when an employee leaves his employer prior to retirement, he does not get any benefit from his

[19]The Old-Age benefit in the United States is paid at age 65, subject to a retirement test. Women have the option of taking their pension or survivors' benefit as early as age 62, provided that they take it at an actuarially reduced rate for life. (Clark, *Economic Security*, I, para. 244–5, 247, 249–51, 254, 257, 282–90.)

[20]*Ibid.*, II, para. 2034.

[21]*Ibid.*, para. 1559–61.

employer's pension plan unless he has been with the employer for 10 years or more.[22] Employees who change jobs many times in the course of their lives may work for a succession of employers with good pension plans, yet reach retirement with only a meagre pension to supplement their Old Age Security. Likewise undesirable from the above-mentioned viewpoint is the fact that the vast majority of employees covered by pension plans, confronted when they leave their employer with the choice of cash or a deferred annuity, take cash.[23] As a consequence of these factors, to an extent which is impossible to determine, most employee pension plans restrict the mobility of labour. Although the point is readily exaggerated, most pension plans also give employers an incentive to discriminate in hiring personnel against persons over age 40.[24] These disadvantages are likely to be more serious in non-contributory pension plans.

It is too early to tell as of this date[25] what will be accomplished by the Ontario Government in its announced intention of adopting legislation to regulate employee pension plans in Ontario.[26] I am hopeful that these disadvantages of employer pension plans can be very substantially reduced and the coverage of such plans broadened greatly. The regulation of employee pension plans is, as I understand it, a matter of property and civil rights, and hence a provincial responsibility under the British North America Act.[27] Provincial regulation of employee pension plans has some obvious disadvantages which

[22]*Ibid.*, para. 1474–7; and National Trust Company, *Study of Canadian Pension Plans*, Table VII.

[23]Clark, *Economic Security*, II, para. 1483–6.

[24]This statement applies to unit benefit pension plans, which constitute the majority of pension plans, but not to money purchase plans. (*Ibid.*, para. 1449–52, 1483, and National Trust Company, *Study of Canadian Pension Plans*, Table V.)

Under a unit benefit plan, the employer's contribution for any covered employee increases with the employee's age, while under a money purchase plan the employer's contribution is independent of his age.

[25]October 6, 1960.

[26]In his statement in the Legislative Assembly of Ontario on April 7, 1960, the Honourable Leslie M. Frost, Prime Minister of Ontario, referred to the work of the advisory committee he had appointed as follows: "The purpose of our technical Committee on Portable Pensions is to explore ways and means by which retirement pension plans can be made more effective, provide more security for our older people and minimize those inhibitions which militate against the employment of the older worker."

[27]Clark, *Economic Security*, II, para. 1531.

can be obviated to a very large degree if other provincial governments are willing to enact legislation similar to that which is being considered in Ontario.

LACK OF SURVIVOR BENEFITS

While Canada does provide family allowances, it is one of the very few nations of the western world that has no survivor benefits programme. Denmark is the only other country with which comparisons frequently are made that provides no survivor benefits. In Belgium, France, West Germany, Italy, the Netherlands, Norway, Sweden, Switzerland, the United Kingdom, and the United States survivor benefits are provided without a means test.[28]

Who need survivor benefits? There are three categories of persons among whom are very many who for one reason or another are not adequately provided for. The first category consists of widowed mothers with one or more children of or under school age. Children in such families constitute a second category. In the third are women who have become widows at an age when, if they have not been recently employed, it would be difficult for them to enter or re-enter the labour market.

The increasing discrepancy between average life expectancies of women and men referred to earlier[29] has meant that the proportion of widows in the age group 50 and over has been increasing.

The statistics in Table I, taken from the 1956 Canadian census, show the number of widows and widowers by age groups. No statistics are available, so far as I know, to show the approximate numbers in the three categories of survivors mentioned, but these will be useful in giving the roughest sort of indication of the numbers of women involved. I have not estimated the number of children living with widowed mothers.

This table shows that at June 1, 1956, there were 292,907 widows and 87,979 widowers under age 70. The ratio of widows to widowers under 70 was 3.3:1. By age groups the number of widows and widowers increased until the maximum numbers were in the age group 70–74.

[28]United States, Social Security Administration, Division of Program Research, *Social Security Programs throughout the World 1958* (Washington: U.S.G.P.O., 1958), Chart I, pp. 1–31.

[29]See p. 326.

TABLE I

NUMBER OF WIDOWS AND WIDOWERS IN CANADA BY FIVE-YEAR AGE GROUPS, 1956

Age group	Number of Widows	Number of Widowers
15–19	99	39
20–24	858	186
25–29	2,429	684
30–34	5,690	1,408
35–39	10,586	2,516
40–44	17,782	4,235
45–49	25,704	6,625
50–54	36,685	9,908
55–59	51,701	14,455
60–64	63,608	19,496
65–69	77,765	28,427
70–74	84,814	35,680
75–79	66,591	32,529
80–84	42,994	22,733
85–89	20,929	11,630
90–94	6,779	3,400
95 and over	1,475	771
TOTAL	516,489	194,722

SOURCE: Canada, Dominion Bureau of Statistics, *Census of Canada 1956: Population: Marital Status by Age Groups* (Bulletin 1–12, Ottawa: Queen's Printer, 1957), Table 28.

While, as explained below, I do not think all widows under age 70 should receive survivor benefits, it is instructive to make a few comparisons using the statistics for the total number of widows less than 70 years of age. On June 1, 1956, the total number of widows in this category constituted 1.8 per cent of the population.[30] There were 771,793 persons receiving Old Age Security in March 31, 1956.[31] The number of widows under age 70 on June 1, 1956, was equal to 38 per cent of this number. This fact indicates that a survivor benefits programme is likely to be costly.

The number of widows under age 50 on June 1, 1956, constituted 22 per cent of the total number of widows under age 70. If the amount of survivor benefits were the same for eligible widowed mothers and

[30]The census population figure for Canada on June 1, 1956, was 16,080,791. (Canada, Dominion Bureau of Statistics, *Census of Canada 1956: Population: Marital Status by Age Groups* (Bulletin 1–12, Ottawa: Queen's Printer, 1957), Table 28.)

[31]Clark, *Economic Security*, I, Table 45, p. 261.

for eligible widows, as it is in Great Britain and the United States,[32] the cost of providing benefits for women widowed in their fifties and sixties would be substantially greater than the cost of paying survivor benefits to widowed mothers.

The provision of survivor pensions can be fitted readily into the existing Old Age Security programme or into a contributory government pension programme with graduated benefits. The philosophy of survivor benefits under the two approaches is rather different.

If the example of the American Social Security Act were followed on this point, survivor benefits, like old-age benefits, would be related to prior contributions. This means that the minimum survivor benefit presumably would be very small, and that the amount of survivor benefits would build up slowly over the working life of contributors. Periods of maturity of benefits of 40 years or more under a contributory programme with graduated benefits are likely to be avoided only in one of two ways, or by a combination of them. One is by having large subsidies paid in the first instance from the general revenues of the government. The other is to require future generations of contributors to pay contributions at a substantially higher rate for a given level of benefits than the first and second generation of contributors are required to pay.[33] Both alternatives have an obvious political appeal in the short run, but significant disadvantages in higher taxation or contributions in the long run. Since entitlement to survivor benefits would depend on prior contributions, logically no minimum residence requirement would be needed.

My preference is to have survivor pensions provided without a means test on a flat-benefit basis, for essentially the same reasons that led the political parties in the Canadian House of Commons in 1950 and 1951 to favour old age pensions for persons age 70 and over.[34]

[32]In Great Britain a widow receives an additional allowance for the first 13 weeks of widowhood. (Great Britain, Ministry of Pensions and National Insurance, *Report of the Ministry of Pensions and National Insurance for the Year 1959* (London: H.M.S.O., 1960), p. 97; and Clark, *Economic Security*, I, Table 4, p. 67.)

[33]The latter alternative was followed in the United States, and a combination of the two alternatives in Great Britain. (Clark, *Economic Security*, I, para. 545–8; and Great Britain, Ministry of Pensions and National Insurance, *Provision for Old Age: The Future Development of the National Insurance Scheme* (London: H.M.S.O., 1958, Cmnd. 538), para. 9–13.

[34]Canada, Parliament, Senate and House of Commons, Joint Com-

The provision of survivor benefits is a logical extension of the philosophy now generally accepted in Canada[35] of providing old age pensions subject to a residence requirement but without a means test. This philosophy rests on the belief that a majority of persons in the categories concerned need the type of benefits described, and that the Canadian people through government can afford and should provide such benefits.

In framing a survivor benefits programmes it would be necessary to decide, rather arbitrarily at best, which categories of survivors were entitled to benefits. Probably the residence requirements should be the same as for Old Age Security.

How long should survivor pensions be paid to widowed mothers and to their children? It might be appropriate to pay such benefits to a widowed mother with one or more children until her last child reaches some appropriate age. The survivor pension for each dependent child might reasonably be paid to the same age. I suggest that this age be 16, which is the age limit for family allowances in Canada, but that the pension to a widow and her children be extended to age 18 in all cases where a child continues in full-time education until this age. The justification for attaching such a condition for extending widowed mothers' and children's benefits is twofold. First is the desirability of encouraging children concerned to continue their full-time education up to the age limit. This is not incompatible with limited part-time employment. Second, if a child is no longer at school or college but is working full-time, the need for survivor benefits

---

mittee on Old Age Security, *Report*, J. H. King and Jean Lesage, Chairmen (Ottawa: King's Printer, 1950), pp. 104–10, para. 27–70, esp. para. 54.

[35]The Canadian Institute of Public Opinion Poll of Canada on October 24, 1951, asked a representative sample of Canadians:

> Next year, every Canadian 70 years of age or over will start getting a pension of $40 per month, regardless of their [*sic*] financial position. Do you approve or disapprove of this?

The answers were as follows:

Approve	81 per cent
Disapprove	17
No opinion	2
	100

(Cited in Clark, *Economic Security*, II, para. 1572, n. 3.)
I do not know of any later public opinion poll on this subject.

is reduced.[36] Logically this survivor pension to widowed mothers should be discontinued, as it is in the United Kingdom and the United States, if a widow remarries, although this creates unpleasant administrative problems in a very small proportion of cases. For both of these types of survivor benefit, the payment should be contingent upon the child's continuing to reside with the mother, or upon the mother's contributing to the support of the child an amount at least equal to the child's survivor benefit.

Who should get widow's pensions as distinct from widowed mother's benefits? This is a more difficult question to answer.

It seems reasonable to contend that not all widows should get a widow's pension for life. Sir William (now Lord) Beveridge, in his famous report to the British Government in 1942, wrote: "There is no reason why a childless widow should get a pension for life; if she is able to work, she should work."[37] This viewpoint was accepted by the British National Insurance Advisory Committee in 1956.[38]

A good case can be made for the opinion that the appropriate age at which widows' benefits should begin would be that at which a majority of women would find it difficult to enter or re-enter the labour market if they have not been employed in recent years. This

[36]Under the American Social Security Act a widowed mother, irrespective of her age, receives a widowed mother's benefit if she has in her care a child under age 18, or regardless of age if the child is over 18 but under a disability which began before age 18. (United States, Department of Health, Education, and Welfare, Social Security Administration, *Social Security Handbook: On Old-Age, Survivors, And Disability Insurance* (Washington: U.S.G.P.O., 1960), p. 48.)

In Great Britain under the National Insurance Act a widowed mother, regardless of her age, receives a widowed mother's "allowance" payable until her child is 18, provided the child is residing with her. The National Insurance Advisory Committee in 1956 unanimously recommended that the payment to a widowed mother should only be payable "so long as the child is in full-time education or apprenticeship" (Great Britain, National Insurance Advisory Committee, *Report of the National Insurance Advisory Committee . . . on the Question of Widow's Benefits* (London: H.M.S.O., 1956, Cmnd. 9684), para. 39–41.)

[37]Sir William Beveridge, *Social Insurance and Allied Services* (London: H.M.S.O., 1942, Cmnd. 6404), para. 153. He favoured widowed mothers' benefits and an allowance for all widows for their first 13 weeks of widowhood.

[38]*Report . . . on Question of Widow's Benefits*, para. 24–7. This committee, composed of nine members, includes a minority of persons who are active supporters of the Labour party.

criterion has not been followed in the United States, where benefits to widows, as distinct from widowed mothers, are not payable until age 62. After careful study the National Insurance Advisory Committee in Great Britain endorsed in 1956 the existing British law under which widows' pensions are payable at age 50.[39]

Research would be necessary to determine whether this would be an appropriate age in Canada. In arriving at this age, one of the factors to consider is the increase in the proportion of married women who are working. Unfortunately no detailed statistical breakdown of the labour force by age and marital status is available. The proportion of married women in the labour force in 1931 was 3 per cent. By 1941 it was 3.7 per cent. Wartime conditions led to a sharp increase in the numbers of married women working, and after the war there was no general return to pre-war attitudes towards married women in employment. The proportion of married women in the labour force has increased steadily from 11.8 per cent in 1953 to 18.6 per cent in 1960.[40] I do not know of any conclusive evidence to indicate whether it is becoming easier for married women in their fifties and sixties to find employment.

It would seem very arbitrary to provide a widow's pension to a woman becoming a widow at, for example, age 50, but no pension for a women widowed at age 48 or 49. This arbitrariness could be mitigated by providing smaller widows' benefits for women who become widows in the very few years before they reach age 50. Thus it would be possible to pay a survivor pension of one-third to a woman becoming a widow at age 48, two-thirds to a woman widowed at age 49, and the full pension to a woman who becomes a widow at age 50.

In the case of widowed mothers who are no longer in receipt of widowed mothers' benefits, it would seem reasonable that they should become eligible for widows' benefits at the same age as childless widows.

In order to qualify for a widow's benefits, it probably would be desirable to require that a widow had been married to her deceased husband for at least one year just before he died.[41] I do not think that a similar provision is necessary for widowed mothers.

The payment of widows' pensions would terminate when the widow died, remarried, or began to receive Old Age Security. Provision for

[39]*Ibid.*, para. 46–7.

[40]Communication to the author from Mr. H. G. Page, September 8, 1960.

[41]This is a requirement for widows' benefits in the United States under the Social Security Act. (United States, *Social Security Handbook*, p. 48.)

paying widows' pensions outside Canada presumably would follow the rules adopted for paying Old Age Security outside the country.

Research would be desirable in order to arrive at appropriate amounts for pensions for the three categories of survivors. Because of the desirability of helping the widowed mother to maintain a house for her family, the amount paid to her should at the least be equal to the amount of Old Age Security payable at age 70 to a single person. The amount payable for each surviving child would need to be significantly greater than the amounts of family allowances now payable in Canada. Probably the amount payable in widows' benefits should be the same as the amount of Old Age Security.[42]

An amendment to the British North America Act would be essential in order to provide the types of survivor benefits advocated.[43]

THE ILLOGICAL BASIS OF FINANCING OLD AGE SECURITY

The basis for financing Old Age Security was adopted, in my opinion, as a matter of political and administrative convenience. It did enable revenues to be collected economically and without necessity of resorting to any new taxes. It was not so widely removed from accepted principles of justice that any Member of Parliament felt moved to vote against the Old Age Security Bill when it was passed in 1951.[44] As far as I know, there have been no widespread objections since 1951 to the use of the personal income tax, corporation income, and sales tax to provide revenue for Old Age Security. All these points are substantial merits.

What criteria may reasonably be used to appraise alternative methods of paying for a flat benefit old age pension and survivor benefit programme in Canada? I suggest that there are seven, not all of which are of equal importance.

(i) All persons, save those with extremely low incomes, should be required to contribute.[45]

[42]If, as I recommend on p. 347, persons eligible for Old Age Security should have the option of obtaining it at actuarially reduced rates from age 67 onwards, it might be desirable to make the widows' benefit equal the actuarially discounted value of a woman's Old Age Security pension at age 67.

[43]Clark, *Economic Security*, II, para. 2023.

[44]*Ibid.*, I, para. 979–81.

[45]The Honourable Douglas Abbott, Minister of Finance, said in the debate on financing Old Age Security in 1951: "Where under social security provisions the benefits are to be universal it is only right that

(ii) All employers should be required to contribute. The logic of requiring employers to contribute is fully as strong as, if not stronger than, the logic of asking them to contribute to unemployment insurance. It is as logical to require the employer to share, in the first instance, in the cost of a government pension and survivor benefit programme as it is to expect him to provide for the depreciation of his plant and equipment.

(iii) All contributors for such a government programme should be aware of the fact that they are contributing for this purpose through the particular earmarked tax or taxes used to pay for it. A simple revenue system of direct taxes for a programme is desirable, not only because it will be more widely understood than a complicated system, but also because it should be more economical to administer. It is only by being aware of the cost of various alternative welfare policies that the people as a whole through their elected representatives can choose intelligently among these policies and among the alternatives for more government spending in other fields or for reducing taxation. Moreover, unless the costs of Old Age Security to individual families are widely known among the public, many people are likely to demand more in pensions than they are prepared to pay for. Since existing Old Age Security pensions already are costly, ranking second only to national defence among federal expenditures, this is a risk that should not be taken lightly.[46] Application of this third criterion would preclude the financing of Old Age Security from the Consolidated Revenue Fund of the federal government, since, under such a system of financing, the public understandably would not know what they as individuals were contributing to this programme.

(iv) If employers and employees are both to contribute directly to such a programme, there is much to be said for requiring them to contribute equally. This is done, for example, in the United States under the Social Security Act and in Great Britain with regard to graduated retirement pensions under the National Insurance Act.

(v) Since the benefits to be provided are flat amounts, there should be an upper limit to the amount required from each individual contributor and from each employer on his behalf.

(vi) Since the programme is designed primarily for the benefit of

---

contributions to the fund should likewise be universal." (Canada, House of Commons, *Debates*, 1951, I, p. 388.)

[46]The estimated amount of Old Age Security payments for the year ended March 31, 1960, was $574 million. (Bank of Canada, *Statistical Summary Financial Supplement 1959*, pp. 102–3.)

lower income groups, there should be some element of subsidy in it to them from those in above-average income groups.

(vii) The costs of administration of the programme should be as low as possible, consistent with the above principles. This criterion would provide an argument against a contributory pension programme with graduated benefits, which, if the British or American programmes were followed, would require the maintenance of records of contributions for the self-employed and for individual employees, made by themselves and their employers.

Let us apply these criteria to the three earmarked taxes used to finance Old Age Security in Canada.

The personal income tax with a ceiling on income taxed for Old Age Security comes close to meeting most of these criteria. The use of it does involve discrimination against the majority of single men in favour of the majority of married men. More specifically, a single person with no dependents and an income, after permissible deductions, over $1,000 and up to $4,000 pays more than a married man with the same earnings who has a dependent wife. Yet on average life expectancies at age 70, a married couple in any income bracket will get somewhat more than double the total amount of pension payable to the single man. This discrimination against single persons would be increased if survivor benefits were provided for widowed mothers and other widows, and the present system of financing Old Age Security were extended to pay for the new types of benefits. Some measure of discrimination against single persons in favour of married couples is doubtless desirable on social grounds. I suggest that it is doubtful, however, if it should be extended.

The sales tax does secure universal contributions, is very economical to collect, and, generally speaking, obtains increasing contributions from individuals as their incomes rise. It was such considerations that led the Honourable Douglas Abbott, Minister of Finance in the Liberal Government when Old Age Security was introduced, to say in the House of Commons: "The sales tax more nearly approaches the ideal levy for financing social security than any other tax in our system."[47] In the same speech he vigorously defended the sales tax against the widespread mistaken notion that it is regressive in its effects on low income groups.[48]

[47]House of Commons, *Debates*, 1951, I, p. 388.

[48]On this topic Mr. Abbott said: ". . . our sales tax . . . does not discriminate against low income groups. . . . in the lower ranges of income

The great majority of those who are paying the federal sales tax, to the extent it is shifted to them, are not aware of how much they are paying. This, in my opinion, is a serious disadvantage in using this tax to pay a substantial share of the costs of Old Age Security. The use of the sales tax prevents the realization of the fourth criterion of equal contributions in the first instance from employers and employees.

The use of the corporation income tax is the least logical of the three taxes earmarked for Old Age Security. It offends against the second criterion and the fourth. If the second criterion is valid, then all employers should be required to contribute. Governments as employers, government-owned businesses, non-profit institutions, corporations that lose money in a particular year, co-operatives, partnerships, and individual proprietorships—none of these as employers should be able to avoid contributions to a government programme providing pensions and survivor benefits for the aged.

The discrimination against corporations making a profit has been, in my opinion, already carried too far in our federal tax system by both Liberals and Conservatives, with enthusiastic C.C.F. support. I believe that there is no valid economic or moral justification for increasing this discrimination every time it is desired to increase pensions for the aged or to add new benefits such as survivors pensions.

One argument against requiring all employers to contribute is that it does not really matter whether a tax for the programme is paid only by profitable corporations or by all employers, since employers in any case will attempt to shift the tax. The reply to this is not to deny that attempts to shift any tax for Old Age Security are made, with widely varying degrees of success, among different employers at different times. The important point that is overlooked in this argument is that the first incidence of any contribution or tax to government, to one's parents, to a church, trade union, or professional association, is of great psychological importance.

Given the decision to earmark part of the personal income tax, corporation income tax, and sales tax to finance Old Age Security, there has never been any obvious logic to the requirement that the rates for the three taxes should be kept equal. In the fiscal years ended March 31,

---

the tax is progressive rather than regressive. What is frequently overlooked is that practically all foods are exempt from sales tax, all fuel is exempt, building materials are exempt, and through wide income ranges not more than one-third of consumer expenditure is on goods subject to sales tax."

1954 to 1960, the sales tax has always been the most important source of revenue for the programme, providing between 37 and 48 per cent of the amount spent in any year on Old Age Security payments. In each of these seven years the personal income tax has provided between 27 and 33 per cent, the corporation income tax between 13 and 16 per cent. Since the yield of the three earmarked taxes combined was insufficient in each of these years, a payment from the Consolidated Revenue Fund was necessary; this varied from 2 to 22 per cent of the amount spent in Old Age Security payments.[49] In raising the rates of the three earmarked taxes from 2 to 3 per cent in his 1959 Budget, the Honourable Mr. Fleming, Minister of Finance, expressed the opinion that by this action "we shall have provided for the necessary revenues to bring the [Old Age Security] fund into balance over the next two or three years."[50]

An alternative source of revenue for Old Age Security and survivor benefits is a tax on earnings, subject to a ceiling, and imposed equally on employers and employees, plus a tax on the earnings of the self-employed. Such a tax would be proportional to earnings. The ceiling on earnings should be related to average earnings of employees. On one alternative there would be no lower income exemption, but the self-employed, employees, and employers would not be required to contribute on earnings below some low figure. In the United States, for example, a self-employed farmer is required to pay contributions on his total net earnings up to a ceiling of $4,800 if his net earnings from self-employment amount to at least $400.[51] Alternatively there could be one low earnings exemption with respect to contributions by or on behalf of each individual contributor.[52]

One of the questions to be answered, if such a tax is used, is whether the self-employed should be taxed at the same rate as employees, at double the rate, or at some rate between these two.

[49]Clark, *Economic Security*, I, Table 43, p. 257; and Bank of Canada, *Statistical Summary Financial Supplement 1959*, op. cit., pp. 102–3.

[50]House of Commons, *Debates*, 1959, p. 2,416. It appears that the earmarked revenues for Old Age Security will exceed the Old Age Security pension payments in the fiscal year 1960–61 by about $40 million. (Canadian Tax Foundation, *The National Finances 1960–61*, 1960, Toronto, Table 54, p. 92.)

[51]Clark, *Economic Security*, I, para. 224.

[52]This would create some administrative problems, which British experience with the National Insurance Act of 1959 suggests can be solved. These problems arise where a person works in rapid succession for different employers.

Under the Social Security Act in the United States the self-employed pay at a rate 50 per cent higher than that of employees. Such an arrangement discriminates in favour of the self-employed, since their average life expectancies at various ages are not very different from those of employees. As far as I have been able to ascertain, this compromise has proved to be generally acceptable in the United States.

The type of taxes here proposed meet all seven of the criteria suggested as relevant for financing pensions for the aged and survivor benefits. The proposals put forward here would be in accord with the views expressed by members of the Joint Committee of the Senate and House of Commons on Old Age Security. This committee did not consider itself responsible for detailed recommendations on financing the flat pensions they favoured. It did, however, suggest that both employers and employees ought to contribute directly to the programme, and appeared to favour a payroll tax on employers as a means of obtaining a contribution from them.[53]

The type of levies proposed here was rejected in 1951 essentially for two reasons. The first was that it would be difficult to tax some categories of employers, such as provincial and municipal governments and non-profit institutions.[54] The administrative problems are far from insuperable, as the experience of the United States and the United Kingdom clearly demonstrates.[55] For constitutional as well as political reasons it would be necessary for the federal Government to get the consent of the provincial governments before it obtains contributions from them as employers.

The other major argument used in rejecting the payroll tax was that "it would increase production costs for our exporters."[56] While

[53]King and Lesage, *Report*, pp. 110–11, para. 66(1) and (2) and 67.

[54]House of Commons, *Debates*, 1951, I, pp. 387–8.

[55]In the United States the federal Government does not have the authority under the American Constitution to levy on state or municipal governments the employer tax for Old-Age, Survivors, and Disability Insurance. By June, 1958, coverage had been obtained by means of voluntary agreements between the federal government and 47 states, and Hawaii, Puerto Rico, and the Virgin Islands. To obtain coverage for its employees, a non-profit institution must file a certificate stating that it wishes its employees to contribute, that at least two-thirds of them concur, and that it waives its exemption from the employer payroll tax for the programme. The problem of taxing the various religious denominations has been avoided by adopting the fiction that each priest or minister is self-employed. (Clark, *Economic Security*, I, para. 206, 219, 220, 226.)

[56]House of Commons, *Debates*, 1951, I, pp. 357–8.

this argument has some merit, I do not consider that it is a conclusive argument against the use of such a tax. The proposed taxes would replace the existing taxes for the programme. For some firms it would mean somewhat heavier taxes, for others, lighter. Such taxes as are recommended here are used in other countries with which Canada is in competition. Both employers and employees in the United States are paying, in 1960, contributions of 3 per cent on earnings up to a ceiling of $4,800 per employee. Amendments to the Social Security Act in 1958 provided that this rate of contributions will rise to 4½ per cent by 1969 in order to finance the level of benefits in effect in 1959.[57] Employers and employees in West Germany contribute at even higher rates on earnings up to twice the national average in the past three years.[58] I do not consider that we should refrain from adopting what is a more equitable system partly for the sake of retaining a system which treats somewhat more leniently those export industries where the labour costs are a relatively high proportion of total costs.

The chief practical argument against changing the basis of financing Old Age Security is doubtless political. Why change a system when there are no widespread complaints against it, especially when it is realized that any change in taxes which requires some to pay more and others to pay less is bound to raise complaints?

THE HARDSHIP CREATED FOR SOME PERSONS WHO DO NOT QUITE QUALIFY FOR OLD AGE ASSISTANCE BY THE FACT THAT OLD AGE SECURITY IS NOT PAYABLE UNTIL AGE 70

The right decision, in my opinion, was taken in 1951 when the age limit for Old Age Security was set at 70. There were then and still are limits to the amount people are prepared to pay for a government pension programme. We have no adequate over-all Canadian statistics, so far as I know, on the average age at retirement of men and women with jobs. I deem it highly probable, however, that a substantial proportion of men continue to work after age 65, especially among farmers, merchants, and professional men.[59] Postponing the

[57]Clark, *Economic Security*, I, Table 18, pp. 118–19; and para. 512.

[58]United States, *Social Security Programs throughout the World 1958*, Chart I, p. 12.

[59]The normal retirement age for men under most Canadian pension plans is 65. According to a survey by the Canadian Department of Labour for 1951 of pension plans in companies with 500 employees or more, 77 per cent had provision for deferred retirement. In the recent National

payment of Old Age Security does, I believe, make it possible to have a larger pension at age 70 than would be possible at age 65. It is reasonable to expect that the proportion of the population living beyond age 70 will continue to increase, as it has already done to a remarkable degree in the past 25 years.[60]

In my opinion it is much more important to place the emphasis on raising the amount of Old Age Security than to divert the significant amount of revenue that would be needed to lower the age limit by two or three years. At the same time, however, there is a strong case for making Old Age Security available at a somewhat lower age to those that want it, provided there is no substantial increase in the cost of doing so. Fortunately this is entirely feasible, from both a financial and an administrative viewpoint.

I believe that persons eligible for Old Age Security should be allowed to get an actuarially reduced pension at any age between 67 and 70. Table II, calculated from the *Canadian Life Tables 1955–57*,

TABLE II

ACTUARIAL EQUIVALENT OF A MONTHLY PENSION OF $55 AT AGE 70[a]

Commencement age	Pension for males	Pension for females
65	$36.04	$38.24
66	38.90	40.83
67	42.14	43.74
68	45.85	47.04
69	50.10	50.76

[a]Computed at zero rate of interest and using the *Canadian Life Tables 1955–57*.

SOURCE: Mr. Geoffrey B. White, F.I.A.

Trust Company study of 117 pension plans, a majority of which were trusteed plans, 76 per cent "made reference to postponed retirement, which as a rule requires the mutual consent of the employer and the employee." In the United States men are eligible to receive Old-Age benefits at age 65, provided they have retired. A person "retired under the Act is permitted to earn up to $1,200 a year without having his Old-Age benefit reduced. That a majority of men covered by the programme work full time beyond age 65 is indicated by the fact that the average age at which men are awarded Old-Age benefits in 1957 was 69.0. (Clark, *Economic Security*, II, para. 1468; National Trust Company, *Study of Canadian Pension Plans*, Table III; Clark, *Economic Security*, I, para. 282–9 and Table 5, p. 70.)

[60]See p. 326.

gives the actuarial equivalent at a zero rate of interest of $55 payable for life at age 70. The figures for women are slightly greater than the figures for men because of a greater average life expectancy for women at age 70.

Any person choosing to take Old Age Security before age 70 would get an actuarially reduced pension for the rest of his life. He could expect to share in any future pension increase.[61] From decade to decade as new mortality tables are computed, the actuarial discounts would have to be recomputed. Each increase in average life expectancy for those at age 70 would raise the actuarial value of the pension before age 70.

Who would be the persons most likely to take advantage of the opportunity to get their pensions on an actuarially reduced basis before age 70? I suggest that the largest group would be widows. A considerable proportion of these have a little life insurance and other assets which prevent their qualifying for Old Age Assistance between the ages of 65 and 70. Another fairly large group would be those who, having reached age 67 or 68, do not expect to live very long thereafter.

If survivor benefits for widows were introduced, and were as great as or greater than the actuarially reduced pension payable to women at age 67, widows presumably would have no incentive to apply for Old Age Security before age 70. Under such circumstances the case for providing the option of taking an actuarially reduced pension, while still strong, is not as striking.

The question will be asked: why not make Old Age Security available on an actuarially reduced basis as early as age 65? The chief reason, I suggest, is that, for the next few years at least, the value of the Old Age Security pension is likely to be too low.

One of the consequences of adopting proposals such as the above for survivor benefits and for permitting persons to obtain Old Age Security as early as age 67 is that the proportion of the population receiving Old Age Assistance should decline. This would save a limited amount of money for both the federal government and the provincial governments. Partially offsetting this saving, however, would be an increase in the number of persons needing small amounts of Old Age Assistance after age 70. One of the logical concomitants of allowing persons to obtain Old Age Security at an actuarially

[61]It would have to be decided whether he would share fully or on an actuarially reduced basis in future pension increases which might take place before or after he was 70.

reduced age from 67 onwards is that the federal and the provincial governments should be prepared to pay Old Age Assistance to persons over age 70 who qualify for it. As I shall argue below, this latter policy is desirable for other reasons than the one implied here.

THE DISCRIMINATION AGAINST SINGLE PERSONS IN RELATION TO MARRIED PERSONS UNDER THE OLD AGE SECURITY AND THE OLD AGE ASSISTANCE ACTS

Dr. Brian Abel-Smith of the London School of Economics recently wrote a stimulating article in which he analysed provisions for pensions to dependent wives in 26 countries in 1958. Only two of these countries gave the wife the same pension as her husband received. Canada was one of these countries, New Zealand the other. Ten countries gave the wife less than 45 per cent of the single person's pension. The remaining 14 countries provided a wife's benefit between 45 and 65 per cent of a single person's benefit.[62] Neither Canada nor New Zealand had a contributory pension programme.[63] Most of the other 26 countries had a contributory programme, some with flat benefits, others with graduated benefits.

The justification in Canada for paying double the pension to a married couple that is paid to a single person is, I assume, that any person becomes entitled to the pension by fulfilling the residence requirement and applying for Old Age Security. When this pension was only $40 a month one can readily understand why the pension for a married couple should not be reduced below $80. The larger the Old Age Security pension becomes in future, the less justification there is, in my opinion, for continuing this policy.

A typical married retired couple can live more cheaply than two typical single persons living alone in the same locality, because of savings in rent, heating, electricity, and other costs.[64] Lord Beveridge

[62]Brian Abel-Smith, *Pensions for Dependent Wives*, a mimeographed address delivered to the International Gerontological Conference in San Francisco, August, 1960, pp. 3–4.

[63]See p. 330 for the definition of the contributory pension programme used in this article.

[64]The Ontario Welfare Council published in April, 1958, the results of a detailed study by a large committee of the Council of living costs for the aged in Toronto. In drawing up budgets for single persons and married couples the Committee adopted the following criterion: "The total amounts . . . are average figures intended to suggest income require-

in his report to the British Government recommended that the pension for a dependent wife should be 66 per cent of the pension for her husband.[65] Research into the living costs of single and married pensioners with no other income than Old Age Security would be highly desirable in order to provide the basis for a reasonable recommendation.

When Old Age Security is raised, the increase presumably could be appreciably greater if single persons and married couples received the same increment, rather than providing double the increase for married couples.

The same problem arises in connection with Old Age Assistance in Canada. A married couple with no other income than the assistance receives twice as much as a single person without any resources. There is a possible inconsistency in policy here, since if the applicant for Old Age Assistance has a limited income from other sources a different policy is followed. The maximum income including Old Age Assistance allowed to a single person is $960 a year, as compared with $1,620 for a married couple. Here the additional income including Old Age Assistance allowed to the wife is 69 per cent of the total income allowed to a single person.[66]

The question may be raised: even if the policy you advocate is logical, could it be introduced when the idea of double pensions for married couples is well established? Dr. Abel-Smith writes:

> The United Kingdom has already undergone almost unnoticed, the transition from equal pensions for men and women to a wife's benefit of about 60 per cent of her husband's benefit. . . .
>
> British experience shows that it is not difficult to make the transition from equal pensions to a lower *proportionate* level of pension for a dependent wife. This could presumably be done in Canada or New Zealand providing the increase in the basic

ments for single men and women, and couples, such that a minimum adequate living standard can be maintained. In this respect, it is not a subsistence budget, but rather a somewhat higher level which may be generally regarded as consistent with health, decency, and self-respect."

In applying this criterion, the Committee concluded that a single elderly man required $92.97 a month, a single elderly woman, $90.74, and an aged couple, $142.10. The additional income required by a wife living with her husband was 35 per cent of the income required by her husband. (Ontario Welfare Council, Committee on Public Welfare Policy, *Economic Needs and Resources of Older People* (Toronto, 1958), pp. EN 8 and 9. The Committee chairman was Gower Markle.)

[65]Beveridge, *Social Insurance and Allied Services*, para. 229–31.

[66]Clark, *Economic Security*, I, Table 47, p. 270.

benefit was considerable and provided the whole emphasis were placed upon this aspect of the change.[67]

I believe he is right.

THE DISCRIMINATION AGAINST THOSE IN RECEIPT OF OLD AGE SECURITY OR OF MEANS-TEST BENEFITS WHO LIVE IN RELATIVELY HIGH COST AREAS

One of the more important arguments against a flat-benefits system of pensions or allowances is that it does not take into consideration differences in living costs in various parts of the country.

There are, to the best of my knowledge, no really satisfactory statistics on the extent of these differences. It is generally accepted that of the various major components of living costs in Canada, the category with the largest variation is the cost of shelter. I estimated in 1958, on the basis of inadequate evidence, that average shelter costs were about 20 to 25 per cent higher in the few largest cities than in the rural areas for single aged persons with incomes of less than $1,000 a year and for married aged couples with incomes of less than $2,000 annually.[68]

The relative weight given to shelter in the Canadian consumer price index is 15 per cent. This excludes the cost of household operations, such as fuel and electricity. This relative weight slightly underestimates the present importance of shelter in the typical urban budget, because since 1949, the base year for the index, the shelter component has risen more than any of the other four component groups in the index.[69]

It is widely known that, especially in the largest urban areas, shelter costs for the lowest income groups are a larger fraction of their total expenditures than they are for middle and upper income groups. For example, in the study by a committee of the Ontario Welfare Council in 1958 of the economic needs of the aged in Toronto, the amount allocated for shelter was equal to slightly more than 38 per cent of the proposed total budget for single women, slightly less than 38 per cent

[67]Abel-Smith, *Pensions for Dependent Wives*, pp. 8, 11.

[68]Clark, *Economic Security*, II, para. 1875.

[69]As compared with the base period of 1949 = 100, the shelter component of the consumer price index rose by 44 per cent to August, 1960, as compared with 28 per cent for the entire index (Canada, Dominion Bureau of Statistics, *Canadian Statistical Review Weekly Supplement, September 13, 1960* (Ottawa: Queen's Printer, 1960), p. 3).

for single men, and 28 per cent for married couples. These shelter costs were based on rentals in limited-dividend housing projects.[70]

It is not only with regard to Old Age Security that no consideration is given to differences in living costs. The amounts paid to individuals under the federal Old Age Assistance Act, the Disabled Persons Act, and the Blind Persons Act are not varied to take into consideration differences in living costs. This failure to take into consideration these differences is a much more serious problem for those with low incomes than for those farther up the income scale.

I know of no way that is likely to be politically acceptable whereby the federal Government could vary its flat Old Age Security pension to allow for differences in living costs within and between provinces. There are, I believe, no comparable obstacles to varying the payments under the three means-test programmes. If this can be done for individuals up to age 70 under the Old Age Assistance Act, there are no compelling reasons why it should not be done for persons beyond age 70.

What I am advocating here is simply what has become accepted practice in Great Britain under the National Assistance Act of 1948. The variations in shelter costs for assistance recipients in Britain is greater than in Canada. In 1959 the average weekly rent paid by assistance recipients in Scotland was 14 shillings 8 pence. It was 24 shillings 3 pence in the regions including London, East Anglia, the southern and southeastern counties.[71]

The British policy has been to divide the basic National Assistance grant into two parts.[72] One of these, which covers all ordinary expenditures except rent, is uniform throughout the country. The other, the rent component, varies ". . . where the applicant . . . is responsible for rent . . . the amount which may be allowed on this account is the net rent payable or such part thereof 'as is reasonable in the circumstances.' "[73] My understanding, based upon personal inquiries in Great Britain in the summer of 1960, is that the British Government has been able to administer this policy effectively and in the way that is acceptable to assistance recipients generally.

[70]Clark, *Economic Security*, II, para. 1869. See also footnote 64.

[71]Great Britain, Ministry of Pensions and National Insurance, *Report of the National Assistance Board for the Year Ended 31st December, 1959* (London: H.M.S.O., 1960, Cmnd. 1085), p. 17.

[72]In addition to the basic grant the National Assistance Board makes discretionary additions for such needs as special diet, laundry, exceptional food requirements, and domestic help (*ibid.*, p. 20).

[73]*Ibid.*, p. 16.

The budgetary deficiency method generally used in determining the amount of Old Age Assistance in the United States is similar to the British method in allowing within broad limits for differences in living costs.[74]

Changing the basis of calculating assistance in Canada under the three means-test programmes would in practice require the consent of the provincial governments who administer these programmes in co-operation with the federal government.

THE UNDESIRABLE EQUATING OF THE MAXIMUM AMOUNT OF OLD AGE SECURITY AND OLD AGE ASSISTANCE, AND THE LIMITATION OF OLD AGE ASSISTANCE TO THOSE BETWEEN THE AGES OF 65 AND 69

What can reasonably be expected of a means-test programme such as Old Age Assistance? The answer partly depends upon the premise with which one considers it. I start from the assumption that, given the continuing variation in needs of aged persons in various parts of Canada, the amount of Old Age Security is unlikely in the foreseeable future to be large enough to provide a subsistence income for *all* needy persons age 65 and over. If this is a valid assumption, then there is a positive and constructive, though limited role for Old Age Assistance to fulfil.

Since the purpose of assistance programmes is to help those who are by definition in need, it is reasonable to expect that no requirement of residence in Canada should be set up as a barrier to providing assistance.[75] This principle is accepted in the federal Unemployment Assistance Act, which contains a provision which has eliminated any residence requirement.[76] The Old Age Assistance Act, the Disabled

[74]Clark, *Economic Security*, I, para. 800–1, 803–10.

[75]In 1958 the Canadian Welfare Council recommended that: "Length of residence shall not be a condition for the receipt of assistance." (Canadian Welfare Council, *Social Security for Canada: A Policy Statement Adopted at the Annual Meeting, 2 June 1958* (Ottawa, 1958, p. 10).

[76]1956, c. 26, amended 1957, c. 20, Schedule s. 4. This section is as follows:

"Length of residence shall not be made a condition for the receipt of assistance if

"(a) the applicant has come from a province whose government has entered into an agreement similar to this respecting unemployment assistance, and

"(b) such agreement includes a like clause as herein contained in respect of length of residence not being a condition for receipt of assistance."

Persons Act, and the Blind Persons Act violate this principle. Each of these acts requires that a recipient must have resided in Canada for ten years immediately preceding the date of the proposed commencement of assistance payments to him.[77] The reason for this provision presumably is to protect Canadian taxpayers against the risk of having hordes of poor foreigners come to Canada where they would live at public expense. Such a reason, in my opinion, does not carry conviction. It is the responsibility of the federal Department of Citizenship and Immigration acting for the citizens of the nation to decide who shall be admitted to Canada. Once a person has been legally admitted to take up residence in Canada, then he should be entitled to assistance under any federal or provincial means-test programme on the same basis as any other Canadian resident. Even if this principle be unacceptable, a requirement of a year's residence in Canada should be ample to discourage the excessive influx of needy immigrants.

There is a strong case for believing that the amount of Old Age Assistance should be sufficient to provide a subsistence income for those who have no other financial resources. This case, however, has not been accepted by any Canadian political party when it formed the Government of Canada. Dr. George Davidson, as Deputy Minister of Welfare in 1958, stated:

> The Old Age Assistance payments has never purported to be an amount calculated to be sufficient for the maintenance of an aged needy person. It has been stated repeatedly in Parliament by the responsible ministers both in respect of the original old age means test pension and more recently in respect of the Old Age Assistance payment that these payments

---

All ten provincial governments have made the requisite agreement with the federal Government.

[77]R.S.C. 1952, c. 199, s. 3(2)(a), amended 1957–8, c. 6, s. 1(2); 1953–4, c. 55, s. 3(2)(a); R.S.C. 1952, c. 17, s. 3(2)(a).

The residence requirement for Old Age Assistance in Canada was reduced from twenty to ten years by the Conservative Government in 1957. At that time the ten-year residence requirement was already in effect under the Blind Persons Act and the Disabled Persons Act.

In each of these sections it is provided that if the applicant for assistance has not resided in Canada for the ten years immediately preceding the date of the proposed commencement of assistance payments to him, he can qualify if he "has been present in Canada prior to those ten years for an aggregate period equal to twice the aggregate periods of absences from Canada during those ten years."

are intended merely as a grant to assist the needy aged in their efforts to maintain themselves.[78]

One readily can understand the important reasons which have led successive federal governments to take such a position. The provision of assistance to the needy is not the responsibility of the federal Government alone. The administration of assistance programmes is largely a responsibility of the provincial governments and this is entirely appropriate in view of their closer contacts with the needy. The provincial governments do share and should share with the federal Government the financial responsibility for assistance programmes. The term "subsistence" is most difficult to define. For the federal Government and the provincal governments to accept responsibility for providing a subsistence standard for the needy would leave these governments open to endless objections that the definition of subsistence was too niggardly or that it was being applied in a parsimonious and arbitrary way. Moreover, the needs of individuals without any financial resources vary greatly. An amount of assistance which would provide a subsistence income for the great majority of the destitute presumably would fail to meet the needs of a small minority with exceptionally great needs. For a government to accept any particular definition of subsistence would be to reduce its freedom in making future policy changes. Finally, apart from the cost of providing a more generous measure of assistance, there is a further political difficulty. Could the federal Government pay out more to Old Age Assistance recipients, who have paid no taxes directly to support this programme, than to Old Age Security pensioners, most of whom during their working lives will have paid the earmarked personal income tax for the latter programme?

Significant as these arguments are, I do not think all of them together justify the continuance of the policy of the federal Government in selecting the maximum amount of assistance payable under the Old Age Assistance Act. The $55 maximum, after allowing for inflation, is greater than the maximum payable by the previous Government. But this fact, and the further fact that in some provinces the federal Government supplements Old Age Assistance payments under the provisions of the Unemployment Assistance Act, do not provide, I suggest, an adequate defense for the method of determining the upper limit of payments under Old Age Assistance.

It is easier to criticize the existing policy than to propose acceptable

[78]Clark, *Economic Security*, I, para. 1037.

practical alternatives. In considering such alternatives, it is desirable to examine various meanings of the term "subsistence." Older definitions of it described subsistence in terms of the cost of the minimum necessities required for the maintenance of merely physical efficiency. Such a definition, or less severe versions of it, suggest that subsistence is to be measured by comparing costs over a period of time of a list of goods and services. Although the items in the list or their relative importance may be changed from time to time, there are inevitably many arbitrary decisions to be made in applying this type of definition.

Another approach to subsistence is to define it for an individual family as some fraction of the family income before retirement. The British Labour party, in its important publication, *National Superannuation,* contends that the average worker's family is receiving "minimum subsistence" if the family income in retirement is about 25 per cent of what it was before the worker retired.[79] This statement, though not written in connection with assistance programmes, can be interpreted in two ways. It can be taken to suggest that subsistence should be related to the income of the individual family before the wage earner retires. Alternatively it can be interpreted to suggest that subsistence should be defined as a fraction of the average income of wage earners in the country. The former interpretation is too relative, and hence inappropriate for determining the maximum amounts to be paid under a means-test programme such as Old Age Assistance. It would be accepted generally that payments under a means-test programme should not be varied to provide more generous treatment for those who have been more fortunate than other recipients of assistance. It is at least administratively feasible to relate the maximum amount of assistance to the average income of wage earners in a country or province. But this leaves the major problem of deciding what fraction of average incomes should be chosen, and in itself points to the need for research if the question is not to be decided in an arbitrary way.

A more promising approach, though not without difficulties, has been proposed by a British sociologist, Peter Townsend. He suggests a method of measuring subsistence apart from "one or two fixed in-

[79]"In Britain today old age, for the average worker, means a fall of nearly 75 per cent in the standard of life for which he has worked and to which he and his wife have become accustomed. This is poverty. No arbitrary and sophisticated attempts to draw lines of minimum subsistence could supply a better definition." (*National Superannuation* (2nd ed., London, 1958), p. 30; italicized in original.)

voluntary overheads," of which rent is the more important.[80] Rent is not included because of the wide variations in rent in Britain. As mentioned earlier, in the basic National Assistance payments in Britain, the grant for rent is determined on a different basis from the remainder of the basic payment.[81] Mr. Townsend suggests that subsistence, apart from these exclusions, should be regarded as equal to the average expenditure, less the same exclusions, of a defined category of wage earners' families. This method involves collecting data for wage-earning households on incomes, expenditures, and consumption of food. Food consumption data for families classified by size and income group are compared with a recognized scale of minimum nutritional standards. Such a scale was prepared by a committee of the British Medical Association. Comparisons with a scale such as this would make it possible to divide the families studied into the categories of those who did and those who did not secure this minimum nutrition. For all the families who obtained the minimum it would be possible to isolate some percentage—he suggests 25 per cent—of the total number of families who achieve this standard on the smallest incomes less the fixed overhead expenditures referred to above. The average total expenditures of these households less the overheads, classified by size of family, can be taken as the subsistence income for these various sizes of family.

In this method of measuring subsistence Mr. Townsend gives prominence to food expenditures partly because of their importance in family expenditures and partly because nutritional needs can be measured more readily than clothing, fuel, and other needs.

He comments:

> Such a standard may be justified on the ground that it is, in fact, attained by a fair proportion of working-class people, and is therefore realistic. It would obviate the need for subjective decisions about the sums of money required for clothing, fuel and light and so on. Inevitably, a subjective element remains, and this is involved in the choice of the proportion of working-class households whose members have an adequate diet and whose spending is to be considered in fixing the standard. But this element need not be obtrusive. . . .[82]

[80]Peter Townsend, "Measuring Poverty," *British Journal of Sociology*, V (June, 1954), p. 135.

[81]See p. 352.

[82]Townsend, "Measuring Poverty," p. 135.

Mr. Townsend did not suggest this method of measuring subsistence with the needs of the aged as his sole concern. Rather he was concerned with the needs of families in poverty at any age. The method he proposes is capable of numerous modifications. In spite of the statistical difficulties involved it would be, in my opinion, a useful basis for some of the research work that is required to carry out the reasonable recommendation of the Canadian Welfare Council in 1958 that:

> The operation of all public assistance programs should be based upon sound and clearly defined standards, particularly with respect to:
> a. Amount of assistance. The appropriate federal or provincial authorities should determine, on a continuing basis, the minimum costs of individual and family maintenance at level consistent with health and decency. This implies:
> (i) A definition of what constitutes a minimum level of health and decency.
> (ii) A schedule of minimum requirements based upon this definition, and related to the age and size of the family unit.
> (iii) The periodic translation of minimum requirements into monetary terms, appropriate to the specific community, which would form the basis of public assistance payments.[83]

Suppose that the maximum amount of Old Age Assistance is to be established by methods such as that outlined above, and that, as I have advocated, the rent or housing component of assistance is determined separately from the remainder of the assistance grant to allow for a range of differences in the housing accommodation costs. Then at least in the high cost of living areas the maximum amount of Old Age Assistance will exceed the amount of the current Old Age Security pension. I know of no compelling reason in principle why the maximum amount of Old Age Assistance should be limited to the amount of a flat Old Age Security pension: nor of any cogent reason why some Old Age Assistance should not be payable to persons in need of it who are receiving Old Age Security. There is nothing in the present federal Old Age Assistance Act or Regulations to prevent the payment of assistance to persons age 70 and over who are receiving Old Age

[83]Canadian Welfare Council, *Social Security for Canada*, p. 12 (italicized in original).

Security. A provision in the regulations under the Old Age Security Act permits the provincial authority administering Old Age Assistance to apply for Old Age Security for assistance recipients who have reached the age of 69 years and six months. Since the provincial governments are responsible for raising revenue to meet half of the Old Age Assistance payments and since they have no financial or other responsibility regarding Old Age Security payments, they all have a natural incentive to transfer Old Age Assistance recipients to Old Age Security as soon as they can do so. They have an incentive to do this even if they supplement Old Age Security on a means-test basis, as is done in varying degrees in the four western provinces and Ontario.[84]

Persons in the United States age 65 and over may be eligible for both Old-Age Insurance and Old-Age Assistance. Especially in the early decades of a contributory social insurance programme with graduated retirement and survivor benefits, such as Old-Age Insurance, it is to be expected that many aged persons would need to have their Old-Age Insurance benefits supplemented by Old-Age Assistance. The proportion of the American population age 65 and over receiving Old-Age Assistance had declined from 22.6 per cent at the end of June, 1950, to 15.6 per cent at June 30, 1959.[85] Of all those receiving Old-Age Assistance in March, 1959, 26.7 per cent were also receiving Old-Age Insurance.[86]

A comparison with Great Britain is more relevant, because up to the present time the contributory National Insurance programme has provided only flat benefits. Persons in Britain may apply for National Assistance at any age from 16 onwards. The basic National Assistance grant plus average rent payment have been consistently above National Insurance retirement pension.[87] Of all the recipients of the

[84]Clark, *Economic Security*, I, para. 1173–1209.

[85]United States, Department of Health, Education, and Welfare, Social Security Administration, "Persons Receiving OASDI, OAA, or both, June 30, 1959," *Social Security Bulletin*, XXIII (July, 1960), Table 3, p. 17.

[86]Sue Ossman, "Concurrent Receipt of Public Assistance and Old-Age Survivors, and Disability Insurance," *Social Security Bulletin*, XXII (Nov., 1959), Table I, p. 7.

[87]Great Britain, *Report of the Ministry of Pensions and National Insurance for the Year 1959*, Table 29, p. 101; *Report of the National Assistance Board for the Year Ended 31st December, 1959*, pp. 14–17. At the end of 1959 a married couple receiving a retirement pension at age 65 under National Insurance Act were getting 80 shillings a week. The basic weekly

latter pension at the end of 1959, about 22 per cent had these pensions supplemented by National Assistance.[88]

I am far from suggesting that it would be a matter of indifference whether the proportion of persons receiving both Old Age Security and Old Age Assistance was high or low. Indeed if the proportion of persons age 70 and over getting benefits under both programmes were as high as 20 per cent, I should regard it as a *prima facie* indication that the Old Age Security pension was too low. Opinions would vary, of course, as to what was a tolerable proportion of the aged to benefit under both programmes. But in the interests of assisting those who most need assistance there is a strong practical case for not limiting the maximum amount of assistance under the federal Old Age Assistance Act to the amount of the Old Age Security pension.

If this case is accepted for eligible persons age 65 to 69, it is equally valid in principle for persons age 70 and over. This argument points directly to the desirability of removing the *de facto* upper age limit as a condition of eligibility for Old Age Assistance.

As explained below, the need for the two changes advocated here is reduced by the operation of the Unemployment Assistance Act. The need for these changes could be met entirely under a general federal assistance act accepted by all the provincial governments under which the category of Old Age Assistance was replaced by the broader category of public assistance.

THE UNNECESSARY DISTINCTION BETWEEN OLD AGE ASSISTANCE, UNEMPLOYMENT ASSISTANCE, AND SOCIAL ASSISTANCE

The major purpose of the Parliament of Canada in passing the Unemployment Assistance Act of 1956 was to enable the federal Government to share the cost of assistance payments to persons who either have exhausted their Unemployment Insurance benefits or who have not established eligibility for such benefits. Under this Act the

---

National Assistance payment at the same date for a married couple was 85 shillings. In addition to this a rent allowance was payable to most National Assistance recipients, the average weekly rent paid being 19 shillings 7 pence. (*Report of the National Assistance Board*, pp. 14–17.) Additional discretionary National Assistance payments were being made at the end of 1959 to about 63 per cent of the cases where the retirement pension under the National Insurance Act was being supplemented by a basic National Assistance grant. (*Ibid.*, pp. 19–20.)

[88]*Ibid.*, appendix III, p. 45.

federal Government makes no distinction between unemployable persons and those who are capable of working. Thus for the first time the federal Government has been willing to share directly in the cost of a programme to aid the unemployable, namely Social Assistance, a programme hitherto regarded by the federal Government as solely a provincial responsibility.

The title of the Unemployment Assistance Act is misleading because the scope of the Act is greater than the title suggests. In addition to this basic purpose of aiding unemployed persons able to work, the federal government under the Act also shares in the cost of supplementary allowances to persons who are in receipt of Old Age Security, Old Age Assistance, Disabled Persons Allowances, or Blind Persons Allowances, provided they are "unemployed and in need."[89] The federal Government has acknowledged the principle of supplementation to persons where the total assistance payment including the supplementary allowance is made on a means-test basis applied to each individual recipient. This basis is followed in Ontario and Manitoba, and accordingly the federal Government shares in the cost of supplementary allowances in these provinces. By contrast it does not share in the cost of supplementary allowances in British Columbia, Alberta, and Saskatchewan, where these allowances are flat amounts payable to all persons whose income and property are less than certain specified amounts. It is to be hoped that modifications in legislation in the three western provinces will be introduced which will induce the federal Government to share in the cost of the supplementary allowances in these provinces.

The federal Government pays three-quarters of the cost of payments made to individuals under the Blind Persons Act, and one-half of the costs of similar payments under the Old Age Assistance Act and the Disabled Persons Act. It reimburses the provincial governments for 50 per cent of the payments made to individuals receiving Unemployment Assistance. This amounts to paying one-half of the cost of provincial Social Assistance payments excluding the cost of Mothers' Allowances in those provinces which retain separate Mothers' Allowances programmes.[90]

There is much to be said for having one federal public assistance act providing federal sharing in the cost of providing assistance on a means-test basis to all categories of needy persons. The basic premise

[89]1957, c. 20, s. 4 Schedule, s. 8.
[90]*Ibid.*, ss. 7–14.

of the proposal is the belief that the payment of assistance to a person should be based on the fact that he is in need and the extent of his need, not on the particular reason why he is needy. The adoption of such an act should lead to savings in administrative costs. It should help to remove existing anomalies which occur in the administration of four separate means-test programmes, each of which has its own eligibility requirements.

In Great Britain there is only one assistance act, the National Assistance Act. The duty of the National Assistance Board operating under the Act is "to assist persons in Great Britain who are without resources to meet their requirements, or whose resources (including benefits receivable under the National Insurance Acts, 1946) must be supplemented in order to meet their requirements."[91] The adoption of a single federal public assistance act to replace the four existing federal assistance acts would not be as easy as it was in Great Britain, partly because of the different viewpoints of the provincial authorities responsible for the administration of the means-test programmes.

As the Canadian Welfare Council recommended in 1958, in advocating a single federal public assistance act, the federal Government could offer each province the option of continuing to receive grants under the four separate assistance programmes or under one new generalized assistance programme.[92]

Under each of the present four federal assistance acts the federal Government pays the same proportion of assistance costs in each province. The desirability of this policy has been questioned on the ground that the burden of the provincial share of assistance costs is

[91] 1948, c. 29, s. 4.

[92] The specific recommendation of the Canadian Welfare Council was: "There should be a federal Public Assistance Act which would be, in effect, an extension of the Unemployment Assistance Act and which would enable the Dominion government to share the aggregate costs to a province, and to the municipalities in a province, of providing financial assistance to all persons who are in need. The Old Age Assistance Act, the Blind Persons' Allowances Act and the Disabled Persons' Allowances Act should be incorporated as specific sections of this general Public Assistance Act. The proposed Act should . . . provide the provinces with the option of continuing old age assistance, blind persons' allowances and disabled persons' allowances as separate programs, or of incorporating these categories in a generalized public assistance program with the same provisions respecting the sharing of costs as in the Unemployment Assistance Act." (*Social Security for Canada*, p. 10; italicized in original.)

much greater in the provinces with lower average personal incomes. Not only is it more burdensome in these provinces to raise any given per capita amount in taxes to pay for assistance, but the proportion of the population needing assistance is likely to be much higher. Among the provinces of Canada in 1959 the average personal income ranged from a low of $842 in Newfoundland, $912 in Prince Edward Island and $968 in New Brunswick to a high of $1,729 in British Columbia and $1,768 in Ontario.[93] At March 31, 1959, the proportion of the population aged 65 to 69 receiving Old Age Assistance ranged from 13 per cent in Ontario and 14 per cent in British Columbia up to 38 per cent in New Brunswick and 61 per cent in Newfoundland.[94]

On the basis of statistics such as these some have argued that the federal share of assistance costs should be inversely proportional to the per capita incomes in each province. It is pointed out that in the United States the federal formula for sharing in Old-Age Assistance payments made by state governments does within very narrow limits recognize the difference in average personal incomes in the different states.[95] The Canadian Welfare Council has taken a somewhat different viewpoint, advocating that the federal Government should progressively increase its share of the total cost of all assistance payments in each province as the total number of persons receiving assistance increases.[96] An advantage of the proposal is that it would provide an automatic increase in federal aid at times when provincial governments presumably would particularly need it. Under this proposal if in two provinces the same proportion of the population was receiving assistance, the two provincial governments would receive the same proportion of their total assistance payments from the federal Government, regardless of any differences in per capita incomes in the two provinces.

There is no doubt that it is desirable for the federal Government to

[93]Canada, Dominion Bureau of Statistics, *National Accounts Income and Expenditure 1959* (Ottawa: Queen's Printer, 1960), Table 29, p. 38.

[94]Canada, Department of National Health and Welfare, *Report of the Administration of Old Age Assistance in Canada, Fiscal Year Ended March 31, 1959* (Ottawa: Queen's Printer, 1959), p. 12.

[95]For a description of the American federal sharing formula for Old-Age Assistance payments introduced in 1958, see Clark, *Economic Security*, I, para. 742–8. There are no federal grants to the American states corresponding with the federal equalization grants to the provincial governments in Canada.

[96]Canadian Welfare Council, *Social Security for Canada*, pp. 10–11.

recognize the substantial differences in fiscal capacity of the various provincial governments to finance not only assistance, but also health and hospital services, education, roads, and other provincial services. Recognition of these differences in fiscal capacity can be met by federal conditional grants which are varied to allow for differences in provincial needs for government expenditures on various services. Under this approach federal grants for each service—assistance, education, and so on—are very probably determined separately.

Alternatively recognition of these differences in fiscal policy can be met by equalization formulae which are based on differences in the revenue-producing capacity of certain taxes in each province. It is this approach which is taken in the present federal equalization grants payable to all provinces except Ontario. These unconditional grants to the provinces are designed to increase their per capita revenues from federal personal income tax, corporation income tax, and succession duties. The amount of these grants is equal to the difference between the per capita yield at specified rates of the three taxes in the two provinces with the highest per capita revenues from these taxes, and the per capita yield at the same stipulated rates of these taxes in each province. The two provinces with the highest per capita yields from these taxes have been Ontario and British Columbia. This formula is necessarily arbitrary in that some tax rate has to be specified for each of the taxes in working out an equalization formula. It is unnecessarily arbitrary in being restricted to the operation of three federal taxes and to the yield of these at the stipulated rates in the two provinces with the highest per capita revenue from them. Why should the equalization formula be related to the yield of these taxes in two provinces?

While the formula can also be criticized on other grounds, it does have the great advantage of providing all provincial governments except Ontario and British Columbia with very substantial sums which they can spend as they see fit.[97] Since public opinion on the

[97]The following table provides a comparison of the estimated per capita equalization payments to the provincial governments for the fiscal year 1960–61 and the estimated per capita personal incomes in the provinces for 1959. Column 1 gives the estimates made by the Canadian Tax Foundation of the federal unconditional equalization payments payable for the fiscal year ended March 31, 1961. The federal unconditional Atlantic Provinces Adjustment Grants for the same fiscal year are given in column 2. Column 3 is the total of columns 1 and 2. Column 4 consists of the figures in column 3 divided by the population estimates for June 1,

relative priorities of provincially administered services varies considerably from province to province, this freedom for provincial governments to spend the unconditional grants as they think best is a very great advantage.[98]

How far the federal Government should go in providing equalization payments related to provincial expenditures or revenues is a question on which a high degree of agreement is scarcely to be expected from one province to another. My own preference is to have federal equalization payments based on provincial revenues rather than on provincial expenditures on various services. This is because I think prevailing opinions on the relative priorities of provincial services differ considerably, and that it is desirable for provincial governments to have a very large measure of freedom in deciding how to

---

1960. The average personal incomes in each province for the latest year available, the calendar year 1959, are given in column 5. Both of these federal grants are entirely separate from the federal tax rental payments to all the provincial governments.

Province	(1) *Estimated equalization grant for the year 1960–61 (millions of dollars)*	(2) *Atlantic Provinces Adjustment grant for the year 1960–61 (millions of dollars)*	(3) *Columns (1)+(2) (millions of dollars)*	(4) *Estimated per capita grants for the year 1960–61 (dollars)*	(5) *Average personal incomes for 1959 (dollars)*
Newfoundland	14.7	7.5	22.2	48	842
Prince Edward Island	3.3	2.5	5.8	56	912
Nova Scotia	20.3	7.5	27.8	38	1,116
New Brunswick	17.4	7.5	24.9	42	968
Quebec	70.6		70.6	14	1,268
Ontario					1,768
Manitoba	14.3		14.3	16	1,488
Saskatchewan	21.7		21.7	24	1,309
Alberta	15.8		15.8	12	1,574
British Columbia	8.4		8.4	5	1,729
TOTAL	186.6	25.0	211.6		

SOURCES:
Columns 1 and 2: Canadian Tax Foundation, *The National Finances, 1960–61* (Toronto, 1960), Table 65, p. 114.
Column 4: column 3; Canada, Dominion Bureau of Statistics, *Estimated Population of Canada by Provinces at June 1, 1960* (Ottawa: Queen's Printer, 1960).
Column 5: Canada, Dominion Bureau of Statistics, *National Accounts Income and Expenditure 1959* (Ottawa: Queen's Printer, 1960), Table 29, p. 38.

[98]For a theoretical economic comparison of the conditional and unconditional grants, see A. D. Scott, "The Evaluation of Federal Grants," *Economics*, Nov., 1952, pp. 377–94.

spend their revenues. But if this approach is to be followed, substantial work remains to be done to gain acceptance for a new equalization formula less restricted by arbitrary factors. Within such a framework there is scope for the continuation of uniform federal conditional grants to the provincial governments, such as those under the four federal assistance acts.

I have written this essay in the belief that it is desirable that the problems dealt with here should be more widely understood and discussed. These problems are likely to receive inadequate public consideration in the continuing and more dramatic controversies over the relative merits of a contributory government pension plan with graduated benefits and the present type of flat Old Age Security pension.

I am confident that answers can be found to the problems considered in this essay. The answers will not satisfy everyone, but in attempting to work them out the federal and provincial governments can create a greatly improved system of welfare legislation. I believe that the Canadian people as a whole can afford such an improved system, and would be willing to pay the costs to make it a reality.

Bibliography of Publications by Henry F. Angus

BOOKS

1926

Citizenship in British Columbia. Victoria: Charles F. Banfield (printer).

1937

The Problem of Peaceful Change in the Pacific Area. London: Oxford University Press.

Canada and the Doctrine of Peaceful Change, edited by H. F. Angus, submitted to the conference by the Canadian Institute of International Affairs. Paris: International Institute of Intellectual Co-operation (mimeographed).

1938

Canada and Her Great Neighbour, edited by H. F. Angus. Toronto: Ryerson.

1942

British Columbia and the United States: The North Pacific Slope from Fur Trade to Aviation, by F. W. Howey, W. N. Sage and H. F. Angus; edited by H. F. Angus. Toronto: Ryerson.

1953

Canada and the Far East, 1940–53. Toronto: University of Toronto Press.

ARTICLES AND PAMPHLETS

1920

"Next for Duty," *University Magazine,* edited by Andrew MacPhail.

1921

"Pay" (by a university professor), *Pacific Review* 1:464–72 (March).

1922

"Standardized Hot Air," *Pacific Review* 2:631–42 (March).

1929

"A Summary of Economic Problems Awaiting Investigation in British Columbia," in *Contributions to Canadian Economics* 2:45–51.

1930

"Kyoto," *Canadian Forum* 10:196–7 (March).

"Pacific Relations," Canadian Political Science Association, *Papers and Proceedings* 2:74–80 (May).

"Canadian Affairs Affecting the Pacific," *Pacific Affairs* 3:735–9 (August).

1931

"The Legal Status in British Columbia of Residents of Oriental Race and Their Descendants," *Canadian Bar Review* 9:1–12 (January).

"The Legal Status in British Columbia of Residents of Oriental Race and Their Descendants," in *Legal Status of Aliens Resident in Canada*, introduced by Gordon Lindsay and D. R. Michener. Toronto: Canadian Institute of International Affairs.

"Canadians of Oriental Race," *Anvil* 1(1):2–4 (January).

"Underprivileged Canadians," *Queen's Quarterly* 38:445–60 (Summer).

"Survey of Canadian Affairs," *Pacific Affairs* 4:1082–4 (December).

1932

"Do We Need an Economic Dictator?" *Canadian Forum* 13:247–9 (April).

"The Economic Theory of a State-Supported University," *Queen's Quarterly* 39:261–71 (May).

"Kidd Report in British Columbia," *Canadian Forum* 13:47–9 (November).

1933

"A Contribution to International Ill-will," *Dalhousie Review* 13:23–33 (April).

"Dr. Inazo Nitobe: A Canadian Farewell," *Pacific Affairs* 6:548–9 (November-December).

1934

"The Responsibility for Peace and War in the Pacific," *Pacific Far Eastern Review* 30:4–7 (January).

"Canadian Immigration: The Law and Its Administration," *American Journal of International Law* 28:74–89 (January).

"The Economy Campaign on the Western Front," *Canadian Forum* 14:257–60 (April).

"Canada and a Foreign Policy," *Dalhousie Review* 14:265–75 (October).

1935

"Canada and Naval Rivalry in the Pacific," *Pacific Affairs* 8:176–84 (June).

"Beating Swords into Ploughshares," *Dalhousie Review* 15:265–74 (October).

"Liberalism Stoops to Conquer," *Canadian Forum* 15:389 (December).

1936

"The Portent of Social Credit in Alberta," *Pacific Affairs* 9:381–7 (September).

The Responsibility for Peace and War in the Pacific. Minneapolis: University of Minnesota Press.

1937

"Health Insurance in British Columbia," *Canadian Forum* 17:12–14 (April).

"Are We at War?" *Dalhousie Review* 17:147–54 (July).

"The Working of Confederation," pt. II, "A Western View," *Canadian Journal of Economics and Political Science* 3:345–53 (August).

1940

"An Analysis of the Report of the Royal Commission on Dominion-Provincial Relations," *Industrial Canada* 41:34–7 (August).

1941

"The Effect of the War on Oriental Minorities in Canada," *Canadian Journal of Economics and Political Science* 7:506–16 (November).

1944

"Immigration Policies, Canadian and American," by "Verax" (pen name) and Bruno Lasker, *Contemporary Affairs*, no. 19.

1946

"Immigration," *International Journal* 1:65–7 (Winter, 1945/6).

"The Canadian Constitution and the United Nations Charter," *Canadian Journal of Economics and Political Science* 12:127–35 (May).

"The Future of Immigration into Canada," *Canadian Journal of Economics and Political Science* 12:379–86 (August).

"Asiatics in Canada," *Pacific Affairs* 19:402–8 (December).

Japan–Our Problem. Toronto: Canadian Institute of International Affairs.

1947

"Need for an Immigration Policy," *Annals of the American Academy* 253:16–21 (September).

"East Indians in Canada," *International Journal* 2(1):47–50 (Winter, 1946/7).

1948

"United Nations," *Canadian Journal of Economics and Political Science* 14:312–20 (August).

"Canada's Interest in Multilateral Trade," in *Canada's Economy in a Changing World*, edited by J. Douglas Gibson. Toronto: Macmillan.

1949

"Malthus Today," Royal Society of Canada, *Transactions* (Section 2) 43 (3rd series):35–43.

"Graduate Studies in the Social Sciences," *Canadian Journal of Economics and Political Science* 15:299–309 (August).

1951

"Dangers of Declaring Human Rights," *Canadian Journal of Economics and Political Science* 17:218–21 (May).

"Balance of Power," *Queen's Quarterly* 58:305–11 (Autumn).

"The Canadian Royal Commission on the Arts, Letters & Sciences," *Western Political Quarterly* 4:577–82 (December).

1952

"Common Sense about Inflation," Royal Society of Canada, *Proceedings* 46(3rd series):57–65. Presidential address read June 2, 1952, before the Royal Society of Canada.

"Harry Ashton (1882–1952)," Royal Society of Canada, *Proceedings* 46(3rd series):69–74.

"Japan's Economic Challenge," *International Journal* 7:253–7 (Autumn).

"British Columbia Election, June 1952," *Canadian Journal of Economics and Political Science* 18:518–25 (November).

"Note on the British Columbia Election in June 1952," *Western Political Quarterly* 5:585–91 (December).

"The Commonwealth Trade and Economic Conference," *Round Table* 169:41–7 (December).

1953

"The Development of Canadian Far Eastern Policy," in 25 *Years of Canadian Foreign Policy*. Toronto: Canadian Broadcasting Corporation.

"The Fiction of the Dollar," *Canadian Bar Review* 31:295–303 (March).

"Dependence on World Trade," *Round Table* 171:274–81 (June).

"Stars and Stripes in Asia: Review Article," *International Journal* 8:193–9 (Summer).

"An Echo of the Past: The Rowell-Sirois Commission," *Canadian Tax Journal* 1:439–49 (September/October).

"Does Freedom Require a Bill of Rights," *Saturday Night* 69:7–8 (November 14).

1954

"A Reply to Mr. Forsey," *Canadian Journal of Economics and Political Science* 20:87–9 (February).

"Asia in Revolt: Review Article," *International Journal* 9:220–9 (Summer).

"Canada and Colombo: A Symposium–Political Aims and Effects," *Queen's Quarterly* 61:337–44 (Autumn).

"Damnosa Hereditas of Empires: Review Article," *International Journal* 10:288–90 (Autumn).

1955

"Rights!!" *University of British Columbia Legal Notes* 2:149–53 (March).

"Colombo Plan," *B.C. Professional Engineer* 6:18–21 (March).

"The Great Canadian Housing Subsidy," *Canadian Tax Journal* 3:178–80 (May/June).

"Japan Today and the West," *Saturday Night* 70:34–5 (November 26).

"Two Restrictions on Provincial Autonomy" (a reply to "What Price Provincial Autonomy," by J. Harvey Perry), *Canadian Journal of Economics and Political Science*, 21:445–6 (November).

1956

"Federal-Provincial Finance: Attitudes of the Provinces toward Federal-Provincial Tax Agreements Pin-pointed," *Industrial Report* 3 (February).

1957

"Administration and Democracy," an address to the Institute of Public Administration of Canada, Vancouver Regional Group, May 22.

1958

"Administrative Decision and the Law: The Views of an Administrator," *Canadian Journal of Economics and Political Science* 24(4): 512–18 (November).

Review of the *Report of the Royal Commission on Canada's Economic Prospects* in the *Canadian Banker* (Winter).

1959

"Canada as a Phenomenon for Political Scientists," *Western Political Quarterly* 12(2): 548–53 (June).

www.ingramcontent.com/pod-product-compliance
Lightning Source LLC
LaVergne TN
LVHW090802070826
844660LV00022B/1058